Preferential Trade Agreements

This book assembles a stellar group of scholars and experts to examine preferential trade agreements (PTAs), a topic that has repeatedly attracted the interest of analysts. It presents a discussion of the evolving economic analysis regarding PTAs and the various dysfunctions that continually place them among the priority items for (re)negotiation by the World Trade Organization (WTO). The book explores recent empirical research that casts doubt on the old "trade diversion" school. It debates why the WTO should deal with PTAs and if PTAs belong under the mandate of the WTO as we now know it.

Kyle W. Bagwell is the Donald L. Lucas Professor of Economics at Stanford University. Professor Bagwell was a reporter for the American Law Institute in its study "Principles of International Trade: The WTO." He also serves as a Research Associate at the National Bureau of Economic Research (International Trade Program). In his research, Professor Bagwell uses economic analysis to interpret and evaluate the design of the WTO. He is a Fellow of the Econometric Society.

Petros C. Mavroidis is the Edwin B. Parker Professor of Law at Columbia University. He also serves as Professor of Law at the University of Neuchâtel and is Research Fellow at the Centre for Economic Policy Research, London. He specializes in the law and the WTO and serves as the Legal Advisor to the WTO in the Technical Cooperation Division, where he assists developing countries in WTO dispute settlement proceedings. He was also the chief coreporter of the American Law Institute project "Principles of International Trade: The WTO."

Preferential Trade Agreements

A Law and Economics Analysis

Edited by

Kyle W. Bagwell

Stanford University

Petros C. Mavroidis

Columbia University, School of Law

CAMBRIDGE UNIVERSITY PRESS
Cambridge, New York, Melbourne, Madrid, Cape Town,
Singapore, São Paulo, Delhi, Tokyo, Mexico City

Cambridge University Press
32 Avenue of the Americas, New York, NY 10013-2473, USA

www.cambridge.org
Information on this title: www.cambridge.org/9781107000339

© Cambridge University Press 2011

First published 2011

Printed in the United States of America

A catalog record for this publication is available from the British Library.

Library of Congress Cataloging in Publication data

Bagwell, Kyle
Preferential trade agreements : a law and economics analysis / edited by Kyle W.
Bagwell, Petros C. Mavroidis.
    p. cm.
Includes bibliographical references and index.
ISBN 978-1-107-00033-9 (hardback)
1. Commercial treaties.   2. Tariff preferences.   3. Foreign trade regulation.
I. Mavroidis, Petros C.   II. Title.
K4600.B34   2011
382′.9 – dc22   2010041883

ISBN 978-1-107-00033-9 Hardback

Contents

Contributors

Kyle W. Bagwell
Donald L. Lucas Professor of Economics, Stanford University

William J. Davey
Guy Raymond Jones Chair in Law Emeritus, University of Illinois
College of Law

Caroline Freund
Lead Economist, International Trade Team, Development Research Group,
World Bank

David A. Gantz
Samuel M. Fegtly Professor of Law, James E. Rogers College of Law,
University of Arizona

Gary N. Horlick
Adjunct Professor of Law, Georgetown University; International Trade Lawyer,
Washington, D.C.

Henrik Horn
Non-Resident Senior Fellow, BRUEGEL, Brussels, Professor of International
Economics; Senior Research Fellow, Research Institute of Industrial Economics,
Stockholm; Research Fellow, Centre for Economic Policy Research (CEPR),
London

Jeff Kenner
Professor of European Law, University of Nottingham

Nuno Limão
Associate Professor, Department of Economics, University of Maryland;
CEPR, NBER

Juan A. Marchetti
Economist, WTO, Trade in Services Division

James H. Mathis
Associate Professor, Department of International Law, University of Amsterdam;
Research Fellow, Amsterdam Center for International Law,
The Netherlands

Petros C. Mavroidis
Edwin B. Parker Professor of Foreign and Comparative Law, Columbia
University, New York; Professor of Law, University of Neuchâtel, Neuchâtel;
Research Fellow, CEPR, London

Thomas J. Prusa
Professor of Economics, Department of Economics, Rutgers University, New
Brunswick, NJ

André Sapir
Professor of Economics, Solvay Brussels School of Economics and
Management, Université Libre de Bruxelles; Senior Fellow, Brussels European
and Global Economic Laboratory (BRUEGEL); Research Fellow, CEPR

T. N. Srinivasan
Samuel C. Park, Junior Professor of Economics, Yale University

Robert Teh
World Trade Organization, Economics and Research Analysis Division, Geneva,
Switzerland

Joel P. Trachtman
Professor of International Law, The Fletcher School of Law and Diplomacy, Tufts
University

L. Alan Winters
Professor of Economics, Department of Economics, University of Sussex;
Chief Economist, Department for International Development, London

KYLE W. BAGWELL AND PETROS C. MAVROIDIS

Introduction: The Law and Economics of Contingent Protection

An Introduction to the Volume

The chapters assembled in this volume deal with preferential trade agreements (PTAs), a topic that has repeatedly attracted the interest of analysts. One might naturally wonder why we need to revisit this issue once again. We believe that there are various good reasons, not necessarily mutually coherent. First, from a pure policy perspective, it is the World Trade Organization (WTO) through its Director General that has placed this item among the priority items for (re)negotiation. Obviously, the feeling must be that something has not been functioning as expected. We want to explore the legitimacy of this claim. On the other hand, recent empirical research casts doubt to the old "trade diversion" school: papers have seen the light of day arguing that no (or insignificant) trade diversion has resulted from the formation of recent PTAs. If so, why should we deal with PTAs at all? Then there is the issue of content of PTAs: many recent PTAs (i.e., after the advent of the WTO) have a subject matter that does not come under the mandate of the WTO as we now know it. The obvious question in this context is what the role should be of the WTO when dealing with issues such as environmental protection or macroeconomic cooperation.

We have put together a stellar group of researchers to discuss this topic.

In his introductory piece, **Alan Winters** provides a helicopter view of the economics and policy issues surrounding PTAs. He notes at the outset that virtually all countries are members of a trade bloc and many belong to more than one; he goes on to introduce some of the main arguments that have been advanced for and against such regionalism. The author considers not only the traditional economic issues such as trade creation and trade diversion, but also more recent economic arguments such as whether PTAs stimulate investment and growth or promote economic and political credibility, peace, and stability.

James Mathis was invited to write the corresponding legal introductory piece. In his chapter, he considers some implications of the process of legalization of Article XXIV (the legal provision that sets out the requirements that PTAs must meet to be judged consistent with the multilateral trading system) for the so-called friends-or-foes debate between regionalism and multilateralism.

1

He recounts some of the legal and systemic issues that have concerned General Agreement on Tariffs and Trade (GATT) Article XXIV to show the trend that Article XXIV has been clarified over time and has become a legalized regime in the sense that WTO members are becoming aware of its requirements and (maybe) responding accordingly in their PTA formations. He notes that the recent WTO case of *Brazil–Tyres* is another step in this process where the European Community (EC) made some direct claims challenging the qualification and legal status of the Mercosur customs union under Article XXIV. Also in this case, the author underlines the importance of the Appellate Body's issuing a ruling that establishes GATT Article XX requirements as having a distinct priority over inconsistent regional arbitral rulings.

Caroline Freund discusses third-country effects of PTAs. She asks the question of whether or not regionalism negatively affects nonmembers (of the PTAs). To answer this question, she examines the effect of regional trade agreements on imports from nonmembers and the tariffs that they face. Using data from six regional trade agreements in Latin America and Europe, she does not find evidence that implementation of the regional agreements is associated with trade diversion from third countries to regional members. Using detailed industry data on preference margins and most-favored-nation (MFN) tariffs for three trade agreements in Latin America over twelve years, she finds that greater preference margins do not significantly reduce imports from third countries. She also looks at the effect of preferences on external tariffs. She finds evidence that preferential tariff reduction tends to precede the reduction of external MFN tariffs in a given sector, offering evidence of tariff complementarity. Overall, the results suggest that regionalism does not significantly harm nonmembers.

Thomas J. Prusa and **Robert Teh** in their chapter examine the provisions on antidumping, countervailing duties, and safeguards in seventy-four PTAs. A number of PTAs have succeeded in abolishing contingent protection measures. In addition, about half of PTAs have adopted PTA-specific rules that tighten discipline on the application of contingent protection measures on PTA members. This is most especially the case for antidumping. There is less of an impact for countervailing duty; this is likely because the economic impact of subsidies is global and there is an absence of commitments in PTAs on meaningful curbs on subsidies or state aid. It is very difficult, they argue, to offer a simple summary characterization of the provisions in PTAs. PTAs vary in size, degree of integration, geographic scope, and the level of economic development of their members. Contingent protection provisions vary greatly from one PTA to the next. In fact, contingent protection provisions differ for the *same* country across different PTAs. Some PTAs have additional rules; some have no rules; and others prohibit the use of these actions. Even if we focus only on the PTAs that incorporate additional rules it is hard to characterize what happens; there is no consensus set of provisions that are found in all (or even most) PTAs. The results of the mappings suggest the need to be vigilant about increased discrimination arising from trade remedy rules in PTAs. If nothing else, the complicated pattern of inclusion of these provisions threatens the delicate give-and-take balancing of incentives that is at the crux of the GATT/WTO agreements. An ongoing policy concern is that the elastic and selective nature of trade remedies may lead to more discrimination, with reduced trade remedy actions against PTA partners, but a greater frequency of trade remedy actions against nonmembers. The adoption of PTA-specific trade remedy rules increases this risk of discrimination, with trade remedies against PTA members being abolished outright or being subjected to greater discipline. In turn, this makes it more difficult for non-PTA members to agree to WTO liberalization because the requisite quid pro quo from PTA members may not be realized. Said differently, PTAs may erode the market access that nonmembers thought they had secured in prior WTO rounds, not primarily because of the discriminatory tariffs but rather because of contingent protection rules.

In his comment to the chapter by Prusa and Teh, **David Gantz** provides some contextual background on major trade remedies sanctioned by the WTO, antidumping actions, countervailing duty (antisubsidy) actions, and safeguards. He also examines in some detail the North American Free Trade Agreement (NAFTA) Chapter 19 dispute settlement mechanism for review of national administrative determinations in antidumping and countervailing duty cases and provides a few observations on specific aspects of the Prusa/Teh study.

Joel Trachtman provides a legal analysis of the significance of standards, technical regulations, and sanitary and phytosanitary provisions (collectively, TBTSPS provisions) in PTAs in relation to the multilateral trading system. He first examines the ways in which PTA regulation of national TBTSPS measures may contribute to or detract from liberalization goals. He then describes how GATT Article XXIV and the Understanding on the Interpretation of Article XXIV (the "Understanding"), as presently understood, regulate PTA regulation of national TBTSPS measures. This issue is increasingly important with the growth of PTAs, raising the question of whether and to what extent PTA internal integration is inconsistent with WTO law. There are two main concerns, in the author's view: first, PTAs may engage in internal integration of TPTSPS measures in a way that disadvantages suppliers from third states; second, PTAs may establish internal disciplines on TBTSPS measures by member-states that strike down these member-state measures as applied to suppliers from PTA partners, but not as applied to suppliers from third states. Thus, internal integration might require the nonapplication of a regulatory measure to a PTA partner, while allowing the application of the measure to third countries. For example, in the 2007 *Brazil–Tyres* case, one of the interesting questions was whether Brazil's Mercosur obligations provide it with an exception from its MFN obligations under GATT, allowing Brazil to discriminate in favor of Mercosur-origin retreaded tires. On the basis of this analysis, the author makes a series of recommendations regarding reinterpretation of some key GATT provisions.

Henrik Horn, Petros C. Mavroidis, and **André Sapir** argue that the growing concern about PTAs stems not only from their increasing number, but also from a perception that many recent PTAs go far beyond the scope of the current WTO agreements. This study examines in detail the coverage of all European Union (EU) and U.S. PTAs by distinguishing two categories of obligations: those already covered by the existing WTO agreements (WTO+), and those falling outside the current WTO (WTO-X). There are two main findings. First, both EU and U.S. PTAs cover a significant number of WTO+ areas, but EU agreements cover many more WTO-X areas than U.S. PTAs. Adjusting for legal inflation, U.S. agreements actually contain more legally binding provisions, both in WTO+ and WTO-X areas, than EU agreements. Second, although EU and U.S. PTAs go significantly beyond the WTO agreements, the number of legally enforceable WTO-X provisions contained in these agreements is in fact quite small. Provisions that can be regarded as really breaking new ground compared to existing WTO agreements only concern three regulatory issues: environment and labor standards for U.S. agreements and competition policy for EC agreements. Both sets of agreements also contain legally enforceable WTO-X provisions in three other regulatory areas, but these are already partly included in existing WTO agreements: investment, capital movement, and intellectual property.

In his comment, **Nuno Limão** states that the chapter provides a careful and systematic classification of the policy areas covered by the reciprocal preferential trade agreements of the United States and European Union as well as the extent of their legal enforceability. Given how unexplored this topic is, he provides suggestions for further research regarding the scope of agreements and countries that could be analyzed and the implications of the analysis for the interaction between preferential and multilateral trade liberalization.

Jeff Kenner deals with labor clauses in EU PTAs focusing on the Cotonou Partnership Agreement. The EU, as the world's largest trading bloc and foremost donor of development aid, seeks to exercise its expanding external powers to promote partnerships with countries that are willing to share its common values. To achieve consistency in its policy approach, the EU has adopted the mainstreaming method to balance the imperative of trade liberalization, in accordance with its WTO obligations, with the promotion of sustainable development, human rights, and foreign policy objectives. Requiring labor clauses as a standard feature of trade agreements has emerged as a central feature of this strategy, justified on the basis that it addresses the social dimension of globalization and is consistent with the International Labor Organization's (ILO) agenda. The Cotonou Partnership Agreement with the African, Caribbean, and Pacific (ACP) group of countries represents the EU's most ambitious attempt to promote market liberalization and development cooperation hand in hand with "positive conditionality, including "fundamental social rights" and international labor standards. Analysis of the agreement reveals that, although the location of the labor clause is somewhat remote, it provides a basis for promoting the ILO's

Core Labor Standards in addition to the parties' obligations under ratified conventions. Complex procedures and the difficulty of warding off charges of protectionism are likely to preempt a sanctions-based response to violations of labor rights. The alternative is a positive approach under which the EU recognizes that it is the stronger partner and should not coerce developing countries by seeking to promote its own values as universal or by exporting its social model. The recent Economic Partnership Agreement between the EU and Caribbean ACP countries could yet prove a model for just such a positive shift under which more confident partners recognize that improvements in labor standards have a beneficial effect on both economic efficiency and competitiveness within a more equitable trading framework.

Juan A. Marchetti deals with preferential liberalization of trade in services. He notes at the outset that it is not a new phenomenon but has become a more common and prominent feature of the latest generation of bilateral PTAs negotiated in this decade. As of September 15, 2010, fifty-six such accords have been notified to the WTO under Article V of the General Agreement on Trade and Services (GATS). Most of those notifications arrived after 2001, and many more agreements are currently being negotiated. One might expect, the author argues, that countries entering these PTAs do so with the objective of eliminating barriers to trade in services, but more importantly, in the hope that the agreements will actually increase bilateral services trade between the parties. Lack of reliable data on trade in services (especially of bilateral flows) has made it almost impossible to carry out empirical studies of the determinants of bilateral services trade flows and – in particular – of the effects of PTAs on trade flows in services. However, the availability of statistics on trade in services has improved over the last year, particularly among Organization for Economic Cooperation and Development (OECD) countries. Taking those developments in the statistical field into account, the main purpose of this chapter is to provide an initial quantitative estimate of the effect of PTAs on bilateral trade in services, using the standard gravity model. Another very important question, particularly when analyzing PTAs from a law and economics perspective, is whether different PTAs have a different impact on trade in services – in other words, whether some of them are more effective than others in promoting trade in services. This question will also be addressed in the chapter by first describing the different modalities adopted by PTAs and second by factoring those differences into the gravity equation.

William J. Davey, in his chapter, tries to advance some thoughts on a model GATT Article XXIV. He notes that the 1995 creation of the WTO in the Uruguay Round of multilateral trade negotiations was a spectacular success, and it appeared to usher into existence a new era of comprehensive multilateralism in world trade. However, viewed a decade and a half later in 2010, the plodding, on-again, off-again WTO Doha negotiations do not compare well at all in terms of effectiveness with the negotiating processes that have led in recent years to a rapid expansion in the number of PTAs. PTAs pose a serious problem for the WTO. Although their economic impacts may not be that negative, they undermine the multilateral trading system in various ways. They create trade diversion and discrimination problems, lead to greatly increased trade complexity through detailed origin rules and varying standards, lead to instability because each new PTA reshuffles the deck in terms of comparative advantage, and directly undermine the multilateral system by competing for negotiating resources and weakening coalitions in favor of multilateral trade liberalization. Because of the inherent superiority of the multilateral trading system, it is essential to blunt the deleterious effects of PTAs on that system and to try, at a minimum, to ensure that PTAs comply with existing WTO rules. Unfortunately, that may be difficult to do. Whereas it would be preferable to strengthen and clarify the existing WTO rules, that does not seem achievable in the near-to-medium term. Indeed, two recent high-profile reports of leading experts on the future of the WTO have concluded that PTAs represent a serious problem for the multilateral trading system, but they were unable to come up with viable proposals to improve the situation. Thus, this chapter attempts to fashion some more modest proposals that are more likely to be acceptable and yet still have some desirable benefits for the multilateral system in its struggle with the proliferation of PTAs.

In his comment to the chapter, **T. N. Srinivasan** underlines the importance of nondiscriminatory trade liberalization and briefly goes through the danger posed by PTAs. In his view, most of the PTAs in force are not only not free trade agreements (FTAs), but some also go beyond matters relating to trade in goods and services and into investment, competition policy, labor, and environmental standards and intellectual property that may or may not be trade related. He concludes that merely improving Article XXIV, which at best covers Customs Unions (CUS) and FTAs limited to trade, is not enough. Moreover, he is not convinced that clarifying the terms used and making other technical improvements in Article XXIV will obviate all the "long-standing, institutional, political, and legal" difficulties. Although he had no expectation that the Rules negotiations in the Doha Round would have effectively addressed them, as Professor Davey points out, the latest negotiation draft of the chair of the Rules negotiation group does not say anything on Article XXIV.

L. ALAN WINTERS

1 Preferential Trading Agreements: Friend or Foe?

Preferential trading agreements (PTAs) have proliferated inexorably during recent years. Virtually all countries are members of a trade bloc and many belong to more than one; more than two-fifths of world trade takes place within such agreements; PTAs are often advanced as a route to development for poor countries, both PTAs with other poor countries and with richer neighbors.

This chapter introduces some of the main arguments that have been advanced for and against such regionalism, especially, because this is my principal interest, as a tool of development policy. It briefly considers not only the traditional economic issues such as trade creation and trade diversion, but also more recent economic arguments such as whether PTAs stimulate investment and growth or promote economic and political credibility, peace, and stability. PTAs matter for individual countries: for potential members there are questions of whether to join (or perhaps with whom to join) and on what terms; for non-members, questions of whether others' PTAs will have adverse effect on them. In addition, PTAs matter systemically: here the issue is whether they strengthen or weaken the multilateral trading system that has served the world well for the past six decades. In the terminology of Baldwin's (2008) excellent recent survey, there are both "small-think" (individual) and "big-think" (systemic) dimensions to the question of regionalism, although I do not accept the implication that the former are uninteresting or unimportant.

The literature on PTAs has proliferated even faster than the phenomenon itself, but not the set of convincing general results to which one can appeal for policy guidance. There are at least two reasons for this. First, the question is complicated compared with normal trade policy analysis: it necessarily involves three parties – a home country, a partner country, and an excluded country – and it inevitably involves the general theory of second best where one set of distortions to trade (tariffs on the partner's sales in the home country) is examined

I am grateful to Emily Blanchard, Jim Mathias, and Petros Mavroidis for stimulating comments on the first version of this chapter, and to Gemechu Ayana for logistical help with it.

in the presence of another (tariffs on excluded country sales).[1] The analysis of
PTAs now also wrestles with inherently complex issues such as multidimensional
negotiations and the effects of regulation.

Second, there is not a great deal of experience from which to draw empirical
conclusions. Partly this is because (nearly) every PTA is *sui generis* to a significant
extent, and it is not clear how to simplify them analytically into a common form
in an innocuous way. In addition, for systematic questions, which are generally of
a very long-term nature, we have no data on a trading system containing a large
number of effective PTAs. Because the big question is whether to head further
in this direction, this is a serious shortcoming. Thus, this introduction is neither
comprehensive nor unambiguous. I will – simply, I hope – lay out a few theoretical constructs, consider some of the more important empirical results, and
sketch some of the policy debate. I hope that this chapter will provide a context
into which to fit the more specialized chapters that follow.

1. Member Countries

1.1. Trade Effects

The modern economic analysis of tariff preferences dates back to Viner
(1950).[2] As many economists have observed, Viner's formal treatment is incomplete and rather confusing (the book is nonetheless a great and wise contribution), but it is so intuitive and so central to the discourse that I reiterate it here.

A PTA, by removing barriers on trade between members of the PTA but not
on trade with excluded (nonmember) countries, almost always increases trade
between the members. The issue, however, is whether it "creates" trade by allowing cheaper products from other bloc members to substitute for more expen-
sive domestic production, or "diverts" it by substituting intra-bloc imports for
imports from outside the group. The latter can happen when outside goods
would be cheaper if all suppliers faced equal tariffs, but because inside goods
no longer face tariffs this gives them a competitive edge. In that case, the pref-
erence-granting country ends up paying more for the imports, the increase being
financed by monies that were initially going to the government in tariff revenues
now accruing to producers in the partner countries. Part of this extra cost is a
simple transfer from the taxpayers in the importing country to producers in the
newly exporting partner, but because the real cost of imports has risen (the partner is less efficient than outside producers, for otherwise it would have been
supplying the goods in the first place), real resources are also wasted by the

---

[1] Second-best theory argues that although removing all distortions in an economy may be
  shown to be welfare improving, removing some while leaving others may or may not be.
[2] Baldwin (2008) cites earlier contributions, notably Adam Smith's "certainty" that partners
  gain when they get preferential access to home markets, and Gottfried Haberler's "spillover," which indicated that excluded countries lose from this.

diversion. When all the commodities covered by the PTA are considered together, if trade diversion predominates, a PTA can reduce the welfare of all or some of the member countries.

Identifying and distinguishing between trade creation and trade diversion is not straightforward empirically. The greatest difficulty is deciding what trade would have looked like if no PTA had been formed – the counterfactual or what the Europeans refer to as the *anti-monde*. This is more a matter of judgment than of science, particularly when it comes to considering whether regionalism is central or incidental to the general liberalization of trade. The evidence on the balance between trade creation and diversion in trade blocs is mixed, but recent research shows that diversion can be quite significant – see for example Soloaga and Winters (2001).

A common way of establishing the *anti-monde* is by comparing the trade of PTA members with that of nonmembers, allowing for various other explanatory factors. These days, the standard tool for doing this is the so-called gravity model of international trade, which explains trade between countries in terms of their gross domestic products (GDPs), populations, distance from each other, contiguity, remoteness from markets, and various trade agreements.[3] Over time, these exercises have shown quite mixed results on the extent to which PTAs increase trade between members and reduce it between members and nonmembers. Recently, however, it has been observed that this ambiguity might be because PTAs are "endogenous," that is, caused by the same set of factors as determine trade flow. Suppose that countries sign PTAs with countries with whom their trade is significantly below what one might expect on the basis of gravity model (i.e., with partners with whom they apparently have a high potential to increase trade). The PTA might bring trade up to normal levels, but precisely because it now looks normal the estimated gravity model will not find anything special about having a PTA and suggest that PTAs have no effect. Baier and Bergstrand (2007) make this argument and find that, allowing for it, PTAs roughly double the amount of trade between members. (I will return to the factors that influence PTA formation in a later section.)

The traditional analysis of trade creation and diversion is based on a view of the world in which intercountry trade is driven entirely by differences in productivity and factor endowments. In fact, trade can also arise from product differentiation and economies of scale, which reduce costs as production grows. Import barriers in such worlds are additionally costly because competition between firms is weakened and consumers lose from the resulting cuts in output and increases in price. International trade offers an important means of increasing competition by allowing new suppliers to enter markets. PTAs can generate such benefits by fostering trade between members, combining larger firm sizes (which increases economies of scale) with competition between larger numbers of firms

---

[3] See Winters (1987) for an accessible discussion of other approaches to the *anti-monde*.

(which increases competition). This is possible because by combining several national markets, the number of producers in each country might fall while the number of sellers with reasonable access to each market rises (because producers from partner countries now have access).

These so-called pro-competitive effects are believed to have been strong during the course of European economic integration, but the empirical evidence that developing countries will be able to reap them in large amounts is not complete. This partly reflects the latter's production structure, with fewer goods in which differentiation and economies of scale are important, and also that significant increases in competition eventually depend on far more than merely removing tariffs and import quotas. Also, of course, if the aim is large markets and buying from firms that supply large markets, no market is larger than the world as a whole. That is, pro-competitive effects will be larger from nondiscriminatory trade liberalization than from discriminatory or restricted liberalization.

1.2. Why Join a PTA – and with Whom?

Why is regionalism so popular if it is just a pale imitation of nondiscriminatory free trade? This subsection briefly considers the basic international trade aspects of the question and then asks how various design features of a PTA might affect its net benefits for members. Section 3, which deals with systemic effects, considers many of the same arguments but places them in context of the trading system as a whole. As with the Vinerian effects, the key analytical step in *ex post* studies of PTA is the definition of *anti-monde*.

The obvious starting point is the hypothesis that if PTAs increase welfare, governments will pursue them. If there are different costs to reducing different trade barriers – even just perceived political costs – it may be that devoting effort to PTAs rather than multilateral or unilateral liberalization will look desirable.

The previous subsection noted Baier and Bergstand's argument that PTAs were endogenous. Baier and Bergstrand (2004) used a simple general equilibrium model with two factors, two monopolistically competitive product sectors, several countries and continents, and different inter- and intracontinental transport costs to derive predictions about who will pair off with whom if they aim to maximize welfare. This suggested that the following increased the probability of countries i and j signing a PTA:

- The smaller the distance between them,
- The greater their remoteness from the rest of the world,
- The larger i and j are,
- The more similar their size (real GDP),
- The less similar their factor endowments (up to the point where we get complete specialization), and
- The more similar is the combined endowment of i and j to the rest of the world's.

Of course, such predictions are just the function of the details of the theoretical model underlying them, but Baier and Bergstrand do have the advantage of having estimated their model on real data and found a very respectable degree of fit: 85 percent of the PTAs and 95 percent of the non-PTA country-pairs in the world were correctly forecast.

In terms of the current discussion, this is not really a test of what determines PTA formation because different theories could have produced similar estimating equations and no alternative variables were contrasted with the selected ones. However, their work certainly suggests that economic factors play a major role in determining our current set of PTAs and that, if they are right, it may be time to stop creating PTAs because all the best ones have been done already!

Although the welfare implications of PTAs are ambiguous in general, one general result is that small countries (for which world prices are given) are likely to lose from a PTA between themselves unless they lower trade barriers with respect to excluded countries (Schiff, 1997; Winters and Schiff, 2003). Moreover, if external trade barriers are not reduced, not only is the bloc as a whole likely to lose, but the distribution of loss is likely to be highly asymmetric, with the more developed members gaining at the expense of the poorer, less developed ones (because their manufacturing exports gain access to the latter's markets). Examples of such problems include the East African Community in the 1960s, where Kenya gained at the expense of Uganda and Tanzania, and the Central American Common Market, where El Salvador gained at the expense of Honduras.

This is essentially the reasoning behind an interesting recent result that if two countries form a PTA, the one whose endowments are more similar to the world average will tend to gain more than the one that is less similar (Venables, 2003). If the two countries have above-average incomes and endowments, this tends to lead to convergence between the two partners, but if they have below-average incomes (i.e., the PTA is between developing countries), it causes divergence.

Related to the size effect, there are benefits of signing a PTA with a large open neighbor – for example, Mexico signed with the United States. This is because an economically large country is more likely to be able to supply all its partner's needs with no increase in marginal costs; and if it is open as well, it will tend to be a more efficient supplier of most goods and a source of greater competition.

An important distinction is between free trade areas (FTAs) that have free trade between members, and customs unions (CUs) that have that plus a common external tariff or, strictly, common trade policy toward excluded countries. FTAs are easier to create and can be institutionally very light, whereas CUs require the negotiation of the common external tariff and coordination of all future trade policy changes. FTAs, however, face the danger of trade deflection – goods entering the member with the lowest tariff and transferring, tax free, to other members from there. Except for the extra transportation cost, this is efficient economically because it lowers the effective tariff, but it undermines the protective effect of some members' own tariff structures. Therefore, governments seek to prevent it by imposing rules of origin (RoOs) to ensure that only goods produced locally in the partner country get tariff exemptions. Such rules are often cumbersome, arbitrary, and protectionist and can greatly reduce the value of the FTA (see, e.g., Anson et al., 2005). CUs avoid this problem if they are complete and can thus induce a greater degree of integration.

There is a huge literature on RoOs (e.g., Krueger, 1999; Augier et al., 2005). It is important in that RoOs are self-imposed trade barriers that take no resources or technical skills to reform (although doing so imposes a political cost, of course). Thus, they are prime candidates for reform. Also, RoOs can be very distortive of markets for particular intermediate inputs. Suppose home's tariff on widgets is $10 and that its RoOs offer its partner exemption from the tariff only on condition that input x, which costs $10 if produced outside the PTA, is produced within the PTA (which comprises home and partner). Meeting the RoO saves producers $10 if they purchase x within the PTA and they will be willing to transfer nearly all of that saving to local x producers in order to do so. Relative to there being no RoO, the x producers essentially get a transfer of $10 on top of the $10 that would have been paid for x abroad. Local producers might be only half as efficient as external producers are and yet still make the sale!

On the other hand, the $10 per widget tariff is the maximum distortion that the RoOs can cause – no one will spend $11 of real resources to avoid a $10 tax. Thus, if tariffs on excluded countries are low, and if there are no other barriers to trade, the damage that a RoO can cause is relatively small.

Another important difference between FTAs and CUs lies in the incentives they create for operating a liberal (i.e., low barrier) trade policy toward nonmembers; it has been argued that there is a tendency for FTAs to be more liberal than CUs. They have less market power and members might compete with each other to reduce tariffs and so enlarge their share of the PTA's imports and hence tariff revenue. Once we recognize that lobbying influences tariffs, it becomes plain that it will affect FTAs and CUs too. For both, there is a presumption that the exceptions to internal free trade negotiated as the PTA is formed will tend to reduce the degree of trade creation, and so reduce the potential benefits. Grossman and Helpman (1995) analyze this in theory, while Olarreaga and Soloaga (1998) and Olarreaga, Soloaga, and Winters (1999) show the importance of these political factors in the determination of the internal and external trade policies of Mercosur countries. Moreover, in the case of CUs, the PTA will change the environment for future lobbying, for decisions are made collectively, although whether this will be toward or away from greater protectionism is impossible to say *a priori*.

1.3. Investment

Raising investment is a prominent objective of many regional agreements. The logic is that larger markets, greater competition, and improved policy credibility will increase the incentives for investment and so raise incomes. The argument applies to all investment but is most explicitly applied to regionalism as a means of attracting foreign direct investment. Ethier (1998a, b) composes a paean to regionalism on this basis. It has some validity in that integration into production chains and the credibility of reforms undoubtedly are important for developing countries. Whether it really captures the motivation for PTAs or whether it is a satisfactory normative to justification of regionalism is quite unclear; however, see Winters (1998).

Early Latin American PTAs were highly interventionist, co-opting regional integration into import substitution at a regional level. Such policies failed almost completely and have now been superseded by a much more market-friendly approach. Part of the latter has been a greater emphasis on policies guaranteeing the fair treatment of investment. These guarantees are often embodied in bilateral investment treaties (BITs), or, where they exist, the investment chapters of PTA. BITs typically contribute to negative integration – that is, precluding certain policies rather than requiring policies to actively encourage investment – but they may play an important facilitating role in investment flows (see Hallward-Driemeier, 2003).

Far more positive in intent is the common argument that PTAs add credibility to government policies in general and thus help to raise investment and attract foreign direct investment (FDI). In fact, however, South–South PTAs are unlikely to do this and may hinder investment if they are not accompanied by trade liberalization with the rest of the world. North–South PTAs, on the other hand, can enhance a Southern country's credibility, but typically only if the PTA is likely to enhance economic performance in its own right and if the large Northern partner is willing to enforce investment-encouraging "club rules." The latter is more likely to be true if the policies on which a developing country wants to gain credibility are specified explicitly in the agreement, if the Northern partner has an identified interest in the Southern partner's success (e.g., alleviating pressures to migrate), and if the Northern partner is naturally "an enforcer." The contrast between the United States and the European Union (EU) is instructive in this regard. The United States typically calls much more explicitly for reforms in investment and other areas than does the EU and shows a much greater willingness to engage developing partners if they appear to be failing to deliver. Having watched the sad spectacle of the EU negotiating new reciprocal PTAs with the Africa, Caribbean, and Pacific (ACP) states over the past decade, one can hardly expect any increase in credibility from these agreements.[4]

Unfortunately, there are few empirical studies of the impact of PTAs on investment. Where we do have evidence, it tends to suggest mild positive effects on investment, but there is no evidence that this translates into higher economic growth. Firmer evidence is available that PTAs boost FDI from

---

[4] Indeed, one can expect little good at all – a perfectly foreseeable outcome as shown, for example, in Winters (2001).

nonmember countries, however, at least for a period. In Mexico, most of the post-North American Free Trade Agreement (NAFTA) boom in FDI went to exportable sectors and seems to have generated large benefits. In Mercosur, it seemed to go to protected (and thus inefficient) import-competing sectors, and protection was even increased to attract FDI in some sectors (e.g., automotive sector) with a likely negative impact on welfare.

The real key to investment is the general policy stance in areas such as sound macroeconomic policies, well-defined property rights, and efficient financial and banking sectors. A PTA may foster investment if it significantly raises policy credibility and market size, but it needs to be accompanied by reasonable conditions overall.

Investment patterns can be seriously affected by the so-called hub-and-spoke phenomenon. This occurs when a country (the hub) signs FTAs with various countries (the spokes) that do not sign FTAs among themselves. Other things being equal, investors will prefer to invest in the exporting sectors of the hub than in those of the spokes, because they can reach all the spokes from the hub but cannot do so from one of the spokes. One way to minimize this effect is for the spokes to sign FTAs with each other's countries. Another is nondiscriminatory most-favored-nation (MFN) trade liberalization.

1.4. Industrial Location and Growth

Economists have long been aware that industry tends to cluster into particular locations to reap economies of agglomeration such as better and cheaper access to inputs, thick labor markets, and access to informal knowledge exchanges. Against these benefits must be balanced congestion costs, the greater competition that is experienced when firms are clustered, and the transport/transaction cost of serving the market that is not the production center. When economic integration occurs, the reductions in the transaction costs disturb previous equilibria with sometimes very large effects. The economics profession has only recently learned to model these phenomenon formally and thus to start to identify precisely how they interact. The theory arose – with Krugman and Venables (1990) – from attempts to understand the possible effects of the enlargement and deepening of the EU and so lends itself directly to the consideration of PTAs. The models do not yet appear to be very realistic and have not yet been accompanied by much empirical evidence. Thus, they are more parables than forecasts. However, they do shed light on qualitative factors and they address such a major concern of policy makers that it is useful to explore their implications for developing countries.[5]

Creating a PTA will change the incentives for industry to agglomerate, because it increases market size and allows the more effective exploitation of the

[5] The most comprehensive treatment is still Fujita, Krugman, and Venables (1999).

links between firms (Fujita et al., 1999). As just noted, a PTA may attract industry into member countries at the expense of nonmembers, but it will also frequently cause industry to relocate between the members. For PTAs between poor countries, this seems likely to increase intermember inequalities because it makes it easier for firms to agglomerate in the more prosperous countries while still selling in the others. For PTAs involving richer members, on the other hand, the results are less clear-cut, and it is quite possible that poorer members will experience strong catch-up following entry to a PTA. This is the case for Spain and Portugal following their accession to the EU in 1986 and is certainly the hope for the countries of Central Europe and the Baltic following theirs in 2004.[6]

Puga and Venables (1998) use this theory of the economic geography of PTAs to suggest that, as trade barriers fall within a North–South PTA, industry will eventually start to grow in a Southern partner as its lower factor costs outweigh the (falling) cost of exporting to the larger Northern market. If there are two (or more) Southern partners, agglomeration economies will limit industrialization to just one of them initially, causing divergence among them. If being the "winner" among Southern partners depends on having a head start over one's rivals, there is clearly an incentive for Southern countries to try to sign PTAs with a Northern partner before their rivals do. This might be one factor behind the recent rush into North–South arrangements. Puga and Venables also suggest that the best outcome for a Southern country is to be in such a PTA while other Southern countries are excluded.

1.5. "Deep Integration"

The discussion so far has concentrated on trade and investment policies, the standard building blocks for analyzing international policy, and also implicitly on the market for goods. However, as trade barriers have come down the important role that domestic regulation plays in economic integration has become plain, especially in services, trade in which is growing faster than in goods. Cooperation on, and the liberalization of, domestic policies can substantially increase the gains from forming a trade bloc. It can lift barriers that isolate national markets for similar goods and services and deliver economic benefits many times larger than those available from mere tariff agreements. Intergovernmental cooperation in designing and applying domestic policies such as taxes, health and safety regulations, and environmental standards – so-called "deep integration" – increases competition in domestic markets by reducing transaction costs and allowing new suppliers to enter markets. It can also help to overcome market failures and ensure that trade restrictions are not reimposed through the back door. Evans et al. (2006) make this case in detail.

---

[6] Ireland's take-off came too late to be attributed directly to its accession to the EU, but without the membership it would almost certainly not have occurred.

Experience with deep integration is very mixed. Until the 1990s, few PTAs contemplated it at all and in the main example – what we now call the European Union – the deep intentions of the original (1957) Treaty of Rome were largely ignored until the Single Market Program (SMP) of the late 1980s. (The main exceptions were the Common Agricultural Policy and the Competition regime.) Even since the SMP, deep integration has proved hard to achieve, and there remain many areas in which the European market is segmented by regulatory differences. In its many PTAs with other countries, the EU genuflects toward deep integration but actually seeks very little.

The United States has pursued deep integration in a number of areas such as investment and intellectual property, using the NAFTA as a model (see World Bank, 2005). In other areas, however, it has shown little interest because it does not wish to compromise its own policies (e.g., competition) and because it does not welcome the institutional burden of joint decision making. Other PTAs are increasingly mentioning areas of deep integration and services trade liberalization. The agreements are said in some cases to cover more services areas than World Trade Organization (WTO) concessions have – for example, Roy, Marchetti, and Lim (2007) – and in others to entail deeper integration than the latter do (e.g., Houde et al., 2007). What is missing so far, however, is evidence that they have resulted in much liberalization of either a bilateral or multilateral nature. (Many argue that deep integration is more difficult to pursue in a discriminatory way so that it is, in fact, much more compatible with multilateralism than are tariff preferences. For example, unifying standards across a PTA benefits excluded county exporters to the region as well as members, and relaxing investment establishment rules benefits all potential entrants.)

Experience suggests that negotiated policy integration is very demanding both politically and technically. Hence, without specific timetables for progress and further negotiation, PTAs are unlikely to make only very slow progress. Merely writing deep integration into an agreement is not sufficient to achieve it. Moreover, PTAs are not the only game in town. Indeed, independent decisions to adopt policies used elsewhere and to pursue multilateral efforts on international technical and regulatory standards have been at least as common as regional efforts. Developing countries can do much to achieve the benefits of policy integration unilaterally by adopting international standards and recognizing the regulatory norms of their major markets, such as the EU and the United States. This is often rejected by governments as slight on their sovereignty; the appropriate policy response to such a concern is "get real."

If developing countries can pursue elements of deep integration unilaterally, the question arises as to why they might combine them with a PTA. The tariff preference component of a PTA might provide benefits to help overcome opposition to necessary domestic policy reforms, and deep integration might assist the implementation and enforcement of PTA trade policies. Of course, such linkage does not excuse selecting suboptimal trade and domestic reforms, but if both are desirable in their own right, combining them might be politically efficient. Fundamentally, there is no technical reason why integrating domestic policies should require trade preferences. For instance, the EU and the United States have drawn up a series of mutual recognition agreements for sectoral product standards completely outside a PTA context. To date, however, developing countries have been entirely excluded from such initiatives.

2. Excluded Countries

I have already noted that nearly every country is excluded from nearly every PTA. Hence in terms of frequency, the discussion in this section will be relevant far more often than that in the previous one. In terms of the depth of the effects, however, it will generally not be more relevant – that is, effects on members are generally larger than those on nonmembers. This has the attraction that it is easier to specify the *anti-mode*: in this section I assume that the excluded country governments do not change their policies at all because of confronting a PTA.

The most common assertion about the way in which a PTA hurts an excluded country is that trade diversion curtails its exports to the PTA (relative to a counterfactual). However, if the price of the lost exports equaled their marginal cost of production and sale (including normal profit) and the loss of exports was not very large, then apart from costs of adjustment as factors of production have to move from one activity to another, the excluded country does not suffer any first-order welfare loss. The resources released by not producing the export are just as valuable as selling the export and buying an import instead. If, on the other hand, export prices exceed marginal costs, then for each unit of exports lost, real income is lost; it falls by the difference between the value of exports in terms of the imports they finance and the value of the resources that foregoing them releases into the domestic economy.[7]

One way in which export prices may exceed marginal cost is if exporting generates supernormal profits because export markets are imperfectly competitive. Such profits are then lost on any trade that is diverted and cannot be replaced by alternative sales at the same price. Similar is the case with industries having economies of scale. If the creation of a PTA causes industry in the rest of the world to contract, then the cost of all its output increases, imposing costs on its other customers and reducing its profit margins. Haaland and Norman (1992), for instance, predicted that European Free Trade Association (EFTA) countries would lose in this way from the creation of the single market in the EU, but the evidence for these effects is generally rather weak despite the frequency with which they are referred to.

Another important source of difference between export values and marginal costs is export taxes. If a PTA cuts an excluded country's exports, the released

---

[7] This section is based on Chang and Winters (2002a) and related papers.

resources cover the cost of production, but not the tax, and aggregate income falls. Related to this – and potentially more important practically – the so-called Lerner symmetry theorem states that export taxes are equivalent to import taxes. This suggests that a country that taxes imports – that is, has tariffs – can lose from its neighbors' PTAs. The story is as follows: tariffs reduce the level of imports below the optimal level and mean that a unit of imports is valued by consumers at more than it costs the country as a whole to buy it. Consumers value it at $(p + t)$ – the price plus the tariff, which is what they are willing to pay for it, but it costs the country only p, the tax just being recycled by government to consumers in their role as taxpayers. If, for extraneous reasons like a PTA, exports fall, imports must eventually follow. Because these imports are worth more than they cost, welfare is lost as they fall.

The second way in which a loss of exports can affect an excluded country is via the prices at which exporters can sell their products. This depends partly on the size of the PTA in question, or more specifically on the importance of the trade flow on which a preference is granted. Although small PTAs will rarely matter because they generally will not affect the prices at which trade occurs, large agreements like the EU or the Free Trade Area of the Americas (FTAA) are large enough to affect world prices. Their existence has implications for everyone in the market – positive for buyers if prices fall and negative for sellers – whether or not they deal with the PTA itself. The significance of price changes is that they affect not just marginal trade, but the whole volume of existing trade.

Looking at the large country case, Robert Mundell (1964) illustrates the terms of trade effects of a PTA in a three-country general-equilibrium model with goods being gross substitutes and price changes occurring to restore balance of payments equilibrium in response to an initial preferential tariff shock. He showed that for a single preferential tariff change by one member, the preferred exporting partner's terms of trade improved, while those of the excluded country deteriorated. Because a PTA amounts essentially to the two partners' swapping such concessions, the excluded country potentially loses at every turn.

Expressing this in terms of firm behavior, when a member-country firm benefits from a preferential tariff concession it becomes more competitive in the PTA market, and excluded country firms may have to respond by reducing their prices in compensation. This is a simple terms of trade change for the exporter – it now gets less for every unit that it sells in that market – and we could measure the loss as $x^* dp$, where x is the volume of exports and dp is the induced change in price. Exporters may be able to avoid some of the loss by redirecting exports to other markets or switching resources to producing other goods, but unless these are easily achieved and generate the same revenue as the lost exports, there will be a loss. If markets are segmented so that prices depend only on local market conditions, even small PTAs may affect the pricing behavior of suppliers to the preferred market. These effects are likely to be larger if not only markets are segmented, but goods are differentiated by place of production and/or place of sale so that each trade is, strictly speaking, unique. If the trade flows affected by this are large relative to the economies concerned, the PTA could lead to an appreciable loss of welfare for the excluded countries.

Despite the importance of price effects like this in the theoretical literature on trade policy, not much empirical work was done on the terms of trade effects of PTA until the past decade. Winters and Chang (2000) examined the price effects of Spanish accession to the EC in 1986 on the exports of major excluded Organization for Economic Cooperation and Development (OECD) countries. This work established beyond doubt that, as Spain offered preferential access to European Community suppliers, U.S. pre-tariff export prices to Spain fell relative to EC prices, but it recognized that it had not unambiguously proven that this reflected falling U.S. prices rather than rising EC ones. For a variety of reasons, however, there seemed most likely to be an element of falling U.S. prices, so the authors felt able to suggest that the PTA had had an adverse effect on the excluded countries, "reducing the pre-tariff price of U.S. exports relative to that of member country exports by nearly half of any tariff differential."

A more thorough exercise was conducted by Chang and Winters (2002b), which examined the creation of Mercosur. They postulated that excluded countries' firms' export prices to Brazil would be influenced not only by the tariffs that they faced, but also by the tariffs that their rivals in member countries faced, via the effect of the latter on the rivals' prices. Thus, in the case of Mercosur, excluded countries suffered a decline in their terms of trade as they reduced prices in reaction to the improved market access that their competitors from Argentina received within Brazil. In this study, Chang and Winters were able to look at U.S. export prices to Brazil relative to U.S. export prices to other markets as well as relative to those of Argentinian exports to Brazil. The comparisons between different U.S. export markets made it clear that U.S. firms had discounted sales to Brazil, with an estimated loss of $600 million per annum in the terms of trade.

Romalis (2007) investigates the terms of trade effects of NAFTA, using quite different methods from Chang and Winters. He finds them to exist but to be smaller than the latter's, plausibly, he speculates, because the United States was already a highly competitive market so that margins could not be squeezed much further. Romalis also finds plenty of cases where imports from excluded countries disappeared, arguably an extreme form of terms of trade effect.

3. PTAs and the Trading System

Whereas Section 2 considered the effects of PTAs on individual excluded countries, this section considers how regionalism affects the interactions between countries within the international economy and community. Regrettably, many of the arguments are only theoretical, for we just do not have enough observations of long-lived regionalism to make empirical judgments, and as we enter the twenty-first century, we are dealing with a completely new world of many active trade blocs as opposed to the late-twentieth-century model of a multilateral world with a few blocs. The essential question is whether the growth of PTAs helps or hinders progress toward nondiscriminatory trade liberalization – building blocks versus stumbling blocks in Bhagwati's phrase, stepping-stones versus millstones in Schiff and Winters'. In some expositions, this question is expressed as "regionalism versus multilateralism," but as I showed in Winters (1997) it is difficult to capture all the dimensions of multilateralism in a single concept (still less a single number), so this lens has not proved to be of much more than rhetorical use. Richard Baldwin (2008) has recently produced an interesting survey of the area, so I shall be brief.

The key difference between this and the previous section is that here the issue is how excluded governments react to the PTA. Thus, defining the *anti-mode*, and even more so, measuring it, is very complex.

3.1 Millstones

Following Baldwin we can identify three mechanisms whereby creating PTAs influences the political incentives to move toward multilateral free (or freer) trade. First, a terms-of-trade logic. Given that creating a PTA often entails improving members' terms of trade vis-à-vis the rest of the world, – bluntly, exploiting the rest of the world – members lose something when they reduce tariffs on excluded countries below some threshold and this could be enough to discourage them from doing so. For sure, the same phenomenon affects each country individually, but it will be smaller in this case because individual countries will not have the market power that they have collectively. Thus, it may be that the market power held by a PTA provides an incentive to resist multilateral overtures to liberalization that no member acting alone would reject.

It is sometimes argued that this outcome requires greater coordination than most groups of countries can muster, but this is not obvious. It does not require that all members have the same tariff (i.e., form a custom union) or that they raise tariffs when the PTA is formed (which historically we have not observed – quite possibly because the General Agreement on Tariffs and Trade [GATT]/WTO forbids it). Given that the modern world started in 1945 from tariffs that were too high for global efficiency, and that for a variety of reasons tariffs are gradually falling, it is perfectly possible that the market power of PTAs is reflected in the progress of liberalization stopping before it would have done if every country had only MFN trade policies. It is quite conceivable that a PTA settles at a point at which its welfare exceeds what its members would get under multilateral free trade. That is, one or more PTAs will block the multilateral outcome.

The second millstone effect is essentially political. Inelegantly termed the "goodies bag" by Baldwin, this argues that a PTA delivers something else of value to members other than the immediate effect of the trade preferences. One example would be using a PTA to foster contacts and understanding between former enemies; the classic case of this is the EU whose earlier incarnations were aimed at reconciling France and Germany. Other examples and the general case are discussed in Schiff and Winters (1998). A second example would be in highly asymmetrical PTAs: for these, it is difficult to see any economic return to the much larger country, so that, the argument goes, the motivation for the PTA must be political. Consider the EU's Economic Partnership Agreement (EPAs) with the small ACP states, or even more obviously, the unilateral (i.e., unreciprocated) preferences that the EU granted them before the EPAs. Limao (2006, 2007) and Limao and Karasaovali (2008) find evidence that tariff headings on which the United States and the EU had previously granted preferences were subject to smaller reductions than other heading in the Uruguay Round. Limao (2007) and Limao and Olarreaga (2006) draw the obvious policy conclusion that if *A* wishes to favor *B* in a way that is not eroded by trade talks, it should use import subsidies rather than preferences to do so. This is not likely to catch on in practice, but it admirably illustrates the nature of the problem. Moreover, even if the grantor of preferences is happy to see them eroded, the recipients may not, and hence seek to block multilateral liberalization. This almost certainly lies behind the least developed countries (LDCs) and ACP countries' lack of enthusiasm for the Doha Round.

A fascinating variant of the "goodies bag" hypothesis concerns the form of multilateralism. Chase (2006) argues cogently that the reason that the GATT (and its precursor, the Havana Charter for the aborted International Trade Organization) permits FTAs as well as customs unions is that the United States had strong reasons to sign an FTA with Canada. That is, the United States was willing to shackle multilateralism with an exception contrary to its public adherence to the principle of nondiscrimination because political imperatives – binding together the noncommunist coalition – called for preferences. It is true that (shackled) multilateralism prevailed and that for many years the exception lay dormant (the U.S.–Canada FTA did not progress for more than forty years), but this was a case not of regional negotiations helping multilateralism along, but the opposite.

The third millstone arises if, starting from MFN restricted trade, a PTA delivers a set of benefits at low political cost from which the net benefits of moving to full free trade would not outweigh the political cost, but where a move from MFN restriction straight to free trade would have been worthwhile (Levy, 1997). Baldwin suggests that reaping the benefits of intra-industry trade within a PTA may be attractive because it entails little intersectoral adjustment and that moving from there to full MFN free trade is unattractive because it is likely to increase inter-industry trade and hence adjustment costs. If countries had started from tariff-ridden trade and had no PTA option, however, the net political benefit of achieving both intra- and interindustry by moving straight to MFN free trade may have been positive.

3.2. Stepping-Stones

The notion that PTAs could be stepping-stones to multilateral free trade dates back to Kemp and Wan (1976) or even, according Baldwin (2008), to Meade (1955). If a PTA selects its external tariffs in such a way that its collective trade with the rest of the world is identical to its pre-PTA (or strictly non-PTA) trade, the rest of the world is unaffected by it. However, within the bloc, liberalizing trade between members enhances efficiency, so that, with suitable (lump-sum) redistribution between countries, every member gains. Through a series of such welfare-enhancing deals, a PTA could expand until it included the whole world, that is, achieved global free trade. The practical problems with this elegant piece of theory include that calculating the "Kemp–Wan" tariff would be too complex in reality, and that nothing obliges the PTA to choose its external tariff in this way – certainly not the WTO. Indeed, in any case where the PTA has market power it forgoes welfare by choosing the Kemp–Wan tariff and so may be reluctant to do so.[8]

The essence of the modern stepping-stones argument is that each creation or expansion of a PTA changes something that makes a further act of regionalism or liberalization suddenly appear attractive, and so on all the way to free trade. Suppose that policy emerges from a political equilibrium that balances sector-specific pro- and antiprotection forces. If a PTA has any efficiency benefits (i.e., trade creation), it will tend to shift resources out of import-competing and into exporting sectors. If political power is based on capital invested or numbers employed, this switches the political equilibrium toward greater openness and may thus induce a next act of liberalization. Baldwin and Robert-Nicoud (2008) christen this the juggernaut theory – a process that generates its own momentum toward free trade. The theory has significant historical resonance in both the nineteenth and twentieth centuries and may well be significant even if the juggernaut gets stuck along the way by political interests with power beyond their numbers (farmers?) or not defined by sectoral loyalties.

The second thing that a PTA might change is the trading conditions faced by excluded countries. Being left out of all blocs in a fragmenting world is a fear frequently expressed by policy makers, and so as one act of regionalism occurs it may create conditions for the next. The economics of this arise because, as a bloc enlarges, it tends to have stronger adverse effects on excluded countries' terms of trade or levels of imports. Thus, the incentives to join the bloc to overcome these effects increase, eventually overcoming other discouragements – say fears about loss of sovereignty. Baldwin (1995) formulated this so-called domino theory to explain European enlargement, which it very plausibly does for richer members such as the UK and the Scandinavians. It also seems to lie behind much of the

---

[8] Kemp and Wan (1976) referred to a customs union. Only years later was the same result proved for free trade areas by Panagariya and Krishna (2002).

spread of regionalism over the 1980s and 1990s – for example, when Canada sought access to the U.S.–Mexican talks that eventually created NAFTA, and with several Latin American and Caribbean countries seeking accession afterward. It is important to note, however, that even though every act of accession is voluntary and increases the accedant's welfare, we cannot infer that, because regionalism is spreading, it is benign. If everyone in your neighborhood is in a street gang, you may want to belong to one yourself, but that does not make gangs a good thing.

One of the analytical problems with domino regionalism is that although enlarging a PTA might increase the incentives for new members to join, it does not correspondingly increase the incentives for existing members to let them in. Given that PTAs discriminate against excluded countries, insiders will want to stop expansion well short of the whole world: there is no point being on the inside if there is no one on the outside to exploit. As Baldwin (2008) notes, existing members cannot stop the others from going off to form their own blocs, however, and this may indeed counter some of the original PTA's market power. However, it is far from guaranteed that once the world has split into several competing blocs, these will combine to create global free trade – see, for example, Campa and Sorenson (1996). Antras, Aghion, and Helpman (2007) give a high-octane version of this issue.

It is sometimes argued that one way around the problem of blockaded entry would be to insist on open access to all PTAs – that is, that any country that could adhere to the rules of a PTA could join it and reap its benefits. In theory, this may be true; indeed it is true in Yi's (1996) very special model, although as Loke (2006) shows, the finding is very fragile. However, in practice, given that accession has to be negotiated because the rules of nearly all PTAs entail more than just tariff reductions, there is no operational way to insist on such access. The concept of "open regionalism," which has several definitions, is related to this (Bergsten, 1997). I see this as more of a slogan than an analytical tool, for, according to the definition, it either reduces to something else (e.g., multilateralism) or it does not separate "good" PTAs from "bad." Fortunately, it seems to be falling out of fashion.

3.3. Equilibrium Tariff

The previous discussion has seen the regionalism versus multilateralism question in terms of PTAs versus multilateral trade rounds. However, there is also the question of whether PTAs affect the tariffs that their members levy on excluded countries in the absence of negotiations. Unfortunately, this is just as ambiguous as the previous discussion. As we saw earlier, signing a PTA might raise members' optimal tariffs on outsiders (or cause them to fall less far) to exploit the market power of the PTA. Second, if members and nonmembers provide different varieties of a good, governments might be able to mitigate the political cost of having a zero tariff on a member's variety by having a higher one on a nonmember's one.

Equally, however, the welfare cost of a multi-product tariff structure typically increases the greater the dispersion of the rates. Thus, if one has to have zero on partners' varieties, economic logic tends to dictate having lower tariffs on nonpartners' to reduce the cost of trade diversion. A variant of this argument pertains only to the FTAs: once your partner has captured your market for X and pays you no tariff, it pays you to reduce your tariff on X sufficiently to return the market to (tariff-paying) excluded country suppliers. If there were no RoOs, your partner would then reduce its tariff to just below yours so that X entered via its customs posts and was then transshipped to you.[9]

A variant of this model notes that trade agreements need to be self-enforcing (incentive compatible) and considers this in the context of repeated games. Suppose that countries gain from their own tariffs but lose when others impose tariffs on them (a terms-of-trade model). They may be able to agree to reduce tariffs below the one-time noncompetitive game level through punishment (so-called trigger) strategies. Assume that tariffs are set for finite periods. If both countries impose the low cooperative tariff in period t, both do so again in period $(t + 1)$ and cooperation is sustained. However, suppose A cheats and raises its tariff in period t while B maintains its low tariff; in period $(t + 1)$ B raises its tariff to the noncompetitive level, and anticipating this, A does so too. Cooperation is withdrawn for some period, possibly infinitely, while this punishment proceeds. The trade-off for A in deciding whether to cheat is whether one period's gain while it cheats is offset by the losses in the period of punishment that follows. It depends on the level of the cooperative tariffs (cheating is more attractive the lower the tariff that B maintains during the period t), the length of the period during which cheating is possible, the number of periods that punishment is expected to continue for, and its discount rate (because gains come before the losses). The less attractive is cheating, the lower the level of the cooperative tariff that can be maintained by the threats of retaliation.

Signing a PTA changes trade flows and hence affects the benefits of cheating and the cost of punishment. Thus, it can change the cooperative tariff that trigger strategies can maintain. If a PTA increases the benefits of cheating by more than the cost of punishment, the cooperative tariffs will rise – that is, the world system will have higher tariffs between a PTA and excluded countries than would its members have maintained in the absence of the PTA.

Two reservations about this approach have been registered. First, Baldwin (2008) argues that because tariffs are obvious and can be changed overnight, the period for which cheating is feasible is infinitesimal so that the criterion in the negotiating game just becomes whether welfare under cooperation exceeds

---

[9] In fact, this works even with RoOs if the partner is large but still imports X. It reduces its tariff on X (just below yours, rendering its internal price just below yours, sells its own output to you at that price, and imports more from outside the PTA to satisfy domestic consumption).

that under noncooperation. For large partners with market power, it may not do so, for the reasons spelled out earlier, whereas for small ones it typically will. The intellectual point, however, is that if cheating induces immediate retaliation, the methodology of trigger strategies breaks down and offers no additional insight as to what tariff will be.

The Baldwin critique is certainly powerful but possibly overstated. In the real world, the WTO has rules about retaliation that slow it down (and preclude the plaintiff from receiving compensation for the period between the onset of the violation and its removal). In at least some cases, the desire to preserve the system – that is, the cooperation that parties value – may allow finite periods of cheating. Second, not all real-world violations are as obvious as the negotiating model assumes. The application of antidumping duties and the manipulation of standards restrict trade but may not trigger immediate responses.

The second reservation is that the results of this approach are not very definitive. Thus, for example, Bagwell and Staiger 2002), its initiators, find that FTAs tend to undermine multilateral cooperation whereas customs unions do not. The differences are clear in their models, but are possibly not very significant quantitatively and depend, anyway, on the precise details of the negotiating game assumed. Thus, one emerges feeling that the results are fragile.

The economics of the tariff negotiating model are very simple. One realistic extension is foreign direct investment, which modifies the incentives for governments to protect industries. If tariff increases merely create profits that flow out to overseas owners, they may be less attractive. Blanchard (2007) suggests that, in such a world, allowing preferences can lower equilibrium tariffs.

3.4. Trade Negotiations

If PTAs made trade negotiations easier, perhaps they would help the world evolve toward freer trade. Coordinated coalitions may have greater negotiating power than their members individually, and such coalitions may facilitate progress just by reducing the number of players represented in a negotiation – as, for example, Krugman (1993) and Kahler (1995) argue. However, the gains from having fewer players in the last stage of a negotiation may well be offset by the complexity of agreeing joint positions in the first phase. The difficulties of achieving a European position on agriculture and cultural protection in the Uruguay Round are well known, and formulating European Economic Community (EEC) positions in the Tokyo Round also proved complex (Winham, 1986).

Setting aside the complexity of agreeing positions within a PTA, the PTA's institutions may impart a particular bias in negotiations. Winters (1994) argues that European decision-making conventions make it difficult to resist protectionist policies, especially in agriculture. A proposal to restrict trade emerges in the Council of Ministers and any government uneasy about it must decide between two strategies: either to reject it but run the risk that, if it nonetheless passes, its country will be effectively excluded from its "benefits," or to support it conditional on receiving part of the "benefits." Even if total cost exceeds total benefits, it might find the latter more attractive and so the measure passes.[10] De Melo et al. (1993), on the other hand, argue that creating a PTA dilutes the power of special interests in lobbying for protectionism and hence reduces protectionist pressures.

A third argument is that the creation of PTAs increases the pressure to complete multilateral liberalization to mitigate the margins of preference they create. This has been advanced for the Kennedy Round (the EEC; see WTO, 1995), the Tokyo Round (EEC deepening and enlargement; Winham, 1986) and the Uruguay Round (NAFTA; Bergsten, 1997). There is some plausibility to this view but I have argued elsewhere that as a strategy for completing trade talks it is both a high risk and limited to only a few countries, because it relies on the threats, and that it probably overstates the influence of PTAs. For example, in the Uruguay Round the event that made completion possible was European agricultural reform in 1991–92, which pre-dated NAFTA.

3.5. Depth and Breadth in Integration

PTAs are sometimes suggested as ways of developing blueprints for technically complex issues before they come to the global level, or as ways of tackling politically difficult issues that cannot yet be agreed on globally. In fact, such benefits have not been as widespread as is sometimes thought, for PTAs often avoided difficult issues, although there is some evidence of their going further more recently. However, even where they do break new ground, we need to ensure that the PTAs created do not subsequently slow it down for the reasons discussed earlier. We need to ensure that the subsequent switch from regionalism to multilateralism is managed effectively by building it into the initial terms of PTA.

One also periodically hears that PTA negotiation is one means of bringing developing countries "up to speed" on the art of trade negotiating.[11] This seems misguided: the improvement in capacity may or may not occur, but where it does, it provides training for a quite different environment from that of the WTO.[12] Far better would be to build capacity for assessing nondiscriminatory trade policy directly.

---

[10] Once it passes, the costs of protection are proportional to consumption, whereas the benefits are related to production. Measures can exclude countries from benefits by restricting their coverage to certain varieties of a product or certain producers – e.g., small farms. In 1992, the UK set aside its objection to the Common Agricultural Policy per se in favor of a position that permitted the policy to continue provided that large farms (abundant in the UK) benefitted as well as small ones.

[11] I hear this in Europe about, for example, the EPA negotiations.

[12] It also arguably imbues policy makers with exactly the wrong set of values (mercantilist ones) for achieving efficient policy outcomes.

The benefits of developing regional blueprints depend heavily on whether they are liberalizing and whether they are otherwise well suited to developing country needs and capacities. Major powers already use access to the GSP to impose environmental and labor conditions on developing countries; the EU looks for action in such areas and on intellectual property in the Europe Agreements and the United States has used NAFTA as a tool for enforcing Mexican labor and environmental standards. By picking off developing countries one by one on these topics, PTAs could lead to very different outcomes than would straight multilateralism. It seems very likely that the outcome will suit developing countries less well, and it may be less open and liberal as well.

Moreover, there are dangers in too great a reliance on PTAs as a precursor to multilateral rounds. Even if the major powers' aspirations are desirable in their own terms, building up rival regional teams could make final negotiations more, rather than less, difficult. And when only one regional bloc is advocating a policy, other countries might sufficiently resent the pressure to adopt it that they pull back. Developing country de facto rejection of the OECD draft Multilateral Agreement on Investment in 1998 contains a strong element of this. The time it takes to build regional coalitions can delay multilateral talks, and coalitions rooted in formal PTAs are here to stay, so that if multilateral processes fail, the blocs remain. This is quite different from a negotiating coalition, which dissolves if it fails to gain its objectives.

To be sure, progress is required in "new" areas such as services and standards, but it is frequently better pursued independently of tariff preferences. Thus, although we may as well learn from PTAs about how to tackle particular aspects of liberalization, this is not a persuasive reason for pursuing PTA per se.

REFERENCES

Anson, José, Olivier Cadot, Antoni Estevadeordal, Jaime de Melo, Akiko Suwa-Eisenmann, and Bolormaa Tumurchudur, 2005. "Rules of Origin in North–South Preferential Trading Arrangements with an Application to NAFTA," *Review of International Economics*, 13(3):501–17.

Antras, P., Philippe Aghion, and Elhanan Helpman, 2007. "Negotiating Free Trade," *Journal of International Economics*, 73(1):1–30.

Augier, Patricia, Michael Gasiorek, and Charles Lai Tong, 2005. "The Impact of Rules of Origin on Trade Flows," *Economic Policy* (July): 567–624.

Bagwell, K., and Robert Staiger, 2001. "Strategic Trade, Competitive Industries, and Agricultural Trade Disputes," *Economics and Politics*, 13(2):113–28.

Baier, Scott L., and Jeffrey H. Bergstrand, 2004. "Economic Determinants of Free Trade Agreements," *Journal of International Economics*, 64(1):29–63.

Baier, Scott L., and Jeffrey H. Bergstrand, 2007. "Do Free Trade Agreements Actually Increase Members' International Trade?," *Journal of International Economics*, 71(1):72–95.

Baldwin, Richard, 2008. "Big-Think Regionalism: A Critical Survey," NBER Working Papers 14056, National Bureau of Economic Research.

Baldwin R. E., and F. Robert-Nicoud, 2008. "A Simple Model of the Juggernaut Effect of Trade Liberalisation," CEP Discussion Paper No. 845, London School of Economics.

Baldwin, Richard, 1995. "A Domino Theory of Regionalism," in Richard E. Baldwin, P. Haaparanta, and J. Kiander (eds.), *Expanding Membership of the European Union*. Cambridge: Cambridge University Press.

Bergsten, Fred, 1997. "Open Regionalism," *World Economy*, 20:545–65.

Campa, Jose Manuel, and Timothy L. Sorenson, 1996. "Are Trade Blocs Conducive to Free Trade?," *Scandinavian Journal of Economics*, 98(2):263–73.

Chang, W., and L. A. Winters, 2002a. "Preferential Trading Arrangements and Excluded Countries: Ex-Post Estimates of the Effects on Prices," *World Economy*, 24(6):797–807.

Chang, W., and L. A. Winters, 2002b. "How Regional Blocs Affect Excluded Countries: The Price Effects of MERCOSUR," *American Economic Review*, 92(4):889–904.

Chase, Kerry, 2006. "Multilateralism Compromised: The Mysterious Origins of GATT Article XXIV," *World Trade Review*, 5(1):1–30.

De Melo, Jaime, Arvind Panagariya, and Dani Rodrik, 1993. "The New Regionalism: A Country Perspective," in Jaime De Melo and Arvind Panagariya (eds.), *New Dimensions in Regional Integration*. Cambridge: Cambridge University Press.

Ethier, Wilfred, 1998a. "The New Regionalism," *Economic Journal*, 108(449):1149–61.

Ethier, Wilfred J., 1998b. "Regionalism in a Multilateral World," *Journal of Political Economy*, 106(6):1214–45.

Evans et al., 2006. "Assessing Region Trade Agreement with Developing Countries: Shallow and Deep Integration, Trade, Productivity, and Economic Performance" Report for DFID. Located at www.sussex.ac.uk/Units/caris/CARIS/DFIF-RTA-REPORT.pdf.

Fujita, Masahisa, Paul Krugman, and Anthony J. Venable, 1999. *The Spatial Economy: Cities, Regions, and International Trade*. Cambridge, MA: MIT Press.

Grossman, Gene, and Elhanan Helpman, 1995. "The Politics of Free-Trade Agreements," *American Economic Review*, 85(4):667–90.

Haaland, J., and V. Norman, 1992. "Global Production Effects of European Integration," in L. A. Winters (ed.), *Trade Flows and Trade Policy After*. Cambridge: Cambridge University Press.

Hallward-Driemeier, Mary, 2003. "Do Bilateral Investment Treaties Attract Foreign Direct Investment? Only a Bit – and They Could Bite," Policy Research Working Paper Series 3121.

Houde, Marie-France, Akshay Kolse-Patiland, and Sébastien Miroudot, 2007. "The Interaction between Investment and Services Chapters in Selected Regional Trade Agreements," OECD Working Paper 55.

Kahler, Miles, 1995. *International Institutions and the Political Economy of Integration*, Washington: Brookings Institution

Kemp, Murray C., and Henry Wan, Jr. 1976. "An Elementary Proposition Concerning the Formation of Customs Unions," *Journal of International Economics*, 6(1):95–7.

Krueger, Anne, 1999. "Are Preferential Trading Arrangements Trade-Liberalizing or Protectionist?" *Journal of Economic Perspectives*, 13(4):105–24.

Krugman, Paul 1993. "Regionalism versus Multilateralism: Analytical Notes," in Jaime De Melo and Arvind Panagariya (eds.), *New Dimension in Regional Integration*.

Krugman, Paul, and Anthony J. Venables, 1990. "Integration and the Competitiveness of Peripheral Industry," in Christopher Bliss and Jaime De Macedo (eds.), *Unity with Diversity in the European Community*.

Levy, Philip I., 1997. "A Political-Economic Analysis of Free-Trade Agreements," *American Economic Review*, 87(4):506–19.

Limao, N., 2006. "Preferential Trade Agreements as Stumbling Blocks for Multilateral Trade Liberalization: Evidence for the U.S.," *American Economic Review*, 96(3):896–914.

Limao, N., 2007. "Are Preferential Trade Agreements with Nontrade Objectives a Stumbling Block for Multilateral Liberalization?," *Review of Economic Studies*, 74(3):821–55.

Limao, N., and Baybars Karacaovali, 2008. "The Clash of Liberalizations: Preferential vs. Multilateral Trade Liberalization in the European Union," *Journal of International Economics*, 74(2): 299–327.

Limao, N., and Marcelo Olarreaga, 2006. "Trade Preferences to Small Developing Countries and the Welfare Costs of Lost Multilateral Liberalization," *World Bank Economic Review*, 20(2):217–40.

Loke W. H., 2006. "Apec Trade Liberalisation: Open Regionalism, Nonbinding Liberalisation, and Unconditional MFN," Doctoral dissertation, University of Sussex.

Meade J. E., 1955. *Trade and Welfare*. Oxford: Oxford University Press.

Mundell, Robert, 1964. "Tariff Preferences and the Terms of Trade," Manchester School of Economic and Social Studies, 1–13.

Olarreaga, Marcelo, Isidro Soloaga, and L. Alan Winters, 1999. "What's behind Mercosur's Common External Tariff?," CEPR Discussion Paper No. 2310.

Olarreaga, Marcelo, and Isidro Soloaga, 1998. "Endogenous Tariff Formation: The Case of Mercosur," *World Bank Economic Review*, 12(2):297–320.

Panagariya, Arvind, and Pravin Krishna, 2002. "On Necessarily Welfare-Enhancing Free Trade Areas," *Journal of International Economics*, 57(2):353–67.

Puga, Diego, and Anthony J. Venables, 1998. "Trading Arrangements and Industrial Development," *World Bank Economic Review*, 12(2):221–49.

Roy, Martin, Juan Marchetti, and Aik Hoe Lim, 2007. "Services Liberalization in the New Generation of Preferential Trade Agreements (PTAs): How Much Further than the GATS?" *World Trade Review*, 6(2):155–92.

Romalis, John, 2007. "NAFTA's and CUSFTA's Impact on International Trade," *Review of Economics and Statistics*, 89(3):416–35.

Schiff, Maurice, 1997. "'Small is Beautiful' Preferential Trade Agreements and the Impact of Country Size, Market Share, and Smuggling," *Journal of Economic Integration*, 12(3):359–87.

Schiff, Maurice, and L. Alan Winters, 1998. "Regional Integration as Diplomacy," *The World Bank Economic Review*, 12(2):271–96.

Soloaga, Isidro, and L. Alan Winters, 2001. "Regionalism in the Nineties: What Effect on Trade?" *North American Journal of Economics and Finance*, 12:1–29.

Venables, Anthony, 2003. "Winners and Losers from Regional Integration Agreements," *Economic Journal*, 113(490):747–61.

Viner, Jacob, 1950. *The Custom Union Issue*, New York: Carnegie Endowment for International Peace.

Winham, Gilbert, 1986. *International Trade and the Tokyo Round Negotiations*. Princeton: Princeton University Press.

Winters, L. A., 1987. "Britain in Europe: A Survey of Quantitative Trade Studies," *Journal of Common Market Studies*, 25:315–35.

Winters, L. A., 1994. "The EC and Protectionism: The Political Economy," *European Economic Review*, 38:596–603.

Winters L. A., 1997a. "Regionalism versus Multilateralism," in R. Baldwin, D. Cole, A. Sapir, and A. Venables (eds.), *Market Integration, Regionalism, and the Global Economy.* Cambridge: Cambridge University Press, 7–49.

Winters, L. A., 1997b. "Regionalism and the Rest of the World: The Irrelevance of the Kemp-Wan Theorem," *Oxford Economics Papers,* 49:228–34.

Winters, L. A., 1997c. "Regionalism and the Rest of the World: Theory and Estimates of the Effects of European Integration," *Review of International Economics,* 5(4):134–47.

Winters, L. A., 1998. "A Comment on 'Regional Roads to Multilateralism' by W. Ethier," in J. Piggott and A. Woodland (eds.), *International Trade Policy and the Pacific Rim.* MacMillan for International Economics Association, 153–6.

Winters, L. A., 2001. "Post-Lome Trading Arrangements: The Multilateral Alternative," in J. von Hagen and M. Widgren (eds.), *Regionalism in Europe: Geometries and Strategies after 2000.* Kluwer: Dordrecht, 221–60.

Winters, L. A., and Won Chang, 2000. "Regional Integration and Import Prices: An Empirical Investigation." *Journal of International Economics,* 51(2):363–77.

Winters, L. A., and M. W. Schiff, 2003. (eds.) *Regional Integration and Development,* Oxford: Oxford University Press for World Bank.

World Bank, 2005. *World Bank Economic Prospect: Trade, Regionalism, and Development,* The World Bank.

WTO, 1995. *Regionalism and the World Trading System.* Geneva: WTO.

Yi, Sang-Seung, 1996. "Endogenous Formation of Customs Unions Under Imperfect Competition: Open Regionalism Is Good," *Journal of International Economics,* 41:153–77.

JAMES H. MATHIS

The "Legalization" of GATT Article XXIV – Can Foes Become Friends?

Introduction

It was a pleasure to have the opportunity to appear at the Columbia Law School seminar on regional trade agreements and to provide comments on the theme of whether regional trade agreements (RTAs) are "friends or foes" of the multilateral trading system. I am also grateful to have Alan Winters' most thorough review of the economic issues regarding RTAs in hand – even though as a lawyer I am also poorly qualified to make comments on most of his points.

At the same time, there are themes raised by Winters that allow me to suggest a complementary legal theme for this seminar subject. This first discusses how Article XXIV has gradually achieved a certain degree of "legalization" within the WTO system and then raises for your consideration how this more legalistic application of the regional exception may bear on the question of whether RTAs are "stumbling blocks or building blocks" in the multilateral trading system. The results of dispute settlement cases in the WTO are tending to show that the regional exception is more narrow than many regional members once believed it to be – that higher degrees of regional trade liberalization are required to form a qualified RTA, and that the burden of demonstrating whether regional members have satisfactorily eliminated their duties and other restrictive regulations of commerce is upon them. This suggests a systemic resolution of the "friends or foes" debate that would tend to favor a smaller number of successful RTAs that contain higher levels of freely traded products. From an economic perspective these legal and systemic developments could have positive implications by reducing the number of noodles in the "spaghetti bowl" even while the remaining qualified agreements could also generate more external trade diversion.

1. Regional Trade Law and Economics – "Friends or Foes"?

The view of GATT Article XXIV as requiring a very high degree of trade liberalization among regional members recalls a fundamental tension between the text of the Article and its earliest economic assessments, going back to Viner (1950), an economist, and Dam (1963), a lawyer applying Viner's assessment.[13] Both of them grappled with the recognition that a completed customs union (or free trade agreement) that "eliminates duties" on "all the trade" can also be a highly trade-diverting arrangement affecting more efficient nonregional producers. The more "complete" a regional arrangement, the more potential for external trade diversion.

After a decade of frustrated working group reviews dealing with incomplete EEC Associations and other regional arrangements that clearly fell short of Article XXIV's "substantially all trade" (SAT) requirement, Haight (1972) reviewed the institutional situation and coined the phrase "paradox of Article XXIV." This is where GATT working group review members were expected to endorse only those RTAs that discriminated against more of their trade and object to those arrangements that discriminated against less of their trade.[14] Although this summarized the frustration among the GATT parties, the economists were also delivering the theoretical basis for a regional exception that would ameliorate what was perceived to be the primary weakness of GATT's regional exception – the SAT requirement. A personal favorite comes from Harry Johnson (1976), who declared that

> The speciousness of the principle of nondiscrimination is only exceeded by the irrationality of permitting nothing less than 100 percent discrimination in the case of customs unions and free-trade areas.[15]

The economic approach to dealing with the SAT requirement was to design a regional exception that would eliminate it – in favor of a "no harm done" standard at the practical level of implementation. As recited by McMillan:

> It is always possible for a regional integration agreement ... to structure itself in such a way as to make the member countries better off without making any of the nonmember countries worse off.[16]

The essence of this reformulation is that when external trade flows were being diverted by an RTA, then the requirement for liberalization in those sectors

---

[13] J. Viner (1950), The Customs Union Issue, Carnegie Endowment. K. Dam (1963), "Regional Economic Arrangements and the GATT, the Legacy of a Misconception," *University of Chicago Law Review*, 30(4):615–65.

[14] F. Haight (1972), "Customs Unions and Free Trade Areas Under GATT: A Reappraisal," *Journal of World Trade Law*, 6(4):391–404.

[15] Recited in R. Snape (1993), "History and Economics of GATT's Article XXIV," in K. Anderson and R. Blackhurst (eds.), *Regional Integration and the Global Trading System*, Harvester Wheatsheaf, 273–91, at p. 273.

[16] J. McMillan (1993), "Does Regional Integration Foster Open Trade? Economic Theory and GATT's Article XXIV," in K. Anderson and R. Blackhurst (eds.), Ibid., 292–310, at p. 293. He refers to the first expression of the proposition by Kemp (1964), and Vanek (1965), his note 2 at p. 307.

among the RTA members would be reduced or eliminated. This would allow for "partial" tariff reductions as contrasted with Article XXIV:8's requirement to "eliminate" duties. Dam had earlier suggested the same in calling for a functional reinterpretation of paragraph 4 of the Article so as to permit a greater degree of flexibility in the Article's SAT requirements. To review, paragraph 4 states that the purpose of an RTA should be to facilitate trade among its members and not to raise barriers to the trade of the other contracting parties. In light of a strict SAT requirement, this is a nearly schizophrenic expression because regional trade liberalization will always raise a "relative" barrier to the trade of nonmembers.[17]

Article XXIV clarification was on the agenda during the Uruguay Round (1986–94). Although a number of changes were made to clarify customs union formations, GATT parties neither addressed the deadlocked institutional review mechanism nor took up any of the suggestions calling for a modification of the SAT requirement. Rather, the results of those discussions appear to confirm the notion that somehow "completed" RTAs were less threatening to the system than "uncompleted" RTAs. Thus, the Preamble to the 1994 "Understanding on the Interpretation of Article XXIV" restated the paragraph 4 sentiment that closer integration between free trade area and customs union members contributes to the expansion of world trade, but then goes on to recognize that this contribution is increased when the elimination of duties and other restrictive regulations of commerce between regional members "extends to all trade, and (is) diminished if any major sector of trade is excluded." This appears to reflect a systemic sentiment that may well diverge from economic welfare considerations – that because RTA members deny MFN treatment to all other GATT parties, this "exception" from MFN should not come on the cheap – that the price for regional members to deny everyone else their MFN rights is that they complete a (very) high degree of regional trade liberalization.

2. The Troublesome Development Dimension

Winters also recognizes the developing country dimension as an important context for the RTA "friend or foe" discussion. Developing countries since the beginning of the GATT system have always argued for a flexible interpretation of Article XXIV that would recognize their special trade and development needs. For the major European Communities' arrangements from the Overseas Association (1958) through to the present time in the Cotonou framework, the issue of trade flexibility for the ACP members has always been a paramount consideration in the review of their trading arrangements with the EEC, the EC, and now the EU. When a more benign sense of the development perspective took

---

[17] Viner did provide one rationale for such a 100 percent trade requirement – that when regional members were free to pick and choose their preferences, "that it is possible, and in practice probable, that the preferences selected will be predominantly of the trade-diverting or injurious kind." J. Viner, *supra* note 1 at p. 51.

hold in the 1980s, the EC was widely applauded for its revision of Lome' IV to specifically exempt developing countries from the rigors of Article XXIV's SAT requirements – as they were now allowed to reintroduce duties and other restrictions in accord with their developmental requirements.

This led to a first "shock" in the prevailing European view of Article XXIV when in 1993 and 1994 the (unadopted) Bananas I and II panels[18] found that they had an obligation according to GATT Article XXIII to at least facially review the provisions of a free trade area that had been raised as a defense to an MFN violation. Prior to this ruling, it had been the established mantra (as ruled by the 1986 Citrus panel) that a panel had no capacity to review or substitute itself for the "special procedures" for qualifying an RTA according to Article XXIV (paragraph 7). In other words, the compatibility of an RTA was essentially a political and diplomatic exercise where the "contracting parties" only had the capacity to form recommendations to regional members regarding the implementation of their arrangements. Because these recommendations could only be generated on the basis of consensus (including regional members), the overall legal theory of an RTA's relationship to the GATT, according to the prevailing view of the time, was that of the "autonomous regime." Once notified and made available for examination, the regional members had done all that the GATT required, and any further actions (inevitably not forthcoming) were up to the General Council to determine and enunciate.

Why the EC and ACP group did not simply amend the Lome' provisions to eliminate the offending paragraph we do not know, but the course of action chosen was to obtain the Lome' waiver at the outset of the Doha Round (2001) and to proceed with the negotiations of free trade areas with the ACP group in the Cotonou framework for fully compatible Article XXIV free trade areas. As such, there has been criticism of complete arrangements for the extent of market openings required of marginal developing (and some least-developed) territories and for the potential trade diversion possible when these high-tariff developing countries make significant market-opening commitments to the European Union.[19]

In the meantime, Doha Round (2001) paragraph 29 also called for a clarification and improvement of the disciplines and procedures for the WTO provisions applying to regional trade agreements, and taking into account the "developmental aspects" of RTAs. ACP countries have invested significant energy into the RTA rules negotiations in the Round to raise points where flexibility could be institutionalized for the benefit of developing countries in a North–South RTA. Many developing WTO members (who are not in the ACP group) have not been very sympathetic. Although the developmental "flexibility" issues have tended to

---

[18] *EEC – Member States' Import Regimes for Bananas.* DS32/R June 3, 1993, and DS38/R, February 11, 1994 (Unadopted).

[19] See, for example, M. McQueen (1999), *The Impact Studies on the Effects of REPAs between the ACP and the EU,* ECDPM Discussion Paper 3, Maastricht.

dominate the Article XXIV negotiations, the EPA waiver clock has also been ticking. It ran out as of January 1, 2008, before any negotiated results for the term SAT were realized in the Doha Round and before any developmental dimension were agreed upon in the light of the SAT requirement.

3.   "Legalization" Arrives

This "legislative" track has all been operating in the shadow of the 1999 *Turkey–Textiles* case, which was the first WTO dispute settlement Appellate Body report to consider the parameters for Article XXIV in the WTO system.[20] Although it took a few years for the implications of this case to sink into the delegate negotiations and the behavior of members within RTA formations, it has been occurring and continues to evolve. For this, I note only the primary points that were determined by the Appellate Body in that case.[21]

1. Article XXIV is a "defense" to violations of GATT obligations owed to other WTO members. There is no autonomous-regime theory and an Article XXIV arrangement is fully reviewable by a panel to determine whether the conditions required by Article XXIV have been met and whether the exception can be applied as a defense.
2. If an RTA member raises the Article XXIV defense, that party then has the burden to go forward to demonstrate that the regional agreement meets all the requirements of paragraphs 5 and 8 of the Article. There is no deference to any special review procedures included in Article XXIV (at least when these have been inconclusive). Dispute resolution procedures are a distinct and independent track of action.
3. There is no implied "no harm done" standard expressed by Article XXIV. "Paragraph 4 contains purposive, and not operative, language. It does not set forth a separate obligation itself but, rather, sets forth the overriding and pervasive purpose for Article XXIV which is manifested in operative language in the specific obligations that are found elsewhere in Article XXIV."

The term "SAT" was not directly at issue in the case. However, the Appellate Body did make remarks on the word "substantially," noting that while flexibility was intended by the term, that this flexibility was limited, as "we caution that the degree of 'flexibility' that subparagraph 8(a)(i) allows is limited by the requirement that 'duties and other restrictive regulations of commerce' be 'eliminated with respect to substantially all' internal trade." (Appellate Body report, para. 48.)

---

[20] *WTO, Turkey – Restrictions on Imports of Textile and Clothing Products*, Report of the Panel, May 31, 1999, WT/DS34/R, Report of the Appellate Body, October, 22, 1999, AB-1999–5, WT/DS34/AB/R.

[21] *Turkey–Textiles*, AB Report, summarizing paras. 48, 58, 59, and 60.

The case has had a significant institutional impact. By ruling that a respondent, when invoking the Article XXIV exception, would carry the full burden to establish – before the panel – that the RTA in question has fully complied with the provisions of paragraphs 8 and 5, the Appellate Body has changed the institutional game for RTAs in the WTO. Rather than promoting a lack of clarity for the formation requirements, which always benefited regional members, now that same lack of clarity and defective institutional process works against regional members, because they have no history of receiving positive recommendations on the compatibility of their trade agreements and worse, no clear criteria available to use as legal benchmarks when going before a panel. Above all, it also raised the frightening prospects for WTO members that it would be a dispute settlement body – a panel or the Appellate Body – that would ultimately settle the criteria for what constitutes a qualified formation.

4. Doha Round Transparency Developments

The responsive developments have been slow but certain in the Doha Round, where there is a meaningful (but yet inconclusive) negotiation on the requirements to be settled for SAT, a term that never made it to the active agenda in the previous Uruguay Round. Along the way, the review procedures in the Committee on Regional Trade Agreements (CRTA) have also been changed to drop the requirement of forming recommendations in favor of a new transparency and notification procedure and the composition of a purely factual report to be drawn by the WTO Secretariat.[22] The transparency instrument is a prerequisite to any further institutional progress on the treatment of RTAs in the WTO.

5. Recent Dispute Developments, *Brazil–Tyres*

Except for the cases dealing with regional safeguard measures, dispute cases concerning Article XXIV have been rare since the *Turkey–Textiles* case. Anecdotally, some members have suggested that the reason for this is that no one in the WTO wants to be the first respondent to raise the Article XXIV defense and actually find out what a panel and the Appellate Body might do to their RTA.

This ducking strategy may be over. In the 2007 case of *Brazil–Tyres*, the EC directly attacked the qualifications of the Mercosur customs union when Brazil raised the Article XXIV defense to excuse its exemption of other Mercosur

---

[22] Transparency Requirement for Regional Trade Agreements, Decision of December 18, 2006, WT/L/671. The requirement may also promote dispute settlement. The mechanism indicates that the Secretariat factual report cannot be used in dispute settlement (para. 10). This author thinks that the disclosed data in the report could be used in a proceeding even if the report could not.

members from the challenged import prohibition.[23] On the basis of judicial efficiency the panel avoided assessing the Mercosur exemption. The Appellate Body suggested at the end of its report that this examination should have been completed: "we have difficulty seeing how the Panel could have been justified in not addressing the separate claims of inconsistency under Article I:1 and Article XIII:1 directed at the Mercosur exemption."[24]

That is wholly in accord with the earlier *Turkey–Textiles* ruling that panels have to deal with the terms of Article XXIV if the defense is raised.

5.1 The EC Points of Attack

What is of interest here are the arguments the EC put to the panel challenge of Mercosur. Here we see all the elements of how a direct attack on an RTA defense will work. The major submission points raised include the following:

- a failure on the part of Brazil to carry its overall burden to establish the underlying qualification of the Mercosur arrangement. Mere submissions and statements made to the CRTA will not suffice as a form of proof in the absence of CRTA recommendations. An incomplete CRTA examination does not qualify as a recommendation for a regional trade agreement. Moreover, submissions made years before to the CRTA did not provide an indication of the qualifying status of the customs union at the time of the exemption and the treatment of the issue by the panel;
- a challenge to the legality of the original Mercosur notification, which was notified according to the Enabling Clause rather than as a customs union;
- a failure on the part of Mercosur to eliminate duties on internal trade (exemption of the auto and sugar sectors in the customs union), and within a reasonable period of time (ten years) as required by Article XXIV;
- a failure as a customs union to properly harmonize its external tariff and commercial policy to the trade of nonmembers within a reasonable period of time.[25]

It is not only an indicator of how far things have progressed that these claims are being brought before a panel, but also that the EC is bringing them. The EC is capable of screening these arguments prior to its submission to ensure that – if and when the same case is raised against it – that these points can all be adequately defended. In short, the EC has put other regional systems on notice that it is prepared to attack the quality of other RTAs based on Article XXIV and to likewise defend its own regional arrangements accordingly.

---

[23] *Brazil – Measures Affecting Imports of Retreaded Tyres*, WT/DS332/R, June 12, 2007, WT/DS332/AB/R, December 3, 2007.
[24] *Brazil–Tyres*, AB Report, para. 257.
[25] *Brazil–Tyres*, Panel Report, generally from para. 4.378.

5.2. The Appellate Body Ruling on Article XX

A second issue of equal importance was treated by the Appellate Body in reversing the panel's rulings on the GATT Article XX chapeau and its requirement that an exceptional measure not be applied in a manner that would "constitute a means of arbitrary or unjustifiable discrimination between countries where the same conditions prevail." Here, the panel found that an earlier Mercosur Court ruling requiring Brazil to exempt its regional partners from the *Tyre* prohibition was not "arbitrary discrimination" – essentially deferring to the ruling of another arbitral body and its members' required compliance with it.[26] The Appellate Body rejected this line entirely in ruling that the only discrimination allowable by the chapeau would be those actions that were causally related to the objectives of the underlying qualified exception – in this case Article XX(b) measures necessary to protect human health.[27]

A regional treaty's free movement provision and a regional arbitral body's ruling enforcing free movement in light of that treaty's own stated health and safety exceptions is not going to qualify as being causally directed to the GATT Article XX exception in question. The Appellate Body has effectively ruled that the GATT Article XX chapeau expresses a hierarchy between this general GATT obligation and whatever inconsistent provisions or rulings may occur under a regional system. The regional member has a choice to comply with the regional findings and then either grant to other WTO members that same degree of free movement, or compensate them if the discrimination is retained. Alternatively, the regional member can comply with the WTO ruling and disregard its own regional provisions and the ruling of its arbitral body. Either way, Article XX and its chapeau provision has been determined to be the "priority provision." For those interested in the spaghetti bowl of inconsistent regional provisions and the multiplicity of regional dispute settlement mechanisms, this is a striking development strongly favoring an international legal hierarchy with the WTO on top.

6. Conclusion: On to the Future

From a treaty law perspective, it is becoming easier to take the position that Article XXIV constitutes *the* constitutive legal expression of today's WTO members regarding the legal relationship between preferential trading systems and the General Agreement. I am suggesting by this that it is the legal text of the Article itself that informs the "friend or foe" discussion and that delineates the nature of this relationship. This continues to be expressed by paragraph 4 of Article XXIV, which acknowledges the desirability of increasing freedom of trade

---

[26] *Brazil–Tyres*, Panel Report, paras. 7.270 to 7.283.
[27] *Brazil–Tyres*, AB Report, para. 246.

through the voluntary agreements of closer integration between regional parties, and that the purpose of a customs union or free trade area is to facilitate trade between the regional parties and not to raise barriers to the trade of non-members. This remains the essence of what GATT and now WTO members have settled on – irrespective of the welfare implications.

It has taken a few generations to determine what this bifurcated expression means in the legal relationship between RTAs and the multilateral trading system. Like other statutes and treaties, it also takes a certain amount of case development for the terms of the legal rule to find their interpretative meaning. One hopes that the points made earlier begin to demonstrate that this type of evolution is not only possible in the WTO setting, but occurs in actual practice thanks in large part to its dispute settlement system.

As we move along to the next generation of RTAs that contemplate roles for advanced harmonization of domestic regulations as well as economic integration agreements for services in the General Agreement on Trade in Services (GATS), we see even less previous institutional review practice to outline the possible definitions than was available in the GATT review history for Article XXIV's SAT requirement. The Article XXIV:8 term "other restrictive regulations of commerce" and the paragraph 5 term "other regulations of commerce" are on the active Doha Rules Committee agenda, but they are also further down the list. They may not receive active negotiation treatment this time around. For the GATS, there are far fewer working group reviews in the practice to clarify the issues on the primary coverage terms. We do not know what "substantial sectoral coverage" might mean in a qualified GATS integration agreement. Nor do we have much insight into the nature of the MFN/exceptional relationship that may be evident in the relationships between GATS Article VII (Recognition) and/or GATS Article VI (Domestic Regulation), and as these both might relate to the regional exception of GATS Article V.

Just as the SAT term may be moving toward some negotiated resolution, these other terms are also surfacing as the key components in defining the legal relationship between more advanced RTAs and the WTO.

Although this suggests that there may be another one or two generations of uncertainty about the RTA rules in WTO, one also takes note that for even the "new issues," the larger legal framework has already been set. The old argument of whether or not the WTO RTA provisions are "exceptional" or "autonomous" is settled. Whether a panel has a right (or an obligation) to review the quality of an RTA when raised on a defense is settled.

This means that the next generation of legal developments for RTAs in the WTO may not take as long to develop as did the last, and that the ongoing "friends or foes" discussion may be increasingly informed by the WTO legal framework.

2 Third-Country Effects of Regional Trade Agreements

1. Introduction

More than 200 regional trade agreements are currently in force. More than half of these agreements were implemented after the conclusion of the Uruguay Round in 1995, and many new agreements are currently under negotiation. In contrast, multilateral liberalization through the WTO has stalled: after seven years of negotiation, agreement among members on further multilateral trade liberalization remains unattainable. These facts speak for themselves; regionalism has been the dominant force for negotiated trade liberalization in recent years. This has led economists to reexamine the implications of regionalism both theoretically and empirically for trade, welfare, and the world trade system. Many concerns have arisen, leading many prominent trade economists to oppose regionalism as a means of trade liberalization.

At issue is the discriminatory nature of regional trade agreements (RTAs).[1] Although tariff preferences stimulate trade among bloc members, they can have deleterious effects on nonmembers, potentially even on members, and on the political economy of trade policy formation. There are three main concerns.[2] The first is trade diversion: RTAs may lead to diversion of imports away from the most efficient global producers to regional partners. This means that the formation of trade blocs can be welfare reducing (even for the member countries) if little new trade is created. The second concern is that regionalism may hinder unilateral and multilateral tariff reduction, leading to a bad equilibrium, with several trade blocs maintaining high external trade barriers. This would happen if trade

I am grateful for comments from Kyle Bagwell, Petros Mavroidis, Kamal Saggi, and participants in the WTO seminar at Columbia Law School. The views presented in this chapter are the views of the author and do not reflect the views of the World Bank.

[1] I use RTA to refer to all types of discriminatory reciprocal trade agreements.

[2] Bhagwati (2008) and Bhagwati and Panagariya (1999) provide in-depth discussions of these concerns. Frankel (1997) summarizes theoretical and empirical issues, Pomfret (2003) presents the literature on the theory of RTAs, and Schiff and Winters (2003) extend the literature to focus on developing countries.

bloc members have less incentive to lower external tariffs than individual countries. Alternatively, regionalism could hinder multilateralism simply by detracting from the multilateral process, especially in countries where government
resources for trade initiatives are limited. Third, the creation of regional agreements may result in cumbersome new trade barriers being erected against nonregional members. One oft-cited example of this is rules of origin that abound
in RTA countries to prevent imports of goods into a high-tariff country via a low-
tariff member.

A more sanguine view maintains that, as a form of trade liberalization,
regionalism should generate growth effects commonly associated with increased
trade. By providing competition to the multilateral system, expanding regionalism may also lead to a redoubling of multilateral efforts. Increased trade diversion costs are likely to be small or will push countries to lower external tariffs to
minimize them. The General Agreement on Tariffs and Trade (GATT) founders
clearly saw regionalism and multilateralism as complementary, or rules for creating free trade agreements (FTAs) and customs unions would not have been formalized in Article XXIV. Indeed, Snape (1993) discusses the history of Article XXIV
and argues that this exception to nondiscrimination is vital to maintaining the
multilateral club. Some members might opt out of the multilateral agreements if
RTAs were not permitted.

In this chapter, I focus on the effects of regionalism on trade with third countries. In particular, have regional agreements led to significant trade diversion –
sharp drops in trade with nonmembers? How have regional agreements affected
the members' external tariffs that nonmembers face? Much of the existing work
on the effects of regional agreements on trade is theoretical – this literature is discussed in the next section. A few empirical papers have begun analyzing the consequences of regional agreements in depth. These are discussed in Section III.
Section IV provides some new evidence on these questions. Section V concludes.

2. Theoretical Foundations for Trade Diversion and Trade Policy

Two key questions are raised by the formation of a regional agreement: Will it
make the member countries better off? Will nonmembers be severely damaged?
It turns out that these two questions are related. In his seminal work, Jacob Viner
(1950) shows that the preferential removal of tariffs can lead to trade diversion –
where goods that formerly were imported from a low-cost producer outside the
agreement are now sourced from the high-cost member of the trade agreement.
If there is significant trade diversion, both member countries and nonmember
countries will be worse off.

To see how trade diversion affects members and nonmembers, and the conditions under which diversion is more likely to occur, let us consider three hypothetical cases involving trade discrimination in a particular product, say shoes.

In particular, we examine how trade patterns change following the initiation of a FTA between Mexico and the United States.

In Case I, the United States is a price taker and importer of shoes. When there are no regional agreements, Brazil is the lowest cost producer and all shoes are imported from Brazil for $10 a pair. Shoes face a 10 percent tariff in the United States, implying that U.S. consumers pay $11 for a pair of shoes. Now, the United States signs a FTA with Mexico and eliminates all tariffs on Mexican goods. Assume Mexican shoes cost $10.99 a pair. After the agreement is implemented, the United States imports all shoes from Mexico. U.S. consumers pay $10.99 for a pair of shoes. In this case, the United States loses because it formerly received tariff revenue of $1 for each pair of shoes, which is now lost. At the same time, the price to consumers has hardly changed, meaning there is no real gain in consumer surplus. Thus, the United States loses significant tariff revenue without any substantial offsetting gains. Similarly, Brazil loses because of lost exports to the United States. The more trade diversion there is, the greater the loss will be (or the smaller the gain) to both the United States and Brazil (i.e., the member and the nonmember).

In Case II, everything is the same as in Case I, except the U.S. tariff is 5 percent. Now, consumers initially pay $10.50 for shoes and all shoes are imported from Brazil. The agreement does not affect this relationship because Brazilian shoes with tariff are cheaper than Mexican shoes without tariff. There is no trade diversion, and the relationship between Brazil and the United States is unaffected by the RTA between Mexico and the United States.

In Case III, Mexico is the low-cost provider. Mexico exports shoes to the United States at $10 before the agreement, the tariff is 10 percent, and consumers pay $11 for a pair of shoes. After the agreement, the price of shoes falls to $10, leading to a large consumer gain, more than offsetting the tariff loss because consumers can afford more shoes at the lower price. This is a case of pure trade creation by the agreement. Again, there is no effect on Brazil.

These cases highlight three important implications of regional liberalization. First, trade diversion is costly to members and nonmembers alike. Trade diversion is costly to members because imports are shifted from efficient third-country producers to less efficient regional producers, which leads to relatively small gains in consumer surplus coupled with large losses in tariff revenue. Second, trade diversion is more likely if the external tariff is high. When the external tariff is high, preferential tariff elimination puts a bigger wedge between the members and nonmembers, providing a large scope for trade diversion. Third, trade diversion is absent when the members are low-cost providers. In the extreme case, when all exports come from the members then preferential tariff elimination is akin to free trade.

We have seen that when external tariffs are low, trade diversion is unlikely. This means that how regionalism affects member countries' incentives to alter their external most-favored-nation (MFN) trade barriers is extremely important in determining whether regionalism is harmful. The effects on incentives can also be seen in the previous example. In Case I, there is a large cost to the United States from trade diversion. This implies there is an incentive for the United States to reduce its external tariff. Following implementation of the trade agreement, if the U.S. external tariff is reduced from 10 percent to 5 percent, then the situation changes from Case I to Case II and there is a real welfare gain. Moreover, if the agreement facilitates this reduction, it implies that the preferential trade agreement was a building bloc to freer trade.

If the formation of a preferential trading bloc is accompanied by reductions in external tariffs, the arrangement is more likely to enhance aggregate world welfare without harming excluded countries. In contrast, if the trading bloc raises trade barriers against the excluded countries (or fails to reduce them deeply enough), diversion of external trade to bloc members is more likely, harming countries in the bloc as well as those in the rest of the world. The welfare consequences of an RTA therefore depend on the member countries' tariff response.

There is a considerable theoretical literature that explores the optimal tariff response of countries. In a standard model, with a welfare-maximizing government, optimal tariffs are likely to fall in a free trade area precisely because of the welfare costs outlined in Case I (Bagwell and Staiger, 1999; Freund, 2000; Bond et al., 2002; Ornelas, 2005). The intuition is that the welfare cost of trade diversion leads countries to lower external tariffs to recapture tariff revenue and improve efficiency. Put another way, losses to nonmembers are limited precisely because trade diversion lowers welfare for both the nonmembers and the members. This means that the members' optimal tariff response will limit trade diversion and potential losses to nonmembers.

However, when political-economy effects are incorporated, the results are ambiguous. For example, Richardson (1993) and Cadot, de Melo, and Olarreaga (2001) find that, following the initiation of a free trade area, lobbying will decline and external tariffs will fall, as the import-competing sector contracts. However, in a different model, Panagariya and Findlay (1996) find that countries in a free trade area will raise tariffs because lobbying in favor of tariffs against the partner will be diverted to lobbying for a greater external tariff.[3]

Incentives are also different in a customs union, where members set a common external tariff. Members of a customs union maximize welfare jointly, and if the union is relatively large, optimal tariffs are likely to rise because of enhanced market power (Syropoulos, 1999; Freund, 2000, Bond et al., 2001). The basic intuition is that the trade agreement expands the market for goods produced in the bloc, resulting in a decline in demand for third-country goods, which will cause an improvement in the bloc's terms of trade if it is large enough. Moreover, it is

---

[3] A large literature addresses the related question of whether allowing countries to form RTAs helps or hinders the viability of a multilateral free trade agreement (Grossman and Helpman, 1995; Levy, 1997; Krishna, 1998; Ornelas, 2005; Aghion, Antràs, and Helpman, 2007; Saggi and Yildiz, 2007).

not just *existing* trade blocs that matter; Bagwell and Staiger (2004) show that the mere potential for a future trade agreement may affect the extent of current tariff reduction that can be negotiated multilaterally. The threat of "bilateral opportunism" will reduce the extent of multilateral tariff reduction because current global trade agreements can be diluted by bilateral preferences.

3.   Empirical Evidence on Trade Diversion and Trade Policy

There is some evidence that trade diversion may be of concern in high-tariff countries, but obtaining reliable estimates of diversion is difficult. The problem is that to estimate diversion, trade flows both in the absence and presence of an RTA are required. Because this is not possible, trade diversion is estimated from comparisons between predicted trade and actual trade. In general, results suggest that trade diversion is minimal, except when external tariffs are high.

Using highly disaggregated bilateral trade data from fourteen countries, Leamer (1990) finds little evidence of trade diversion. Frankel, Stein, and Wei (1995) also find little evidence from aggregate bilateral trade data from fifty-six countries. Krishna (2003) estimates trade diversion and trade creation in twenty-four hypothetical bilateral trade agreements and finds that in 80 percent of the cases, trade creation outweighs trade diversion. Srinivasan, Whalley, and Wooton (1993) survey the results from numerous studies and show that regionalism has had little effect on trade patterns, suggesting that concerns over diversion are somewhat "overblown." There are, however, some exceptions. For example, Yeats (1998) and Haveman, Nair-Reichert, and Thursby (2003) find evidence of trade diversion, using disaggregated trade data for Mercosur.

The empirical literature on the effect of RTA formation on external tariffs is in its infancy. Foroutan (1998) provides a general account of how countries forming regional trade blocs have adjusted their external tariffs. Using data on trade and trade policy in fifty countries, she finds that both integrating and nonintegrating countries have reduced their trade barriers, suggesting that regionalism is relatively benign. Bohara et al. (2004) examine tariff adjustment in Argentina following the formation of Mercosur and find some support for Richardson's (1993) hypothesis that the decline of some industries will lead to a reduction in their lobbying and lower tariffs. Similarly, Estevadeordal, Freund, and Ornelas (2008) examine changes in preferential tariffs and MFN tariffs in ten Latin American countries and 100 industries over twelve years. Using a number of empirical techniques to extract causality, they find that free trade areas lead to a decline in external tariffs; however, these results are much weaker in customs unions. Their results are consistent with the model of Bagwell and Staiger (1999), which suggests that tariff complementarity will dominate in FTAs but not in customs unions. In contrast, Limao (2006) finds that the United States was more reluctant to lower tariffs in the Uruguay Round for products that offered preferences. His results imply that trade preferences lead to less multilateral tariff reduction. Karacaovali and Limao (2008) find similar results for the European Union (EU).

The findings of Foroutan (1998), Bohara et al. (2004), and Estevadeordal, Freund, and Ornelas (2008), which imply that regionalism is a building bloc to external liberalization in developing countries, contrast sharply with those of Limao (2006) and Karacaovali and Limao (2008), which find that the United States and the EU liberalized less during the Uruguay Round in sectors where preferences were granted. One reason that the results may differ is that the countries analyzed are very different. Because the multilateral system has not enforced much tariff reduction on developing countries, tariffs are relatively high there, creating a large potential for trade diversion. Lower external tariffs moderate that loss. The results of Foroutan (1998), Bohara et al. (2004), and Estevadeordal, Freund, and Ornelas (2008) suggest that this force is important in explaining changes in MFN tariffs of developing countries involved in free trade areas. In contrast, the work of Limao focuses on the industrial countries. Tariffs were already quite low in the United States and the EU at the onset of the Uruguay Round, which reduces the importance of this channel. In addition, the theoretical underpinnings in Limao's work used to justify the importance of preferences in North–South agreements rely on RTAs being formed for noneconomic reasons – preferential treatment is given in exchange for noneconomic benefits, such as cooperation on migration, drug trafficking, or a global political agenda. This is not the case in South–South RTAs, where the goal is exchanging market access and improving regional economic cooperation.

Even if trade barriers are not altered when a trade bloc is formed, Chang and Winters (2002) show that nonmembers can be negatively affected because of price competition with member countries. Nonmembers may reduce prices to compete with member producers that face a lower tariff. Although this is good for the members who face lower import prices, this negatively impacts welfare of nonmembers.

4. Evidence on Diversion and Trade Liberalization in RTAs

In this section, I use trade data for three regional accords and three accessions to existing agreements to examine how trade patterns change following the implementation of trade preferences. The regional agreements are NAFTA (North American Free Trade Agreement; Canada, Mexico, and the United States, 1994), Mercosur (Argentina, Brazil, Paraguay, and Uruguay, 1991), and the Andean Community (Bolivia, Colombia, Ecuador, Peru, and Venezuela, 1991).[4]

---

[4] Peru left the group in 1992, but it maintained bilateral agreements with all other CAN members.

I also examine three accessions to the EU, including the first wave, Denmark, Great Britain, and Ireland (1973); the second wave, Portugal and Spain (1986);[5] and the third wave, Austria, Finland, and Sweden (1995). All data for this part are from Comtrade and are recorded in U.S. dollars. The purpose is to identify whether and how trade growth with members and nonmembers changed subsequent to the agreement.

I also want to look at the effect of regional agreements on external tariffs. I use detailed industry data on preferential tariffs and MFN tariffs over twelve years for Mercosur, the Andean Community, and NAFTA to examine how preferences affect trade with members and nonmembers and also the path of the external tariff.

Figures 2.1–2.6 show total imports and import growth from nonmembers and internal imports, ten years before and after the six agreements (or accessions) were implemented. There is no evidence that trend import growth with nonmembers fell sharply following the implementation of the agreements. Moreover, internal import growth and import growth with nonmembers are highly correlated, following very similar paths, implying that other factors besides the RTA tend to drive aggregate trade growth.

Table 2.1 shows the mean growth rates of external and internal imports before and after the regional agreements were implemented. A few things are interesting. First, the RTA does not always lead to higher internal trade growth. In half of the RTAs, trade growth declines. Of interest, external import growth slows in only two of the episodes. Second, in the post-RTA period, internal trade grows faster than external trade only half of the time. In contrast, in the pre-RTA period, internal trade growth was faster than external import growth in five out of six cases. Thus, looking at import growth there is little evidence that the trade agreement led to higher trade growth among members at the expense of nonmembers.

Although the sample is small, to more rigorously test whether import growth from nonmembers was retarded, I performed t-tests on the difference in the means of the pre-union and post-union growth rates and between the growth rate of internal trade and trade with nonmembers. Results are reported in Table 2.1. The t-tests of the difference in the mean growth rates show that growth rates of members and nonmembers are never significantly different from each other. In addition, only in one case is mean growth after the agreement significantly different (at the 10 percent level) for nonmembers, and that is in Mercosur, but growth is significantly higher in the period after the agreement was formed. This was largely because of large (unilateral) external trade liberalization that accompanied the agreement.

---

[5] Greece also joined in 1981 and is sometimes considered with Portugal and Spain as part of the second wave.

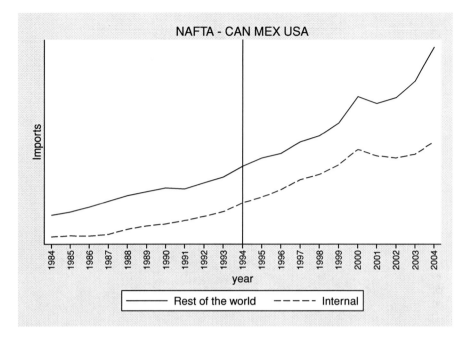

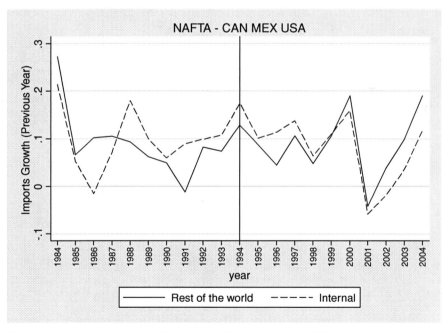

Figure 2.1. Internal and external imports and import growth in NAFTA.

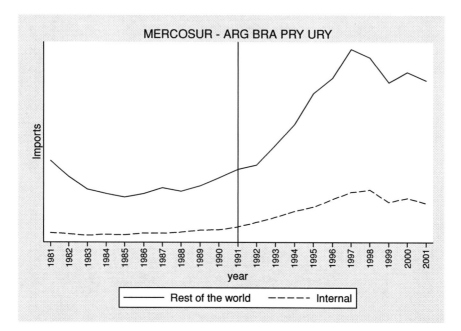

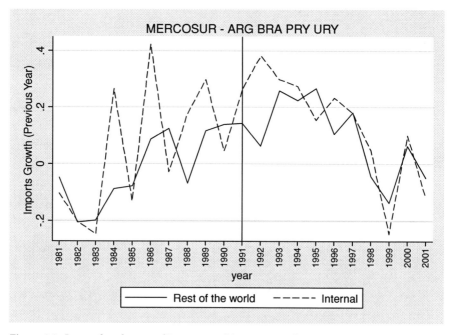

Figure 2.2. Internal and external imports and import growth in Mercosur.

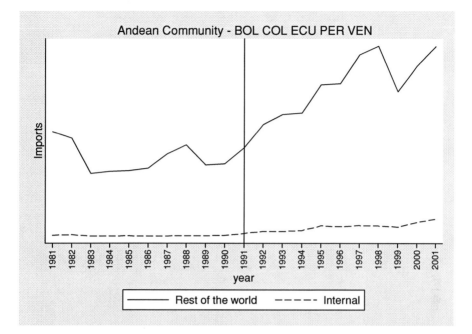

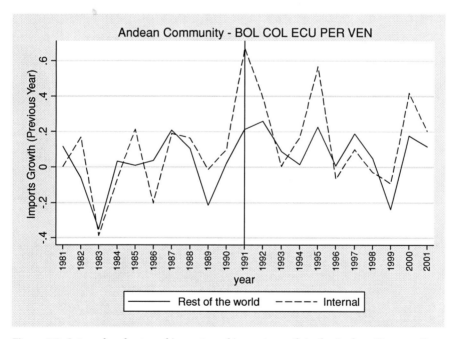

Figure 2.3. Internal and external imports and import growth in the Andean Community.

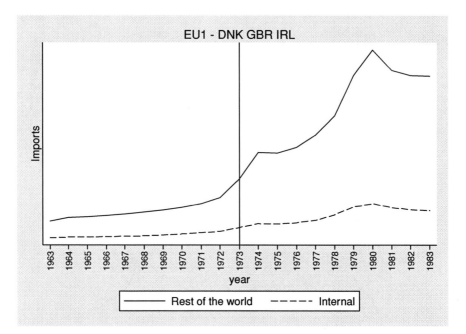

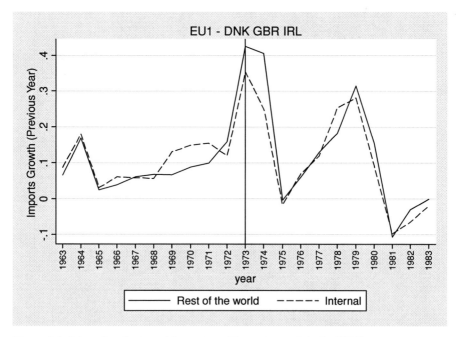

Figure 2.4. Internal and external imports and import growth in the EU, first wave.

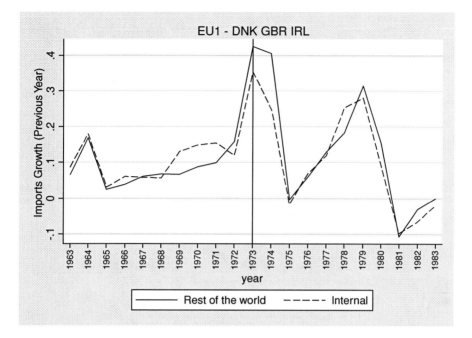

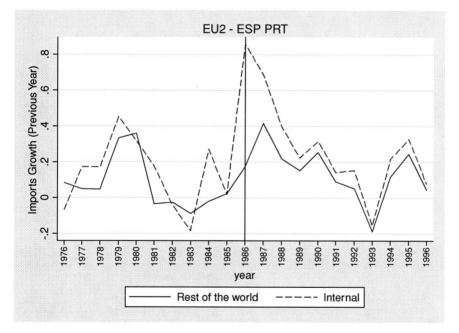

Figure 2.5. Internal and external imports and import growth in the EU, second wave.

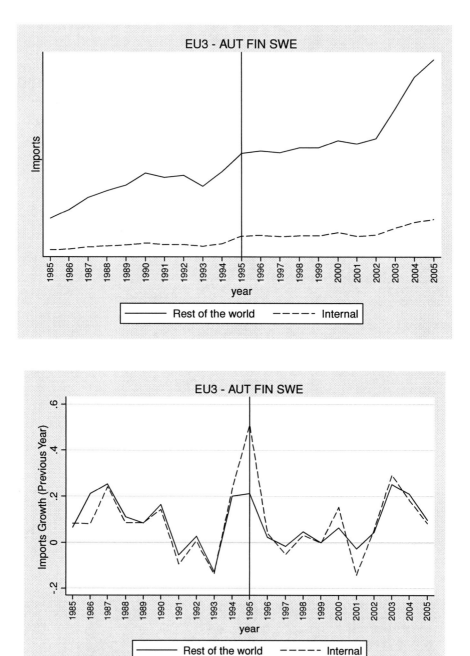

Figure 2.6. Internal and external imports and import growth in the EU, third wave.

Table 2.1. *Growth rates of imports*

	Internal	External	*t*-test	*p*-value	Correlation
		NAFTA			
Before RTA	0.096	0.089	0.199	0.844	0.958
After RTA	0.076	0.087	−0.338	0.739	0.943
t-test	0.654	0.093			
p-value	0.522	0.927			
		Mercosur			
Before RTA	0.049	−0.021	0.845	0.409	0.338
After RTA	0.131	0.093	0.497	0.625	0.980
t-test	−0.855	−1.889			
p-value	0.404	0.075			
		Andean Community			
Before RTA	0.016	−0.010	0.327	0.748	0.754
After RTA	0.166	0.088	0.917	0.371	0.858
t-test	−1.592	−1.423			
p-value	0.129	0.172			
		EU1			
Before RTA	0.103	0.084	0.860	0.401	0.994
After RTA	0.086	0.110	−0.358	0.724	0.991
t-test	0.352	−0.500			
p-value	0.729	0.623			
		EU2			
Before RTA	0.129	0.073	0.711	0.486	0.924
After RTA	0.237	0.139	1.140	0.269	0.969
t-test	−1.172	−0.948			
p-value	0.256	0.356			
		EU3			
Before RTA	0.072	0.093	−0.382	0.707	0.983
After RTA	0.064	0.070	−0.109	0.915	0.990
t-test	0.148	0.490			
p-value	0.884	0.630			

Note: Author's calculations based on bilateral import data (CIF US $), using the DOT-IMF database.

Finally, if increased trade with bloc members were displacing imports from third countries, we would expect to see a decline in the correlation between internal and external trade growth subsequent to the formation of the RTA. However, as shown in the last column of Table 2.1, the correlation between external trade growth and internal trade goes up in four out of the six agreements – and by a large amount for Mercosur and the Andean Community. In the two episodes where the correlations fell, NAFTA and EU1, the changes were marginal.

Next, I examine in more detail the relationship between third-country imports and preferential and MFN tariffs. In particular, I examine how MFN and preferential tariffs affect import growth by using detailed industry data from Estevadeordal, Freund, and Ornelas (2008) on tariffs in nine Latin-American countries. The data set includes Argentina, Brazil, Colombia, Ecuador, Mexico,

Table 2.2. *Correlation between tariffs and trade in Latin America*

	ln (internal imports)	ln (external imports)	Margin
ln (internal imports)	0.57		
	(0.00)		
	107.52		
Margin	0.20	0.14	
	(0.00)	(0.00)	
	7790	8199	
MFN	0.04	0.04	0.42
	(0.00)	(0.00)	(0.00)
	7925	8353	10168

Note: The *p*-values are in parentheses. The number of observations are below *p*-values.

Paraguay, Peru, Uruguay, and Venezuela.[6] The data are reported at the ISIC 4-digit level (ninety-six industries) and include data on preferential tariffs and MFN tariffs from 1990 to 2001.

Table 2.2 shows correlations among MFN tariffs, preference margins, internal trade, and imports from the rest of the world. Imports from regional members are positively correlated with imports from nonmembers. This is not too surprising because some categories of imports are much larger. Preference margin and MFN tariffs are positively correlated; this is in part because preference margins can only be large when MFN tariffs are high. Finally, tariffs and margins are positively correlated with imports from both members and nonmembers. This suggests that tariffs tend to be set slightly higher on large imported goods. The correlation between member trade and preference margins is higher than the correlation between nonmember trade and margins, suggesting that margins are larger on goods that are more important to members, or that because of margins these goods have become more important to members.

To control for other factors that might affect trade patterns, I use regression analysis. First, I examine the effect of trade preferences and MFN tariffs on internal imports and imports from third countries. Specifically, I run the following regression:

$$\ln M_{ijtg} = \gamma_{ijg} + \gamma_{jtg} + \beta_1 \mathrm{marg}_{ijt} + \beta_2 \mathrm{MFN}_{ijt} + \varepsilon_{ijt}, \tag{1}$$

where M_{ijtg} are imports in industry i, country j, year t, from group g (members or nonmembers). The variable γ_{ijg} is a country-industry fixed effect for group g and γ_{jtg} is a country-year fixed effect for group g. The country-industry effects will

[6] Estevadeordal, Freund, and Ornelas (2008) present a detailed discussion of the data. There are ten countries in the full data set. In the results presented here, Chile is excluded because it is not part of a major trade bloc. Each of the nine countries has preferences to Bolivia, but data for Bolivia's preferences were not available.

Table 2.3. *The effect of tariffs and preference margins on imports*

	Dependent variable					
	Ln (Internal imports)			ln (External imports)		
	(1)	(2)	(3)	(4)	(5)	(6
Margin	0.02***		0.03***	0.00		0.01***
	[0.01]		[0.01]	[0.00]		[0.00]
MFN		−0.01***	−0.03***		−0.02***	−0.02***
		[0.00]	[0.01]		[0.00]	[0.00]
Observations	7790	7790	7790	8199	8199	8199
R^2	0.918	0.918	0.919	0.932	0.932	0.932

Note: Country-industry and country-year fixed effects are used in all regressions. Robust standard errors are in brackets.
*** $p < 0.01$, ** $p < 0.05$, * $p < 0.1$.

control for average demand for products from that group in the country industry, and the country-year effects will control for general liberalization and business cycle effects. A positive and significant β_1 implies that a higher preference margin leads to more imports from the group. We expect β_1 to be positive for members, who can take advantage of the preferential treatment. The coefficient, β_1, will be negative and significant for nonmembers if trade is being diverted and insignificant if there is mostly trade creation from the RTA. The coefficient on the applied MFN tariff, β_2, is likely to be negative for both groups, implying that a higher tariff leads to lower imports.

Table 2.3 reports the results. As expected, preference margins are correlated with higher internal trade (column 1) and MFN tariffs with lower internal trade (column 2). When we include both variables in the regression (column 3), we find a stronger effect of MFN on internal trade than when it is included alone. This makes sense because some high MFN sectors will have low preferential tariffs, which is especially good for internal trade. The results suggest that a 1 percentage point higher preference margin leads to 3 percent more internal trade. In addition, a 1 percentage point higher MFN tariff, controlling for preference margins, leads to 3 percent less internal trade.

With respect to nonmembers, we see no significant effect of preference margins on imports (column 4) and a more negative effect of MFN tariffs (column 5). Surprisingly, when we include both variables in the regression (column 6), the preference margin has a small but significant *positive* effect on imports from nonmembers. This suggests that, controlling for the MFN tariff level, preference margins tend to stimulate imports from nonmembers. One potential explanation is that more trade with members could lead to more imports from nonmembers if goods are complements in production. For example, if goods produced by members use inputs from nonmembers, then more regional trade (and production of tradables) will lead to more imported inputs from nonmembers. At the

Table 2.4. *The effect of preferential tariff reduction on MFN tariff reduction*

	\multicolumn{4}{c}{Dependent variable: d MFN}			
	(1)	(2)	(3)	(4)
L.dmargin	−0.28***			
	[0.03]			
L2.dmargin		−0.13***		
		[0.02]		
L.dpref			0.15***	
			[0.02]	
L2.dpref				0.06***
				[0.01]
Observations	8349	7445	8349	7445
R-squared	0.555	0.45	0.532	0.439

Note: Country-industry and country-year fixed effects are used in all regressions; robust standard errors are given in brackets.
*** $p < 0.01$, ** $p < 0.05$, * $p < 0.1$.

level of aggregation of the data, many of the inputs will be in the same industry so a greater preference margin could stimulate imports from nonmembers through this channel. Alternatively, there may be improvements in the general trade environment – such as harmonizing product standards or improving customs procedures for some sectors – that coincide with the preferential tariff reduction. Overall, the results imply that greater preference margins do not negatively affect imports from nonmembers. As expected, applied MFN tariffs do restrict imports from nonmembers. Specifically, results suggest that a 1 percentage point higher MFN tariff leads to 2 percent less trade.

In Table 2.4, let us examine the effect of preference margins on MFN tariffs. The regression we estimate is

$$d\,\mathrm{MFN}_{ijt} = \gamma_{ij} + \gamma_{jt} + \beta_0\,l.d\mathrm{marg}_{ijt} + \varepsilon_{ijt}, \qquad (2)$$

where MFN_{ijt} is the MFN tariff in industry i, of country j and year t. The variable $l.d$marg is the lagged change in the preference margin. The variable γ_{ij} is a country-industry fixed effect and γ_{jtg} is a country-year fixed effect. A positive coefficient on the lagged change in margin, β_0, implies that increases in the preference margin are followed by increases in the MFN tariff – a stumbling bloc effect. A negative coefficient points to a building bloc effect. The change in margin is lagged (I also report results with two lags) to control for unobserved factors that might affect all tariffs, both preferential and MFN, simultaneously. For example, assume preferential tariffs and MFN tariffs are reduced together because some industries are easier to liberalize. In this case, the change in the margin and the change in the MFN tariff will be negatively correlated, provided preferential tariffs are cut more sharply, but the relationship may not be a causal one. Because the change in the margin (margin = MFN – preferential tariff) is a function of the change in the MFN tariff (the dependent variable), which may cause econometric problems, I also report results using the lagged (and twice lagged) change in the preferential tariff as the independent variable of interest. In this case, the coefficient on the change in the preferential tariff will have a positive sign for a building bloc effect and negative for a stumbling bloc effect. These regressions are similar to the regressions reported in Estevadeordal, Ornelas, and Freund (2008).[7]

Table 2.4 shows results for the effect of lagged changes in preference margins on MFN tariffs. The table shows complementarity between preferential liberalization and unilateral tariff reduction. A past increase in the preference margin, or a decline in the preferential tariff, precedes a decline in the MFN tariff. In particular, the results from column 1 suggest that a 1 percentage point increase in the preference margin is associated with about a 0.3 percentage point cut in the MFN tariff in the following year.

The findings of no significant trade diversion and external liberalization following preferential liberalization are likely to be related. Countries that lower both preferential tariffs and MFN applied tariffs will experience less diversion. Moreover, if they are setting external tariffs optimally, it may be the potential cost of diversion that encourages them to lower MFN tariffs subsequent to preferential liberalization. In this case, preferential liberalization generates external trade liberalization to prevent trade diversion, and regionalism serves as a mechanism for freer trade with the world.

5. Conclusion

This chapter explores third-country effects of regional integration. Concerns have been raised that regional integration will harm outsiders through trade diversion and potentially less external liberalization by members. In the six agreements that I examined, there is no evidence of trade diversion. I also find no evidence that trade preferences have reduced imports from nonmembers in Latin America. Finally, I present evidence that preferential tariff reduction tends to be followed by MFN tariff reduction in Latin America. These findings may be related: preferential liberalization enhances the incentives for external trade liberalization to prevent trade diversion. Thus, in products where pre-regional agreement tariffs were high, the regional agreement creates incentives to reduce them and observed diversion is limited. As a result, regionalism serves as a mechanism for freer trade with the world.

Considering the collapse of the Doha Round, the move to regionalism may be beneficial. RTAs offer an alternative forum for negotiation to further trade

---

[7] Estevadeordal, Freund, and Ornelas (2008) focus on effects in customs unions versus free trade areas. They show that complementary effect of preferential tariff reduction does not extend to customs unions. In addition, the authors use theoretical underpinnings and econometric techniques to provide strong evidence that the relationship is causal – preferential tariff reduction leads to a reduction of the applied MFN tariff in free trade areas.

liberalization. Although there are sure to be some costs, the costs associated with trade diversion and potential stumbling bloc effects are absent in the data presented here. In most other areas of economics we focus on first-order effects, with only a few words for second-order concerns – it appears as if regionalism may not be the exception that people once thought. If trade liberalization does not happen through multilateral negotiation, regional agreements do not appear to be so worrisome to be avoided.

REFERENCES

Aghion, P., P. Antràs, and E. Helpman, 2007. "Negotiating free trade," *Journal of International Economics*, 73:1–30.
Bagwell, K., and R. Staiger, 1999. "Regionalism and Multilateral Tariff Cooperation," in J. Piggott and A. Woodland (eds.), *International Trade Policy and the Pacific Rim*. London: Macmillan.
Bagwell, K., and R. Staiger, 2004. "Multilateral Trade Negotiations, Bilateral Opportunism, and the Rules of GATT/WTO," *Journal of International Economics*, 63(1):1–29.
Bhagwati, J., 2008. *Termites in the World Trading System*. New York: Oxford University Press.
Bhagwati, J., and A. Panagariya, 1999. "Preferential Trading Areas and Multilateralism: Strangers, Friends, or Foes?" Regionalism in trade policy: Essays on preferential trading." Singapore; River Edge, NJ; and London: World Scientific: 47–111.
Bohara, A., K. Gawande, and P. Sanguinetti, 2004. "Trade Diversion and Declining Tariffs: Evidence from Mercosur," *Journal of International Economics*, 64:65–88.
Bond, E., C. Syropoulos, and A. Winters, 2001. "Deepening of Regional Integration and Multilateral Trade Agreements," *Journal of International Economics*, 53(2):335–61.
Bond, E., R. Riezman, and C. Syropoulos, 2002. "A Strategic and Welfare Theoretic Analysis of Free Trade Areas." Mimeo.
Cadot, O., J. de Melo, and M. Olarreaga, 2001. "Can Bilateralism Ease the Pains of Multilateral Trade Liberalization?," *European Economic Review*, 45(1):27–44.
Chang, W., and A. Winters, 2002. "How Regional Blocs Affect Excluded Countries: The Price Effects of Mercosur," *American Economic Review*, 92(4):889–904.
Estevadeordal, A., C. Freund., and E. Ornelas, 2008. "Does Regulation Affect Trade Liberalization Toward Novembers?," *Quarterly Journal of Economics*, 123:1531–75.
Foroutan, F., 1998. "Does Membership in a Regional Preferential Trade Arrangement Make a Country More or Less Protectionist?" *The World Economy*, 21:305–35.
Frankel, J., 1997. *Regional Trade Blocs in the World Economic System*. Washington, DC: Institute for International Economics.
Frankel, J., E. Stein, and S. Wei, 1995. "Trading Blocs and the Americas: The Natural, The Unnatural, and the Supernatural," *Journal of Development Economics*, 47(10): 61–95.
Freund, C., 2000. "Multilateralism and the Endogenous Formation of Free Trade Agreements," *Journal of International Economics*, 115:1317–41.
Grossman, G., and E. Helpman, 1995. "The Politics of Free Trade Agreements," *American Economic Review*, 85:667–90.
Haveman, J., U. Nair-Reichert, and J. Thursby, 2003. "How Effective Are Trade Barriers? An Empirical Analysis of Trade Reduction, Diversion, and Compression," *Review of Economics and Statistics*, 85(2):480–85.

Krishna, P., 1998. "Regionalism and Multilateralism: A Political Economy Approach," *The Quarterly Journal of Economics*, 113:227–52.

Krishna, P., 2003. "Are Regional Trading Partners Natural?," *Journal of Political Economy*, 111(1):202–26.

Karacaovali, B., and N. Limão, 2008. "The Clash of Liberalizations: Preferential vs. Multilateral Trade Liberalization in the European Union," *Journal of International Economics*, 74:299–327.

Leamer, E. 1990. "The Structure and Effect of Tariff and Non-Tariff Barriers in 1983," in R. Jones and A. Krueger (eds.), *The Political Economy of International Trade: Essays in Honor of Robest E. Baldwin*. Cambridge, MA: Blackwell.

Levy, P., 1997. "A Political-Economic Analysis of Free Trade Agreements," *American Economic Review*, 87:506–19.

Limão, N., 2006. "Preferential Trade Agreements as Stumbling Blocks for Multilateral Trade Liberalization: Evidence for the U.S.," *American Economic Review*, 96:896–914.

Ornelas, E., 2005. "Rent Destruction and the Political Viability of Free Trade Agreements," *Quarterly Journal of Economics*, 120:1475–1506.

Panagariya, A., and R. Findlay, 1996. "A Political-Economy Analysis of Free Trade Areas and Customs Unions," in R. Feenstra, G. Grossman, and D. Irwin (eds.), *The Political Economy of Trade Reform: Essays in Honor of J. Bhagwati*. Cambridge, MA: MIT Press.

Pomfret, R. 2003. *Economic Analysis of Regional Trading Arrangements*. Cheltenham, UK: Elgar Reference Collection.

Richardson, M., 1993. "Endogenous Protection and Trade Diversion," *Journal of International Economics*, 34(3–4):309–24.

Saggi, K., and H. M. Yildiz, 2007. "Bilateral Trade Agreements and the Feasibility of Multilateral Free Trade." Mimeo.

Schiff, M., and A. Winters, 2003. *Regional Integration and Development*. Washington, DC: The World Bank and Oxford University Press.

Snape R. 1993. "The History and Economics of GATT's Article XXIV." *Regional Integration and the Global Trading System*. New York: St. Martin's Press, 273–91.

Srinivasan, S., J. Whalley, and I. Wooton, 1993. "Measuring the Effects of Regionalism on Trade and Welfare. Regional Integration and the Global Trading System." New York: St. Martin's Press, 52–80.

Syropoulos, C. 1999. "Customs Unions and Comparative Advantage." *Oxford Economic Papers*, 51(2):239–66.

Viner, J., 1950. *The Customs Union Issue*, Chapter 4. New York: Carnegie Endowment for International Peace.

Yeats, S., 1998. "Does Mercosur's Trade Performance Raise Concerns about the Effects of Regional Trade Agreements?," *World Bank Economic Review*, 12(1):1–28.

THOMAS J. PRUSA AND ROBERT TEH

3 Contingent Protection Rules in Regional Trade Agreements

1. Introduction

This chapter examines contingent protection provisions in seventy-four regional trade agreements (RTAs). Before we discuss any motivation or results, we will make two comments on our terminology. First, we use the term "regional trade agreements" in a broad sense.[1] For purposes of this chapter we use the term to refer to customs unions (where tariffs are zero for intra-RTA trade and are set at a common level for external trade), free trade areas (where tariffs are zero for intra-RTA trade and each member is free to set its own tariffs for external trade), and preferential trade agreements (where tariffs are lowered but not necessarily zero for intra-RTA trade and each member is free to set its own tariffs for external trade).[2] Whether member-states are in the same regional or geographical area does not matter for our purposes. As RTAs have proliferated many, perhaps even most, RTAs involve countries in geographically distinct areas.

Second, by "contingent" protection we mean antidumping (AD), countervailing duties (CVD), and emergency or safeguard measures. Because the World Trade Organization (WTO) agreement requires a link between trade volume and the imposition of trade protection for all of these trade remedies, they are referred to as *contingent* protection. Although other forms of protection often garner more attention (e.g., Super 301, TRIPs), the statutes mapped in this chapter account for most of the discretionary border protection beyond

The authors would like to thank staff of the WTO Secretariat. They are absolved of any errors and omissions in this chapter. The views expressed in this chapter are not meant to represent the positions or opinions of the WTO Secretariat nor of its members and are without prejudice to members' rights and obligations under the WTO. We would also like to thank David Gantz for his comments and suggestions on an earlier draft.

[1] We follow the WTO's own practice of using the term "RTA" to refer to all types of preferential agreements.

[2] According to the WTO, customs unions account for less than 10 percent of RTAs; the rest are free trade agreements and partial scope agreements.

Table 3.1. *Trade contingent actions, initiations, and measures: 1995–2006*

Trade contingent instrument	Initiations	Measures
Antidumping	3,220	2,052
Countervailing duty	201	119
Global safeguards	163	83

Source: WTO Secretariat.

WTO-negotiated tariff rates.[3] As shown in Table 3.1, there have been more than 3,000 AD initiations and a few hundred CVD and safeguard initiations since 1995. Official statistics on other border measures are not reported to the WTO, but extrapolating from our review of U.S. border measures, it is doubtful that there are more than a few hundred disputes involving all other trade statutes *combined.*

AD and CVD can be levied on exporters who engage in "unfair" trading practices that cause material injury to domestic producers. These unfair trading practices can take the form of selling products below their "normal" price or of benefiting from government-provided subsidies. Before levying either AD duties or CVD, countries must also show that the unfairly traded goods have caused material injury. The rules governing how governments calculate normal and export prices, compute the difference, determine subsidy amounts, and assess the injury or impact of the unfair trade and the duration of the duties are all contained in the General Agreement on Tariffs and Trade (GATT) and WTO agreements.[4]

Global safeguard actions do not require any evidence of unfair trade. A WTO member may temporarily restrict imports of a product if its domestic industry is injured or threatened with injury caused by a surge in imports. Here, the injury has to be serious, although the text of the agreement only vaguely describes what is required to show that injury is serious.[5] Although safeguard measures have been included in every GATT agreement (Article XIX), they have been relatively infrequently used especially as compared to AD or CVD.[6]

---

[3] Data on disputes can be found at www.wto.org/english/tratop_e/tratop_e.htm.

[4] Article VI of the GATT provides for the right of contracting parties to apply AD measures; the Agreement on Subsidies and Countervailing Measures addresses multilateral disciplines regulating the provision of subsidies and the use of countervailing measures to offset injury caused by subsidized imports.

[5] However, WTO jurisprudence does clarify that there is a "much higher standard" of injury for the imposition of a safeguard measure in comparison to that required in antidumping or countervailing measures; (see para. 124 of the WTO (2001) U.S.-Lamb, Appellate Body Report.

[6] Instead some governments preferred to protect their industries through "grey area" measures ("voluntary" export restraint arrangements on products such as cars, steel, and semiconductors). The WTO safeguards agreement broke new ground in prohibiting "gray area" measures and setting time limits on all safeguard actions.

No matter the difference in conditions under which they can be triggered, all three policy instruments represent internationally agreed means for a country to temporarily increase the level of trade protection granted to an injured domestic industry. Moreover, given that all three trade remedy provisions are governed by existing GATT/WTO agreements, RTAs with no additional language and provisions simply fall back to their preexisting WTO commitments. In other words, the status quo is WTO rules. If member countries choose, RTAs can impose additional rules for levying contingent protection or even prohibit the use of contingent protection against RTA members. As a general rule, these provisions typically make it more difficult to levy duties on RTA members than under WTO rules. In addition, such provisions can make intra-RTA contingent protection less attractive if they impose rules on the size of the margins and/or the duration of the duties. Hence, it is our working hypothesis that additional rules in RTAs tend to reduce contingent protection among RTA members.[7]

Bilateral safeguard provisions are an important exception. As we will discuss next, many RTAs have adopted bilateral safeguards rules that allow RTA members to temporarily delay some of the commitments under the agreement with the period of relief providing the domestic industry the opportunity to adjust toward free trade. In contrast with the other contingent protection rules in RTA, bilateral safeguards are responses to cuts in preferential tariffs and RTA rules that apply to them will not lead to more favorable treatment of intra-bloc members. A conceptual distinction between bilateral and global safeguards will be maintained in this chapter with the concern about discrimination focusing on RTA provisions on global safeguard actions.

There are several key findings from this study.

First, a relatively small number of RTAs (less than 10 percent of RTAs) have succeeded in abolishing contingent protection measures. Our econometric estimations suggest that these RTAs are characterized by a higher share of intra-RTA trade and deeper forms of integration that go well beyond the dismantling of border measures.

Second, a large number of RTAs have adopted RTA-specific rules that tighten discipline on the application of contingent protection measures on RTA members. More than half of RTAs include some additional rules on applying contingent measures. In the case of AD, key provisions increase the *de minimis* volume, tighten dumping margin requirements, and shorten the duration for applying AD relative to the WTO Antidumping Agreement. In similar fashion, exceptions to WTO global safeguard rules allow RTA partners to be excluded from what

---

[7] One possible exception is the special safeguard measure (SSM). The SSM is present in sixteen of the RTAs in the sample. It is triggered by a price or volume of imports threshold and a country is not required to show injury to the domestic industry. The country within the RTA that invokes the measure can apply tariffs up to the MFN level. The SSM applies mostly on a subset of agricultural products and textiles and clothing. It is not included in the WTO agreement.

otherwise are most-favored-nation (MFN) restraints. Examples of such exceptions include provisions that limit safeguard measures unless the RTA member is among the top five suppliers in most recent three-year period and/or account for at least 80 percent of total imports. Such provisions conflict with multilateral rules that require that safeguard measures be applied to all sources of imports and highlight the problem of nontariff discrimination emanating from RTAs. The WTO Appellate Body has repeatedly found such provisions "as applied" violate WTO rules, but they continue to be included in RTAs. With respect to CVD, we are unable to find major innovations in CVD rules and practice by past and present RTAs. We believe there are two reasons for the lack of CVD rules. First, few RTAs contain rules that meaningfully curb subsidies or state aid. Without such commitments, it is more difficult for negotiators to include CVD provisions. Second, the economic impact of subsidies is rarely confined to just intra-RTA trade; subsidies affect global trade. Hence, there is little economic justification for their inclusion in a RTA.

Third, a small number of RTAs give a role to regional institutions to conduct AD and CVD investigations and to review final determinations of national authorities. There is a theoretical presumption and some empirical evidence to suggest that this reduces the frequency of antidumping initiations and final determinations against RTA members (Blonigen, 2005).

Fourth, and perhaps the major lesson we have learned, is that it is very difficult to produce a simple summary of the contingent protection provisions in RTAs. RTAs vary in size, degree of integration, geographic scope, and the level of economic development of their members. What RTAs do with contingent protection provisions varies greatly from one RTA to the next, and even for the same country across different RTAs. Although it may not be surprising to learn that RTAs involving the European Union (EU) and United States have significantly different provisions, it is also important to realize that a country's attitude toward RTA provisions is a moving target. The United States' stance, for instance, has clearly evolved and its most recent RTAs lack many provisions included in its early RTAs.

Fifth, even if we focus only on the RTAs that incorporate additional rules it is hard to characterize what happens. Most RTAs have bilateral and/or global safeguard rules, but these same RTAs often do not have AD or CVD rules. There is a stronger connection between RTAs that have AD and CVD rules – most RTAs that have AD provisions also have CVD provisions. Nevertheless, there is a weak relationship between the particular provisions incorporated. For example, just because the CVD section includes additional injury provisions does not mean that the AD section will have the same injury provisions.

The results of the mappings suggest the need to be vigilant about increased discrimination arising from trade remedy rules in RTAs. If nothing else, the complicated pattern of inclusion of these provisions threatens the delicate give-and-take balancing of incentives that is at the crux of the GATT/WTO agreements.

An ongoing policy concern is that the elastic and selective nature of trade remedies may lead to more discrimination, with reduced trade remedy actions against
RTA partners, but a greater frequency of trade remedy actions against nonmembers. The adoption of RTA-specific trade remedy rules increases this risk of discrimination, with trade remedies against RTA members being abolished outright
or being subjected to greater discipline. In turn, this makes it more difficult for
non-RTA members to agree to WTO liberalization as the requisite quid pro quo
from RTA members may not be realized. Said differently, market access that non-
RTA members thought they had secured in prior WTO rounds may be eroded not
primarily because of the discriminatory tariffs but rather because of contingent
protection rules.

1.1. Brief Introduction of the Issues

Despite the extensive literature on regionalism, not much is known about
the actual content of many RTAs. This is certainly true about trade remedy provisions. Thus, one of the contributions of this chapter is to provide baseline information about the contents of the trade remedy provisions in RTAs. How many
have been able to abolish trade remedies and how many maintain the need for
these instruments? What are common features of trade remedy provisions in
RTAs?

Beyond this role of filling gaps in our knowledge about the contents of RTA,
this chapter also attempts to answer a range of other questions. Are there iden-
tifiable families of trade remedy provisions (families differing by geographical
regions or nature of RTA, for example)? What role do trade remedies play in RTAs?
Are there economic characteristics of the RTA members that are able to statistically explain some key features of the trade remedy provisions? Will the frequency of their use change as a consequence of RTA proliferation?

1.2. Survey of Analytical and Policy Discussions Surrounding
   Trade Remedies

1.2.1. Why Are Trade Remedies Needed in RTAs?

Why do trade agreements need trade remedy provisions? One explanation
for the high proportion of trade agreements with trade remedy provisions is the
political economy of protectionism. The long-term process of tariff liberalization
in the post-World War II era has successfully reduced tariff rates to very low levels
worldwide. Despite the tariff liberalization, or perhaps because of the liberalization, import-competing sectors continue to have an incentive to secure protection through whatever means they can find. Although trade remedy measures
are typically administered by bureaucracies that appear to be insulated from
political pressure, influence can be brought to bear on them indirectly "through
the shaping of the laws and regulations" that govern their work (Finger, Hall,

and Nelson, 1982). One of the advantages offered by administered protection to import-competing sectors is that it is inherently biased in their favor because it is a channel for complaints about an excess of import competition and not of its lack. By design, the trade remedy bureaucracy can only impose protection and not remove it (other than that which it imposes itself).[8]

A second explanation sees trade remedy measures as a pragmatic tool to deal with the political demands for protection that trade liberalization provokes (Jackson, 1997). Trade liberalization may lead to costs of adjustment. If nothing is done to manage those costs, political pressure may build up to a point where protectionist forces would be able to engineer a permanent reversal of trade liberalization. The introduction of trade remedy measures in a trade agreement may be thought of as anticipating the possibility of such difficult adjustments, the political pressure for protection that they give rise to, and providing a means to deflate this pressure with a temporary reversal of liberalization. This implies that the depth of liberalization that can be achieved by a trade agreement *ex ante* may depend on whether there are built-in escape clauses that allow governments to depart temporarily from their liberalization commitments under well-defined and circumscribed conditions. Trade remedy measures address this need. Whereas the use of the trade remedy measures may result in *ex post* welfare losses during periods when the level of protection is temporarily increased, the deeper liberalization that is allowed *ex ante* means that this could be outweighed by the long-term welfare gains.[9] Jackson's argument seems especially relevant for explaining why so many RTAs include bilateral safeguard provisions.

Paradoxically, these arguments suggest RTAs should generally make it easier for member-states to grant contingent protection. Empirically, however, we find that in general trade, remedy rules in RTAs work in the opposite direction: RTA rules often make protection more difficult to grant. With respect to AD, the inclusion of such rules is consistent with the view that dumping is driven by closed home markets (Mastel, 1988). The elimination of barriers for intra-RTA trade reduces the ability of firms to dump because they no longer have a protected home market where they can earn supernormal profits. More generally, the opening of markets via the RTA preferences reduces the ability for countries to price discriminate. This logic is also consistent with the lack of CVD rules in RTAs. Because most RTAs have failed to strengthen antisubsidy rules, the notion that there will be fewer subsidies, and in turn less need for CVD, is

---

[8] See Finger, Hall, and Nelson (1982, p. 454). Moore (2002, 2006) offers an excellent overview of U.S. sunset policy.

[9] A recent paper by Moore and Zanardi (2007) has examined whether this particular explanation for trade remedy measures can be empirically verified. They find that the evidence for a sample of twenty-three developing countries is not supportive of the argument that the availability of AD measures has contributed to tariff reductions. Instead, they conclude that past use of AD may have led to less trade liberalization.

not supported. Nevertheless, standard theory suggests political pressure should make it harder to include contingent protection rules in RTAs.

1.2.2. Legal Issues Surrounding Trade Remedies in RTAs

Because RTAs have the objective of dismantling barriers to intra-regional trade, one might expect RTA members would abolish the use of trade remedies against intra-bloc trade. In fact, there are those who view the elimination of trade remedies, in particular AD actions, as a requirement under Article XXIV of GATT 1994, which deals with customs unions and free trade areas. Paragraph 8(b) of GATT Article XXIV requires WTO members, who form a preferential trade area, to "eliminate duties and other regulations restricting trade."[10] Marceau (1994) interprets the reference to "other regulations restricting trade" to include trade remedies, specifically AD actions. This view is strengthened in that paragraph 8(b) of GATT Article XXIV allows, when necessary, RTA members to exclude certain GATT articles from the general requirement to "eliminate other regulations restricting trade."[11] It would have been easy to include GATT Articles VI (Antidumping and Countervailing Duties) and XIX (Emergency Action on Imports of Particular Products) to the excluded GATT articles, if that had been the intention of the framers of the GATT. That they are not excluded suggests that RTAs that retain the use of trade remedy instruments are inconsistent with GATT rules (Marceau, 1994).

1.2.3. Demand for Trade Remedies in RTAs

As mentioned earlier, the elimination of intra-RTA tariffs may create new demands for the protective effects of trade remedies. For a government entering into a RTA, import-competing sectors need to be given assurance that they have the means to protect themselves from the unanticipated consequences of the regional liberalization program. Retaining trade remedies in the RTA serves the useful purpose of soliciting political support for the agreement.

In these circumstances, trade remedies might be akin to other provisions in RTAs that limit or delay the possible deleterious effects of the RTA's liberalization, for example, long transition periods, complicated rules of origin, and carve-outs for sensitive sectors in RTAs; all result in a slower process of liberalization for sensitive import-competing sectors.

---

[10] Article XXIV: 8(b) states that "A free-trade area shall be understood to mean a group of two or more customs territories in which the duties and other restrictive regulations of commerce (except, where necessary, those permitted under Articles XI, XII, XIII, XIV, XV, and XX) are eliminated on substantially all the trade between the constituent territories in products originating in such territories."

[11] The GATT articles not covered by the requirement to eliminate "other regulations restricting trade" include Article XI (General Elimination of Quantitative Restrictions), XII (Restrictions to Safeguard the Balance of Payments), XIII (Nondiscriminatory Administration of Quantitative Restrictions), XIV (Exceptions to the Rule of Nondiscrimination), XV (Exchange Arrangements), and XX (General Exceptions).

Instead of directly cushioning the effects of the RTA by drawing out the process of tariff elimination, trade remedies achieve a different cushioning effect by specifying a set of conditions – injury to the domestic industry – under which the regional liberalization program may be temporarily suspended or partially reversed. Bilateral safeguard rules are the clearest examples of this idea, but one can interpret other forms of contingent protection as having a similar purpose.

1.2.4. Welfare Effects of Trade Remedy Provisions in RTAs

Whereas abolishing trade remedies on RTA partners' imports will most likely increase intra-bloc trade, this does not necessarily mean that abolition would raise welfare. The ambiguity of the welfare impact stems from the well-known insight that preferential trade arrangements have both trade-creation and trade-diversion effects (Viner, 1950). The impetus given to intra-regional trade by the abolition of trade remedy actions on RTA partners' trade may be at the expense of cheaper sources of imports that come from nonmembers.

The danger in fact is that as intra-regional trade expands because of falling intra-regional tariffs, contingent protection becomes increasingly directed at the imports of nonmembers. Bhagwati (1992, 1993) and Bhagwati and Panagariya (1996) have argued that as a result of their elastic and selective nature, administered protection can increase the risk of trade diversion from RTAs. Bhagwati (1993, p. 37) makes this statement:

> My belief that FTAs will lead to considerable trade diversion because of modern methods of protection, which are inherently selective and can be captured readily by protectionist purposes is one that may have been borne out in the European Community. It is well known that the European Community has used antidumping actions and VERs profusely to erect Fortress Europe against the Far East. Cannot much of this be a trade-diverting policy in response to the intensification of internal competition among member states of the European Community?

So apart from discrimination introduced by preferential tariffs, the establishment of RTAs can lead to more discrimination against nonmembers of the RTA through more frequent trade remedy actions. Thus, one key conclusion from Bhagwati's hypothesis is that in a world teeming with RTAs, there is greater need for stronger multilateral disciplines on trade remedies. It appears that Bhagwati (1992, 1993) and Bhagwati and Panagariya (1996) envisioned that this increase in discrimination against nonmembers can take place without necessarily requiring the adoption of special RTA rules on trade remedies. The elastic and selective nature of trade remedy protection allows nonmembers to be targeted more frequently.

To the extent that RTAs adopt special or additional rules on trade remedy actions against members' trade, they can effectively increase the level of discrimination against nonmembers. This increase in discrimination can occur when

RTA members abolish trade remedy actions against the trade of RTA members but not against nonmembers' trade. It could also occur when RTA members adopt rules that strengthen disciplines on trade remedy actions against the trade of RTA members but not against the trade of nonmembers.

At first blush, moves to strengthen disciplines on trade remedy actions against RTA partners or to abolish trade remedy actions against RTA partners appear good for trade. However, the welfare effects are ambiguous. Such rules may simply lead to intra-regional imports substituting for cheaper sources of imports from nonmembers (i.e., trade diversion). Because RTAs thrust us into the world of the second best, actions that look like they will lead to an increase in economic efficiency may achieve exactly the opposite effect.

2. RTAs Included in the Mapping

Seventy-four RTAs were surveyed for this chapter. The list of the RTAs appears in Table 3.2. To our knowledge, our database of contingent protection rules in RTAs is the most comprehensive available. Our database includes all of the economically large RTAs and all of the most active users of contingent protection.

The RTAs were selected according to a number of criteria. First, with a few exceptions, the RTAs mapped were notified to the WTO. As is well known, many RTAs have never been formally notified to the WTO. Without notification, the challenge for us to access the text of the agreement is limited. Second, we wanted a geographically diverse sample. Our current database involves RTAs from all major regions and has North–North, South–South, and North–South RTAs. Third, the sample includes the most economically important RTAs; these RTAs account for a large amount of trade and also the bulk of contingent trade measures.

In Table 3.2 we also list some key information about the RTAs: the date of entry into force; the relevant provision for GATT/WTO notification; the type of agreement; the development status of the members; and a general description of whether the RTA provisions governor AD, CVD, or safeguard.

2.1. Key Economic Characteristics of the RTAs

As shown in Table 3.3, of the seventy-four RTAs included in this survey, only four have not yet been notified to the WTO as of July 18, 2007. They are the Andean Community, the Group of Three, Mexico-Northern Triangle, and Mexico-Uruguay.

Collectively, the notified RTAs in our survey represent about half of the total number of RTAs notified to the WTO under Article XXIV of GATT 1994 and the Enabling Clause.[12] As shown in Table 3.3, about 82 percent of the RTAs in our

---

[12] As of July 18, 2007, 157 RTAs in force have been notified to the WTO under either Article XXIV of GATT 1994 or the Enabling Clause of 1979. A further 48 RTAs in force have been notified under Article V of the General Agreement on Trade in Services (GATS).

Table 3.2. *Contingent protection rules in selected RTAs*

RTA	Date of entry into force	Relevant GATT provision	Type of agreement	Development status of members	AD	CVD	Bilateral safeguards	Global safeguards
AFTA	1992	Enabling Clause	FTA	Developing	No rules	No rules	Rules	No rules
ALADI	1981	Enabling Clause	PTA	Developing	No rules	No rules	Rules	No rules
Andean Community	1993	—	CU	Developing	Rules	Rules	Rules	No rules
Australia–Singapore	2003	Article XXIV	FTA	Mixed	Rules	Rules	Disallowed	No rules
Australia–Thailand	2005	Article XXIV	FTA	Mixed	Rules	Rules	Rules	Rules
Australia–U.S.	2005	Article XXIV	FTA	Developed	No rules	No rules	Rules	Rules
CACM	1961	Article XXIV	CU	Developing	Rules	Rules	No rules	No rules
Canada–Chile	1997	Article XXIV	FTA	Mixed	Disallowed	No rules	Rules	Rules
Canada–Costa Rica	2002	Article XXIV	FTA	Mixed	Rules	No rules	Rules	Rules
Canada–Israel	1997	Article XXIV	FTA	Mixed	No rules	Rules	Disallowed	Rules
CARICOM	1973	Article XXIV	CU	Developing	Rules	Rules	Rules	No rules
CEMAC	1999	Enabling Clause	PTA	Developing	No rules	No rules	No rules	No rules
CER	1990	Article XXIV	FTA	Developed	Disallowed	Rules	Rules	No rules
China–Hong Kong	2004	Article XXIV	FTA	Developing	Disallowed	Disallowed	Rules	No rules
China–Macao	2004	Article XXIV	FTA	Developing	Disallowed	Disallowed	Rules	No rules
COMESA	1994	Enabling Clause	PTA	Developing	Rules	Rules	Rules	No rules
EC–Algeria	1976	Article XXIV	FTA	Mixed	Rules	Rules	Rules	Rules
EC–Andorra	1991	Article XXIV	CU	Mixed	No rules	No rules	No rules	No rules
EC–Chile	2003	Article XXIV	FTA	Mixed	Rules	Rules	Rules	Rules
EC–Croatia	2002	Article XXIV	FTA	Mixed	Rules	Rules	Rules	No rules
EC–Egypt	2004	Article XXIV	FTA	Mixed	Rules	Rules	Rules	Rules
EC–Faroe Islands	1997	Article XXIV	FTA	Mixed	Rules	No rules	Rules	No rules
EC–FYROM	2001	Article XXIV	FTA	Mixed	Rules	No rules	Rules	No rules
EC–Israel	2000	Article XXIV	FTA	Mixed	Rules	No rules	Rules	No rules
EC–Jordan	2002	Article XXIV	FTA	Mixed	Rules	No rules	Rules	No rules
EC–Lebanon	2003	Article XXIV	FTA	Mixed	Rules	Rules	Rules	Rules

(continued)

Table 3.2 *(continued)*

RTA	Date of entry into force	Relevant GATT provision	Type of agreement	Development status of members	AD	CVD	Bilateral safeguards	Global safeguards
EC–Mexico	2000	Article XXIV	FTA	Mixed	Rules	Rules	Rules	No rules
EC–Morocco	2000	Article XXIV	FTA	Mixed	Rules	No rules	Rules	No rules
EC–OCT	1971	Article XXIV	FTA	Mixed	No rules	No rules	Rules	No rules
EC–Palestine Authority	1997	Article XXIV	FTA	Mixed	Rules	No rules	Rules	No rules
EC–South Africa	2000	Article XXIV	FTA	Mixed	Rules	Rules	Rules	Rules
EC–Switzerland– Liechtenstein	1973	Article XXIV	FTA	Developed	Rules	No rules	Rules	No rules
EC–Syria	1977	Article XXIV	FTA	Mixed	Rules	Rules	Rules	No rules
EC–Tunisia	1998	Article XXIV	FTA	Mixed	Rules	No rules	Rules	No rules
EC–Turkey	1996	Article XXIV	CU	Mixed	Rules	No rules	Rules	No rules
EEA	1994	Article XXIV	FTA	Developed	Disallowed	Disallowed	Rules	No rules
EFTA	2001	Article XXIV	FTA	Developed	Disallowed	Disallowed	Rules	No rules
EFTA–Chile	2004	Article XXIV	FTA	Mixed	Disallowed	Rules	Rules	Rules
EFTA–Croatia	2002	Article XXIV	FTA	Mixed	Rules	Rules	Rules	No rules
EFTA–FYROM	2001	Article XXIV	FTA	Mixed	Rules	Rules	Rules	No rules
EFTA–Israel	1993	Article XXIV	FTA	Mixed	Rules	Rules	Rules	No rules
EFTA–Jordan	2002	Article XXIV	FTA	Mixed	Rules	Rules	Rules	No rules
EFTA–Morocco	1999	Article XXIV	FTA	Mixed	Rules	Rules	Rules	No rules
EFTA–Palestine Authority	1999	Article XXIV	FTA	Mixed	Rules	Rules	Rules	No rules
EFTA–Singapore	2003	Article XXIV	FTA	Mixed	Disallowed	Rules	Rules	No rules
EFTA–Tunisia	2005	Article XXIV	FTA	Mixed	Rules	Rules	Rules	Rules
EFTA–Turkey	1992	Article XXIV	FTA	Mixed	Rules	Rules	Rules	No rules
European Communities	1958	Article XXIV	CU	Developed	Disallowed	Disallowed	Disallowed	No rules
GCC	1981	Enabling Clause	PTA	Developing	No rules	No rules	No rules	No rules

Agreement	Year	Legal basis	Type	Development					
Japan–Singapore	2002	Article XXIV	FTA	Mixed	No rules	No rules	No rules	Rules	Rules
Korea–Chile	2004	Article XXIV	FTA	Developing	Rules	Rules	Rules	Rules	Rules
Mercosur	1991	Enabling Clause	CU	Developing	Rules	Rules	Rules	Disallowed	No rules
Mexico–Chile	1999	Article XXIV	FTA	Developing	No rules	No rules	No rules	Rules	Rules
Mexico–EFTA	2001	Article XXIV	FTA	Mixed	Rules	Rules	Rules	Rules	No rules
Mexico–Israel	2000	Article XXIV	FTA	Developing	Rules	Rules	Rules	Rules	Rules
Mexico–Japan	2005	Article XXIV	FTA	Mixed	No rules	No rules	No rules	Rules	Rules
Mexico–Nicaragua	1998	Article XXIV	FTA	Developing	Rules	Rules	Rules	Rules	Rules
Mexico–Northern Triangle	2001	—	FTA	Developing	Rules	Rules	Rules	Rules	Rules
Mexico–Uruguay	2004	—	FTA	Developing	Rules	Rules	Rules	Rules	Rules
NAFTA	1994	Article XXIV	FTA	Mixed	Rules	Rules	Rules	Rules	Rules
New Zealand–Singapore	2001	Article XXIV	FTA	Mixed	Rules	No rules	No rules	Disallowed	No rules
SADC	2000	Article XXIV	FTA	Developing	Rules	Rules	Rules	Rules	No rules
SAFTA	1995	Enabling Clause	PTA	Developing	Rules	Rules	Rules	Rules	Rules
SPARTECA	1981	Enabling Clause	PTA	Mixed	Rules	No rules	No rules	Rules	No rules
Turkey–Israel	1997	Article XXIV	FTA	Developing	Rules	No rules	No rules	Rules	No rules
UEMOA	2000	Enabling Clause	PTA	Developing	Rules	No rules	No rules	Rules	Rules
U.S.–Bahrain	2006	Article XXIV	FTA	Mixed	No rules	No rules	No rules	Rules	Rules
U.S.–CAFTA & Dom. Republic	2006	Article XXIV	FTA	Mixed	No rules	Rules	Rules	Rules	Rules
U.S.–Chile	2004	Article XXIV	FTA	Mixed	No rules	Rules	Rules	Rules	Rules
U.S.–Israel	1985	Article XXIV	FTA	Mixed	No rules	No rules	No rules	Rules	No rules
U.S.–Jordan	2001	Article XXIV	FTA	Mixed	No rules	No rules	No rules	Rules	Rules
U.S.–Morocco	2006	Article XXIV	FTA	Mixed	No rules	No rules	No rules	Rules	Rules
U.S.–Singapore	2004	Article XXIV	FTA	Mixed	No rules	No rules	No rules	Rules	Rules

Note: CU = customs union; FTA = free trade area; PTA = preferential trade agreement.

Table 3.3. *Characteristics of RTAs*

Relevant GATT provision	Number	Percent	
Article XXIV	61	82.4	
Enabling Clause	9	12.2	
Unknown	4	5.4	
Type of agreement	Number	Percent	
Customs Union	7	9.5	
FTA	60	81.1	
PTA	7	9.5	
Development status of members	Number	Percent	2005 Intra-RTA imports ($ Billion)
Developed/developing mixed	6	8.1	$2,932.4
Developing	22	29.7	$501.0
Mixed	46	62.2	$1,307.7

sample were notified to the WTO under Article XXIV of GATT 1994; about 12 percent were notified to the WTO under the Enabling Clause.[13] The Enabling Clause permits developed countries to discriminate between different categories of trading partner (i.e., between developed, developing, and least developed countries) that would otherwise violate Article I of the GATT. Article I stipulates that no GATT contracting party be treated worse than any other (i.e., MFN treatment). In effect, this allows developed countries to give preferential treatment to poorer countries, particularly to least developed countries. Given its roots, our conjecture is that RTAs notified under the Enabling Clause will tend to have fewer rules.

The RTAs surveyed accounted for about 52.5 percent ($4.7 trillion) of global merchandise import flows in 2005.[14] Intra-RTA imports in 2005 for the surveyed RTAs ranged from a high of $2.4 trillion (for the European Community or EC) to a low of $73 million for the arrangement involving European Free Trade Association (EFTA) and the Former Yugoslav Republic of Macedonia (FYROM). The share of intra-RTA trade was largest (61 percent) for the EC and North American Free Trade Agreement (NAFTA; 34.5 percent) while the smallest share was for the FTA involving the EC with the Faroe Islands.

2.2. Other Stylized Facts

Crawford and Fiorentino (2005) and Fiorentino, Verdeja, and Toqueboeuf (2007) have provided a comprehensive picture of the current RTA landscape. They document the continuing increase in the number of RTAs being formed. Even countries in East Asia that have traditionally eschewed preferential trade

[13] These percentages are very comparable to those for all notified RTAs. Of the 157 RTAs notified to the WTO under either Article XXIV of GATT 1994 or the Enabling Clause of 1979, 82 percent were notified under Article XXIV of GATT 1994.
[14] Not all intra-RTA trade receives preferential treatment.

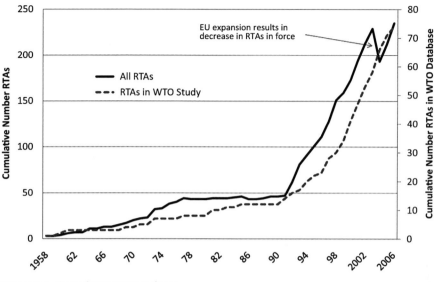

Figure 3.1. Cumulative RTAs in force.

arrangements have now become active players in regional trade negotiations. RTAs between developed and developing countries and cross-regional agreements are on the increase. Many of the patterns they document are also apparent in the list of RTAs included in our survey. A large number of the RTAs were formed just recently. Forty came into force at the beginning of the current decade and twenty-two in the 1990s. Only four came into force in the 1980s; four in the 1970s; and four before 1970 (see Figure 3.1).

The sample is also geographically diverse with RTAs from North America, the Caribbean, Latin America, Asia and the Pacific, Africa, the Middle East, Western Europe, and Central and Eastern Europe. Of the seventy-four RTAs, six (8 percent) involved only developed countries, twenty-two (30 percent) were composed of purely developing countries, and forty-six (62 percent) involved a mixture of developed and developing countries (Table 3.3).[15] When we weigh the RTAs by trade value, we see that 62 percent of intra-RTA trade involve the developed country RTAs, 28 percent involve mixed RTAs, and just 10 percent involve developing country RTAs.

The sample is dominated by free trade agreements – 80 percent of the RTAs in our sample are free trade areas, 10 percent are customs unions, and, 10 percent are preferential trade areas.[16] We emphasize that the RTAs self-report whether

---

[15] "Developed countries" refer to Australia, Canada, EC, the members of EFTA, Japan, New Zealand, and the United States. All other countries are classified as developing countries.

[16] This distribution reflects the distribution for all notified RTAs, where 10 percent are customs unions, 60 percent are free trade areas, and 30 percent are partial.

they are free trade or preferential trade areas. It appears that many RTAs that declare themselves to be free trade areas do not lower tariffs to zero on substantially all tariff lines, even many years after the FTA is enacted.

3. Methodological Approach to the Mapping

3.1. Review of Previous Approaches to Examining Contingent Protection Rules in RTAs

We know of no previous attempt to comprehensively and systematically analyze trade remedy rules in RTAs. However, the AD rules in NAFTA have received some research attention. NAFTA provides for the creation of binational panels that have the authority to review AD determinations made by national authorities. To what extent can the existence of such a regional institution affect the frequency of AD initiations and measures against RTA partners?

The key policy concern is the elastic and selective nature of trade remedies that can lead to more discrimination, with reduced trade remedy actions against RTA partners, but a greater frequency of trade remedy actions against nonmembers. Although reduced trade remedy actions against RTA members may lead to more intra-regional trade, the welfare effects of this increased trade are ambiguous depending on the trade-creation and trade-diversion effects.

The economic literature suggests one important avenue through which the specific trade remedy rules in RTAs can reduce actions against imports from RTA partners. It appears that the existence of a regional body that has the power to review the determinations of national investigating authorities can reduce the incidence of trade remedy actions against intra-RTA imports.

In the cases of NAFTA and the Canada–U.S. Free Trade Agreement (CUSFTA), a member-state can request a review of the final AD or CVD determination made by the authority of another NAFTA partner. Under Chapter 19 of NAFTA, this would be undertaken by a binational panel, composed of five experts designated by the concerned NAFTA members. Although the scope of the review is limited to determining whether the decision of the trade remedy authority is in accordance with national laws, the panel has the authority to remand it to the concerned authority for action if it judges that the determination has not been in accord with national laws. Chapter 19 also allows NAFTA partners to request a binational panel review of a proposed amendment of AD or CVD statutes. The creation of binational panels in NAFTA appears to have reflected Canadian concerns over U.S. AD and CVD actions (Gagné, 2000; Jones, 2000). If final determinations can be subject to review not only by the courts or tribunals of the country whose authorities imposed the measure but by a regional body as well, it may provide an additional layer of objectivity (Gagné, 2000). The existence of regional review bodies might also change the incentives for filing unfair trade petitions by reducing the likelihood of an affirmative finding of injurious unfair trade (Jones, 2000).

A number of empirical studies have tried to ascertain whether this specific provision in CUSFTA and NAFTA have had a discernible effect on the number of U.S. trade remedy actions against NAFTA partners and on the final determinations by U.S. authorities.

One possible test is to see whether there is a significant difference in outcome of the appeals before binational panels as opposed to national tribunals. Goldstein (1996) computes the ratio of the share of U.S. unfair trade orders against Canada as a proportion of Canadian imports to the United States. She found that, in 1987, before the FTA, the Canadian ratio of AD orders to its share of U.S. imports was 0.83. By the end of 1990, that number had been reduced to 0.33. This reduction in unfair trade orders occurred only in Canadian trade as the same ratio computed for the EC and Japan rose during the same period. She attributes this shift to the rulings of the binational panels. Rugman and Anderson (1997) reviewed the initial five-year period (1989–1994) of the operation of CUSFTA. They noted that two-thirds of Canadian appeals of U.S. trade remedy actions before binational panels were remanded, compared with one-third for non-NAFTA countries before U.S. tribunals (i.e., the Court of International Trade). Although Rugman and Anderson are critical of the binational panels and make a number of recommendations for improving them, given this evidence they acknowledged that Canada obtained a unique benefit from the binational panels under CUSFTA.

Neither the Goldstein paper nor the Rugman and Anderson papers applied any statistical tests to the data. Using AD and CVD filings of the United States from 1980–1997 and similar data of Canada for 1985–1997, Jones (2000) estimated a Poisson regression with macroeconomic variables, imports, industry characteristics, and an FTA dummy as regressors. He found a robust inverse relationship between the introduction of NAFTA Chapter 19 and the number of unfair trade petition filings. He also found that there was a statistically significant reduction in both U.S. AD filings against Canada and Canadian AD filings against the United States after NAFTA took effect.

Blonigen (2005) extended the study by Jones in a number of ways. First, Mexico was included in the study. Second, instead of representing Chapter 19 as a time dummy, he used the number of requests for panels and/or remands, so more closely measuring the amount of Chapter 19 activity. Third, Blonigen not only examined the possible effect of Chapter 19 on the number of AD/CVD filings but also on the outcome of the reviews. Unlike Jones, he found no evidence that binational reviews under Chapter 19 of NAFTA affected the frequency of U.S. filings or affirmative determinations against Canada and Mexico. However, he did discover some indication that cumulative remands by Chapter 19 dispute panels to review U.S. decisions against Canada have led to fewer affirmative decisions against Canada.

Because of this literature, our mapping includes information on whether a provision giving regional institutions the authority to review decisions made by national authorities.

3.2. Benchmarks (Templates) Used for the Mapping

3.2.1. Introduction

The mappings that are presented in this chapter are drawn almost exclusively from the legal text of the RTAs. In a small number of instances primarily involving older RTAs, the mapping has also relied on directives or decisions that were enacted subsequently, several years after the RTA came into force. The primary purpose of the mappings is to understand the nature of these rules.[17] Admittedly, we are assuming that legal provisions in the RTAs coincide with actual practice. We recognize the potential gap between the language contained in the agreements and how the provisions are actually implemented. This is true in any legal document and it is particularly pertinent for any study of RTAs. It is well known that some promised tariffs concessions are not enacted in a timely fashion. In addition, although the legal text controlling trade remedy practice may sometimes be similar across RTAs, there could be large variation in trade remedy practices that in turn generate differences in outcomes.

Blonigen and Prusa (2003) have emphasized the importance of the institutional process surrounding the AD investigation and determinations and argued that these have significant impacts beyond the AD duty finally observed. They pointed to the substantial discretion enjoyed by authorities in their decisions on dumping margins and injury determinations. They identified a number of differences in AD practices across countries. The level of transparency varied and seemed to be a problem for new users. Price undertakings were common in some countries but not in others. Some countries began collecting AD duties only a few days after a petition was filed, although most countries waited until a preliminary injury determination was made. Some countries levied an AD duty equal to the full dumping margin while others levied a lesser amount.

Blonigen (2006) noted that the average dumping margin calculated by the U.S. Department of Commerce (DOC) had risen from an average of 15.5 percent in the early 1980s to an average of 63 percent by 2000. He concluded that DOC discretionary practices have played the major role in rising dumping margins. During the same time, the proportion of cases which the U.S. International Trade Commission found material injury rose from 45 percent in the early 1980s to 60 percent by 2000. Importantly, the evolving effect of discretionary practices was due not only to increasing use of these practices over time, but apparent changes in implementation of these practices that meant a higher increase in the dumping margin whenever they were applied.

The recent survey by Horlick and Vermulst (2005) of the AD practices in ten major user countries – Australia, Brazil, China, the EC, India, Indonesia,

---

[17] Secondarily, the mapping makes it possible to test empirically testable hypotheses about trade remedies in RTAs.

Table 3.4. *Summary of contingent protection rules in RTAs*

	AD	CVD	Bilateral Safeguard	Global Safeguard
Disallowed	9 (12.2%)	5 (6.8%)	5 (6.8%)	0 (0.0%)
Rules	47 (63.5%)	39 (52.7%)	65 (87.8%)	29 (39.2%)
No rules	18 (24.3%)	30 (40.5%)	4 (5.4%)	45 (60.8%)

Mexico, South Africa, Thailand, and the United States – showed that this problem extended to many countries. They identified a number of problem areas: procedural issues, determination of dumping margins, and injury determinations. They found that the increasing use of constructed normal values gave too much discretion to AD authorities in determining the existence of dumping. They reached a similar conclusion that there was too much administrative discretion in the determination of injury, injury margins, and causation.

What these studies imply is that although the legal provisions on trade remedies in RTAs provide important information, they may not be enough. The institutional setting, the administrative procedures, and practices will need to be examined to ascertain what part they play in determining the trade and welfare effects of trade remedy actions. Unfortunately, we are unable to take these factors into account in this chapter. While acknowledging this concern, we nevertheless think that the mapping of trade remedy provisions continues to be a useful exercise, and the only test of whether there is predictive power from the mapping will come from empirically grounded tests of specific hypothesis about trade remedy practice in regional trade agreements.

3.2.2. Antidumping

We developed a two-level template for the comparative analysis of AD provisions. In the first level of the template, the key questions that are asked are (i) whether AD is disallowed among the members and (ii) if specific rules on AD apply to RTA members' trade. If specific AD rules apply to RTA members, the second level of the template maps these specific provisions of the agreement.

Level 1 elements: The first and more important level of the template classifies AD provisions in RTAs into three mutually exclusive categories. The first category of RTAs includes those that disallow AD actions among the RTA members. The second category includes RTAs that have no such prohibition and have no specific language or provisions on AD. The final category is made up of RTAs that allow AD against RTA members and contain specific provisions on AD.

In Table 3.2 we list for each RTA the level 1 coding for AD provisions. As shown in Table 3.4 we find about two-thirds of the RTAs have additional AD rules and about one-fourth have no AD rules (i.e., do not mention AD in the RTA). Only a small number (nine) of RTAs prohibit the use of AD. These are Canada–Chile, CER (Australia–New Zealand), China–Hong Kong, China–Macao, the EC, European Economic Area (EEA), EFTA, EFTA–Chile, and EFTA–Singapore. In the case of the EEA, the prohibition on AD applies only to intra-regional trade of goods that fall under Chapters 25 to 97 of the harmonized system. In other words, AD measures can still be taken against agricultural and fishery goods.[18] The Chile-Mexico FTA, which came into force in 1999, stipulated future negotiations between the partners that will lead to the removal of AD actions. However, it appears that the negotiations to achieve this goal have not been successfully concluded.

Level 2 elements: For those RTAs that contain specific rules on AD, the second level of the template maps these specific provisions in some detail. The second-level template is patterned after the Antidumping Agreement of the WTO. It includes elements such as determination of dumping, determination of injury, evidence, provisional measures, price undertakings, duration and review of AD duties and price undertakings, and notification and consultation. However, it includes elements that are either quite unique in regional agreements or that have been highlighted in the literature that is available on AD in RTAs.

As noted earlier, one important avenue through which trade remedy rules in RTAs can affect the probability of trade remedy actions among RTA partners is through the establishment of a regional body that has the power to conduct investigations or has the authority to review or remand final determinations of national authorities.

The level 2 template used to map the AD provisions of the RTAs appears in Table 3.5.

Discussion: Some of the specific language in the RTAs clearly makes AD a less attractive option for domestic petitioners. For example, the Andean Community requires a higher *de minimis* volume (6 percent) and mandates a shorter period (three years) for applying AD than does the WTO Antidumping Agreement. The New Zealand–Singapore FTA has a higher *de minimis* dumping margin (5 percent) and a higher *de minimis* volume requirement (5 percent) than the WTO benchmark. Mercosur also limits the duration of AD duties to three years (compared to five years in the WTO agreement).

Regional oversight bodies also will likely reduce the amount intra-RTA AD activity. Five of the seventy-four RTAs included in the survey (Andean Community, Central American Common Market [CACM], Caribbean Community [CARICOM], NAFTA, and West African Economic and Monetary Union [UEMOA]) give a role to regional bodies to conduct investigations and/or review

---

[18] This is based on communication with the EFTA Secretariat.

Table 3.5. *Abridged antidumping template*

1. AD actions disallowed
2. AD actions allowed but with no specific provisions
3. AD actions allowed and with specific provisions
   a) Determination of dumping
   b) Determination of injury
   c) Definition of domestic industry
   d) Mutually acceptable solution
   e) Initiation and conduct of investigations
   f) Evidence
   g) Provisional measures
   h) Price undertakings
   i) Imposition and collection of AD duties
   j) Retroactivity
   k) Duration and review of AD duties and price undertakings
   l) Public notice and explanation of determinations
   m) AD action on behalf of a third country
   n) Regional body/committee
   o) Notification/Consultation
   p) Dispute settlement
   q) In accordance with GATT Article VI/AD Agreement

the final determinations of national authorities. In the Andean Community, the Secretary-General of the Andean Community is given the authority to open and conduct AD investigations and decide on provisional and final AD duties. The Secretariat for Central American Economic Integration (SIECA) is the regional body given the authority to conduct AD investigations in the CACM. In the CARICOM, one of the regional organs – the Council for Trade and Development (COTED) – has the authority to conduct AD investigations, to authorize member-states to apply AD measures, and to keep such measures under review. The UEMOA Commission is the regional body in charge of AD in UEMOA. In the case of NAFTA, the establishment of binational panels can be requested by any of the members to review final AD determinations.

With the exception of NAFTA, the four other RTAs with provisions for regional bodies are customs unions. Some of these regional groupings have a history of relying heavily on regional institutions in the integration process. The Andean Community and the CARICOM, in particular, are composed of small member-states and it could be argued that certain public goods may be better delivered by regional institutions than national ones because of the possibility of pooling expertise and resources. In the context of the current WTO negotiations, for example, CARICOM countries have tabled proposals that will allow WTO members to designate a regional body to carry out the functions necessary to implement the provisions of the Sanitary and Phytosanitary (SPS)

Agreement, Technical Barriers to Trade (TBT) Agreement, and the Trade-Related Intellectual Property Rights (TRIPS) Agreement. These WTO agreements have implementation obligations that seem to pose very high hurdles for developing countries, particularly for the smallest ones. This explanation has some similarity to the argument made by Andriamananjara and Schiff (1999) that a microstate's decision to form, expand, or join a regional organization is based on reduced negotiating costs and increased bargaining power rather than on the traditional costs and benefits of trade integration. Although the use of regional bodies in AD actions in these RTAs may have been intended as a device to lower the cost of public good provision, it also mitigates the ability of domestic producers to inveigle a compliant national investigating authority to find for them in dumping cases. Thus, all things being equal, an RTA that gives a role to regional institutions in conducting investigations and in final determinations may see fewer AD initiations and measures.

Almost all of the RTAs entered into by the EC contain specific language on AD. These provisions have a number of common characteristics. There is a regional body that is established to oversee the whole RTA. When (or even before) an AD petition is initiated, the regional body is informed and attempts are made by the partners to arrive at a mutually agreed solution. If no mutually acceptable solution is found, the action (investigation or final determination) proceeds. Provisional AD measures can be taken if delay will lead to material injury. Almost all of these EC-centered RTAs establish regional bodies (joint committees) to oversee the implementation of the agreement. However, apart from serving as a forum for consultations or notification, they play no central role in how the AD process affecting intra-regional trade unfolds. The RTAs that the EFTA countries have entered into with the same partners as the EC also exhibit similar characteristics.

With the exception of NAFTA, the RTAs entered into by the United States (Australia–United States, United States–Bahrain, United States–Central America Free Trade Agreement [CAFTA] and Dominican Republic, United States–Chile, United States–Jordan, United States–Israel, United States–Morocco, and United States–Singapore) have no specific provisions on AD. All by United States–Israel were negotiated after NAFTA. The change in the United States' position likely reflects unhappiness by large AD users, and in turn unhappiness by key members of Congress, over the perceived loss of autonomy in applying AD against NAFTA partners.

To our mind, the large number of RTAs (fifty-six) that have either abolished AD actions against RTA members or have drawn up specific rules on AD actions against RTA members should raise some concern about increased discrimination, whether per se or de facto, against nonmembers. From a welfare standpoint, the concern is with the likelihood of greater trade diversion arising from the design of the RTA AD rules.

3.2.3. Countervailing Duties

A similar two-level template is adopted for CVD provisions. One addition to the first-level CVD template is information concerning the presence of a common policy or program on subsidies and any additional disciplines that are imposed on the use of subsidies and state aid. Under multilateral rules, CVDs can be levied on imports that benefit from subsidies if they cause or threaten material injury to an established domestic industry, or if they retard materially the establishment of a domestic industry. If the RTA members have a common policy on subsidies or state aid, or if the RTA members are able to agree on additional disciplines that apply to subsidies or state aid, they may be able to dispense with the use of CVDs. However, absent a common subsidy policy or additional disciplines on subsidies, it is unlikely for the provisions governing CVDs in the RTA to depart from multilateral rules or practice. Even if the RTA members have a common policy on subsidies or state aid, it may be difficult for RTAs to negotiate CVD rules because the economic impact of subsidies is global and is not confined to intra-RTA trade.

Level 1 elements: The first level classifies CVD provisions in RTAs into three mutually exclusive categories. The first group of RTAs is those RTAs that disallow CVD actions against RTA members. The second category includes RTAs with no specific CVD provisions. The third are RTAs with specific CVD rules. As previously discussed, additional information about regional disciplines on subsidies and state aid are also included in the first level of the template.

In Table 3.2 we list for each RTA the level 1 coding for CVD provisions. We find about half of the RTAs have additional CVD rules and about 40 percent have no CVD rules (see Table 3.4). Only five RTAs (less than 10 percent of our sample) have abolished CVD. These RTAs are China–Hong Kong, China–Macao, EC, EEA, and EFTA. However, in the case of EFTA and the EEA, CVDs are disallowed only for products falling under Chapters 25 to 97 of the Harmonized System; that is, CVDs can be applied to agricultural and fishery products.[19]

Level 2 elements: The second and more detailed level of the template involves determining whether certain provisions are present in the third category of RTAs and is patterned after the Subsidies and Countervailing Duties Agreement (SCM) of the WTO. These include provisions on conditions for applying CVDs, initiation and subsequent investigation, evidence, consultation, determination of injury, definition of domestic industry, provisional measures, undertakings, imposition and collection of CVDs, retroactivity, duration and review of CVDs and undertakings, special and differential treatment of developing countries, subsidization by third countries, and dispute settlement. We include information on the role of regional institutions in the administration of countervailing

---

[19] This is based on communication with the EFTA Secretariat.

Table 3.6. *Abridged countervailing duties template*

I. Subsidies
  1. Disciplines on subsidies
  2. Disciplines on state aid
II. Countervailing duties
  1. CVD disallowed
  2. CVD allowed but no specific provisions
  3. CVD allowed with specific provisions
    a) Mutually acceptable solution
    b) Conditions for applying countervailing measures
    c) Evidence
    d) Consultation
    e) Provisional measures
    f) Undertakings
    g) Imposition and collection of CVD
    h) Duration and review of CVD and undertakings
    i) Special and differential treatment of developing country members
    j) Subsidization by third countries
    k) Regional body/committee
    l) Dispute settlement
    m) In accordance with GATT Article VI and/or SCM Agreement

duties. Regional bodies that have the authority to conduct CVD investigations and to review and remand final determinations seem to be the most important.

The template used to map the CVD provisions of the RTAs appears in Table 3.6.

Discussion: The great majority of the surveyed RTAs either has no specific CVD provisions (thirty RTAs) or has specific provisions on CVDs that nonetheless allow the use of CVD measures (thirty-nine RTAs). However, of those RTAs with specific provisions on CVDs, seventeen have what we consider "weak" provisions: they only state that all CVD actions should be in accord with GATT Article VI and the SCM Agreement. From our perspective, this language essentially restates the obvious.[20] Under a stronger standard for what constitutes rules, we would have only twenty-two RTAs with any detailed provisions on CVD actions. However, even then, arguably the only interesting RTA provisions are those where regional bodies are allowed to conduct CVD investigations or have the power to review and remand final CVD determinations. The four RTAs with such provisions are the Andean Community, CACM, CARICOM, and NAFTA.

Our study indicates that there has been little tinkering with CVD rules in the sample of RTAs surveyed. We believe this can be traced to the lack of movement at the RTA level in agreeing on additional curbs on subsidies or state aid.

---

[20] Rather than classify such weak rules as "no rules" (which preordains that the provision does not matter), we opted to classify these RTAs as having CVD provisions.

The only quite explicit provision we have found is the prohibition or elimination of export subsidies to agricultural products in sixteen RTAs, none of which involve the EC or EFTA. The RTAs that have prohibited export subsidies on agricultural products are Australia–Singapore, Australia–Thailand, Australia–United States, Canada–Chile, Canada–Costa Rica, CER, Group of Three, Mexico–Chile, Mexico–Nicaragua, Mexico–Northern Triangle, Mexico–Uruguay, New Zealand–Singapore, United States–Bahrain, United States–CAFTA–Dominican Republic, United States–Chile, and United States–Morocco.

Apart from this, there is often only a quite general statement against state aid that distorts competition. It appears that countries have not put subsidy programs on the table in their RTA negotiations and thus feel a continuing need for CVD as a weapon to wield against such support. Although it is possible to agree to a reduction or elimination of subsidies in an RTA negotiation, part of the trade benefits from that will be captured by nonmembers. The reluctance to give away a "freebie" may explain why the only meaningful negotiation on further reductions in agricultural subsidies is occurring at the multilateral level.

The "free rider" problem might also explain why we see so little RTA rules on CVDs. Specifically, in contrast to AD where pricing issues can really be viewed as market-specific issues, the economic consequences of a subsidized industry are likely go beyond any single market and any single RTA. Hence, it may well make less sense to include CVD provisions in RTAs given the nature of the distortion.

Given that only a few RTAs have meaningful CVD rules – perhaps as few as four RTAs – it does not appear that there is increased threat of trade diversion arising from the specific rules adopted on CVD in the RTAs covered in this study.

3.2.4. Safeguards

We distinguished between "bilateral" and "global" safeguard provisions in regional trading agreements.

Bilateral safeguard actions are meant to apply only to the trade of other RTA members. Bilateral actions provide a temporary escape for members when, because of undertaking the commitments under the agreement, increased imports from RTA partners result in serious injury to the domestic industry. Triggering the safeguard provision in the RTA allows a member to relieve itself of its RTA obligations temporarily, with the period of relief providing the beleaguered domestic industry the opportunity to adjust toward free trade. In fact, these actions are worded in that way – bilateral safeguards – in a number of RTA agreements. However, even in those RTAs where this distinction is not made explicitly, the safeguard provision is clearly meant to address emergency situations that occur because of the preferential treatment accorded to partners' imports.

The most common type of bilateral safeguard provision involves transition safeguards. These provisions allow a country to delay implementation during the transition period following inception. The other, and often more widely publicized, bilateral safeguard provision involves special safeguards. Special safeguards identify particular industries that warrant "special" treatment, for example, traditionally sensitive sectors like agricultural products and textiles and clothing. Two characteristics are noteworthy. Firstly, special safeguards are triggered by a different mechanism, typically involving price and/or quantity thresholds. Second, they do not require that injury to the domestic industry be demonstrated.

Global safeguard actions are those actions that are triggered under GATT Article XIX (Emergency Action on Imports of Particular Products) and the Agreement on Safeguards. Multilateral rules require that any safeguard measure be applied on a nondiscriminatory basis.[21] Typically, the RTA provisions on global safeguard actions specify the conditions under which RTA partners could be excluded from multilateral safeguard actions invoked by an RTA member.

Provisions of both bilateral and global actions are included in the safeguard template and mapping.

Level 1 elements: The first level of the template classifies bilateral safeguard provisions in RTAs into three mutually exclusive categories. The first category includes RTAs that disallow bilateral safeguard actions among RTA partners. The second covers RTAs that we believe allow bilateral actions but have no specific provisions. The third category includes those RTAs that allow bilateral safeguard actions and have specific language governing those actions. The second and more detailed level of the template involves a classification of the provisions contained in the third category of RTAs.

In Table 3.2 we list for each RTA the level 1 coding for safeguard provisions. We find about 90 percent of the RTAs have bilateral safeguard provisions and about 5 percent have no safeguard provisions (see Table 3.4). The RTAs with no specific safeguard provisions are CACM, Economic and Monetary Community of Central Africa (CEMAC), EC–Andorra, and Gulf Cooperation Council (GCC).

Only five RTAs (Australia–Singapore, Canada–Israel, European Communities, Mercosur, and New–Zealand–Singapore) have ruled out the use of bilateral safeguard measures against a partner's trade. In the case of Mercosur, Annex IV of the Treaty of Asuncion only allowed the application of bilateral safeguards to imports of products benefiting from the trade liberalization program established under the treaty up to December 31, 1994.

---

[21] Article 2.2 of the Agreement on Safeguards states that "Safeguard measures shall be applied to a product being imported irrespective of its source."

We also note that although great majority of RTAs (sixty-five) surveyed have specific provisions on bilateral safeguards, none of the RTAs included in the survey give a role to regional institutions in conducting bilateral safeguard investigations or in reviewing findings by national authorities.

Level 2 elements: Much of the template used for mapping bilateral safeguard provisions is basically patterned after the Agreement on Safeguards of the WTO, although other elements are included as well. The elements include provisions on conditions for the application of safeguards, determination of injury, investigation, application of safeguard measures, provisional measures, duration and review of safeguard measures, compensation (equivalent level of concession), retaliation (suspension of equivalent concessions), treatment of developing countries, existence of a regional authority, notification and consultation, dispute settlement, special safeguards, and relationship to WTO agreements. Given that many of these elements are familiar from the Safeguards Agreement, we shall highlight those that are not found in that agreement.

Like in the previous two templates, we allowed for a role for regional bodies in bilateral safeguard actions. Regional institutions could have a coordinating function, serving for example, as a clearinghouse for information on emergency action. Or regional authorities could conduct safeguard investigations and/or review safeguard measures taken by national authorities. The template maps information regarding provisions on global safeguard actions, if they exist in the RTA. Finally, given the role of trade remedy instruments in managing regional trade liberalization, the template also takes into account the existence of special safeguard provisions for products or sectors that are politically sensitive.

The template used to map the bilateral safeguard provisions of the RTAs appears in Table 3.7.

Global safeguards template: Unlike the template used for bilateral safeguards, there is only one level in the template on global safeguards. It provides information about RTA provisions that refer to global safeguard actions, or GATT Article XIX or the Agreement on Safeguards.

The key aspect of the template concerns which RTAs exclude members from global safeguard actions and the conditions under which this occurs. The stated conditions under which imports from RTA members can be excluded from a global safeguard action are if those imports do not account for a substantial share of total imports and if they do not contribute to serious injury or the threat thereof.

Most of the RTAs describe very precisely what "substantial share" of total imports and "contribute importantly to serious injury" mean. However, our survey found some RTAs define the terms. In our template we note when "not substantial share of total imports" is defined if that partner is not among the top

Table 3.7. *Abridged safeguards template*

1. Bilateral safeguard measures disallowed
2. Bilateral safeguard measures allowed but with no specific provisions
3. Bilateral safeguard measures allowed and with specific provisions
   a) Conditions for application of transition safeguards
   b) Investigation
   c) Mutually acceptable solution
   d) Application of transition safeguard measures
   e) Provisional measures
   f) Duration and review of transition safeguard measures
   g) Maintain equivalent level of concessions (Compensation)
   h) Suspension of equivalent concessions (Retaliation)
   i) Developing/LDC members
   j) Regional body/committee
   k) Notification and consultation
   l) Special safeguards
4. Global safeguards
   a) Relationship to Article XIX of GATT 1994/Safeguard Agreement
   a1) retains rights and obligations under/in accord with GATT Article XIX/Safeguards Agreement
   a2) with exceptions

five suppliers during the most recent three-year period. We also indicate when "not contribute importantly to serious injury or threat thereof" is defined if the growth rate of imports from an RTA partner is appreciably lower than the growth rate of total imports from all sources.

The template used to map the global safeguard provisions of RTAs appears in Table 3.7.

Discussion: Bilateral safeguards. There is a clear difference between the EC and EFTA-centric RTAs and those involving the other major hubs: the United States, Mexico, Chile, Australia, Singapore, and Canada. In these latter RTAs, bilateral safeguard measures are imposed only during the transition period, the stipulated period for intra-RTA tariffs to be eliminated. For the most part, the bilateral safeguard measure is a suspension of the process of tariff reduction or, at worst, an increase of the preferential rate to the MFN level. RTAs also limit the duration of bilateral safeguard measures to between one and three years. The RTAs require a member to maintain an equivalent level of concession if that member imposes a bilateral safeguard measure. Unlike the Agreement on Safeguards, if no mutually acceptable compensation is agreed upon between the concerned members, the right to retaliation is not restricted.[22]

---

[22] Article 8.3 of the Safeguard Agreement requires that retaliation not be exercised for the first three years that a safeguard measure is in effect, provided that there has been an absolute increase in imports.

Limiting bilateral safeguard measures to the transition period and the shorter duration of such measures lessen the impact of bilateral safeguard actions on intra-regional trade. Further, the provisions on compensation and retaliation provide greater deterrence to the use of bilateral safeguard actions in the RTA. It is possible to argue that these features of the bilateral safeguard provisions in RTAs do not increase discrimination against nonmembers of the RTA. Certainly, if the bilateral safeguard action is triggered by the RTA's tariff reduction program and increased imports from RTA members, the action is solely bilateral (taken only against RTA partners); there is no spillover effect on nonmembers. However, one can contemplate situations where imports are increasing from many sources, RTA and non-RTA members alike, and the higher threshold for successfully mounting a bilateral safeguard action leads a country to invoke a global safeguard action. Thus, differences in the disciplines on safeguard actions applying to imports from RTA and non-RTA sources may lead to more frequent global actions penalizing nonmembers more than would otherwise have been the case.

Special safeguard mechanism: Sixteen RTAs have special safeguard provisions that create a different threshold for imposing additional protective measures on sensitive sectors. The RTAs include ASEAN Free Trade Area (AFTA), Australia–Thailand, Australia–United States, Canada–Chile, Canada–Costa Rica, EC–Chile, EC–South Africa, Group of Three, Korea–Chile, Mexico–Northern Triangle, NAFTA, United States–Bahrain, United States–CAFTA–DR, United States–Chile, United States–Morocco, and United States–Singapore. These special safeguard measures typically allow an RTA member to impose additional duties on sensitive imports, although the tariff should not exceed the MFN rate, once imports cross either a volume or price threshold. They could be imposed even without showing serious injury or threat of serious injury. Further, they normally extend beyond the transition period of the RTA. The sensitive sectors are usually agriculture, textiles, and apparel. These special safeguard provisions should probably be seen as part of the portfolio of trade management instruments, which include long transition periods, sectoral carve-outs, and complex and restrictive rules of origin, to mitigate the effects of the RTA on import-sensitive industries.

Provisions on global safeguards: Whereas most of these RTAs state that their safeguard provisions are in accord with or do not affect their members' rights and obligations under the multilateral agreements, more than half of them go on to exclude the imports of RTA partners from global safeguard actions. The stated conditions under which imports from RTA members can be excluded from a global safeguard action are if those imports do not account for a substantial share of total imports and if they do not contribute to serious injury or the threat thereof. The RTAs that exclude RTA partners from global actions include Australia–Thailand, Australia–United States, Canada–Chile, Canada–Israel,

EU–Chile, Group of Three, Mexico–Chile, Mexico–Israel, Mexico–Nicaragua, Mexico–Northern Triangle, Mexico–Uruguay, NAFTA, United States–CAFTA–DR, United States–Jordan, and United States–Singapore.

The Agreement on Safeguards requires that safeguard measures be applied to all imports irrespective of source (nondiscrimination).[23] Thus, the exclusion of RTA partners from a safeguard action poses a potential conflict between regional and multilateral rules.[24] This conflict has been addressed in a number of WTO dispute cases (*Argentina–Footwear, United States–Wheat Gluten, United States–Line Pipe*, and *United States–Steel*). In these cases, the investigating authority had included imports from all sources in making the determination that imports were entering in such increased quantities so as to cause serious injury to the domestic industry. However, instead of applying safeguard measures to all imports irrespective of their source, the country invoking the safeguard action excluded its RTA partners. In *Argentina–Footwear*, Argentina had included Mercosur imports in the analysis of factors contributing to injury to its domestic industry. Yet it excluded Mercosur countries from the application of the safeguard measure. In *United States–Wheat Gluten*, the United States excluded Canada from the application of its safeguard action although imports of wheat gluten from Canada were included in the investigation phase. In the *United States–Line Pipe* case, the United States excluded imports from its NAFTA partners from the safeguard measure. And in *United States–Steel*, the United States included all sources of imports in its analysis of increasing imports, injury serious injury, and the causal nexus. However, it excluded its NAFTA partners, Israel and Jordan, from the application of its safeguard action. In all four cases, the Appellate Body had ruled against the WTO member that included its RTA partners in the safeguard investigation but excluded them in the application of the safeguard measure.

The key concept that underlines all these cases has been called "parallelism." The WTO's Appellate Body acknowledged that the word "parallelism" is not found in the text of the Agreement on Safeguards; however, it considered that the requirement of parallelism is found in the language used in the first and second paragraphs of Article 2 of the Agreement on Safeguards.[25] In brief, parallelism prohibits any asymmetry in the application of safeguards measures. Regionalism is just the most relevant and prominent application of parallelism to date. In the case of RTAs, parallelism means that when a WTO member has conducted a safeguard investigation considering imports from all sources, it cannot, subsequently, without any further analysis, exclude imports from RTA

---

[23] Article 2, para. 2 of the Safeguards Agreement states that "Safeguard measures shall be applied to a product being imported irrespective of its source."

[24] Bown (2004) discusses the discriminatory protection contained in the 2002 U.S. steel safeguard action.

[25] Appellate Body Report, *U.S.–Steel*, para. 439.

partners from the application of the resulting safeguard measure.[26] To exclude imports from RTA partners, the investigating authority must establish explicitly that imports from non-RTA sources alone caused serious injury or threat of serious injury to the domestic industry. The investigating authority, in its causality analysis, should ensure that the effects of the excluded (RTA) imports are not attributed to the imports included in the safeguard measure.[27]

Although the elaboration of the principle of parallelism by the Appellate Body in these four cases has clarified one issue, WTO jurisprudence has not provided a definitive ruling to what extent GATT Article XXIV could be relied on by a WTO member to exclude RTA partners from the application of a safeguard measure. One dispute (between the United States and Korea) in which this issue was given some consideration was the *U.S.–Line Pipe* case. There the United States argued that GATT Article XXIV gave it the right to exclude its NAFTA partners from the scope of the safeguard measure. The panel accepted the U.S. argument that the exclusion of its RTA partners from safeguard actions forms part of the required elimination of "restrictive regulations of commerce" on "substantially all the trade" among the free trade area members, which is a condition required by GATT Article XXIV. The panel decision was subsequently appealed by Korea. On appeal, the Appellate Body declared the ruling by the panel on Article XXIV as moot and having no legal effect.[28] The question whether Article XXIV of the GATT 1994 permits imports originating from an RTA partner to be exempted from a safeguard measure becomes relevant only in two circumstances. The first was when the imports from RTA members were not included in the safeguard investigation. The second was when imports from RTA members were included in the safeguard investigation; it nevertheless was established explicitly that imports from sources outside the free trade area alone satisfied the conditions for the application of a safeguard measure. Because neither of these applied to the circumstances surrounding the *U.S.–Line Pipe* case, the issue was not relevant to the case. However, the Appellate Body was careful to point out that, in taking this decision, it was not ruling on the question whether Article XXIV of the GATT 1994 permits exempting imports originating in a member of a free trade area from a safeguard measure. This decision thus leaves the question of an appeal to GATT Article XXIV still very much open.[29]

The provisions excluding RTA partners from global safeguard actions raises concerns about increased discrimination against nonmembers and trade diversion. Although WTO dispute settlement panels have ruled against excluding RTA partners from safeguard measures if imports from those RTA partners had been included in the investigation, they appeared to have done so on quite narrow grounds – on the lack of parallelism in the application of safeguard measures.

[26] Appellate Body Report, *U.S.–Steel*, para. 441.
[27] Appellate Body Report, *U.S.–Steel*, para. 453.
[28] Appellate Body Report, *U.S.–Line Pipe*, para. 199.
[29] See Pauwelyn (2004) for a discussion of this issue.

Table 3.8. *Cross-tabulation of contingent protection rules*

		Global safeguard rules (29)			
			Countervailing duty		
		Disallowed	Rules	No rules	TOTAL
	Disallowed	0	1	1	2 (6.9%)
AD	Rules	0	14	2	16 (55.2%)
	No rules	0	3	8	11 (37.9%)
	TOTAL	0	18	11	29
		(0.0%)	(62.1%)	(37.9%)	
		No global safeguard rules (45)			
			Countervailing Duty		
		Disallowed	Rules	No rules	TOTAL
	Disallowed	5	2	0	7 (15.6%)
AD	Rules	0	19	12	31 (68.9%)
	No rules	0	0	7	7 (15.6%)
	TOTAL	5	21	19	45
		(11.1%)	(46.7%)	(42.2%)	

Conceivably, under a different set of circumstances, exclusion of RTA partners from safeguard measures could pass muster.

4. Analysis

4.1. Patterns and Correlations across RTAs

Table 3.2 lists the level 1 mappings for each RTA. As one can see, the provisions vary considerably in almost every dimension. An RTA may have rules for one trade remedy, no rules for another trade remedy, and prohibit a third remedy. In Table 3.8 we take a closer look at the correlation in rules. The table is divided into two parts. At the top we restrict ourselves to the twenty-nine RTAs that have global safeguard rules. At the bottom we look at the forty-five RTAs with no global safeguard language. In each panel we provide a cross-tabulation of the provisions for AD and CVD. This allows us to better identify the similarity of the three trade remedy laws within RTAs.

For instance, looking at the top panel (global safeguard provisions) we see that about half also have CVD and AD rules, but eight have both no AD rules and no CVD rules. The bottom panel is those RTAs with no global safeguard rules. Within this group, we see that nineteen have rules for both AD and CVD. This suggests that there is a rather small link between global safeguard rules and rules on other contingent protection measures. As with the top panel, there is considerable variation. There is no hard and set pattern across provisions.

We also find only modest differences among several other RTA characteristics. For example, we can consider the impact of the GATT/WTO provision justifying the RTA, Article XXIV, and the Enabling Clause. As seen in Table 3.9, there is no clear difference between the two notification methods at least for AD and safeguards. With respect to CVD, however, it appears that RTAs notified under the Enabling Clause tend to more often have no rules.

The type of regional agreement – customs union, free trade agreement, or preferential trade agreement – seems to affect the rules on contingent protection. In general, FTAs are the most likely to have rules or prohibit the trade remedy laws (Table 3.9).

The development status also seems to influence the rules. RTAs involving only developed countries tend to have more additional rules than those involving just developing countries or those with a mixed development status.

4.2. Hubs and Spokes

There is a pronounced hub-and-spoke and cross-regional pattern in the RTAs in the sample (see Table 3.10). The largest constellations are grouped around the EC (future accession countries, Euromed, and others), EFTA, and the United States. However, there are other active RTA players, including Mexico (with ten RTAs), Singapore (with six RTAs), Australia (with five RTAs), Chile (with five RTAs), and Canada (with four RTAs).

The prominent hub-and-spoke and cross-regional pattern of the RTAs in the sample accentuates features of the trade remedy provisions negotiated by the major hubs – the EC, the United States, the EFTA countries – and to a certain extent the other major players. Prior to developing the mapping, our understanding was that each major hub negotiates according to certain key principles in mind. That is, we expected to see that U.S. RTAs have similar provisions governing government procurement rules, labor mobility, foreign direct investment, and so on. Likewise, we expected the same for the other major hubs. The rules and philosophy might vary across hubs, but we expected consistency within a hub.

With respect to the contingent protection statutes, however, the consistency across RTAs is a mixed bag. As shown in Table 3.11, we see examples of strong consistency in provisions. For example, a high fraction of EC RTAs has AD and safeguard rules; EFTA and Mexican RTAs are very likely to have additional rules for all three trade remedy statutes. The U.S. RTAs also have similarities – most U.S. RTAs have bilateral safeguard and AD rules but no CVD rules. On the other hand, the remaining major hubs have much less consistency. For example, the Chilean, Australian, and Canadian RTAs display little real patterns.

If we explore deeper, the lack of consistency within a hub's RTAs becomes more apparent. To see this we examine what level 2 provisions are in each RTA (Tables 3.5–3.7); for each hub we total the RTAs that have each specific provision. In Table 3.12 we report the handful of provisions that appear in the majority of

Table 3.9. *Contingent protection rules*

	Antidumping		
	Article XXIV	Enabling Clause	
Disallowed	7 (11%)	2 (22%)	
Rules	39 (64%)	4 (44%)	
No rules	15 (25%)	3 (33%)	
	CU	FTA	PTA
Disallowed	1 (14%)	6 (10%)	2 (29%)
Rules	5 (71%)	39 (65%)	3 (43%)
No rules	1 (14%)	15 (25%)	2 (29%)
	Developed	Developing	Mixed
Disallowed	3 (50%)	3 (14%)	3 (7%)
Rules	2 (33%)	14 (64%)	31 (67%)
No rules	1 (17%)	5 (23%)	12 (26%)
	Countervailing duty		
	Article XXIV	Enabling Clause	
Disallowed	4 (7%)	1 (11%)	
Rules	33 (54%)	2 (22%)	
No rules	24 (39%)	6 (67%)	
	CU	FTA	PTA
Disallowed	1 (14%)	3 (5%)	1 (14%)
Rules	4 (57%)	34 (57%)	1 (14%)
No rules	2 (29%)	23 (38%)	5 (71%)
	Developed	Developing	Mixed
Disallowed	3 (50%)	2 (9%)	0 (0%)
Rules	0 (0%)	13 (59%)	26 (57%)
No rules	3 (50%)	7 (32%)	20 (43%)
	Bilateral safeguard		
	Article XXIV	Enabling Clause	
Disallowed	4 (7%)	1 (11%)	
Rules	54 (89%)	7 (78%)	
No rules	3 (5%)	1 (11%)	
	CU	FTA	PTA
Disallowed	2 (29%)	3 (5%)	0 (0%)
Rules	3 (43%)	56 (93%)	6 (86%)
No rules	2 (29%)	1 (2%)	1 (14%)
	Developed	Developing	Mixed
Disallowed	1 (17%)	2 (9%)	2 (4%)
Rules	5 (83%)	18 (82%)	42 (91%)
No rules	0 (0%)	2 (9%)	2 (4%)

Table 3.10. *Hub-and-spoke and cross-regional arrangement of RTAs*

EC	EFTA	Mexico	U.S.	Singapore	Chile	Australia	Canada
European Communities	EFTA–Turkey	NAFTA	U.S.–Singapore	U.S.–Singapore	U.S.–Chile	SPARTECA	NAFTA
EEA	EFTA–Tunisia	Mexico–Uruguay	U.S.–Morocco	New Zealand–Singapore	Mexico–Chile	CER	Canada–Israel
EC–Turkey	EFTA–Singapore	Mexico–Northern Triangle	U.S.–Jordan	Japan–Singapore	Korea–Chile	Australia–U.S.	Canada–Costa Rica
EC–Tunisia	EFTA–Palestine Authority	Mexico–Nicaragua	U.S.–Israel	EFTA–Singapore	EC–Chile	Australia–Thailand	Canada–Chile
EC–Syria	EFTA–Morocco	Mexico–Japan	U.S.–Chile	Australia–Singapore	Canada–Chile	Australia–Singapore	
EC–Switzerland–Liechtenstein	EFTA–Jordan	Mexico–Israel	Australia–U.S.	AFTA			
EC–South Africa	EFTA–Israel	Mexico–EFTA	U.S.–CAFTA and Dom. Republic				
EC–Palestine Authority	EFTA–FYROM	Mexico–Chile	U.S.–Bahrain				
EC–OCT	EFTA–Croatia	Group of 3	NAFTA				
EC–Morocco	EFTA–Chile						
EC–Mexico	EFTA						
EC–Lebanon	EEA						
EC–Jordan							
EC–Israel							
EC–Faroe Islands							
EC–FYROM							
EC–Egypt							
EC–Croatia							
EC–Chile							
EC–Andorra							
EC–Algeria							

Table 3.11. *Cross-tabulation of contingent protection rules*

	EC	EFTA	Mexico	U.S.	Singapore	Chile	Australia	Canada
RT# As in hub	21	12	9	9	6	5	5	4
AD disallowed	9.5%	33.3%			16.7%	20%	20%	25%
AD rules	81.0%	66.7%	77.8%	11.1%	33.3%	40%	60%	50%
AD no rules	9.5%		22.2%	88.9%	50%	40%	20%	25%
CVD disallowed	9.5%	16.7%						
CVD rules	38.1%	83.3%	77.8%	33.3%	33.3%	60%	60%	50%
CVD no rules	52.4%		22.2%	6.7%	66.7%	40%	40%	50%
Bilat safeg disallowed	4.8%				33.3%		20%	25%
Bilat safeg rules	90.5%	100%	100%	100%	66.7%	100%	80%	75%
Bilat safeg no rules	4.8%							

Table 3.12. *Primary provisions in RTAs (for each hub)*

Instrument	RTA provision	RTAs with majority inclusion*
AD	Mutually acceptable solution	EC, EFTA
	Provisional measures	EC, EFTA
	Regional body/committee	EC, EFTA
	Notification/ consultation	EC, EFTA, Mexico, Canada
	In accordance with GATT Article VI/AD Agreement	EC, EFTA, Mexico, Canada
CVD	Mutually acceptable solution	EFTA, Mexico
	Consultation	EFTA, Mexico
	Regional body/committee	EFTA
	In accordance with GATT Article VI and/or SCM Agreement	Mexico, Chile, Australia
Safeguards	Conditions for application of safeguard	EC, EFTA, Mexico, U.S., Singapore, Chile, Australia, Canada
	Investigation	Mexico, U.S., Singapore, Chile, Australia, Canada
	Mutually acceptable solution	EC, EFTA
	Application of safeguard measures	EC, EFTA, Mexico, U.S., Singapore, Chile, Australia, Canada
	Provisional measures	EC, EFTA, Australia
	Duration and review of safeguard measures	Mexico, U.S., Singapore, Chile, Australia, Canada
	Maintain equivalent level of concessions (Compensation)	Mexico, U.S., Singapore, Chile, Canada
	Suspension of equivalent concessions (Retaliation)	Mexico, U.S., Singapore, Chile, Canada
	Notification and consultation	EC, EFTA, Mexico, U.S., Singapore, Chile, Australia, Canada
	Regional body/committee	EC, EFTA, Singapore
	Special safeguards	U.S., Chile, Canada
	Relationship to Art. XIX of GATT 1994/Safeguard Agreement	Mexico, U.S., Chile, Canada

* Regional hubs listed if at least 50% of their RTAs include the provision.

any hub's agreements. As seen, only five of the seventeen AD level 2 provisions appear in at least half of any hub's RTAs. And even these five provisions are not seen for most hubs. For instance, some RTAs have a provision that states the parties will seek a "mutually acceptable solution" to the dumping problem. However, this provision is not that common. Only two hubs, the EC and EFTA, include it in at least half of their agreements. Interestingly, we find that the United States, traditionally the world's heaviest user of AD, has no AD provisions that appear in the majority of its agreements.

Similar results are seen for the level 2 provisions for CVD. As seen, only four of the thirteen CVD level 2 provisions appear in at least half of any hub's RTAs. EFTA and Mexico are the hubs with the most conformity across agreements. In the case of CVD, neither the United States nor the EU has any provision that is common in the majority of RTAs.

The safeguard rules are the one area where we see some persuasive evidence of conformity. All thirteen of the level 2 provisions for safeguards appear in the majority of at least one hub. Many of the provisions appear in multiple RTAs. In particular, special rules governing conditions for applying bilateral safeguards and the application of the bilateral safeguard protection itself are found in the majority of RTAs for virtually all major hubs.

4.3. Abolishing Trade Remedies in RTAs

About one-sixth of the RTAs surveyed have managed to abolish the application of trade remedies on intra-regional trade. Only one RTA – the EC – has managed to abolish all three forms of trade remedies on members' trade. Are there any economic factors that distinguish these RTAs and that could explain why they have been able to abolish trade remedy measures against members' trade?

Perhaps the leading candidate to explain the abolition of trade remedy measures, particularly AD, is the depth of market integration envisioned in the RTA. RTAs that aim at deeper integration, going beyond the elimination of border measures, and harmonizing or even in some cases adopting common internal regulations, are more likely to do away with trade remedy measures. We have already alluded to the role of a harmonized or a common subsidy policy in explaining the type of CVD provisions that can be adopted in an RTA. De Araujo et al. (2001) have argued that the implementation of common macro- and microeconomic policies in the EU reduced the social and political cost related to the removal of AD. They point in particular to the role that structural funds played in easing the need for AD as a trade adjustment measure. Wooton and Zanardi (2005) link the phasing out of AD with the creation a single market. They point as examples to the experiences of the EC and the EEA. In their view, the elimination of AD was a necessary step to achieving a common market.

A second explanation that is sometimes provided is the adoption of a common competition policy by members of the RTA. RTAs that adopt a common competition policy may find AD to be redundant. Of course, the two explanations are not mutually exclusive because a common competition policy may not make sense until a sufficiently high level of integration is achieved. However, Hoekman (1998) dismisses the notion of a link between the adoption of a common competition policy and the abolition of AD in a RTA. He argues that the adoption of a common competition policy in a RTA is often motivated by the need to manage the result of deeper integration.[30] Its purpose is not to provide a substitute policy instrument so that AD measures can be abolished (although of course this could be one of the consequences of having a common competition policy). Another argument against this link is that there are important differences between competition policy and AD; for example, competition policy is often concerned with consumer protection but AD is not, which may make one instrument rather than the other more likely to be hostage to protectionist interests. So to the extent for example that AD is being used as a shield against imports, the adoption of a common competition policy need not automatically lead to the abolition of AD.

A growing literature has documented the difference in how developing/developed countries use the three trade remedy instruments (see Miranda et al., 1998; Zanardi, 2004; Prusa, 2005). For instance, developing countries have become more frequent users of AD and safeguard actions. One may therefore also need to examine what effect the development status of the members of the RTA has on the trade remedy rule adopted.

We have conducted more formal tests of what possible explanatory variables affect the decision to abolish trade remedies using a probit model. Explanatory variables that we included were (i) the development level of RTA members, (ii) vintage of the RTA (when it came into force), (iii) average volume (as well as share) of intra-RTA trade prior to the establishment of the RTA, (iv) the existence of a common external tariff, (v) the inclusion of a competition policy provision in the RTA, and (vi) the degree of integration achieved by the members. Many of these variables were never found to be statistically significant and hence we report only the specification with the deep integration variable and common external tariff.

We present the results of the probit estimation for the seventy-four RTAs in the sample in Table 3.13, separately for each trade remedy instrument. For AD

---

[30] Hoekman (1998) defines deep integration as consisting of explicit actions by governments to reduce the market segmenting effect of differences in national regulatory policies that pertain to products, production processes, producers, and natural persons. In practice this will require decisions (i) that a partner's policies are equivalent (mutual recognition) or (ii) to adopt a common regulatory stance in specific areas (harmonization). Also see Lawrence (1996), who uses "deeper" integration to refer to a process in which increased cross-border economic transactions between countries erode the traditional segmentation between areas of domestic policy making and areas of international policies.

Table 3.13. *Probit estimation results – predict abolition of policy*

Explanatory variables	Antidumping	Countervailing duty	Bilateral safeguards
Deep integration (dummy)	0.632	0.528	−0.001
	[0.000]**	[0.000]**	[0.990]
Common external tariff (dummy)	−0.084	−0.029	0.154
	[0.206]	[0.432]	[0.128]
Prob > chi2	0.0001	0.0001	0.3051
Numb of Obs.	74	74	74

Notes: Each column is estimated separately. Reported estimates give the change in probability for a discrete change of dummy variable from 0 to 1; *p*-value corresponds to the test of the underlying coefficient being 0.
* significant at 5%; ** significant at 1%; *p*-values are given in brackets.

and CVD, the only variable that consistently shows economic and statistical significance is the degree of integration. In the case of safeguards, none of the variables that we used were statistically significant, although the common external tariff was on the cusp of being significant at the 10 percent level.

5. Conclusions

Trade remedies seem to be permanent fixtures in international trade agreements. One explanation for their omnipresence is that they provide governments entering into a trade agreement a useful policy tool to manage trade adjustment and the political pressure for protection that is created. They make it easier to obtain political support for the agreement. The trade agreement, in turn, makes possible a more liberal trade regime, although this will be at the cost of episodic recourse to protection during economic downturns.

There is an added layer of complexity to the role of trade remedies introduced by preferential trade agreement, which by nature discriminates between members and nonmembers. Even without modifications to the rules governing trade remedies, their elastic and selective nature may lead to more discrimination against nonmembers through greater frequency of trade remedy actions against them. The adoption of RTA-specific trade remedy rules increases this risk of discrimination, with trade remedies against RTA members being abolished outright or being subjected to greater discipline. As in much of theory of customs unions, the welfare effects of this increased discrimination are unclear. Any increase in intra-regional trade brought about by greater discipline on trade remedy action against RTA members may simply be substituting for cheaper sources of imports from nonmembers.

Based on the result of this mapping, about one-sixth of the RTAs surveyed have dispensed with at least one type of trade remedy. What these RTAs seem to share in common is a greater level of integration ("deep" integration) as evidenced either by the adoption of common or harmonized behind-the-border policies and high shares of intra-regional trade.

There appears to be a large number of RTAs that have adopted RTA-specific rules that have tightened discipline on the application of these remedies on RTA members. In the case of AD for example, we noted that some specific provisions tightened discipline by increasing *de minimis* volume and dumping margin requirements, and shortening the duration for applying AD duties relative to the WTO Antidumping Agreement. We have also highlighted the possible contribution by regional bodies to reducing action against RTA members. In the EC-centered and EFTA-centered RTAs, members acting through a regional body notify and consult one another to arrive at a mutually acceptable outcome short of applying the measure. In the Andean Community, CACM, CARICOM, NAFTA, and UEMOA, regional bodies have the authority to conduct their own investigations or to review conclusions reached by national bodies.

In similar fashion, many of the provisions on bilateral safeguards lead to tightened discipline or reduce the incentives to take safeguard actions. Bilateral safeguard measures can be imposed only during the transition period, have shorter duration periods, and require compensation if put in place. Further, retaliation is allowed if there is no agreement on compensation. A final concern is with the exclusion of RTA partners in safeguard actions triggered under GATT Article XIX and the Agreement on Safeguards. This puts RTA rules on safeguards in conflict with the nondiscriminatory principle that underlies multilateral rules on safeguard action and squarely raises the problem of trade diversion. Although WTO panels have ruled against such exclusions so far, it is not clear that future panels will do so consistently given the particular ground of parallelism on which previous decisions have been made.

In the case of CVDs, we are unable to find major innovations in CVD rules and practice by past and present RTAs. We suspect that a major reason for this is the absence of agreements in the RTA on meaningful or significant curbs on subsidies or state aid. We have emphasized the possible role of regional bodies in mitigating any abuse of CVDs. However, only four RTAs provide a role for regional institutions as investigating bodies or give it the power to review determinations of national authorities.

The results of the mappings suggest the need to be vigilant about increased discrimination arising from trade remedy rules in RTAs. Discrimination against non-RTA partners through more frequent trade remedy actions can arise from the elastic and selective nature of already existing rules on trade remedies. Designing specific trade remedy rules that apply only to RTA partners increases the likelihood of discrimination. This takes place when an RTA abolishes trade remedy actions against the trade of RTA members but not against nonmembers' trade. It can take place when RTA members adopt rules that strengthen disciplines on trade remedy actions against the trade of RTA members but not against the trade of nonmembers.

REFERENCES

Andriamananjara, Soamiely, and Maurice Schiff, 1999. "Regional Groupings Among Microstates," World Bank Policy Research Working Paper Series No. 1922. Washington, DC: The World Bank.

Bhagwati, Jagdish, 1992. "Regionalism versus multilateralism," World Economy 15(5).

Bhagwati, Jagdish, 1993. "Regionalism and Multilateralism: An Overview," in Jaime de Melo and Arvind Panagariya (eds.), New Dimensions in Regional Integration. Cambridge: Cambridge University Press.

Bhagwati, Jagdish, and Arvind Panagariya (eds.). 1996. The Economics of Preferential Trade Agreements. Washington, DC: AEI Press.

Blonigen, Bruce A., 2005. "The Effects of NAFTA on Antidumping and Countervailing Duty Activity," World Bank Economic Review, 19 (December): 407–24.

Blonigen, Bruce A., 2006. "Evolving Discretionary Practices of U.S. Antidumping Activity," Canadian Journal of Economics, 39 (August): 874–900.

Blonigen, Bruce A., and Thomas J. Prusa, 2003. "Antidumping," in E. K. Choi and J. Harrigan (eds.), Handbook of International Trade. Oxford, UK, and Cambridge, MA: Blackwell Publishers, pp. 251–84.

Bown, Chad P., 2004. "How Different Are Safeguards from Antidumping? Evidence from U.S. Trade Policies Toward Steel." Brandies University Working Paper.

Crawford, Jo-ann, and Roberto V. Fiorentino, 2005. "The Changing Landscape of Regional Trade Agreements." WTO Discussion Paper No. 8. Geneva: WTO.

De Araujo, Jose Tavares Jr., Carla Macario, and Karsten Steinfatt, 2001. "Antidumping in the Americas," Journal of World Trade, 35(4): 555–74.

Finger, J. M., Keith H. Hall, and Douglas R. Nelson, 1982. "The Political Economy of Administered Protection," American Economic Review, 72(3): 452–66.

Fiorentino, Roberto V., Luis Verdeja, and Christelle Toqueboeuf, 2007. "The Changing Landscape of RTAs: 2006 Update," WTO Discussion Paper No. 12. Geneva: WTO.

Gagné, Gilbert, 2000. "North American Free Trade, Canada, and U.S. Trade Remedies: An Assessment After Ten Years," The World Economy, 23(1): 77–91.

Goldstein, Judith, 1996. "International Law and Domestic Institutions: Reconciling North American "Unfair" Trade Laws," International Organization, 50(4): 541–64.

Hoekman, Bernard, 1998. "Free Trade and Deep Integration: Antidumping and Antitrust in RTAs," World Bank Policy Research Working Paper No. 1950. Washington, DC: The World Bank.

Horlick, Gary, and Edwin Vermulst, 2005. "The 10 Major Problems with the Anti-Dumping Instrument: An Attempt at Synthesis," Journal of World Trade, 39(1): 67–73.

Jackson, John H., 1997. The World Trading System: Law and Policy of International Economic Relations. Cambridge, MA: MIT Press.

Jones, Kent, 2000. "Does NAFTA Chapter 19 Make a Difference? Dispute Settlement and the Incentive Structure of U.S./Canada Unfair Trade Petitions," Contemporary Economic Policy, 18(2): 145–58.

Lawrence, Robert Z., 1996. Regionalism, Multilateralism, and Deeper Integration. Washington, DC: Brookings Institution Press.

Marceau, Gabrielle (ed.). 1994. Anti-Dumping and Anti-Trust Issues in Free-Trade Areas. Oxford: Clarendon Press.

Mastel, G., 1998. Antidumping Laws and the U.S. Economy. Armonk, NY: M. E. Sharpe.

Miranda, Jorge, Raul A. Torres, and Mario Ruiz, 1998. "The International Use of Antidumping: 1987–1997," Journal of World Trade, 32(5): 5–71.

Moore, Michael O., 2002. "Commerce Department Antidumping Sunset Reviews: A First Assessment," *Journal of World Trade*, 36(2): 675–98.

Moore, Michael O., 2006. "An Econometric Analysis of U.S. Antidumping Sunset Review Decisions," *Review of World Economics/Weltwirtschaftliches Archiv*, 142(1).

Moore, Michael O., and Maurizio Zanardi, 2007. "Does Antidumping Use Contribute to Trade Liberalization in Developing Countries?" Unpublished manuscript.

Pauwelyn, Joost, 2004. "The Puzzle of WTO Safeguards and Regional Trade Agreements," *Journal of International Economic Law*, 7(1): 109–42.

Prusa, Thomas, 2005. "Antidumping: A Growing Problem in International Trade," *The World Economy*, 28(5): 683–700.

Rugman, Alan M., and Andrew D. M. Anderson, 1997. "NAFTA and the Dispute Settlement Mechanisms: A Transaction Costs Approach," *The World Economy*, 20(7): 935–50.

Viner, Jacob, 1950. *The Theory of Customs Union Issue*. New York: Carnegie Endowment for International Peace.

Wooton, Ian, and Maurizio Zanardi, 2005. "Anti-Dumping versus Anti-Trust: Trade and Competition Policy," with Ian Wooton, in K. Choi and J. Hartigan (eds.), *Handbook of International Trade, Volume II: Economic and Legal Analysis of Laws and Institutions*. Oxford, UK, and Cambridge, MA: Blackwell Publishers.

World Trade Organization, 2001. *United States – Safeguard Measures on Imports of Fresh, Chilled, or Frozen Lamb Meat from New Zealand and Australia (U.S.–Lamb)*, Appellate Body Report WT/DS177/AB/R.

Zanardi, Maurizio, 2004. "Antidumping: What are the Numbers to Discuss at Doha?," *The World Economy* 27(3): 403–33.

DAVID A. GANTZ

3.1 *Commentary on "Contingent Protection Rules in Regional Trade Agreements"*

Introduction

The Prusa/Teh study[31] is a very useful and thorough analysis of a complex topic, one that will be helpful to those of us who research and write about trade remedies and regional trade agreements (RTAs). There is little in the analysis or the conclusions with which I disagree. Consequently, in these comments I offer a few observations that may complement Professor Prusa and Mr. Teh's work.

Part I of this discussion focuses on the context (RTAs whose parties are also WTO members subject to WTO disciplines affecting the use of trade remedies). Part II focuses on Chapter 19 of the North American Free Trade Agreement (NAFTA),[32] certainly the most important RTA after the EU given the huge volume of NAFTA trade, the relatively large number of intra-NAFTA trade actions, and the uniqueness of the Chapter 19 mechanism for appeals of national administrative agency decisions in AD and CVD unfair trade proceedings. Chapter 19 remains the most extensive (and widely used) mechanism relating to resolution of unfair trade actions among RTA partners, except the mechanisms available within the EU to deal with such issues (primarily related to anti-competitive practices).

Part III offers observations on specific sections of the chapter.

A few caveats are appropriate. As a noneconomist, I am more comfortable with discussing the legal and administrative processes and the external factors (primarily political) that affect efforts by RTAs to deal with trade remedy issues than the economic effects. I also tend to view trade remedies from a very practical, and perhaps somewhat cynical, point of view, likely resulting from the fact that for sixteen years I was a practicing trade lawyer in Washington.

[31] Robert Teh and Thomas J. Prusa, *Contingent Protection Provisions in Regional Trade Agreements* (2008, 2009), reproduced in this volume.

[32] North American Free Trade Agreement, December 17, 1992, U.S.–Mexico–Canada, [hereinafter NAFTA], 32 I.L.M. 289 (1993), also available at www.nafta-sec-alena.org/Default Site/index_e.aspx?CategoryId=42 (full text and annexes); (last visited July 20, 2007).

During that period I primarily represented foreign companies, particularly enter-prises exporting to the United States from Asia that were the targets of U.S. dumping, subsidy, and safeguards actions. Had I represented U.S. domestic industries, I might then and now have been more sympathetic to the use of these mechanisms to protect domestic industries despite their trade-distorting effects.

1. General Comments

RTAs are likely to continue to proliferate in the foreseeable future. According to the WTO there are more than 230 in force today, with nearly 200 more likely to be implemented by the end of 2010,[33] particularly if the Doha Round of global trade negotiations remains stalled at least through 2009. The United States under President Obama is highly unlikely to replicate the flurry of new FTA negotia-tions carried out by the George Bush administration, although one can hope that Congress will eventually approve the pending U.S. FTAs with Colombia, Panama, and South Korea. However, United States' reluctance to conclude new RTAs will not affect the enthusiasm of other WTO members, particularly the EU, China, South Korea, Association of Southeast Asian Nations (ASEAN) members, Peru, and Chile, among many others, for concluding new RTAs. Thus, the number of RTAs notified to the WTO – 410 as of late 2008 – will only increase.[34]

RTAs are characterized by their diversity rather than their similarities except with regard to those concluded by a major trading nation or bloc, such as the United States or EU. They range from well-integrated groupings of developed nations such as the EU (with highly sophisticated and powerful institutions) to aggregations of small developing nations such as the members of the Central American Common Market (Costa Rica, El Salvador, Guatemala, Honduras, and Nicaragua), with weak institutions and long-delayed perfection of the RTA, to bilateral FTAs such as United States–Morocco, Chile–China et al., also with weak institutions and the ability to generate only small trade volumes.[35] They involve truly regional groupings such as NAFTA, the EU, and Mercosur, and others that are "regional" (e.g., United States–Israel, United States–Singapore) only in the sense that they are not global. These variations make accurate generalizations about RTAs difficult, as the Prusa/Teh study emphasizes.

With RTAs as with many international agreements, there is often a substan-tial gap between RTA provisions as written and as they are actually applied and

---

[33] WTO, Regional Trade Agreements, available at www.wto.org/english/tratop_e/region_e/ region_e.htm (last visited January 16, 2009).

[34] Ibid. There is some double-counting in the figures; a trade agreement that includes both goods and services commitments is notified twice, once under GATT Article XXIV and again under the General Agreement on Trade in Services (GATS), Article V. *See also* David A. Gantz, *Regional Trade Agreements: Law, Policy, and Practice* (Carolina Academic Press, 2009), chs. 1–2.

[35] Id., ch. 4.

implemented. For example, the CACM's general secretariat (SIECA) and the secretariat in Mercosur have relatively extensive powers on paper that are largely ignored in practice, as in the authority to initiate trade remedy actions for unfair trade practices within the CACM (but not actions against non-Parties). Moreover, with some major RTAs, particularly Mercosur, the ASEAN Free Trade Agreement, and the Southern African Customs Union, there have been persistent delays in ratification and entry into force of the various constituent instruments. Thus, what you see is not always what you get!

Particularly with small developing countries, the *de minimis* rules in the Antidumping Agreement, SCM Agreement, and Agreement on Safeguards, plus special rules for CBI members applicable to U.S. FTAs with CAFTA-DR and Panama, make the risks of AD/CVD actions brought by major trading nations relatively minor, although there are exceptions.[36] Those *de minimis* or "negligible" imports rules that exclude from AD investigations nations responsible for less than 3 percent of the subject imports or 7 percent for groups of nations[37] mean that only very large quantities of exports could be affected. Similar *de minimis* exclusions exist for the Safeguards Agreement and the SCM Agreement.[38] For U.S. AD actions potentially brought by the United States against its CAFTA–DR partners or against Panama, the Caribbean Basin Economic Recovery Act provision against cumulating the effects of imports from small countries for injury purposes further reduces the practical risk of the imposition of AD duties.[39] The exceptions in U.S. and other FTAs with developing nations providing for special safeguards for agriculture and textiles/apparel are likely a greater potential risk.

To state the obvious, the volume of trade actions is influenced significantly by the volume of trade among RTA member nations. NAFTA, for example, has generated a significant number of trade actions among the parties (although perhaps fewer new ones in recent years than in the 1990s), in part because there is almost $1 billion worth of trade within the region annually. RTAs between faraway parties with limited historical two-way trade (e.g., United States–Israel, United States–Chile, Peru–China), even with complementary economies, are somewhat less likely to lead to trade actions, regardless of whether the RTA provides special treatment for AD/CVD actions.

---

[36] See, e.g., *Argentina–Definitive Antidumping Duties on Poultry from Brazil*, WT/DS241/R, adopted May 19, 2003 (brought by one Mercosur partner against another); *Thailand–Anti-Dumping Duties on Angles, Shapes and Sections of Iron or Non-Alloy Steel and H-Beams from Poland*, WT/DS122/AB/R, April 5, 2001.

[37] Agreement on Implementation of Article VI of the General Agreement on Tariffs and Trade 1994, art. 5.8 [hereinafter "Antidumping Agreement" or "ADA"].

[38] Agreement on Safeguards, art. 9 (3%/9%) [hereinafter "Safeguards Agreement"; Agreement on Subsidies and Countervailing Measures, Art. 27.10 (4%/9%) [hereinafter "SCM Agreement"].

[39] See, e.g., United States–Panama Trade Promotion Agreement, June 28, 2007, art. 8.8.1 [not in force], available at http://www.ustr.gov/Trade_Agreements/Bilateral/ Panama_FTA/Final_Text/Section_Index.html (last visited September 26, 2008).

There are relatively few users of CVD laws against actionable government subsidies either within or outside RTAs, except for the United States, EU, and Canada. From 1995 to 2007, of the 202 CVD investigations initiated, 94 were by the United States, 46 by the EU, and 21 by Canada, with those 3 members representing about 75 percent of the total. The only other significant user was South Africa (11); Mexico initiated only 2.[40] The SCM Agreement, more that most of the Uruguay Round accords, reflects U.S. law and practice pre-Uruguay Round. It is difficult to know whether the relatively rare use of CVD actions results from the relative sophistication needed by the administering authority to analyze effects of government subsidies, the fact many members still provide subsidies to domestic producers that might be actionable under the CVD laws,[41] or for some other reason. The fact that the SCM Agreement permits WTO members to challenge government subsidies before the Dispute Settlement Body may also present an alternative to CVD actions.[42]

A significant question exists today whether use of global safeguards under GATT Article XIX and the Safeguards Agreement can ever be GATT/WTO legal. Clearly, the parallelism problem[43] discussed in the Prusa/Teh study is a daunting one for RTA members interested in using safeguards, but other barriers may be more significant. In particular, the Appellate Body has effectively required members applying safeguards measures to demonstrate that the GATT Article XIX requirement that the increase in imports is a result of "unforeseen developments" linked to a reduction in tariffs through tariff concessions be met.[44] This is an almost impossible task. After all, the expectation when a member reduces its tariffs on a particular item in the course of a Round is that imports will increase in the future. The Appellate Body views safeguard measures as "extraordinary remedies"[45] and scrutinizes them very carefully.

The Safeguards Agreement also effectively made it illegal for members to avoid the compensation requirements of Article XIX through "Voluntary Restraint Agreements," "Orderly Marketing Agreements" (OMAs) and the like, as was common in the past.[46] There is also more likely to be a perceived cost to using safeguards measures (compared to AD and CVDs) given the compensation

---

[40] WTO, CV Initiations by Report Member, Jan. 1, 1995 to Dec. 31, 2007, available at www.wto .org/english/tratop_e/scm_e/cvd_init_rep_member_e.xls (last visited September 26, 2008).

[41] And are thus concerned that the target member will retaliate against the member whose enterprises initiated the action.

[42] See SCM Agreement, Parts I–III.

[43] Appellate Body Report, *Argentina – Safeguard Measures on Imports of Footwear*, WT/DS121/ AB/R, adopted January 12, 2000, paras. 111–113 [hereinafter "Argentina – Footwear Safeguards"]; Appellate Body Report, *United States – Definitive Safeguard Measures on Imports of Certain Steel Products*, WT/DS248, 249, 251, 252, 253, 254, 258, 259/AB/R, adopted December 10, 2003, para. 197 [hereinafter "United States-Steel Safeguards"].

[44] See, e.g., Appellate Body Report, *Argentina – Footwear Safeguards*, para. 97.

[45] Appellate Body Report, *United States-Steel Safeguards*, para. 80.

[46] For example, during the Carter administration, Korea and Taiwan concluded formal OMAs limiting color television and footwear exports to the United States. During the 1970s and

requirements (although there is effectively a three-year grace period for compensation in most circumstances),[47] and there are of course significant costs to consumers of products that are subject to any trade remedies (which are arguably easier for governments to ignore).[48]

This compensation requirement in the Safeguards Agreement has likely encouraged domestic industries and investigating authorities to choose to bring AD actions in place of safeguards actions; the members do not wish to risk harm to an unrelated domestic industry or industries through compensation paid after safeguards measures are applied, and counsel and consultants who represent domestic industries know this. Given the discretion enjoyed by investigating authorities under the Antidumping Agreement (ADA) it usually is not that difficult for them to find dumping margins more than the 2 percent *de minimis* level,[49] and material injury or threat thereof.[50]

From a broader trade policy perspective, it may be unfortunate that the Appellate Body has made it so difficult for investigating authorities to impose safeguard measures in a GATT-legal manner. This result has forced members to charge falsely the existence of unfair trade practices (dumping) rather than to carefully consider safeguards actions, with or without the threat of compensation. The Antidumping Agreement, in addition to not requiring compensation, provides an initial period of five years, compared to four years under the Safeguards Agreement.[51]

There are risks of misunderstanding WTO or other global data on AD if one fails to keep in mind that since the mid-1990s in particular about 25 percent of

---

early 1980s it was common practice (discussed with the author) for the Korean and European footwear associations to meet annually in Brussels to decide how many pairs of Korean shoes would be exported to the European Communities during the coming year! The Safeguards Agreement, art. 11.2 & Annex, outlawed such evasions but permitted the EC to maintain its long-standing quotas on Japanese auto imports until December 31, 1999.

[47] Safeguards Agreement, Art. 8. No compensation is required for the first three years "provided that the safeguard measure has been taken as a result of an absolute increase in imports and that such a measure conforms to the provisions of this Agreement."

[48] For example, in a long-standing U.S. antidumping action against Mexican cement, the shortages and high prices caused in the American Southwest by antidumping duties in excess of 50 percent were ignored by U.S. authorities from 1990 until the Katrina hurricane disaster in 2005 made it politically impossible to do so. See Bowman, Covelli, Gantz, and UHM, *Trade Remedies in North America: Laws, Economic Analyses, and Practice* (Kluwer Law Int'l, forthcoming 2010), ch. 14.

[49] Antidumping Agreement, Art. 5.8.

[50] Under U.S. law, there is a risk that the president will decline to impose safeguards despite a finding of injury by the U.S. International Trade Commission, based in part on his assessment of the "national economic interest." *See* 19 U.S.C. §§ 2251, 2253(a)(2)(F). Such an exercise of presidential discretion is avoided under the U.S. Antidumping and Countervailing Duty Laws, 19 U.S.C. §§ 1671–1677n.

[51] Safeguards Agreement, Art. 7.1; the Antidumping Agreement, Art. 11.3, requires that dumping duties be terminated after five years in the absence of a new investigation renewing them.

the total number of AD actions worldwide have been brought against China.[52]
This fact also affects statistics relating to the average dumping margin found by
the investigating authority, such as the Department of Commerce in the United
States. The United States, EU, Mexico (until late 2008), and many other countries
have used a nonmarket economy (NME) methodology for calculating dumping
margins for actions against NME enterprises (including those located in such
countries as Vietnam) that typically exaggerates the AD margins.[53] If one calculates broad averages of global dumping margins without adjusting for China
(e.g., mixing NME and market economy dumping determinations), the results
may well be distorted.

The NME analysis normally is based on an approach in which the labor,
materials, and overhead costs incurred by producing enterprises in China are
ignored and data from supposedly comparable manufacturing operations in a
market economy country, often India or Bangladesh, are substituted to calculate
normal value. This approach provides the investigating authority with even more
opportunities for manipulating the data than when domestic sales or third-party
sales or constructed value are used for normal value calculations.[54] For example,
the Commerce Department only uses publicly available data for factors of production in its NME analyses, which frequently is not broken down into detailed
product subcategories. It may be difficult to find public data as the cost of raw
shrimp by size of shrimp in the surrogate country, with the result that any cost of
production analysis relying on cost of frozen shrimp (as the main raw material)
is distorted.

There is no similar distortion with regard to CVD actions yet. Until very
recently, the U.S. Department of Commerce had taken the position that under
U.S. law CVD actions were not intended to apply to NMEs, a position that had
been upheld by U.S. courts.[55] However, in 2006 the Department of Commerce
changed its policy and initiated a CVD investigation against coated paper from
China.[56] Although that particular case was ultimately terminated for lack of a
showing of material injury to U.S. producers, CVDs (at rates of up to 615 percent)
were recently applied to imports of line pipe into the United States.[57] Other CVD

[52] WTO, Antidumping Investigations by Reporting Country, Jan. 1, 2005–Dec. 31, 2007,
available at www.wto.org/english/tratop_e/adp_e/ad_init_exp_country_e.xls (last visited
September 26, 2008). It indicates that China had been the exporting country in 597 of 3,210
total actions.

[53] The NME methodology is explicitly permitted in China's 2001 WTO Accession Agreement.
See Accession of the People's Republic of China, November 10, 2001, para. 15, available at
docsonline.wto.org/DDFDocuments/t/WT/L/432.doc (last visited January 16, 2009).

[54] See Antidumping Agreement, Art. 2.2.

[55] Georgetown Steel Corp. v. United States, 801 F.2d 1308 (Fed. Cir. 1986).

[56] Department of Commerce, Notice of Investigation of Countervailing Duty Investigations:
Coated Free Sheet Paper from the People's Republic of China, Indonesia and the Republic
of Korea, 71 Fed. Reg. 68,546 (November 27, 2006).

[57] ITC Affirmative Injury Finding in Pipe Case Is First Time CVD Duties to Apply to China, 25
Int'l Trade Rep. (BNA) 960 (June 26, 2008).

actions against China are pending in the United States. To date, the decision to bring CVD cases against NMEs has been limited to China, but the Department of Commerce is being strongly urged by Congress to make the new CVD policy applicable to all NMEs.[58] One can reasonably expect a substantial increase in U.S. CVD actions against China (and some against Vietnam) in the future, perhaps sufficient to affect aggregate global CVD statistics as well.

As one continues to study RTAs and trade remedies, particularly with regard to relations among the FTA parties, it is not difficult to conclude that the European Union is *sui generis* as to addressing unfair trade practices among the member-states. Thus, in the trade remedy area the EU cannot be compared across the board with any of the other RTAs except in the manner in which it addresses unfair trade actions against nonmembers, even if such customs unions as Mercosur, CACM, and the ASEAN Group see the EU as a model. In my view, the only entity that is comparable to the EU regarding regulation of internal trade and eliminating barriers is the oldest of all RTAs, the United States of America, with its strong central government, agencies (supposedly) regulating trade and competition, and federal courts enforcing the Commerce Clause of the U.S. Constitution.[59]

2.   NAFTA, Chapter 19

Given the significance of Chapter 19 as a procedural mechanism for dealing with unfair trade practices in an RTA, one of a few that exist and is functional, some explanation of that mechanism is useful for those not familiar with it. The rationale for Chapter 19's inclusion in the United States–Canada Free Trade Agreement (CFTA)[60] and later in NAFTA was political, legal, and economic. Canada demanded in the course of the CFTA negotiations (the fourth set of U.S.–Canada FTA negotiations over the past 100 years or so[61]) that the United States agree that AD and CVD actions would not be brought against each other by FTA parties. Canadian officials argued with considerable economic justification that price discrimination would be impossible for trade between the two nations, given that most of it moved across the land border in an efficient manner, once all

---

[58] Amy Tusi, *Commerce Announces Significant Shift, Applies CVD Law in Chinese Paper Case,* 24 *Int'l Trade Rep.* (BNA) 495 (April 5, 2007). *See also H.R. 496, The Trade Enforcement Act of 2009,* January 16, 2009, available at www.insidetrade.com/secure/pdf13/wto2009_0254b .pdf (last visited January 26, 2009). The bill would, inter alia, "lock in" Commerce's change in practice so that "Commerce fully captures NME subsidy practices."

[59] David A. Gantz, *Regional Trade Agreements: Law, Policy, and Practice* 11–13 (Carolina Academic Press, 2009), characterizing the United States as the world's most successful customs union and common market.

[60] United States–Canada Free Trade Agreement, December 1997–January 1998 [U.S. –Can.], 27 I.L.M. 281 (1998).

[61] See Ralph Folsom, Michael Gordon, and David Gantz, *NAFTA and Free Trade in the Americas* 10–12, 15–19 (2nd ed., West Publ., 2005).

tariff and nontariff barriers were eliminated on nonagricultural trade (and most of the latter). For example, if a Canadian steel producer tried to dump steel by selling at a lower price in the United States than in Canada, purchasers in the United States would resell the steel to entrepreneurs who would return the steel to Canada and resell it there at the lower prices.

Canada also argued against CVD actions, but less persuasively, because neither nation envisioned a central authority comparable to the European Commission to deal with competition law and restrict state aids or other government subsidies. Thus, there would have been no means for the United States to object to Canadian federal or provincial subsidization of the steel industry in Ontario and Nova Scotia or of the softwood lumber industry in British Columbia and elsewhere in the absence of recourse to national CVD laws or the WTO's Dispute Settlement Body.

The impasse over special treatment for AD/CVD actions threatened to prevent conclusion of the CFTA. Finally, at the eleventh hour, acting on a suggestion originally made by U.S. House Ways and Means Committee Chairman Sam Gibbons, the Chapter 19 mechanism was devised.[62] It was almost entirely procedural; each party preserved its own AD/CVD laws, regulations, and legal precedents (although consultation was required on amendment of national laws). Binational panels are effectively substituted for the national federal courts for review of the actions of the investigating authorities. It is a hybrid procedure, an international/binational arbitration process that applies national laws rather than international dumping or subsidies rules. Canada and the United States agreed in CFTA that the mechanism would be reviewed in five years, presumably because the United States was skeptical about it.

Canada accepted the compromise in part because their producer's frustration with U.S. use of AD/CVD laws was based on the perception that the U.S. federal courts (Court of International Trade, Court of Appeals for the Federal Circuit) responsible for reviewing U.S. Department of Commerce and U.S. International Trade Commission determinations (of dumping and subsidies margins, and material injury, respectively) were too often likely to side with the government. The binational panels would be made up of nonjudges, mostly trade lawyers or law professors who were thought likely by Canada to be more objective in reviewing U.S. Department of Commerce and U.S. International Trade Commission determinations. (Judges are actually preferred as binational panelists "to the fullest extent practicable" under NAFTA,[63] but few have ever consented to serve.)

Essentially the same mechanism, without the five-year review period, was incorporated into NAFTA. Canada could not have sought parliamentary approval

---

[62] See Michael Hart, *Decision at Midnight: Inside the Canada–U.S. Free Trade Negotiations* 321, 334 (Vancouver: UBC Press, 1994), discussing the development of the Gibbons proposal.

[63] NAFTA, annex 1901.2.

of NAFTA had the mechanism it had taken to Parliament less than five years earlier with great fanfare been eliminated. There was no practical way to exclude Mexico, whose negotiators apparently welcomed the idea of avoiding U.S. federal courts,[64] and the U.S. negotiators used Mexico's interest in Chapter 19 as a tool to demand that Mexico make a broad range of procedural due process changes in its administrative procedures in AD/CVD actions. Mexico's unhappiness with a U.S. AD action against Mexican cement producers likely contributed to Mexico's advocacy of the inclusion of Chapter 19 in NAFTA. There is no provision for a five-year or other review; Chapter 19 is here to stay.

Chapter 19 has been extensively used in part because all three parties have used the AD laws frequently against not only their NAFTA parties but worldwide. During the period 1995–2007, the United States reported 402 actions, leading the WTO, with Canada filing 142 and Mexico 94, putting all of them in the top 12 worldwide.[65] Of these, the inter-NAFTA AD actions were as follows:

United States v. Mexico, 15
United States v. Canada, 14
Mexico v. United States, 25
Mexico v. Canada, 1
Canada v. Mexico, 2
Canada v. United States, 16

Still, despite the huge volume of intra-regional trade, these seventy-three intra-NAFTA actions constituted only about 11.4 percent of the AD actions brought by the NAFTA parties worldwide. The intra-NAFTA CVD actions have been much rarer. Canada and Mexico have not used CVD actions within NAFTA; the United States has brought eight actions, all against Canada.[66]

As of mid-2008, 115 Chapter 19 actions had been filed, 76 against the U.S. authorities, 22 against Canadian authorities, and 17 against the Mexican authorities. Of these, more than a third were terminated by the request of the parties, and more than fifty decisions (not including multiple decisions in the same case after remands) had been rendered; a total of twenty-four remained pending.[67] Of

---

[64] Conference Remarks of Beatriz Leycegui, Mexican Secretariat of Commerce and Industrial Development (SECOFI), D.C. Bar Conference, June 2005.

[65] AD Initiatives, Reporting Members vs. Exporting Country, January 1, 1995–December 31, 2007, available at www.wto.org/english/tratop_e/adp_e/ad_init_rep_exp_e.xls (last visited September 26, 2008), showing that during the period the United States had reported 402 actions, leading the WTO, with Canada filing 142 and Mexico, 94, putting all of them in the top 12 worldwide.

[66] CV Initiations: Report Country vs. Exporting Country From January 1, 1995 to January 31, 2007, available at www.wto.org/english/tratop_e/scm_e/cvd_init_rep_member`e.xls (last visited September 26, 2008).

[67] NAFTA Secretariat Status Reports, available at www.nafta-sec-alena.org/DefaultSite/index_e.aspx?DetailID=9 (last visited May 12, 2008).

the panel decisions then rendered, a 2005 study determined that more than 80 percent resulted in unanimous rulings regardless of panelist nationality.[68]

Also, the numbers tend to exaggerate the number of AD/CVD disputes because frequently the final determinations of the Commerce Department or the Canadian Border Services Agency (responsible for the margin determinations) and of the USITC and Canadian International Trade Tribunal (determining material injury or threat thereof) are appealed separately. (In Mexico both determinations are made by the Ministry of Economy.) Controversy has been relatively rare except in a few high-profile cases, including softwood lumber, cement, and pork and live swine.[69]

There is no formal appeal of binational panel decisions; the only available review through the Extraordinary Challenge Committee (ECC) is narrow, and the challenge succeeds only where a panelist is guilty of bias, the panel seriously departed from a fundamental rule of procedure, or the panel manifestly exceeded its powers, *and* such actions materially affected the panel's decision *and* threatens the integrity of the process.[70] Not surprisingly, despite several challenges none have succeeded.[71]

Chapter 19 provides review only of AD/CVD final determinations; panels have no jurisdiction over safeguards actions. The NAFTA parties other than the United States have not used safeguards widely; Mexico brought only one action and Canada three in the 1995–2008 period.[72] The United States brought ten. Of the safeguards actions brought, the United States was the only NAFTA party to impose safeguards measures (six times).[73] One of these, the only one against a NAFTA party, *Broom Corn Brooms*, was reviewed and effectively reversed under NAFTA's Chapter 20 government-to-government dispute settlement mechanism.[74]

Although the NAFTA parties effectively excluded AD/CVD matters from the coverage of the Chapter 20 government-to-government dispute settlement mechanism, leaving such disputes to the WTO's Dispute Settlement Body, they

---

[68] Conference Remarks of Beatriz Leycegui, *supra.*

[69] See U.S. General Accounting Office, *U.S.–Canada Free Trade Agreement, Factors Contributing to Controversy in Appeals of Trade Remedy Cases to Binational Panels*, June 1995.

[70] NAFTA, art. 1904(13).

[71] See, e.g., *Softwood Lumber from Canada*, ECC-2004–1904-01USA (August 10, 2005), at 5–6, available at www.nafta-sec-alena.org/DefaultSite/index_e.aspx?DetailID'796 (last visited March 20, 2006).

[72] WTO, Safeguards Initiations by Reporting Member, January 1, 1995–June 1, 2008, available at www.wto.org/english/tratop_e/safeg_e/safeg_stattab1_e.xls (last visited September 26, 2008).

[73] WTO, Safeguard Measures by Reporting Member, March 29, 1995 to June 19, 2008, available at www.wto.org/english/tratop_e/safeg_e/safeg_stattab4_e.xls (last visited September 26, 2008).

[74] U.S. Safeguard Action Taken on Broomcorn Brooms from Mexico, Case no. USA-97–2008-01 (January 30, 1998), available at www.nafta-sec-alena.org/app/DocRepository/1/Dispute/english/NAFTA_Chapter_20/USA/ub97010e.pdf (last visited September 26, 2008).

did not seek to do the same regarding Chapter 19. This likely seemed reasonable and logical at the time. Chapter 19 and the DSU contemplate different parties (private "interested parties" in the former, governments in the latter) and differing albeit similar bodies of law (national AD/CVD laws in the former, the WTO Agreements in the latter).

However, because two different adjudicatory bodies can address the same matter has resulted in unfortunate conflicts, particularly in the long-running softwood lumber dispute. In at least four DSU actions, the United States generally prevailed, with some exceptions.[75] In a similar number of Chapter 19 panel decisions, including a key one effectively overturning the U.S. International Trade Commission's threat of material injury determination, Canada generally prevailed.[76] In the latest (2006) settlement agreement in Softwood Lumber, disputes are referred neither to the WTO nor Chapter 19, but to the London Court of International Arbitration![77]

There is no explicit judicial review mechanism for safeguards actions under NAFTA. However, the provisions of Chapter 20, the government-to-government dispute settlement mechanism, are sufficiently broad to be applicable to safeguards imposed either under NAFTA's Chapter 8 or under the WTO's Safeguards Agreement. In *Brooms*, Mexico challenged the United States' application of safeguards to corn brooms from Mexico. Mexico argued that the application of the safeguards was inconsistent with NAFTA Chapter 8 and with the WTO Agreement on Safeguards. The panel found unanimously in favor of Mexico, holding that the U.S. International Trade Commission had failed to explain adequately its "domestic industry" determination in violation of NAFTA requirements.[78]

---

[75] Appellate Body Report, *United States–Final Countervailing Duty Determination with Respect to Certain Softwood Lumber from Canada*, WTO Doc. WT/DS257/AB/R, adopted February 17, 2004; Appellate Body Report, *US–Final Dumping Determination on Softwood Lumber from Canada*, WT/DS264/AB/R, adopted August 31, 2004; Panel Report, *United States–Investigation of the International Trade Commission in Softwood Lumber from Canada*, WTO Doc. WT/DS277/R, adopted April 26, 2004; Panel Report, *United States – Preliminary Determinations With Respect to Certain Softwood Lumber from Canada*, WT/DS236/R, adopted November 1, 2002.

[76] See, e.g., *Softwood Lumber Products from Canada (Injury)*, USA-CDA-2002–1904-07, April 19, 2004, August 31, 2004; *Softwood Lumber Products from Canada (CVD)*, USA-CDA-2002–1904-03, June 7, 2004, December 1, 2004; *Softwood Lumber Products from Canada (Dumping)*, USA-CDA-2002–1904-02, June 9, 2005, all available at www.nafta-sec-alena.org/DefaultSite/index_e.aspx?DetailID=76 (last visited June 2, 2008).

[77] Softwood Lumber Agreement between the Government of Canada and the Government of the United States of America, Sep. 12, 2006, art. XIV(2), available at: www.dfait-maeci.gc.ca/eicb/softwood/pdfs/SLA-en.pdf (last visited January 25, 2008). For a thorough discussion of the softwood lumber dispute, *see* Jeffrey L. Dunoff, "The Many Dimensions of Softwood Lumber," 45 *Alberta L. Rev.* 319 (2008).

[78] *U.S. Safeguard Action Taken on Broomcorn Brooms from Mexico*, Case no. USA-97–2008-01 (January 30, 1998), citing NAFTA Annex 803.3(12), available at www.nafta-sec-alena.org/app/DocRepository/1/Dispute/english/NAFTA_Chapter_20/USA/ub97010e.pdf (last visited July 25, 2007).

It is telling that in post-NAFTA FTAs, not only the United States but also Mexico and Canada have chosen not to replicate NAFTA Chapter 19 in any such agreement. For the United States, this is likely due at least in part to the importance that the Congress attaches to preserving U.S. flexibility in continuing to utilize the AD/CVD laws to protect domestic producers. In the Canada–Chile FTA, the Parties agreed to refrain from AD investigations or imposition of AD measures (new or existing) against each other for goods that are freely traded.[79] Presumably, Canada advocated such provisions in an effort to demonstrate post-NAFTA a continuing commitment to avoid AD measures against FTA partners.[80] Those provisions have not been replicated in other Canadian FTAs.

3. Miscellaneous Observations

I am very skeptical of Marceau's assertion, discussed in the Prusa/Teh study, that use by RTA partners of the WTO AD/CVD remedies is inconsistent with GATT Article XXIV, regardless of whether GATT Articles VI and XVI are explicitly listed in Article XXIV:8(b) exceptions. If Marceau is correct, most RTAs notified under GATT Article XXIV are GATT illegal, because they typically preserve explicitly or implicitly the right of parties to bring global unfair trade actions against each other. The issue has never arisen before the Dispute Settlement Body, presumably because there are so few RTAs that seek to exclude GATT/WTO AD/CVD actions (only nine according to the Prusa/Teh study, several of which are agreements effectively within China, i.e., with Chinese Taipei and Hong Kong). One may speculate that the lack of direct attention to this issue in the 1946–1947 negotiations has resulted from the time few of the original GATT Contracting Parties were using AD/CVD actions except the United States, so it really didn't matter.[81] After all, as late as the late 1980s only a handful of GATT contracting parties had AD/CVD statutes (United States, EC, Australia, Canada, and Mexico, the latter only as of 1986).

Could the reduction in the ratio of U.S. unfair trade actions against Canada to Canada's share of U.S. imports be a direct result of the freeing of trade under CFTA and NAFTA, that is, the success of the Agreements? If the elimination of tariffs and nontariff barriers makes it difficult for enterprises one states party to engage in price discrimination in the territory of the other state party, this in itself

---

[79] Canada–Chile Free Trade Agreement, December 5, 1996, Art. M-01.

[80] This assertion is based on the author's discussions of the issue with various Canadian government officials familiar with the negotiations.

[81] Professor Raj Bhala suggests that the right of government to use antidumping duties was not challenged during the negotiation of the Havana Charter, and that no attention was paid to such actions until the Kennedy Round of GATT negotiations in 1964. Up to that time there had been only one GATT dispute settlement proceeding involving an antidumping action, relating to Swedish imposition of AD duties on Italian stockings. Raj Bhala, *International Trade Law: Interdisciplinary Theory and Practice* 873 (3rd ed., Lexis, 2007).

should reduce the incidence of AD actions. I do not have any direct evidence, but I suspect that the existence of the Chapter 19 binational panel review process has been less important to this result than the difficulty of maintaining effective international price discrimination (although perhaps not negligible). In practice tariff-free, quota-free trade may discourage some AD/CVD actions because it is difficult to prove price discrimination, another indication that the FTA is succeeding in reducing trade barriers.

As noted earlier, I suspect that the increase in average dumping margins (15.5 percent to 60 percent) found by the Commerce Department from the 1980s to 2000 is in significant part the result of NME methodology used for determining normal value in AD actions against China. The China effect is exacerbated by the difficulty for U.S. courts of second-guessing the Commerce Department when Chinese respondents have challenged the NME methodology (since it is statutory[82]), and the fact that until China became a member of the WTO in November 2001 it could not challenge U.S. AD methodology in the DSU. (China has not done so since it became a WTO member in late 2001.)

There is probably not a great deal of significance that the United States has agreed in most of the post-NAFTA FTAs not to provide export subsidies to goods exported to member countries. The United States relies primarily on domestic subsidies to support its agricultural exports, and there is no prohibition of them in any of the FTAs (although arguably some are prohibited in the WTO).[83] Moreover, the United States is permitted to use export subsidies in the newer FTAs if they are considered necessary so that U.S. agricultural exports can compete with subsidized agricultural exports from nonparties (read the EU).[84] Many of the other bilateral FTAs, with the exception of Mexico's, that prohibit export subsidies are among parties that by and large do not use agricultural export subsidies extensively in the first place, although the Canada–Chile FTA provided for their removal only seven years after the Agreement was concluded.[85]

Bilateral safeguards, as least as found in U.S. FTAs, are in my view of limited usefulness. In NAFTA and the post-NAFTA U.S. FTAs, they are effective only for the interim period (i.e., until free trade is established for the affected products) and the remedy is increasing tariffs to the party's MFN rate or the rate as of the day the FTA went into effect, whichever is lower.[86] For low-tariff countries such as the United States, this is an ineffective remedy in most instances; the greater flexibility of the WTO Safeguards Agreement and U.S. trade law permitting higher

[82] 19 U.S.C. § 1677(18).
[83] Under the Agreement on Agriculture and/or the SCM Agreement.
[84] See, e.g., Central American–Dominican Republic–United States Free Trade Agreement [hereinafter "CAFTA-DR], United States, Guatemala, El Salvador, Honduras, Nicaragua, Dominican Republic, Aug. 5, 2004, Art. 3.14, available at www.ustr.gov/Trade Agreements/Regional/CAFTA/CAFTA-DR_Final_Texts/Section_Index.html (last visited May 14, 2008).
[85] CCFTA, Art. C-14(2), effective beginning in 2003.
[86] See NAFTA, Art. 801; CAFTA-DR, Art. 8.1.

tariffs or quotas, or a combination of both, is preferable. The difference between the global and regional safeguard alternatives may be less significant for developing country FTA partners, many of whom maintained much higher MFN tariffs applicable to imports from the FTA partners pre-FTA, so that reversion to MFN tariffs could provide a significant degree of protection.

JOEL P. TRACHTMAN

4 The Limits of PTAs

WTO Legal Restrictions on the Use of WTO-Plus Standards Regulation in PTAs

1. Introduction

This chapter provides a legal analysis of the significance of standards, technical regulations, and sanitary and phytosanitary provisions (collectively, TBTSPS provisions) in regional or other preferential trade agreements (PTAs) in relation to the multilateral trading system. This issue is increasingly important with the growth of PTAs, raising the question of whether and to what extent PTA internal integration is inconsistent with World Trade Organization (WTO) law. There are two main concerns. First, PTAs may engage in internal integration of TPTSPS measures in a way that disadvantages suppliers from third states. Second, PTAs may establish internal disciplines on TBTSPS measures by member-states that strike down these member-state measures as applied to suppliers from PTA partners, but not as applied to suppliers from third states. Thus internal integration might require the nonapplication of a regulatory measure to a PTA partner, while allowing the application of the measure to third countries. For example, in the 2007 *Brazil–Tyres* case, one of the interesting questions was whether Brazil's Mercosur obligations provide it with an exception from its most-favored-nation (MFN) obligations under the General Agreement on Tariffs and Trade (GATT), allowing Brazil to discriminate in favor of Mercosur-origin retreaded tires.[1]

This chapter first examines the ways in which PTA regulation of national TBTSPS measures may contribute to or detract from liberalization goals. It then describes how GATT Article XXIV and the Understanding on the Interpretation

This chapter is based on the author's "Toward Open Recognition? Standardization and Regional Integration under Article XXIV of GATT," 6 *Journal of International Economic Law* 459 (2003). I wish to thank Chad Bown and Petros Mavroidis, and other participants in the Columbia WTO Seminar, for helpful comments on an earlier draft.

[1] Brazil–Measures Affecting Imports of Retreaded Tyres, WT/DS332/AB/R, adopted December 17, 2007. The panel applied "judicial economy" to avoid responding to this issue, and thus the Appellate Body had no occasion to address it.

of Article XXIV (the "Understanding"),[2] as presently understood, regulate PTA regulation of national TBTSPS measures. This article concludes by suggesting how Article XXIV and the Understanding might be reinterpreted or revised to conform more closely with the normative goal, expressed in Article XXIV:4, of balancing regional integration goals with multilateral liberalization goals.

This chapter finds that most of the "fortress PTA" types of concerns, as they relate to TBTSPS measures, are addressed if not precluded by WTO law as presently understood, and that the remaining potential "fortress PTA" concerns relating to TBTSPS measures are of uncertain significance. However, policy makers continue to express concern. For example, in 2002, then-United States Trade Representative (USTR) Robert Zoellick, urging the U.S. Senate to approve fast track authority, made the following remarks:

> Each [PTA] agreement without us [the U.S.] may set new rules for intellectual property, emerging high-tech sectors, agriculture standards, customs procedures, or countless other areas of the modern, integrated global economy – rules that will be made without taking account of American interests.[3]

During the late 1980s, there was much concern, associated with the development of the single market in Europe, regarding the process and outcome of standard-setting in a variety of areas. Standards and technical regulations can be used for protectionism, and can also create barriers to trade that exceed in value the benefits they provide, or can create unnecessary barriers to trade. Furthermore, coordination within PTAs may simply have the result of promoting intra-regional trade at the expense of imports from outside the PTA: trade diversion.

The requirements of Article XXIV of GATT and the Understanding with respect to PTA regulation of national TBTSPS measures are somewhat unclear. This chapter suggests that WTO law be read to require PTAs internally to impose two disciplines: national treatment-type nondiscrimination and necessity. However, it must be recognized that the WTO system already provides this anti-protectionism discipline with respect to TBTSPS measures, and so this requirement has little traction.

On the other hand, Article XXIV:8 does not appear to require harmonization or mutual recognition arrangements. To the extent that PTAs engage in harmonization, their harmonized TBTSPS measures must conform to the requirements of WTO law, namely the GATT, the TBT Agreement, and the SPS Agreement. Nor does Article XXIV:8 appear to require national treatment or necessity disciplines that exceed in their rigor those of WTO law. Thus, in the *Brazil–Tyres* case, Brazil should not have been able to succeed with its defense of discriminatory

---

[2] Understanding on the Interpretation of Article XXIV of the General Agreement on Tariffs and Trade 1994.

[3] Robert B. Zoellick, "Falling Behind on Free Trade," *N.Y. Times*, April 14, 2002, sec. 4, p. 13, col. 1.

treatment in favor of Mercosur-origin tires, based on the application of stricter Mercosur disciplines.

The regulation of PTA rules of mutual recognition, under the MFN obligation of Article I:1 of GATT, and under Article XXIV, is unclear, and rules of mutual recognition may present some opportunities for PTA protectionism. It would be useful to clarify the meaning of "other restrictive regulations of commerce" in Article XXIV:8, and "other regulations of commerce" in Article XXIV:5 and 8 in order to clarify what Article XXIV requires and what it prohibits.

2. National TBTSPS Measures, PTA Disciplines on National TBTSPS Measures, and Multilateral Trade: Friends or Fortresses?

This section will examine the ways in which TBTSPS measures, promulgated by either states or PTAs, and PTA disciplines on national TBTSPS measures, may impede multilateral trade. It will also examine how PTA disciplines on national TBTSPS measures may assist in achieving the goal of liberalized trade.

2.1. National and PTA TBTSPS Measures as Barriers to Trade

In regulatory theory, TBTSPS measures are restraints on competition and trade. Of course, this observation does not have a normative impact: there are many instances in which such restraints may be useful. TBTSPS measures may be motivated by public policy goals of addressing information asymmetries between producers and consumers, of internalizing externalities, of redistribution, and so on.[4]

In a public-interest-motivated model of the production of TBTSPS rules, government would engage in a domestic cost–benefit analysis of these rules, in terms of the regulatory benefits versus the costs occasioned by restraint on competition and trade. However, this domestic cost–benefit analysis might not take full account of costs to foreign producers occasioned by national TBTSPS measures.[5] PTA provisions addressing TBTSPS issues, and the relevant GATT, TBT, and SPS Agreements, may be designed either directly to reduce the costs to foreign producers (as by harmonization or recognition requirements), or to cause domestic rule makers to take the costs to foreign producers into account in formulating their TBTSPS measures (as by requirements of proportionality,

---

[4] See Charles P. Kindleberger, "Standards as Public, Collective, and Private Goods," 36 *Kyklos* 377 (1983).

[5] See Joel P. Trachtman, "Trade and ... Problems, Cost-Benefit Analysis, and Subsidiarity," 9 *Eur J. Int'l L.* 32 (1998). However, in Mexico, regulators "are required to check whether relevant international standards provide a least trade-restrictive solution for achieving regulatory objectives." OECD, Working Party of the Trade Committee, Trade and Regulatory Reform: Insights from the OECD Country Reviews and Other Analyses, para. 36, November 3, 2000.

necessity, or balancing). It is in this sense that these PTA provisions are allied with the WTO: they have a common enemy in the form of national TBTSPS measures that excessively burden international trade.

2.2. Potential Threats to Multilateral Trade

To the extent that PTAs substitute PTA-wide TBTSPS measures for national TBTSPS measures, or develop other means of integration in TBTSPS measures, they have the opportunity to disadvantage goods imported from outside the PTA. Chen and Mattoo make this finding:

> Regional harmonization significantly increases intra-regional trade, raising both the likelihood and the volume of trade between participating countries in affected industries. Exports of excluded countries to the region, however, decline on average.[6]

Among excluded countries, Chen and Mattoo find that countries in which firms are better equipped to comply with stricter standards are more likely to increase their exports to the harmonizing PTA. During the preparation of Europe's "single market" initiative from 1988 until 1992, concerns were raised that the single market project had the goal, or would have the effect, of creating a "Fortress Europe." It is worth analyzing the claim of protectionism through integration in the TBTSPS field, as it may apply to PTAs more broadly today.

2.2.1. Discriminatory or Unnecessary Harmonized Rules

A "fortress" might arise through the establishment of harmonized TBTSPS measures that discriminate against outside commerce, or regulate unnecessarily in a way that disproportionately disadvantages outside commerce. This is prohibited by GATT Articles I and III, the TBT Agreement, and the SPS Agreement. Discrimination may be de jure or de facto. De facto discrimination may be more difficult to identify and eliminate. One type of de facto discrimination designs facially neutral TBTSPS measures to favor domestic production over imports. This type of discrimination may be reduced through multilateral rules requiring transparency and access to the process by which TBTSPS measures are established, such as those contained in the TBT Agreement and SPS Agreement. It may also be addressed through negative integration rules at the multilateral level.

In discussions of regional integration, "negative integration" is used to refer to judicially applied standards that have the effect of striking down national regulation. These standards include national treatment, necessity, or balancing rules. These types of negative integration rules are also available in the WTO context. The TBT Agreement and SPS Agreement also discipline the process by which

---

[6] Maggie Xiaoyang Chen and Aaditya Mattoo, "Regionalism in Standards: Good or Bad for Trade," 41:3 *Can. Rev. Econ.* 838, 840 (2008).

positive integration at the PTA level in the form of harmonization takes place. By "positive integration," we mean the "legislation" of harmonized rules or rules of mutual recognition: the "positive" establishment of regulation at the PTA level.

PTAs have no greater formal capacity to disadvantage imports through harmonization than individual states have through their TBTSPS-setting processes. The important point with respect to harmonized rules that discriminate or unnecessarily burden outsiders is that the normal WTO rules apply to discipline these, just as they would if a particular WTO member-state adopted discriminatory or unnecessary regulation.

However, the process of establishing a PTA or of integrating within a PTA may result in a change to national TBTSPS measures that are disadvantageous to outsiders, relative to the status quo. Harmonized PTA TBTSPS measures may disadvantage foreign producers without any discrimination or failure of necessity. That is, it is argued that by virtue of harmonization, and creation of a single market, insiders have an advantage in addressing the single market. However, the advantage depends on an assumption that outsiders cannot take advantage of the single market in the very same way – by imports or by investment.

2.2.2. Discriminatory Access to Benefits of Negative Integration

The PTA may enact a regime of negative integration, applying national treatment, proportionality, necessity, or other disciplines to national regulation. However, the negative integration process may require changes in national TBTSPS measures that, according to the WTO rule of MFN, would seem to be required to be made available to other WTO members. It may be that a PTA could at one time have argued that it is not required to make these changes in TBTSPS measures available to third countries, but this argument would be unlikely to succeed, especially under the relevant recent WTO Appellate Body jurisprudence, for reasons set out in Sections 3 and 4. It is worth noting that within the European Communities, a foreign good, once it has entered any member-state, may freely travel to another member-state according to the principle of "free circulation," taking advantage of European Union (EU) rules of negative integration.

2.2.3 Discriminatory Access to Benefits of Internal Mutual Recognition

A PTA may enact a regime of positive integration through rules of mutual recognition. By excluding non-PTA states from this regime, it may promote intra-PTA trade at the expense of imports from outside the PTA.[7] Intra-PTA mutual recognition regimes, like intra-PTA negative integration regimes, may raise interesting issues under the MFN principle of Article I of GATT, as well as under Article XXIV. Multilateral requirements of recognition based on equivalence or necessity, either applied by courts or imposed by legislation, can address de facto

---

[7] See Joel P. Trachtman, "Embedding Mutual Recognition at the WTO," 14:5 *Journal of European Public Policy* 780 (2007).

discrimination that arises from failure to recognize home country regulation that meets the host country goal.

As discussed in more detail next, the multilateral trade system, via the WTO, may intervene to regulate the PTA regulation of national TBTSPS regulation in connection with any or all of these types of restrictions. In other words, national regulation regulates the market, PTA rules regulate the national regulation, and WTO rules regulate the PTA rules.

In addition to the WTO rules that apply to PTA measures as well as to national measures, Article XXIV of GATT may impose additional restrictions on the formation or operation of PTAs. These additional restrictions relate to Article XXIV:8, "internal requirements" for eliminating most barriers with respect to substantially all intra-PTA trade, as well "external requirements" of a common commercial policy for customs unions. These restrictions may be understood as intended to create hurdles to the creation of PTAs, to protect the operation of the MFN principle.[8] In addition, Article XXIV:5 requires that external barriers not be increased.

From a normative perspective, it is not clear which is better for global welfare, or even for the multilateral trade system: requiring and promoting PTA regulation of national TBTSPS measures, or forbidding or inhibiting this activity. Given this uncertainty, perhaps a first prescription should be "do no harm." In any event, it would appear that the multilateral system poses a greater legal threat to PTA TBTSPS measures than vice versa.

2.3. Potential Benefits to Multilateral Trade

Despite the modest potential that PTA TBTSPS disciplines may have to impede multilateral trade without violating existing WTO law, it should be understood that they also have the capacity to promote multilateral trade (not to mention their capacity to promote regional trade). Following are some potential positive contributions to multilateral liberalization that may arise from PTA TBTSPS disciplines.

2.3.1. PTA-Driven "Autonomous" TBTSPS Liberalization

As noted earlier, to the extent that PTA negative integration disciplines are stricter[9] than WTO disciplines on national TBTSPS measures, and provided that the operation of these disciplines provides MFN benefits, these disciplines would reduce the trade impediments that might result from national TBTSPS measures. Furthermore, in addition to the negative integration measures, positive integration measures in the form of harmonization can also provide benefits to

---

[8] See Jagdish Bhagwati, "Regionalism and Multilateralism: An Overview," in Jaime de Melo and Arvind Panagariya (eds.), *New Dimensions in Regional Integration* (1993).

[9] In order to be "stricter," the substantive rules themselves need not be more rigorous; the intensity and bindingness of enforcement activity could render a PTA discipline "stricter," or, for that matter, less strict.

outsiders. That is, as suggested earlier, to the extent that a PTA harmonizes its approach to a particular TBTSPS measure, outsiders can be expected to realize some economies of scale comparable to those realized by insiders. The expected MFN nature of a substantial segment of PTA TBTSPS liberalization, explained in more detail later, distinguishes TBTSPS measures from tariff reduction within a PTA.

2.3.2. The "Lock-In" Effect

The "lock-in" effect refers to the idea that governments may use PTA obligations to bind subsequent governments to liberalization programs.[10] However, GATT and the WTO can achieve similar lock-in effects,[11] as some observers suggested in connection with China's accession.

2.3.3. "Parallel Processing" in Reduction of Nontariff Barriers

The leading goal of the multilateral trading system is increased welfare through reduction of barriers to trade. It may be that once tariff barriers are eliminated, the most fruitful path to the goal of further reduction of barriers is through reduction of TBTSPS barriers. If PTAs, comprising of smaller groups of states, with greater homogeneity of regulatory preferences, can reduce TBTSPS barriers more efficiently than multilateral efforts, the multilateral system should "use" PTAs to achieve its goals. Furthermore, by diminishing protection on a regional basis, states may reduce the value to their industries of continued protectionism through TBTSPS measures, and thereby reduce the level of political support for such protectionism. This benevolent perspective on regional standardization suggests that regions may be analogized to parallel processors, working out regional solutions that make it easier for multilateral solutions to coalesce later.[12]

There is an alternative interpretation of this prospect: that regional solutions, establishing differing paths, will make later multilateral solutions more difficult. The choice of interpretation will depend on the degree of path dependence involved in regional standardization, compared to the costs of transition to multilateral solutions. Furthermore, regional integration may diminish incentives for multilateral liberalization.

2.3.4. PTAs as "Laboratories" of Integration

PTA TBTSPS disciplines may serve as examples or pathfinders for future multilateral disciplines: as laboratories of integration[13] and sources of intellectual capital. On the other hand, as previously suggested, we have questions about

---

[10] Jeffrey A. Frankel, *Regional Trading Blocs in the World Economic System* 216 (1997).

[11] See Bhagwati, *supra* note 8, at 25.

[12] For a more general statement of this perspective, *see WTO Secretariat, Regionalism, and the World Trading System* (1995).

[13] For an elaboration, see Sungjoon Cho, "Breaking the Barrier Between Regionalism and Multilateralism: A New Perspective on Trade Regionalism," 42 *Harv. Int'l L.J.* 419 (2001).

the extent to which PTA disciplines might result in circumstances where the PTA proceeds along a path that makes multilateral integration more difficult, or that may predetermine the path of multilateral integration:[14] path dependence. Thus, the PTA may take advantage of "first mover" advantages in TBTSPS activities, and use its prior action to impose outcomes on other states.

2.4. The Building Blocks versus Stumbling Blocks Analysis of TBTSPS Measures

Economists have devoted much research to the question of whether regional arrangements for free trade areas or customs unions are welfare enhancing or welfare reducing.[15] This study began with the seminal work of Jacob Viner, comparing the trade-creating (welfare-enhancing) effects with the trade-diverting (welfare-reducing) effects of regional integration. In the years since 1950, economists have critiqued and extended the static Vinerian analysis in a number of ways.[16] Economists have spent much less time considering the effects of regional arrangements relating to TBTSPS measures,[17] yet in a (developed) world where tariffs are already very small, reducing the barrier component of TBTSPS measures takes on greater importance.

The 1988 Cecchini Report, which formed the intellectual basis for the EU's single market program, showed important barriers to trade based on TBT-SPS measures, and substantial benefits accruing to Europe from reduction of TBTSPS-based barriers to trade.[18] Sykes conjectures that barriers in today's multilateral system are even more significant,[19] and the potential benefits even greater, because at the time of the Cecchini Report, Europe had already taken some measures to reduce these barriers, and because intra-European trade was already substantial.[20] This leaves us with two empirical questions: (i) what are the benefits of reduction of TBTSPS barriers in other regions (besides Europe), and (ii) what is the relationship between regional benefits and multilateral benefits? Each of these questions has both a static and dynamic component. To elaborate, is there any inconsistency between regional reduction of TBTSPS barriers and

[14] See Bhagwati, *supra* note 8, at 22.
[15] See Arvind Panagariya, "Preferential Trade Liberalization: The Traditional Theory and New Developments," 36 *J. Econ. Lit* 287 (2000).
[16] Id.
[17] See Note by the Secretariat, *A Brief Review of the Literature on the Trade Effects of Article XXIV Type Regional Agreements*, MTN.GNG/NG7/W/54, October 12, 1989. But see Chen and Mattoo, *supra* note 6.
[18] Paolo Cecchini et al., *The European Challenge 1992: The Benefits of a Single Market* (1988), summarizing results of research project on the "costs of non-Europe."
[19] See Organization for Economic Cooperation and Development, Proceedings of the Conference on Consumer Product Safety Standards and Conformity Assessment: Their Effect on International Trade, Paris: OECD (1996).
[20] Alan O. Sykes, *Product Standards for Internationally Integrated Goods Markets* (1995).

either (i) from a static standpoint, global welfare, or (ii) from a dynamic stand-point, global reduction of TBTSPS barriers? In addition to the potential immediate efficiency gains, is there also a possibility for dynamic institutional gains that will result in efficiency gains, due to learning, institutional innovation, demonstration effects, or other factors?

It is well understood that trade diversion per se is welfare reducing. One way of understanding PTAs is to examine whether the welfare reduction resulting from trade diversion is greater or less than the welfare enhancements resulting from trade creation. This kind of test, though, is difficult enough to apply *ex post*, and seems impossible to apply reliably *ex ante*. Furthermore, it is a rather passive and aggregative test. In analyzing Article XXIV, Bhagwati suggests this:

> A different, and my preferred, approach is not to pretend to find rules of thumb to exclude CUs and FTAs "likely" to be trade-diversionary, but rather to examine the different ways in which trade diversion could arise and then to establish disciplines that would minimize its incidence.[21]

This is a more active and precise approach: a rule of reason rather than a per se test. Bhagwati suggests that Article XXIV:5 operates in this spirit, by seeking to ensure that external barriers are not increased at the formation of a PTA, although "it is evident to trade economists that *maintaining* external tariffs unchanged is, in any event, not the same as eliminating trade diversion."[22] Therefore, Bhagwati recommends rules that would require a reduction in external tariffs.

This approach, while contested in the tariffs field, does not easily translate to the TBTSPS field. What would it mean to require a reduction of external TBTSPS measures? Would they be less onerous than internal TBTSPS measures? Given the existing requirement for national treatment and MFN, distinguishing the TBTSPS context from the tariff context in connection with PTAs,[23] there is little scope for discrimination against outside products. Are there nondiscriminatory PTA measures in the TBTSPS field that result in welfare reduction in a way that is different from the measures that states are permitted to take under current WTO disciplines? As suggested earlier, the main area where this applies seems to be rules of mutual recognition, which may be developed within or without PTAs.

2.5. Market-Access-Based Analysis

Of course, if we consider TBTSPS measures to be comparable in economic effect to a tariff – if we ignore the regulatory motivation of these measures – then

---

[21] Bhagwati, *supra* note 8, at 16.   [22] *Id.*
[23] We argue later that Article XXIV does not provide an exception that would extend to PTA TBTSPS measures that discriminate against outside states. Of course, the purpose of Article XXIV with respect to tariffs is to permit discrimination against outside states.

the analysis of regional versus multilateral tariff reduction is partially applicable.[24] However, TBTSPS measures have a dual character. On the one hand,
they are comparable to taxes, as opposed to tariffs, assuming that they are applied on a national treatment basis – tariffs are obviously inconsistent with national treatment. This perspective does not take into account path dependence,
economies of scale, and other factors that may cause nondiscriminatory TBTSPS
measures to have differential effects.

On the other hand, this type of regulation usually has some nonprotectionist regulatory purpose: to reduce information asymmetries, to require the inter-
nalization of externalities, to establish a focal point rule (such as driving on the
right), or simply to engage in redistribution (a subsidy). It is this regulatory purpose that distinguishes TBTSPS measures from tariffs, and makes the treatment
of the trade barriers caused by TBTSPS measures more complicated.

The expected MFN nature of PTA TBTSPS liberalization, explained in more
detail later, further distinguishes TBTSPS measures from tariff reduction within
a PTA. As illustrated in *Brazil–Tyres*, the negative integration, given WTO disciplines, is expected to raise few unaddressed concerns: it is the positive integration – harmonization and recognition – that provides opportunities for strategic
behavior. Thus, it might be argued that regional disciplines on national TBTSPS
measures in the form of negative integration – striking down discriminatory or
unnecessary national TBTSPS measures – would be expected to do little harm to
the multilateral system of trade. This perspective is congruent with the interpretation of GATT Article XXIV developed later: Article XXIV:8(a)(i) and (b) are best
understood as calling for negative integration, as opposed to positive integration.

Bagwell, Mavroidis, and Staiger consider the effects on trade of environmental and labor "standards," focusing on the reduction of national regulation of
production in ways that enhance the competitive position of import-competing
or export industries.[25] They see the "trade and..." problem as one of incomplete "property rights" in connection with WTO market access commitments –
those commitments may be undermined by modifications of national labor or
environmental regulation. In addition, exporting states may reduce standards in
support of mercantilism: in order to promote exports through reduced domestic labor or environmental protection. Bagwell, Mavroidis, and Staiger are concerned with production standards whereas this chapter focuses (as do the SPS
Agreement and the TBT Agreement) on product standards. However, a similar
analytical technique may apply. That is, we may understand TBTSPS measures
as means of defection from market access commitments.

However, the important distinction is that TBTSPS measures, as product
regulation, result in a relatively level playing field: all competing products in
a given market are subject to the same requirements. As a result of national

[24] See Richard Baldwin, Simon Evenett, and Patrick Low, "Beyond Tariffs: Multilateralizing
Deeper RTA Commitments," working paper dated September 2007.
[25] Kyle Bagwell, Petros C. Mavroidis, and Robert W. Staiger, "It's a Question of Market Access,"
96 *Am. J. Int'l L.* 56 (2002).

treatment and MFN obligations, there is unlikely to be legally valid discrimination in the application of TBTSPS measures except perhaps in the case of recognition arrangements, as discussed in more detail later in the chapter. On the
other hand, tariffs are by definition discriminatory departures from the "national
treatment" principle: domestically produced products are not subject to tariffs.
Of course, an additional important point, as with production standards, is that
their main purpose is or should be independent of their trade effects. Of course,
this chapter is not concerned with national TBTSPS measures as impediments to
trade, but with PTA TBTSPS measures.

Once we understand these measures as potential avenues of defection from
market access commitments, we can see that PTA harmonization could be
designed to erect barriers to imports, and that PTA recognition agreements could
provide differentially enhanced access to internal producers, compared to foreign producers. As previously discussed, the former potential threat is addressed,
at least in part, by WTO regulation of PTA TBTSPS measures as substitutes for
national TBTSPS measures. In *Brazil–Tyres*, the Appellate Body found that the
fact that a certain type of preferential treatment is required under a PTA does not
render it nonarbitrary for purposes of the chapeau of GATT Article XX. In that
case, neither the panel nor the Appellate Body reached the question of whether
this type of preferential treatment is authorized under Article XXIV.

The threat of defection from MFN obligations through mutual recognition
arrangements seems more pressing than the threat of the establishment of standards that have adverse effect on third states, and mutual recognition agreements may be permitted by WTO law. Bagwell, Mavroidis, and Staiger see potential scope for nonviolation complaints and Article XXVIII renegotiations as bases
for "rebalancing" market access after a change in production standards. It is
possible that these types of rebalancing could be applied in respect of recognition arrangements for product standards also. In fact, this may be a basis for
understanding the requirements of Article XXIV:5. However, such an effort would
require difficult calculations as to the magnitude of the shift in relative market
access due to the recognition arrangements.

Although there are some caveats, there may be substantial reasons, in welfare as well as political terms, for the WTO to accept and even foster the negative
and positive integration of TBTSPS regulation within PTAs. In Sections 3 and 4,
we evaluate the ways in which GATT and the Understanding regulate and foster TBTSPS integration in PTAs. In the spirit of Bhagwati's search for precision in
designing the conditionality for PTAs, we suggest conditions that might be established to reduce the possibility that TBTSPS measures may reduce global welfare.

3.   The Relationship among Article XXIV and GATT, the TBT Agreement, and the SPS Agreement

As we consider the relationship between regional TBTSPS measures and
multilateral reduction of trade barriers, it is important to analyze the current

circumstances under WTO law. The sources of law in this area are Article XXIV of GATT 1994, the Understanding, the TBT Agreement, and the SPS Agreement. Article XXIV, of course, dates from the GATT 1947, whereas the rest of these texts came into existence in the Uruguay Round (although the TBT Agreement had a predecessor dating from the Tokyo Round). Of course, they are all annexes to the 1994 WTO Charter, which is a single treaty.

3.1. Article XXIV

Article XXIV of GATT provides a conditional right for members to enter into free trade areas and customs unions: to the extent that its conditions are not met, these arrangements will generally violate other provisions of GATT.[26] With respect to the core internal attribute of a free trade area or customs union – internal tariffs of zero – this right is needed as an exception to allow what would otherwise be a clear violation of the MFN obligation of Article I of GATT. However, one of the most important interpretive questions that remain is, what other attributes are authorized by Article XXIV? This question arises in connection with the subject of this chapter – TBTSPS measures – but also with respect to other types of measures, such as safeguards. Article XXIV also imposes important requirements on free trade areas and customs unions. TBTSPS measures may play a role in the satisfaction of these requirements.

3.2. The Relationship between Article XXIV and the TBT Agreement and SPS Agreement

Does Article XXIV provide an exception from the requirements of the TBT Agreement or the SPS Agreement? Neither Article XXIV nor the TBT and SPS Agreements expressly provide such an exception. What happens when Article XXIV permits what these other agreements prohibit? This could come up in our case where, for example, a PTA SPS measure violates the prohibition under Article 2.3 of the SPS Agreement against arbitrary or unjustifiable discrimination between members where identical or similar conditions prevail. As noted earlier, the Appellate Body's logic in interpreting the chapeau of Article XX in *Brazil–Tyres* suggests that the PTA-based distinction is arbitrary, even though it is required under a PTA.

In the context of an intra-PTA mutual recognition agreement, it is possible that PTA-origin goods might be admitted where external goods are excluded, despite that similar substantive conditions otherwise prevail.[27] On the other hand, it might be argued that Article 4 of the SPS Agreement, or Article 6.3 of the

---

[26] See Gabrielle Marceau and Cornelis Reiman, "When and How is a Regional Trade Agreement Compatible with the WTO?," 3 *Leg. Iss. Econ. Integration* 297 (2001).

[27] This depends on the answer to several interpretative questions, including what is meant by "similar conditions."

TBT Agreement, authorizing recognition arrangements, might serve as a defense. Even if it were clear that Article 4 and Article 6.3 provide defenses under the SPS Agreement and TBT Agreement, it is not clear that they provide a defense under GATT. In fact, a purely textual interpretation argues that they do not.

The *EC–Bananas III* and *Canada–Periodicals* decisions of the Appellate Body in connection with the relationship between GATT and GATS suggest that the obligations under those agreements are cumulative. This conclusion is supported, in the context of the relationship between GATT Article III, the TRIMS Agreement, and the SCM Agreement (*Indonesia–Automobiles*), GATT Article XIII and the Agreement on Agriculture (*EC–Bananas III*), GATT Article XIII and the Safeguards Agreement (*US–Line Pipe*), and GATT Article XIX and the Safeguards Agreement (*Korea–Dairy Safeguards*). The Appellate Body made the following statements in *Korea–Dairy Safeguards*: [28]

> We agree with the statement of the Panel that: It is now well established that the WTO Agreement is a "Single Undertaking" and therefore all WTO obligations are generally cumulative and Members must comply with all of them simultaneously[29] ... In light of the interpretive principle of effectiveness, it is the *duty* of any treaty interpreter to "read all applicable provisions of a treaty in a way that gives meaning to *all of them, harmoniously.*"[30] An important corollary of this principle is that a treaty should be interpreted as a whole, and, in particular, its sections and parts should be read as a whole.[31]

This was a simple application of the principle of effective interpretation. It is suggested that the principle of effective interpretation is relevant both for rights and obligations. In *Brazil–Desiccated Coconut*, the Appellate Body upheld the panel

[28] Korea–Definitive Safeguard Measure on Imports of Certain Dairy Products, WT/DS98/AB/R, paras. 74, 81, adopted January 12, 2000.
[29] Panel Report [Korea–Dairy Safeguards] para. 7.38.
[30] We have emphasized this in Appellate Body Report, *Argentina–Safeguard Measures on Imports of Footwear*, WT/DS121/AB/R, circulated December 14, 1999, para. 81. See also Appellate Body Report, *United States–Gasoline*, p. 23; Appellate Body Report, *Japan–Alcoholic Beverages*, p. 12; and Appellate Body Report, *India–Patents*, para. 45.
[31] The duty to interpret a treaty as a whole has been clarified by the Permanent Court of International Justice in "Competence of the I.L.O. to Regulate Agricultural Labour" (1922), *PCIJ*, Series B, Nos. 2 and 3, p. 23. This approach has been followed by the International Court of Justice in *Ambatielos Case* (1953) *ICJ Reports*, p. 10; *Reservations to the Convention on the Prevention and Punishment of the Crime of Genocide* (1951) *ICJ Reports*, p. 15; and *Case Concerning Rights of United States Nationals in Morocco* (1952) *ICJ Reports*, pp. 196–99. See also I. Brownlie, *Principles of Public International Law*, 5th ed. (Clarendon Press, 1998), p. 634; G. Fitzmaurice, "The Law and Procedure of the International Court of Justice 1951–1954: Treaty Interpretation and Other Treaty Points," 33 *British Yearbook of International Law* (1957), p. 211 at p. 220; A. McNair, *The Law of Treaties* (Clarendon Press, 1961), pp. 381–82; I. Sinclair, *The Vienna Convention on the Law of Treaties* (Manchester University Press, 1984), pp. 127–29; M. O. Hudson, *La Cour Permanente de Justice Internationale* (Editions A Pedone, 1936), pp. 654–59; and L. A. Podesta Costa and J. M. Ruda, *Derecho Internacional Público*, Vol. 2 (Tipográfica, 1985), p. 105.

decision that the transitional rights given in the SCM Agreement could not be nullified by an interpretation of Article VI of GATT 1994.[32]

Thus, we might ask, what does "effective interpretation" require in the context of a modern application of Article XXIV? The WTO's obligations and rights must apply cumulatively and harmoniously unless set aside because of a conflict with another provision, or perhaps because another provision is *lex specialis*.[33] However, the panel in *Turkey–Textiles* also insisted that because the WTO members have a right under Article XXIV to form regional trade agreements, the interpretation of the other WTO provisions should be such as to ensure that this right does not become a "nullity."[34] Should this principle be extended to other WTO provisions, including the SPS Agreement and TBT Agreement? Given an understanding of the SPS Agreement and TBT Agreement as interpretations and extensions of principles that already existed within GATT – Articles I, III, XI, and XX – should we read the statement in the chapeau of Article XXIV:5 to the effect that "nothing in this Agreement [the GATT] shall prevent" to refer to the obligations of the SPS Agreement and the TBT Agreement as well? From the policy standpoint of avoiding unnecessary impediments to PTA integration, the answer would appear to be yes. And we might assume that this was the diplomatic intent. However, the text, which remains the focus of interpretation, is less availing.

The General Interpretative Note to Annex 1A to the WTO Charter (the "General Interpretative Note") provides that "[i]n the event of conflict between a provision of the General Agreement on Tariffs and Trade 1994 and a provision of another agreement in Annex 1A to the Agreement establishing the World Trade Organization (referred to in the agreements in Annex 1A as the 'WTO Agreement'), the provision of the other agreement shall prevail to the extent of the conflict."

The other agreements in Annex 1A include, inter alia, the SPS Agreement and the TBT Agreement. Thus, the latter prevail over GATT in the event of conflict. This raises an important question about what is meant by "conflict."[35] Is the kind of potential overlap, where one agreement authorizes what another agreement forbids, a conflict within the General Interpretative Note?

The answer is likely to be no. In WTO law, the type of conflict that is meant involves a circumstance where one agreement requires what another forbids.[36]

---

[32] Appellate Body Report on *Brazil–Measures Affecting Desiccated Coconut*, WT/DS22/AB/R, adopted March 20, 1997, p. 17.

[33] On this issue see Gabrielle Marceau, "Conflicts of Norms and Conflicts of Jurisdictions," 35 *J. World Trade* 1090 (2001).

[34] Panel Report in *Turkey–Restrictions on Imports of Textiles and Clothing Products*, WT/DS33/R, adopted as amended by the Appellate Body Report, November 19, 1999, paras. 9.96 and 9.103 [hereinafter, *Turkey–Textiles* Panel Report].

[35] See William J. Davey and Werner Zdouc, "The Triangle of TRIPS, GATT and GATS," chapter 2 in Thomas Cottier and Petros C. Mavroidis, (eds.), *Intellectual Property: Trade, Competition, and Sustainable Development* (2003), pp. 53–84.

[36] See Gabrielle Marceau and Joel P. Trachtman, "TBT, SPS, and GATT: A Map of the WTO Law of Domestic Regulation," 36 *J. World Trade* 811 (2002), *citing* Appellate Body Report

This is not the case here. Therefore, the General Interpretative Note is not likely to provide a ready answer, and the correct interpretative principle is that of "effectiveness." This principle would suggest that the TBT Agreement and the SPS Agreement, as part of the single undertaking, should be treated in the same way as the provisions of the GATT, although Article XXIV:5 fails to refer specifically to them. This reading should be clarified through a definitive interpretation or an understanding, or it may be clarified through dispute settlement.

3.3. The Relationship between Article XXIV and Articles I, III, and XI of GATT

In the *Turkey–Restrictions on Imports of Textile and Clothing Products* decision,[37] the Appellate Body examined the relationship between Article XXIV and other provisions of GATT. In particular, the question arose whether Article XXIV applies only to the MFN principle, or whether it provides an exception to other requirements of GATT.

The case concerned the final phase of the creation of a customs union between Turkey and the EU. As of January 1, 1996, Turkey harmonized its tariffs, and its textiles and clothing quantitative restrictions, with those of the EU. India claimed that the imposition of these quantitative restrictions on textiles and clothing violated GATT Articles XI and XIII, as well as Article 2.4 of the Agreement on Textiles and Clothing, and was not justified by Article XXIV.

The Appellate Body found that the words "shall not prevent" (with reference to the formation of a customs union or a free trade area) in the chapeau of Article XXIV:5 are critical to a determination of the scope of the exception under Article XXIV.

The panel had found that Article XXIV does not provide an exception from the rules against quantitative restrictions contained in Articles XI and XIII of GATT 1994.[38] The Appellate Body determined that the panel did not fully analyze the chapeau of Article XXIV:5, and proceeded to do so. The Appellate Body emphasized the words "shall not prevent" and held that "Article XXIV can justify the adoption of a measure which is inconsistent with certain other GATT provisions only if the measure is introduced upon the formation of a customs union, and only to the extent that the formation of the customs union would be

---

on Guatemala – Anti-Dumping Investigation regarding Portland Cement from Mexico, WT/DS60/AB/R, adopted November 25, 1998, para. 65. The same narrow definition of conflict was also used in Indonesia – Certain Measures Affecting the Automobile Industry, WT/DS54, 55, 59 and 64/R, adopted July 23, 1998, paras. 14.29–14.36 and 14.97 to 14.99; Appellate Body Report on United States – Antidumping Measures on Certain Hot-Rolled Steel Products from Japan, WT/DS 184/AB/R, adopted August 23, 2001, at para. 55, 62; Panel Report in Indonesia–Certain Measures Affecting the Automotive Industry, WT/DS54/R, WT/DS55/R, WT/DS59/R, WT/DS64/R, footnote 649, adopted July 23, 1998.

[37] WT/DS34/AB/R, adopted November 19, 1999 [*Turkey–Textiles* Appellate Body Report].

[38] *Turkey–Textiles* Panel Report, *supra* note 34, paras. 9.188 and 9.189.

prevented if the introduction of the measure were not allowed."[39] "It follows necessarily that the text of the chapeau of paragraph 5 of Article XXIV cannot be interpreted without reference to the definition of a "customs union." The definition of a customs union contained in Article XXIV:8 of GATT 1994 is as follows:

A customs union shall be understood to mean the substitution of a single customs territory for two or more customs territories, so that:

   (i) duties and other restrictive regulations of commerce (except, where necessary, those permitted under Articles XI, XII, XIII, XIV, XV, and XX) are eliminated with respect to substantially all the trade between the constituent territories of the union or at least with respect to substantially all the trade in products originating in such territories, and,
  (ii) ...substantially the same duties and other regulations of commerce are applied by each of the members of the union to the trade of territories not included in the union.

Article XXIV:8(a)(i) sets the internal requirement to eliminate duties and other restrictive regulations with respect to substantially all trade. Article XXIV:8(a)(ii) sets the external requirement for a "common external trade regime."[40] In addition, Article XXIV:5(a) imposes an additional external requirement to the effect that duties and other regulations of commerce "shall not on the whole be higher or more restrictive than the general incidence" prior to formation. (We will examine the application of these requirements to TBTSPS measures next.)

The Appellate Body found that Article XXIV:4 and the preamble of the Understanding provide an important part of the context for interpretation of the chapeau of Article XXIV:5, to the effect that a balance must be struck between the positive internal effects of customs unions and any negative trade effects on third parties: this is an economic test.[41]

The Appellate Body held that the state using the Article XXIV defense bears the burden of proving that the requirements of Article XXIV:5 and 8 are met, and that the measure for which the defense is sought is necessary to the customs union: that compliance with the relevant provision of GATT would prevent the formation of the customs union.[42] The panel failed to examine compliance with Article XXIV:5 and 8.[43]

---

[39] *Turkey Textiles*–Appellate Body Report, *supra* note 37, para. 46.
[40] *Turkey–Textiles* Appellate Body Report, *supra* note 37, para. 49.
[41] *Turkey–Textiles* Appellate Body Report, *supra* note 37, paras. 55–57, *citing* Panel Report, para. 9.120.
[42] *Turkey–Textiles* Appellate Body Report, *supra* note 37, para. 58.
[43] The panel suggested that it is arguable that it did not have jurisdiction to consider such compliance, but the Appellate Body noted in this respect its opinion in India– Quantitative Restrictions on Imports of Agricultural, Textile, and Industrial Products, to the effect that a panel has jurisdiction to examine matters that are also committed to political evaluation. WT/DS90/AB/R, adopted September 22, 1999, paras. 80–109.

With respect to the necessity criterion, Turkey asserted that if it had not imposed the quantitative restrictions at issue here, the EU would have "exclud[ed] these products from free trade within the Turkey/EC customs union."[44] The EU would have done so to prevent trade diversion: to prevent these products from flowing into the EU through Turkey, and thereby avoiding the application of the EU's quantitative restrictions. These goods accounted for 40 percent of Turkey's trade with the EU, thus raising concerns that, if they were excluded, Turkey's regional arrangement with the EU would not satisfy the "substantially all trade" criterion.

However, the Appellate Body agreed with the panel that there existed less trade restrictive alternatives, including the use of rules of origin to distinguish between Turkish and third-country textiles.[45] This would have addressed the problem of trade diversion and obviated the need to exclude the textiles and clothing sector from the EU–Turkish customs union. However, the Appellate Body did not address the fact that such rules of origin would require administration and prevent the formation of the kind of customs union that the EU and Turkey wished: one that would not require border controls on goods, consistent with the principle of "free circulation."[46]

Under the Appellate Body's approach, the EU and Turkey are not entitled under Article XXIV to an exception necessary for a customs union with features that go beyond those specified in Article XXIV itself. In the panel decision in *United States–Line Pipe Safeguards*, the panel interpreted the *Turkey–Textiles* necessity test differently. The panel distinguished *Turkey–Textiles* on the basis that the measure there restricted imports, whereas the measure at issue in the Line Pipe case involved the facilitation of internal trade – the "raison d'etre" of an FTA. It concluded, "If the alleged violation of GATT 1994 forms part of the elimination of 'duties and other restrictive regulations of trade,' there can be no question of whether it is necessary for the elimination of 'duties and other restrictive regulations of trade.'"[47] This may be understood as a statement that any measure to comply with Article XXIV:8 is irrefutably "necessary."

---

[44] Turkey appellant's submission, para. 56.

[45] *Turkey–Textiles* Appellate Body Report, *supra* note 37, para. 62–63.

[46] *Turkey–Textiles* Panel Report, *supra* note 34, para. 4.3, quoting a response to written questions by the European Communities as follows: "The use of rules of origin benefiting only Turkish exports would have been an exception to the principle of free circulation within the customs union and would have required the maintenance of customs and border checks within the customs union designed to ensure that Turkey would not become a transit point of goods in circumvention of the Community's quota system arising from Turkey's adoption of the Community's rates of tariffs, etc."

[47] Panel Report, United States–Line Pipe Safeguards, WT/DS202/R, October 29, 2001, para. 7.148 (citation omitted). This holding was determined by the Appellate Body to be moot and without legal effect, as the Article XXIV issues only became relevant if there was no failure of "parallelism." Appellate Body Report, United States–Line Pipe Safeguards, WT/DS202/AB/R, adopted March 8, 2002, para. 199.

The approach of the Appellate Body in *Turkey–Textiles* seems to decline to balance the integration benefits against the detriments to third-party commerce, although the Appellate Body's language, based on Article XXIV:4, seems to call for this type of balancing. In Article XX jurisprudence, under GATT 1947, panels developed the necessity test to require that the measure be the least trade-restrictive alternative reasonably available. The reasonable availability component of this test, if carried over to the necessity test the Appellate Body has developed here, might have provided a different outcome. Furthermore, as noted later, in *Korea–Beef* and *Asbestos*, the Appellate Body has extended the "necessity" criterion to comprehend a kind of balancing test.

The Appellate Body concluded that Turkey failed to satisfy its burden of proof that formation of a customs union between the EU and Turkey would have been prevented if Turkey were not allowed to adopt the quantitative restrictions at issue.

3.4. Necessity and Balancing

In subsequent jurisprudence, the Appellate Body has had occasion to revisit the necessity test in the context of Article XX(b) and (d) of GATT. The Article XX test would certainly not necessarily be applied to Article XXIV. However, there are some interesting similarities, and they are worthy of exploration. In both, the Appellate Body is trying to balance between an "exception" and trade restrictiveness. While in *Turkey–Textiles*, the Appellate Body speaks in terms of a less GATT-inconsistent alternative, it is not clear why the broader balancing developed in *Korea–Beef* and *Asbestos* could not be applied under Article XXIV.

Of course, it is unclear how the *Korea–Beef* and *Asbestos* balancing tests will be used in future cases under Article XX(b) and (d). It is even less clear what implications this jurisprudence will have in connection with Article XXIV. On the one hand, the Appellate Body's interpretation of the language of the chapeau of Article XXIV:5 – "shall not prevent" – provides a link to the "necessity" qualifier of Article XX(b) and (d), and the chapeau of Article XX. Furthermore, in *Turkey–Textiles*, the Appellate Body pointed out that Article XXIV:4 seems to suggest balancing between the dual objective of facilitating internal trade while avoiding raising barriers to external trade:

> This [combined] objective demands that a balance be struck by the constituent members of a customs union, but it should *not* do so in a way that raises barriers to trade with third countries. ... The chapeau cannot be interpreted correctly without constant reference to this purpose.[48]

---

[48] *Turkey–Textiles* Appellate Body Report, *supra* note 37, para. 57.

3.5. Necessity and Article I and III of GATT, the TBT Agreement, and the SPS Agreement

Now that we have reviewed the relevant jurisprudence, we can apply Article XXIV to the specific concerns regarding PTA integration of TBTSPS measures. The *Turkey–Textiles* report would suggest that each case would be required to be examined individually, but that the burden of proof would be on the PTA (or more accurately, except possibly in the case of the European Communities, its member).[49]

To the extent that PTA regulation of TBTSPS measures might violate MFN or national treatment or other obligations in GATT, in the SPS Agreement, or in the TBT Agreement, are these violations eligible for exception under Article XXIV? Are they sufficiently "necessary" under the *Turkey–Textiles* test? The *Turkey–Textiles* "necessity" test could suggest that the exception from these other norms is limited to what is required to form a customs union or free trade area under Article XXIV:8. However, it is not clear that the Appellate Body found that Article XXIV imposes such a limit. In other words, it is not clear that the Appellate Body meant that the only measures that are permitted under the chapeau of Article XXIV:5 are those that form the most minimalist customs union or free trade area that meets the requirements of Article XXIV:8. Could it not be that the measures permitted are those required to form a customs union or free trade area that meets the balancing test articulated by the Appellate Body?

The Appellate Body stated that Article XXIV:4 demands balancing between trade facilitation internally and avoidance of additional barriers externally. It further stated that for this purpose "the chapeau of paragraph 5, and the conditions set forth therein for establishing the availability of a defense under Article XXIV, must be interpreted in the light of the purpose of customs unions set forth in paragraph 4."[50] This approach might lead to an evolving or variable definition of "other restrictive regulations of commerce" (the internal test), as used in Article XXIV:8(a)(i) and (b), and "other regulations of commerce" (the external test), as used in Article XXIV:8(a)(ii) and XXIV:5(a). In *Turkey–Textiles*, the panel suggested that "other regulations of commerce" is an evolving concept.[51] This definition might expand and contract, depending on this balancing test.

To conclude, the question of whether a particular measure is "necessary" depends on the definition of "other restrictive regulations of commerce" and of "other regulations of commerce." Measures that would violate other WTO laws are prohibited, unless they are necessary to form a customs union or free trade area in this sense: if they are not required, they are prohibited. Therefore, if they

[49] *See* Marceau and Reiman, *supra* note 26.
[50] *Turkey–Textiles* Appellate Body Report, *supra* note 37, para. 57.
[51] *Turkey–Textiles* Panel Report, *supra* note 34, para. 9.120.

are not meant to dismantle "other restrictive regulations of commerce" or "other regulations of commerce," they are not permitted.

In Section 4, we review the requirements of Article XXIV:5 and XXIV:8 to determine what integration measures with respect to TBTSPS measures PTAs are required to take. We conclude that Article XXIV:8 most likely does not require either harmonization or rules of recognition, mutual or not.

Nor, given the understanding presented next of Articles XXIV:4 and 5, could one imagine that Article XXIV:8 requires discrimination in providing access to the benefits of negative integration. That is, where a PTA rule of negative integration results in a change in national TBTSPS regulation, that change would be required to be provided on an MFN and national treatment basis to all WTO members, and not just members of the PTA. Therefore, PTA harmonization or recognition of TBTSPS measures would be required to comply with these other norms.

3.6. Is Mutual Recognition a Violation of MFN?

It would not be important to the legality of mutual recognition arrangements whether or not they comply with Article XXIV, unless they violate another provision of WTO law.[52] So we must determine whether these types of arrangements violate the MFN obligation under Article I:1. This analysis raises an interesting question about the scope of MFN obligations.[53] There are two issues. First, does the MFN obligation apply on a product-by-product basis? Second, does the MFN obligation apply to provide non-PTA states an opportunity to qualify for recognition?

Mutual recognition arrangements (MRAs) are an important mechanism, both within and without PTAs,[54] to reduce regulatory barriers to trade.[55] The core of mutual recognition is recognition: the acceptance of foreign regulation as "equivalent" to domestic regulation, and therefore as an adequate and definitive substitute for the otherwise applicable domestic regulation. The "mutual" aspect describes arrangements in which recognition is accorded reciprocally: placing

---

[52] Of course, a somewhat separate, but equally important, question is whether internal mutual recognition agreements are required to constitute a customs union or free trade area.

[53] See generally, William J. Davey and Joost Pauwelyn, "MFN Unconditionality: A Legal Analysis of the Concept in View of its Evolution in the GATT/WTO Jurisprudence with Particular Reference to the Issue of 'Like Product,'" in Thomas Cottier, Petros C. Mavroidis, and Patrick Blatter, (eds.), *Regulatory Barriers and the Principle of Non-Discrimination in World Trade Law* at 13 (2000).

[54] The European Union has entered into a number of MRAs with third states. See, e.g., Agreement on Mutual Recognition Between the European Community and the United States of America, OJEC No. L31, February 4, 1999. The European Union has also entered into similar agreements relating to conformity assessment. These deal largely with conformity assessment, as opposed to recognition of substantive technical regulations themselves.

[55] See Kalypso Nicolaidis, "Non-Discriminatory Mutual Recognition: An Oxymoron in the New WTO Lexicon," in Thomas Cottier, Petros C. Mavroidis, and Patrick Blatter (eds.), *Regulatory Barriers and the Principle of Non-Discrimination in World Trade Law* at 267 (2000).

the condition of reciprocity on recognition would seem inconsistent with the principle of unconditional MFN treatment. The legal question for us is whether, and under what circumstances, a state may recognize some states' TBTSPS measures without recognizing the TBTSPS measures of all WTO members.

Recall that in the *Canada–Autos* case, the Appellate Body confirmed that Article I:1 addresses de facto as well as de jure discrimination. The Appellate Body emphasized the unconditional and broad scope of Article I:1 in finding that mere differential treatment of products originating in different member-states, regardless of the producer-based rationale, violates Article I:1. Although the Appellate Body did not emphasize this, its interpretation is based on the "like products" reference of Article I:1 – automobiles are like products regardless of whether their manufacturers have or have not invested in Canada.[56] Given the focus on Article I:1's reference to the matters referenced in Article III:4, and to "any advantage," it appears possible that "like products" treated differently because of different recognition arrangements might result in a violation of MFN. It appears even more likely that the advantage of inclusion in a regime of recognition might be required to be provided on an MFN basis.

There would seem to be a conflict between mutual recognition and a strict understanding of the MFN and national treatment obligation, to the effect that imported "like" products cannot be treated differently from "like" products from other member-states, or those produced domestically.[57]

In the *Asbestos* case, the Appellate Body articulated a fairly broad definition of "like products" for application under Article III:4.[58] Although the definition of "like products" in Article I:1 may be narrower, the Appellate Body's response to this broad definition may be useful to consider in the Article I:1 context. The Appellate Body recognized that this interpretation of "like products" would result in a relatively broad scope of application of Article III:4. To avoid a commensurately broad scope of invalidation of national law, the Appellate Body focused on the second element required under Article III:4: "A complaining Member must still establish that the measure accords to the group of 'like' imported products

---

[56] Appellate Body Report: Canada–Certain Measures Affecting the Automotive Industry, WT/DS139/AB/R, WT/DS142/AB/R, adopted June 19, 2000, para. 85. See also, Appellate Body Report, European Communities–Regime for the Importation, Sale, and Distribution of Bananas, WT/DS/27/AB/R, adopted September 25, 1997, paras. 205–06, citing United States–Non-Rubber Footwear, adopted June 19, 1992, 39 B.I.S.D. 128, para. 6.9.

[57] For an example of a circumstance where government certification did not provide sufficient distinction, see Panel Report, European Economic Community–Imports of Beef from Canada, adopted March 10, 1981, 28 B.I.S.D. 92. For an example of differential import licensing procedures violating Article I:1, see Panel Report, EC–Regime for the Importation, Sale, and Distribution of Bananas, adopted September 25, 1997, WT/DS27/R, paras. 7.188–7.193; 7.251–7.256; 7.235–7.241.

[58] See Robert E. Hudec, "'Like Product': The Differences in Meaning in GATT Articles I and III," in Thomas Cottier, Petros C. Mavroidis, and Patrick Blatter, (eds.), *Regulatory Barriers and the Principle of Non-Discrimination in World Trade Law* at 101 (2000).

'less favorable treatment' than it accords to the group of 'like' domestic products. The term 'less favorable treatment' expresses the general principle, in Article III:1, that internal regulations 'should not be applied...so as to afford protection to domestic production.'"[59]

Thus, two dimensions of discriminating treatment are required: first, like
products must be treated differently; second, foreign like products as a class
must be treated differently from, and less favorably than, domestic like products.
It is not enough to find a single foreign like product that is treated differently from
a domestic like product. Rather, the class of foreign like products must be treated
less favorably than the class of domestic like products. In order for this to occur,
it would seem necessary that the differential regulatory treatment be predicated,
either intentionally or unintentionally, on the foreign character of the product.
However, in *Korea–Various Measures on Beef,* the Appellate Body made clear that
differential treatment based on nationality alone would not necessarily amount
to "less favorable" treatment.[60] The area left for panel or Appellate Body discretion is in determining, in cases of de facto and unintentional disparate regulatory
treatment, whether there is a violation of the national treatment requirement. It
is possible that this "less favorable treatment" test (even though this language
is not replicated in Article I:1) would apply, *mutatis mutandis,* to protect bona
fide mutual recognition, especially where it is administered on a nonpreferential
basis,[61] from criticism under Article I MFN.

In this light, we might note that the TBT Agreement and the SPS Agreement contain provisions encouraging recognition regimes. This encouragement,
in order to have *effet utile,* must be interpreted as providing some form of protection against Article I:1 challenge. However, the language of these agreements
would not appear to condone artificial, PTA-based limitations on the right to
"qualify" for recognition.[62] Furthermore, any arguable exception under Article XX

---

[59] WTO Appellate Body Report: European Communities – Measures Affecting and Asbestos-
   Containing Products, WT/DS135/AB/R, para. 100, adopted April 5, 2001.
[60] Appellate Body Report, Korea – Various Measures on Beef, WT/DS161/AB/R and WT/
   DS169/AB/R, at para. 134. See also WTO Appellate Body Report, *Dominican Republic–
   Cigarettes,* WT/DS302/AB/R, adopted May 19, 2005, para 96.
[61] Interestingly, as discussed later, this possible approach would be roughly consistent with
   the structure of GATS Article VII.
[62] See Davey and Pauwelyn, *supra* note 53, at 23–24, evaluating mutual recognition agreements under the MFN principle: "On the one hand, such agreements offer an effective
   means of facilitating trade. On the other hand, they also have an impact on the competitive strength of nonparticipating countries. This is why two WTO agreements (TBT and
   SPS) encourage members to negotiate MRAs but at the same time require that they do
   so in a transparent and open way." See also Petros C. Mavroidis, "Transatlantic Regulatory Cooperation: Exclusive Club or 'Open Regionalism,'" in George A. Bermann, Matthias
   Herdegan, and Peter L. Lindseth (eds.), *Transatlantic Regulatory Cooperation: Legal Problems and Political Prospects* 263, 266 (2001): "Any interpretation of the WTO agreements
   that the MFN principle precludes MRAs must be rejected, because it runs counter to the
   principle of 'effective interpretation' of the treaties as laid down in the Vienna Convention
   on the Law of treaties."

of GATT (or compliance with the necessity requirements of the TBT Agreement and SPS Agreement) would require that the recognition regime not discriminate in an arbitrary manner, and may require that the recognition regime be necessary. These requirements would seem to argue that recognition regimes could not be exclusive to members of a PTA, but, as under the GATS, would be required to be offered on an open basis.

Interestingly, this logic would have results similar to those explicitly stated in Article VII of GATS. Indeed, the language of Article 4 of the SPS Agreement requires recognition on an open and objective basis. Under this provision, intra-PTA recognition arrangements would make it more difficult to resist extra-PTA recognition. Article 2.7 of the SPS Agreement does not provide as strong a requirement, calling on members to "give positive consideration" to accepting foreign technical regulations as "equivalent." Furthermore, the application of the necessity requirements in Article 2.2 of the SPS Agreement and Article 2.2 of the TBT Agreement might be affected by PTA recognition arrangements in the following way: Once a state enters into a recognition arrangement, it becomes more difficult to argue that its own regulation must meet complete compliance by other imports, when those other imports are equivalent. In other words, the recognition arrangement may set a lower standard of necessity.

To conclude, although it appears that recognition arrangements may be legal under WTO law, there seems little support for "closed" recognition as it might appear within a PTA. Does Article XXIV provide an exception that would allow closed recognition?

4. The Regional–Multilateral Relationship in the WTO as It Pertains to TBTSPS Measures: Article XXIV and the Understanding

The Appellate Body's decision in *Turkey–Textiles* has important implications for the treatment of TBTSPS measures in PTAs under Article XXIV. As noted, that decision suggests that measures that are not required to form a customs union or free trade area are prohibited, at least insofar as they violate another provision of GATT. However, there may be different ways of understanding what is required. In this section, we examine

- the **internal requirement** for customs union or free trade area status under Article XXIV:8(a)(i) for customs unions and Article XXIV:8(b) for free trade areas,
- the **external requirement** for customs union status under Article XXIV: 8(a)(ii),
- the **requirement not to raise external barriers** under Article XXIV:5, and
- the application of the **necessity test** developed in *Turkey–Textiles*.

Our focus is on what is required to constitute a PTA under Article XXIV, but our second purpose is to explore what is implicitly prohibited under Article XXIV.

4.1. The Internal Requirement for Customs Union or Free Trade Area Status

First, we must analyze how TBTSPS measures relate to the "internal requirement" under Article XXIV:8(a)(i) (customs unions) and Article XXIV:8(b) (free
trade areas) that "duties and other restrictive regulations of commerce (except,
where necessary, those permitted under Articles XI, XII, XIII, XIV, XV, and XX)
are eliminated with respect to substantially all the trade between the constituent
territories."[63] Is PTA regulation of TBTSPS measures, like that imposed by the EU
single market program, required, and if so, to what extent? This first depends on
whether TBTSPS measures are included in "other restrictive regulations of commerce." It is also worth noting the reference to Article XX in the parenthetical;
this suggests that at least some TBTSPS measures might be excluded from the
requirement of elimination.

4.1.1. What is an "Other Restrictive Regulations of Commerce" under Article XXIV:8(a)(i) and (b)? How does it differ from an "Other Regulations of Commerce" Under Article XXIV:5(a) and (b), and Article XXIV:8(a)(ii)?

As previously discussed, there are two similar terms contained in Article
XXIV:8 and Article XXIV:5. They are "other restrictive regulations of commerce"
(ORRCs) and "other regulations of commerce" (ORCs).[64] GATT neither defines
nor specifically distinguishes these terms. ORRC is used to deal with intra-PTA
regulation – the internal requirement – while ORC is used to deal with barriers
to external trade. In the terms of Article XXIV:4, ORRC deals with "facilitating"
intra-PTA trade while ORC deals with avoiding raising barriers to external trade.
However, in substantive terms, both refer to barriers to trade. We deal with both
in this section, for purposes of ease of exposition, as their definitions are linked.
However, our treatment of the definition of ORC is a digression from our analysis
of the internal requirements for FTAs, which depends on the definition of ORRC.

From the most basic interpretive perspective, assuming, based on the principle of effective interpretation, that these terms are intended to have different
meanings, it appears that ORC encompasses a wider scope than ORRC.[65] One
supposes that the *expressio unius* principle of interpretation could be deployed

[63] This language is drawn from Article XXIV:8(a)(i), relating to customs unions, and Article XXIV:8(b), relating to free trade areas. The language is the same.
[64] For the drafting history of Article XXIV and the Understanding in connection with ORCs, see Background Note by the Secretariat, Systemic Issues Related to "Other Regulations of Commerce," WT/REG/W/17/Rev.1, February 5, 1998. For a useful review of the approach taken to these terms by working parties in the GATT years, see Background Note by the Secretariat, Systemic Issues Related to "Other Regulations of Commerce," WT/REG/W/17/Add.1, November 5, 1997.
[65] See Statement by the Representative of Canada to the Committee on Regional Trade Arrangements, WT/REG/M/15, January 13, 1998, para. 26.

to argue that ORCs do not include restrictive regulations, but this would assume great incompetence on the part of the draftsman and would seem contrary to the intent of at least Article XXIV:5.

It should be noted that Article XXIV:5(a), referring to ORCs, sets forth an obligation that duties and ORCs "shall not on the whole be higher or more restrictive" than prior to formation. The reference to restrictiveness here would seem to argue that ORC and ORRC were intended to have similar meaning. That is, as regulations cannot grammatically be "higher," the only obligation under this provision with respect to ORCs is to ensure that they are not "more restrictive." Therefore, the only ORCs actually addressed are those that are "restrictive." Thus, at least in this particular context, there is no particular difference between ORC and ORRC. This argument may be slightly weakened because Article XXIV:8(a)(ii), where ORC is also used, does not refer to restrictiveness, although there is no guarantee that ORC has the same meaning in both provisions.

Toward a Definition of ORRC That Would Include Only "Protectionist" TBTSPS Measures: The text of Article XXIV:8 suggests that the term ORRC would ordinarily include some measures permitted under Articles XI, XII, XIII, XIV, XV, and XX of GATT, but these measures are exceptions from the obligation to dismantle internal barriers. So, for example, it appears that quantitative restrictions would ordinarily be ORRCs, but where there is an exception, as for example under Article XI:2, these would not be required to be eliminated. SPS and TBT measures that are not discriminatory would ordinarily be permitted under Article III, although some discriminatory measures could theoretically be permitted under Article XX.[66] Article III is not referenced, but it is not clear that the list of GATT provisions is intended to be exhaustive.[67] The fact that Article XX is referenced suggests that it is at least possible that TBTSPS measures might be included as ORRCs, except to the extent permitted under Article XX, but this does not allow us to draw a strong inference.

More importantly, it might be argued that TBTSPS measures are not ordinarily "restrictive" or "regulations of commerce,"[68] because they are not intended, as duties are, to reduce market access. (To the extent this argument depends on the

---

[66] There may be a rather metaphysical argument to the effect that these nondiscriminatory SPS and TBT measures, applied at the border, are "permitted" under Article XI because, under an interpretation of *ad* Article III, these measures are subject to Article III and not subject to Article XI.

[67] See Robert E. Hudec and James D. Southwick, "Regionalism and WTO Rules: Problems in the Fine Art of Discriminating Fairly," in Miguel Rodriguez Mendoza, Patrick Low, and Barbara Kotschwar, (eds.), *Trade Rules in the Making: Challenges in Regional and Multilateral Negotiations* 47, 64 (1999).

[68] Within federations like the United States, or within the European Communities, these measures are considered "regulations of commerce," at least for purposes of authority for positive integration and judicial application of negative integration. However, these definitions have shifted over the history of these entities engaging in economic integration. Therefore, a teleological interpretation, in the WTO's current circumstances, might find that TBTSPS measures are not yet "regulations of commerce" in the sense of this requirement.

inclusion of the word "restrictive," this may be an argument for differentiating between ORRCs and ORCs.) Here, the word "other" would be understood to draw this link between duties and the types of "regulations of commerce" covered by Article XXIV:8 – the regulations included are those that are restrictive in the same sense as duties. Perhaps this would include TBTSPS measures that are discriminatory against foreign goods, or that are otherwise "restrictive" in the same sense as a duty.

Moreover, it would be absurd to include all TBTSPS measures as ORRCs, because the implication would be that Article XXIV:8(a)(i) and XXIV:8(b) require their elimination. It must be that if any TBTSPS measures are included, it is a subcategory of them. This would seem to support the interpretation that only discriminatory, or perhaps also unnecessary, TBTSPS measures are ORRCs.

It appears that WTO members have not addressed this particular issue, but their post-1947 discussions seem supportive of the interpretation of ORRC suggested earlier. "Most of the discussion has focused on whether safeguard and antidumping measures should be considered ORRCs. . . . Some Members argued that what is important is whether the application of some specific measures among PTA parties led to restrictions on the trade of third parties, and not whether they constituted ORRCs."[69] Although this article does not deal with the service sector, it is worth noting that the coordinate provision of GATS, Article V:1(b), limits its scope to discriminatory measures.

In the Report of the 1970 Working Party on "EEC–Association with African and Malagasy States," some members opined that the maintenance of fiscal charges on imports from other members was inconsistent with Article XXIV:8(b), *where these charges had no domestic counterpart.*[70] The parties to that convention replied that "so far as they knew, the elimination of fiscal charges had never yet constituted an element necessary for recognition that a free trade area was consistent with the GATT rules . . . The General Agreement made a clear-cut distinction between measures which had a protective effect and other measures applied in like manner to domestic and imported products."[71] Although there appeared to be some disagreement on the facts, both sides seemed to agree on the principle.

This issue came up again soon after in the Report of the Working Party on "EEC–Agreement of Association with Malta." In response to a *reductio ad absurdum* argument to the effect that Malta could replace all its tariffs with "revenue duties," the parties to the association agreement responded that "the existence of revenue duties, which by definition ruled out discriminatory application, could

---

[69] Note by the Secretariat, Synopsis of "Systemic" Issues Related to Regional Trade Agreements, WT/REG/W/37, March 2, 2000, para. 45 and n. 93. The latter part of this quote seems odd in the context of para. 8, which deals with internal restrictive regulations of commerce.

[70] L/3465, adopted December 2, 1970, 18 B.I.S.D. 133, para. 7.

[71] Id., para. 8.

not be regarded as jeopardizing the establishment of free trade."[72] This suggests that discriminatory character is the critical feature.

It may be desirable for the meaning of ORRC to be delineated more clearly in dispute settlement or in a definitive interpretation of GATT. It is also perhaps desirable to take an evolutionary approach to the definition of ORRC. This evolutionary approach, following the *Shrimp–Turtle* decision of the Appellate Body, would recognize that as tariff barriers have declined, nontariff barriers such as TBTSPS measures have become more important barriers to trade, in both relative and absolute terms.

Thus, we might consider the definition of ORRC to depend on what is "inherent" in a customs union or free trade area, as India argued in the *Turkey–Textiles* case.[73] What is "inherent" may depend on the historical moment, and on the circumstances. This interpretation would be consistent with the Appellate Body's call in the *Turkey–Textiles* decision for balancing the objectives of internal trade facilitation and avoiding barriers to external trade. So, a case-by-case approach, recognizing the possibility of evolution in what is "inherent" in a PTA, and balancing these goals, may be the best route to defining ORRCs. This evolutionary approach might lead us to the conclusion that only protectionist (discriminatory or unnecessary) TBTSPS measures are included in ORRC and therefore subject to the requirement of elimination.

Similarly, if PTAs are only required to eliminate protectionist TBTSPS measures, then they are not permitted to violate other provisions of WTO law to engage in harmonization or recognition.

Toward a Definition of ORC: This section is a digression from the issue of the definition of ORRC and the requirements of Article XXIV:8(a)(i) and (b) of GATT, but it is useful to cover the definition of "other regulations of commerce" as used in Article XXIV:5 and XXIV:8(a)(ii) before traveling too far from our discussion of the definition of ORRC. GATT contains no definition of "other regulations of commerce" or ORC.[74] It is not clear whether ORC was intended to have the same meaning as ORRC: "It has been generally recognized that paragraph 8 deals mainly with those measures that are internal to the customs union or FTA, whereas paragraph 5 governs external relations, and that the former paragraph describes the minimum parameters which a PTA must meet."[75] This view seems consistent with the structure of paragraph 8(a), which refers to ORRCs with respect to its internal test and ORCs with respect to its external test. Thus,

---

[72] L/3665, adopted May 29, 1972, 19 B.I.S.D. 90, para. 15. In para. 17, it was noted that "The discussion brought to light the fact that the English and French versions of Article XXIV paragraph 8(a) differed inasmuch as the English text referred only to 'duties,' whereas the French text referred to 'droits de douane' (customs duties). The Working Party did not reach any conclusion on the point."

[73] *Turkey–Textiles* Appellate Body Report, *supra* note 37, para. 21.

[74] For a useful analysis, see Communication from Australia, WT/REG/W/25, April 1, 1998.

[75] Secretariat Synopsis, *supra* note 69, para. 46. See also para. 62.

the purposes of these two provisions seem different: one requires reduction of barriers to intra-PTA imports, and the other requires reduction of barriers to imports from outside the PTA.

In *Turkey–Textiles*, the panel made the following statement:

> While there is no agreed definition between Members as to the scope of this concept of "other regulations of commerce," for our purposes, it is clear that this concept includes quantitative restrictions. More broadly, the ordinary meaning of the terms "other regulations of commerce" could be understood to include any regulation having an impact on trade (such as measures in the fields covered by WTO rules, e.g., *sanitary and phytosanitary*, customs valuation, antidumping, *technical barriers to trade*; as well as any other trade-related domestic regulation, e.g., *environmental standards*, export credit schemes). Given the dynamic nature of regional trade agreements, we consider that this is an evolving concept.[76]

If ORC includes quantitative restrictions, it is difficult to see why it would not also include TBT or SPS measures that amount to or are somehow analogous to quantitative restrictions, as the panel suggests. Thus, while ORC is an evolving concept, at least some TBTSPS measures will be covered. It would seem appropriate to include "protectionist" TBTSPS measures as ORCs, especially if these are included in ORRC, as previously suggested.

4.1.2. The Requirements of Article XXIV:8(a)(i) and Article XXIV:8(b)

We now return to our discussion of the requirements of Article XXIV:8(a)(i) and (b), based on the definition of ORRC. If ORRC were to be interpreted to include all TBTSPS measures, it appears that Article XXIV:8(a)(i) and Article XXIV:8(b) would require that such measures be eliminated with respect to customs unions and free trade areas, respectively. This would obviously go too far. If TBTSPS measures are covered, only some portion of them, such as discriminatory or disproportionate (in the sense of unnecessary) TBTSPS measures, must be included.

It would appear that the better understanding is that only protectionist TBTSPS measures would be seen as "restrictive" and therefore subject to a requirement of elimination. Thus, a PTA would be required to prohibit discrimination (and perhaps "unnecessary" regulation) in this area. However, as WTO law already does so, this requirement would not seem to have much traction, at least in PTAs exclusively among WTO members.[77]

---

[76] *Turkey–Textiles* Panel Report, *supra* note 34, para. 9.120 (emphasis added).

[77] If, alternatively, all TBTSPS measures are included as ORRCs, then (assuming we all agree that elimination is absurd) this provision might require further integration. This further integration might include negative integration in the form of proportionality or other tests (again, to the extent not already included in WTO law), and/or requirements of mutual recognition or harmonization within the PTA.

4.2. The External Requirement for Customs Union Status

Second, we must examine the extent to which failure to engage in PTA regulation of TBTSPS measures may violate the external requirement of Article XXIV:8, as applied to customs unions. Article XXIV:8(a)(ii) requires that "substantially the same duties and other regulations of commerce are applied by each of the members of the union." Does this reference include in the "common external trade regime" the approach to external TBTSPS measures? The answer to this question depends on what is meant by "other regulations of commerce." We refer to the earlier discussion of the meaning of ORC. Although the definition of ORC is not clearly delineated, and may well be in flux, it would seem absurd to require harmonization of TBTSPS measures for external application under clause (ii) of Article XXIV:8(a), while only eliminating protectionist TBTSPS measures internally under clause (i). Thus, whatever the full meaning of ORC, it seems appropriate to expect that in the field of TBTSPS measures, it is not greater than ORRC.

If this is accepted, the combination of these provisions results in what amounts to an MFN requirement: protectionism in TBTSPS measures (argued earlier to be included in ORRC) must be eliminated both internally and, because it is also included within ORC, externally. However, this is largely accomplished already under WTO law. Thus, this requirement too lacks traction given the evolution of WTO law in the Uruguay Round.

In *Turkey–Textiles*, the Appellate Body interpreted "substantially the same" to require a high degree of sameness – "comparable trade regulations having similar effects do not meet this standard."[78] The commonality need not be exact, but the external trade regimes must be substantially the same. According to the Appellate Body, it must "closely approximate 'sameness,'" and the Appellate Body rejected the panel's interpretation to the effect that the external trade regimes of constituent states may be "comparable."[79] This would seem to argue for a requirement that customs unions have uniform external requirements for TBTSPS measures, to the extent that TBTSPS measures are included in ORCs. Given the requirements of MFN and national treatment in the GATT, the TBT Agreement, and the SPS Agreement, a common external regime would require a common internal regime.

However, this outcome would be absurd if ORC goes beyond protectionism. As we have suggested, Article XXIV:8(a)(i) cannot require "elimination" of nonprotectionist TBTSPS measures. It would be odd indeed if Article XXIV:8(a)(ii) required the harmonization externally of nonprotectionist measures that were not required to be harmonized internally under Article XXIV:8(a)(i).

[78] *Turkey–Textiles* Appellate Body Report, *supra* note 37, para. 50.
[79] *Turkey–Textiles* Body Report, *supra* note 37, para. 50, citing Panel Report, para. 9.151.

4.3. The Requirement not to Raise External Barriers

Third, and somewhat inconsistently with the tests discussed previously, to what extent does internal TBTSPS integration impose a risk of violation of the requirement in Article XXIV:5 that the "duties and other regulations of commerce" are on the whole higher or more restrictive than the general incidence prior to formation of the customs union or free trade area? In other words, if common external TBTSPS measures upon formation are higher than the general incidence prior to formation, would this cause the PTA to violate Article XXIV? Would this rule have a deregulatory bias? Would TBTSPS measures be evaluated separately from duties, or on an "aggregate barriers to trade" basis?

Paragraph 2 of the Understanding provides that "for the purpose of the overall assessment of the incidence of other regulations of commerce for which quantification and aggregation are difficult, the examination of individual measures, regulations, products covered, and trade flows affected may be required." This would suggest that these types of measures may be required to be evaluated separately, without quantification or aggregation.[80]

On the other hand, in *Turkey–Textiles*, the Appellate Body found that Article XXIV:5(a) requires "that the effects of the resulting trade measure and policies of the new agreement shall not be more trade restrictive, overall, than were the constituent countries' previous trade policies."[81] This suggests that the test under Article XXIV:5 is something of a balancing test.

The Appellate Body agreed with the panel that Article XXIV:5(a), as elaborated and clarified by paragraph 2 of the Understanding, calls for an "economic" test for assessing the compatibility of a specific customs union with Article XXIV.[82] The Appellate Body referred to Article XXIV:4 as a basis for interpreting the rest of Article XXIV, requiring balancing between positive internal effects and negative trade effects on third parties.

Australia has provided an interesting hypothetical example worth discussing here:

> Country E maintains a strict system of sanitary and phytosanitary regulations that underpins its considerable success on export markets in plant and animal products. It now decides to enter into a free trade agreement with Country F which, for reasons of comparative advantage, has operated under

---

[80] For an argument that import restrictions in the form of quotas or regulations can, at least conceptually, be translated into tariff levels, see Marceau and Reiman, *supra* note 26. Although we have experience, under the Agriculture Agreement, in tariffication of protectionist quotas, it is far more difficult to imagine how a TBTSPS measure might be tariffied, due to its regulatory character.

[81] *Turkey–Textiles* Appellate Body Report, *supra* note 37, para. 55, quoting *Turkey–Textiles* Panel Report, para. 9.121.

[82] *Turkey–Textiles* Appellate Body Report, *supra* note 37, para. 55, quoting *Turkey–Textiles* Panel Report, para. 9.120.

less stringent rules. Both countries agree that there would be considerable efficiency gains through closer economic integration, but that this result was only possible if at the same time there was a harmonization of sanitary and phytosanitary rules at the level of Country E's regulations. Inevitably, this would mean a raising overall in the incidence of restrictive regulation, but how should it be considered in the context of the rules expressed in Article XXIV:8? Obviously, nobody would claim that sanitary and phytosanitary regulations are irrelevant in a free trade area, but here we have the paradoxical situation that imposing them would promote economic integration.[83]

This example is extremely useful, as it points out the inherent potential conflict between the goals of Article XXIV:8 and those of Article XXIV:5. That is, imposing heightened SPS measures might promote economic integration while it might increase barriers to third countries. Would the *Turkey–Textiles* "necessity" test find that raising SPS measures was not necessary? After all, the goals of Article XXIV:8 could be met by harmonization at the (lower) Country F level. Or, if external barriers are evaluated on an aggregate basis, would this PTA be required to "compensate" by reducing barriers in another area?

This may be an absurd result, as Country F had the freedom to raise the level of its SPS measures, within the parameters of the SPS Agreement, separately. In fact, an advisor to this PTA might suggest that Country F raise the level of its SPS measures "autonomously" prior to entering the PTA. On the other hand, its motivation – not being a changed "appropriate level of protection" but being economic integration – might raise concerns under the SPS Agreement.

Does Article XXIV:5 address the circumstance where, by virtue of internal reductions of barriers through positive integration, without increasing absolute barriers, imports are made relatively less competitive? It does not appear intended to do so, as this is the natural implication of Article XXIV: internal barriers may, indeed they must, be dismantled, and external barriers cannot be increased. Therefore, there is no guarantee that imports will remain competitive.

4.4. TBT Agreement

The TBT Agreement contains remarkably little addressing PTAs. Articles 4.1, 9.2, and 9.3 seek to ensure that regional standard-setting and conformity assessment mechanisms comply with certain obligations of the TBT Agreement. Perhaps this is based on an assumption that TBT measures are not subject to Article XXIV, or that the interpretive issues outlined earlier are already well understood.

Of course, Article 2.1 provides a requirement of MFN treatment, as well as national treatment. Earlier we addressed the possibility that PTA arrangements could violate the MFN requirement.

---

[83] Communication from Australia, *supra* note 74, para. 10.

Article 2.7 seeks to promote recognition of other members' technical standards. This could presumably validate a regional arrangement for recognition, but it leaves open the question of compliance with the MFN requirement discussed previously.

Article 2.4 of the TBT Agreement calls for use of international standards in the preparation of technical regulations but does not refer to regional standards.

4.5. SPS Agreement

The SPS Agreement takes a somewhat different approach to drafting, but it covers regional measures in approximately the same substantive way as the TBT Agreement. Article 13 of the SPS Agreement provides that

> Members shall take such reasonable measures as may be available to them to ensure that nongovernmental entities within their territories, as well as regional bodies in which relevant entities within their territories are members, comply with the relevant provisions of this Agreement. In addition, Members shall not take measures which have the effect of, directly or indirectly, requiring or encouraging such regional or nongovernmental entities, or local governmental bodies, to act in a manner inconsistent with the provisions of this Agreement.

Article 2.3 of the SPS Agreement contains a somewhat more nuanced requirement for MFN than that found in the TBT Agreement, providing that "Members shall ensure that their sanitary and phytosanitary measures do not arbitrarily or unjustifiably discriminate between Members where identical or similar conditions prevail, including between their own territory and that of other Members." It specifically allows for justifiable discrimination. It is possible that justifiable discrimination might be found to exist under circumstances of a mutual recognition agreement in connection with a PTA.

The SPS Agreement contains provisions substantively similar, for our purposes, to those of the TBT Agreement relating to harmonization and recognition. Although Article 4 of the SPS Agreement calls for recognition on objective terms, it does not provide sufficient guidance as to whether PTA recognition arrangements would violate MFN obligations.

4.6. Compare GATS Article VII

This chapter is not intended to address GATS per se. The lack of authority for regional integration of TBTSPS measures in the TBT and SPS Agreements contrasts with the treatment of this topic in the GATS.[84] Article V of GATS has a similar structure to Article XXIV of GATT, regulating the formation of PTAs in relation to services. However, Article VII provides an additional facility. It allows

---

[84] This lack of authority supports the argument made earlier in this article that Article XXIV was intended to cover "necessary" exceptions to the TBT and SPS Agreements.

for autonomous, reciprocal, or regional, or even plurilateral, arrangements for recognition of standards or criteria for the authorization, licensing, or certification of services suppliers. It requires that other members be permitted to demonstrate the qualification of their regulatory regime for recognition. Recognition arrangements may not be used as a means of discrimination.

Article VII presumably provides an exception from the requirements of GATS Article II, requiring MFN treatment. One might ask, if this facility was acceptable in the field of services, why was it not provided with respect to TBTSPS measures? It cannot be that its specific inclusion in GATS suggests an interpretation that similar recognition was not intended in the goods sector. Article VII of GATS seems to have struck an appropriate balance, but its relationship to the regional integration provision of GATS, Article V, is unclear.[85]

5. Conclusion

The requirements of Article XXIV of GATT and the Understanding with respect to PTA regulation of national TBTSPS measures are somewhat unclear, in large measure as a result of the imprecision of the definitions of "other restrictive regulations of commerce" in Article XXIV:8, and "other regulations of commerce" in Article XXIV:5 and 8. This article suggests that the WTO law be read to require PTAs internally to impose a rule of national treatment-type nondiscrimination and necessity. However, it must be recognized that the WTO system already provides this antiprotectionism discipline, and so this requirement has little traction.

On the other hand, Article XXIV:8 does not appear to require harmonization or mutual recognition arrangements. To the extent that PTAs engage in harmonization, their harmonized TBTSPS measures must conform to the requirements of WTO law, namely the GATT, the TBT Agreement, and the SPS Agreement. The regulation of PTA rules of mutual recognition, under the MFN obligation of Article I:1 of GATT, and under Article XXIV, is unclear, and rules of mutual recognition may present some opportunities for PTA protectionism. It would be useful to clarify the meaning of "other restrictive regulations of commerce" in Article XXIV:8, and "other regulations of commerce" in Article XXIV:5 and 8 in order to clarify what Article XXIV requires and what it prohibits.

The core question raised by this article has to do with the treatment of recognition arrangements. Should PTAs be permitted to maintain exclusive recognition arrangements, effectively discriminating against similarly situated third-party states and "like" third-state products? Or should they be required, as under Article VII of the GATS, to practice what might be termed "open recognition"? Open recognition would establish PTA conditions for recognition but permit

---

[85] See Aaditya Mattoo, "MFN and the GATS, in Regulatory Barriers and the Principle of Non-Discrimination," in Thomas Cottier, Petros C. Mavroidis, and Patrick Blatter (eds.), *World Trade Law* at 51 (2000).

third-party states to meet those conditions. This article has suggested that, although the legal requirements are not clear, open recognition may be required under Article I:1 and XXIV of GATT. It might be useful to clarify these requirements.

To ensure that PTA TBTSPS measures do not unnecessarily inhibit trade with outside parties, and to ensure that WTO requirements for MFN and Article XXIV requirements do not unnecessarily inhibit regional integration, the following three initiatives are recommended:

1. Interpret Article XXIV:5 to provide an exception from obligations contained in the TBT Agreement and SPS Agreement, principally the MFN obligation, in accordance with the *Turkey–Textiles* necessity test. This avoids imposing an inappropriate barrier to formation of PTAs.
2. Interpret "other restrictive regulations of commerce" and "other regulations of commerce" in Articles XXIV:5 and 8 to include only discriminatory and unnecessary TBT or SPS measures. This avoids requirements to eliminate or harmonize nonprotectionist TBT or SPS measures. It avoids imposing an inappropriate barrier to formation of PTAs.
3. Interpret Article I:1 of GATT and the MFN provisions of the TBT Agreement and SPS Agreement to clarify authorization for only "open" mutual recognition agreements, similar to the permission contained in Article VII of GATS. Today, it is not clear that any mutual recognition agreements are authorized. This ensures that recognition arrangements will not provide an avenue of discrimination or other defection from WTO multilateral free trade principles.

These initiatives could be affected by the dispute settlement process, or by action of the member-states of the WTO.

These initiatives would assist in ensuring that PTA TBTSPS integration contributes to global welfare, and that WTO rules do not inappropriately inhibit the formation of PTAs. However, this article's analysis does not purport to answer the question of building blocks or stumbling blocks in connection with regional integration in the TBTSPS field.

This article has also not addressed the dynamic time path issue: whether PTA integration of TBTSPS issues will help to achieve greater welfare through institutional growth. One problem with this question is that it is not clear that either PTA or multilateral standardization would increase welfare in any particular circumstance. Although Kindleberger suggests that world standards are a public good,[86] Sykes,[87] Stephan,[88] and others point out that harmonization may

---

[86] Kindleberger, *supra* note 4, at 393.   [87] Sykes, *supra* note 20.
[88] Paul B. Stephan, "Regulatory Cooperation and Competition: The Search for Virtue," in George A. Bermann, Matthias Herdegan, and Peter L. Lindseth (eds.), *Transatlantic Regulatory Cooperation: Legal Problems and Political Prospects* 167 (2001).

diminish welfare through suppression of efficient variation and regulatory competition. In a sense, both perspectives are correct, but they depend on the particular type of product and the preferences of individuals and states.[89]

Flexible institutional arrangements are needed to permit the emergence of private, national, regional, and global TBTSPS measures in response to circumstances and preferences as they vary and as they emerge over time. The balancing test enunciated by the Appellate Body in *Turkey–Textiles* may serve to provide an appropriate degree of flexibility. The Appellate Body's "economic test," although neither operational in an economic analysis sense nor formally realizable in a legal sense, may be a useful way forward in the near term.

[89] See Pascal Lamy, "Facing the Challenge of Globalisation: Regional Integration or Multilateral Rules," Buenos Aires, March 1, 2002, available at www.europa.eu.int/comm/trade/speeches_articles/spla99_en.htm.

HENRIK HORN, PETROS C. MAVROIDIS, AND ANDRÉ SAPIR

5 EU and U.S. Preferential Trade Agreements: Deepening or Widening of WTO Commitments

1. Introduction

There is growing concern about preferential trade agreements (PTAs) and the role they should play within the multilateral trading system. This concern stems from both their increasing number and their ever-broader scope.

During the period 1948–94, the General Agreement on Tariffs and Trade (GATT) received 124 notifications of PTAs, of which about 50 were active at the creation of the World Trade Organization (WTO) in 1995. Since then, more than 250 new arrangements have been notified to the WTO, and the number of arrangements active in 2008 was about 200. A large part of this expansion involves agreements where the European Community (EC)[1] or the United States is a partner. As a result, the EC and the United States have become the two main "hubs" in the pattern of PTAs, with the "spokes" represented by agreements with the various partner countries.

Modern PTAs exhibit features that earlier PTAs did not possess. In particular, PTAs formed before 1995 concerned only trade in goods and took the form of (mostly) free trade areas (FTAs) or (more rarely) customs unions (CUs), involving mainly tariff liberalization. Since the creation of the WTO and the extension of multilateral trade agreements to trade in services and trade-related aspects of intellectual property rights, new PTAs also tend to cover these two subjects, which revolve chiefly around regulatory issues. Besides, there are claims that

This chapter draws substantially on a study prepared for Bruegel, a European think tank, to whom we are grateful for financial support. An earlier version was presented at a seminar held at the Columbia Law School in New York on October 14, 2008. We are grateful for constructive comments to our discussants, Gary Horlick and Nuno Limão, and to Kyle Bagwell and Jagdish Bhagwati. We are indebted to Malwina Mejer for superb and meticulous research assistance. Assistance from Vera Squaratti and Anna Wolf is also acknowledged.
    [1] We will generally use the term "European Community" (EC), which is the legally correct expression in the WTO context. However, we will also sometimes use the term "European Union" (EU) where appropriate.

the new preferential agreements signed by the EC or the United States go even further in the coverage of regulatory issues, by including provisions in areas that are not currently covered by the WTO agreements at all, such as investment protection, competition policy, labor standards, and protection of the environment.

This claim has potential systemic implications because, although they jointly account for no more than 40 percent of the world gross domestic product (GDP) (at purchasing power parity [PPP]) and world trade, the EC and the United States are sometimes viewed as the "regulators of the world." It is estimated indeed that, together, they account for around 80 percent of the rules that regulate the functioning of world markets.[2]

The relatively broad scope of PTAs involving the EC and the United States is reflected in the policy debate, and to a lesser extent in the academic literature. Economic scholars have been arguing for some time about the relationship between PTAs and the multilateral trading system, with a clear division into two camps. On one hand, there are those who argue that PTAs, especially those of the "new generation," constitute a dangerous threat to the system.[3] On the other, there are those who feel that such concern is overstated, and that there are potential solutions to reconcile the two, provided that the political will exists.[4]

There is now also an institutional acknowledgment that PTAs should be regarded as a serious concern for the multilateral trading system. Thus, in opening the conference entitled "Multilateralizing Regionalism," held in Geneva in September 2007, WTO Director-General Pascal Lamy reflected "that it would be fair to say that proliferation [of PTAs] is breeding concern – concern about incoherence, confusion, exponential increase of costs for business, unpredictability, and even unfairness in trade relations." Yet no concrete action has been taken so far by the policy community to address this multifaceted concern.

This chapter serves as a building block in this discussion. We believe that, before embarking on a discussion as to whether (new) PTAs should be viewed with concern, one needs to examine the facts in greater detail than is typically done in the debate. Our primary purpose, therefore, is to analyze the precise content of the EC and United States preferential trade agreements. To do this, we divide the subjects covered by these agreements into two categories: WTO plus (WTO+), and WTO extra (WTO-X). The first category corresponds to those provisions of PTAs that come under the current mandate of the WTO, where the parties undertake bilateral commitments going beyond those they have accepted at the multilateral level. An example would be a reduction in tariffs. By contrast, the

---

[2] See Sapir (2007).

[3] See, in particular, Bhagwati (2008).

[4] See, for instance, Baldwin (2006).

WTO-X category comprises those PTA provisions that deal with issues lying outside the current WTO mandate. An example would be a commitment on labor standards.

At the outset it should be emphasized, however, that our aim is not to answer the question why WTO members – and in particular the EC and the United States – include WTO-X obligations in their PTAs. At one end of the spectrum, one might suppose that PTAs serve as a kind of preparation for setting tomorrow's multilateral agenda. According to this argument, assuming consistency in the subject matter across PTAs, it will be easier to interconnect them and multilateralize them in the future, or at least use their subject matter as a basis for negotiating tomorrow's WTO rules.[5] However, one could also argue that the very existence of WTO-X provisions is evidence that the preferential partners do not wish to include certain items in the WTO, and that is why they consistently maintain them in their PTAs.

The study covers all the fourteen EC and fourteen U.S. agreements with WTO partners signed by the parties and, generally, notified to the WTO as of October 2008. In order to fully map these agreements, we proceed in two steps.

The first step consists of listing all the policy areas contained in the twenty-eight agreements. For each of the fifty-two areas identified, we then record whether each agreement specifies obligations.

As a second step, we determine whether each obligation contained in the agreements is *legally enforceable*. We describe more precisely later why we believe that this is an important feature and how we evaluate whether a provision is enforceable or not. Let us simply say for the moment that the general idea is that texts that specify clear legal obligations are more likely to be implemented than highly less hard-edged ones.

In order to shed light on the validity of the claim that the EC and U.S. agreements go substantially beyond the WTO agreements, we divide the fifty-two identified policy areas into two groups as already indicated. The first, labeled WTO+, contains fourteen areas, whereas the second, labeled WTO-X, contains thirty-eight areas.

Applying the WTO+/WTO-X distinction to the EC and the U.S. sets of agreements, our main findings are as follows.

First, we observe that although both sets cover both WTO+ and WTO-X types of provisions, the fourteen EC agreements contain almost four times as many instances of WTO-X provisions as the fourteen U.S. agreements do. This would suggest that EC PTAs extend much more frequently beyond the WTO agreements than U.S. PTAs.

However, second, the picture changes dramatically once the nature of the obligations is taken into account. The EC agreements evidence a very significant amount of "legal inflation," in particular in the parts dealing with development

---

[5] This view can be found, for instance, in Baldwin (2006).

policy. U.S. agreements actually prove to contain more legally enforceable WTO-X provisions than the EC agreements. Hence the latter contain many obligations that have no legal standing.

Third, we also find that both the EC and the U.S. PTAs contain a significant number of legally enforceable, substantive undertakings in WTO+ areas. Fewer obligations contained in EC agreements tend to be enforceable than those of U.S. agreements, but the difference is not as pronounced as for the WTO-X areas.

Finally, we find that there is a difference in the nature of the legally enforceable obligations contained in EC and U.S. agreements, with the latter putting more emphasis on regulatory areas.

The plan of the remainder of the chapter is as follows. Section 2 deals with methodological issues related to the agreements being studied, the classification of policies into either WTO+ or WTO-X areas, and the definition of legally enforceable obligations. Section 3 presents our initial findings concerning the coverage, the legal enforceability, and the depth of obligations for WTO+ areas. Section 4 contains similar findings for WTO-X areas. These two sections prepare the ground for Section 5, which contains our main analyses. Section 6 briefly summarizes the results.

2.   Methodological Issues

The purpose of this section is to describe the set of PTAs under study, to set out how we classify the coverage of these agreements, and to explain how we evaluate whether a covered policy contains legally enforceable obligations.

2.1. PTAs and the WTO

According to WTO rules, members may enter with other WTO members into PTAs either concerning trade in goods, or trade in services, or both. With respect to trade in goods, WTO members that satisfy the requirements included in Article XXIV GATT can legally treat products originating in some WTO member countries (those with which they have formed a PTA) more favorably than like products originating in the other WTO member countries. Article XXIV GATT distinguishes between two forms of PTA: FTAs and CUs. For an FTA to be GATT consistent, its members must liberalize trade between them; for a CU to be GATT consistent, its members must, beyond liberalizing trade between them, agree on a common trade policy vis-à-vis the rest of the WTO membership. All the PTAs that will be considered here are FTAs, with the exception of the EC–Turkey agreement, which is a CU.

In the WTO, it is also possible to form PTAs under a separate legal instrument – the Enabling Clause. However, because this possibility is only available where all members of the PTA are developing countries, such agreements are not relevant to this study.

The specific conditions for satisfying consistency with the multilateral rules concerning goods trade are laid down in Article XXIV.5–8 of GATT. Apart from requesting the PTA to encompass substantially all trade between its members, and not to raise the overall level of protection vis-à-vis the rest of the WTO membership, these provisions oblige WTO members wishing to enter into a PTA to show that they have complied with the relevant multilateral rules.

With respect to trade in services, Article V of the General Agreement on Trade in Services (GATS) mentions only one form of preferential scheme entitled economic integration. It is akin to a GATT FTA because its members are entitled to retain their own trade policies vis-à-vis third countries, although there are also some differences between the two schemes. The disciplines of economic integration echo those preferential schemes that apply to trade in goods: Article V.1 of GATS requires that a PTA has substantial sectoral coverage, and Article V.4 of GATS requires PTA members not to raise the overall level of barriers against non-participants.

2.2. The Agreements under Study

Table 5.1 lists the set of agreements that are scrutinized in this study, which consists of all PTAs signed between the EC and the United States, respectively, and other WTO members as of October 2008. The list includes agreements signed before and after the creation of the WTO but excludes those where the partner is not a WTO member. It also includes agreements signed by the parties but not yet ratified, and therefore not yet notified to the WTO or actually in force. Of the twenty-eight listed agreements, fourteen are EC PTAs and fourteen are U.S. PTAs, counting the EC agreements with individual European Free Trade Association (EFTA) partners (Liechtenstein and Switzerland counting as one, owing to their economic union) and the European Economic Area agreement (between the EC and the EFTA countries, except Switzerland) as one PTA.

2.3. The Coverage of the Agreements

A basic aim of this study is to identify more precisely than has been done in the literature so far the legal obligations imposed by PTAs involving the European Union (EU) and the United States, and to compare the nature of these two sets of agreements. To this end, we have gone through the twenty-eight agreements in their entirety, and characterized the obligations that they impose. The contents of these agreements have been divided into fifty-two policy areas. This characterization is intended to be exhaustive, in the sense that all the provisions contained in the twenty-eight agreements fall under one or other of the areas, except for those that concern the administration of the agreement, which we disregard. The classification is largely based on the article headings in the case of the EC agreements, and on the chapter headings in the case of the U.S. agreements.

Table 5.1. *EC and U.S. PTAs with other WTO members, signed as of October 2008*

EC Agreements	Date of signature by parties	U.S. Agreements	Date of signature by parties
Norway	11/11/1970		
Iceland	22/07/1972		
Switzerland	22/07/1972		
EEA	02/05/1992	Israel	22/04/1985
Turkey	06/03/1995	NAFTA	17/12/1992
Tunisia	17/07/1995	Jordan	24/10/2000
Israel	20/11/1995	Singapore	06/05/2003
Morocco	26/02/1996	Chile	06/06/2003
Jordan	11/24/1997	Australia	18/05/2004
South Africa	11/10/1999	Morocco	15/06/2004
Mexico	23/03/2000	CAFTA-DR	05/08/2004
FYRoM	09/04/2001	Bahrain	14/09/2004
Egypt	25/06/2001	Peru	12/04/2006
Croatia	29/10/2001	Oman	19/01/2006
Chile	18/10/2002	Colombia	22/11/2006
Albania	12/06/2006	Panama	28/06/2007
CARIFORUM	15/10/2008	South Korea	30/06/2007

Notes: The EC also has reciprocal PTAs with several non-WTO members: Algeria, Andorra, Faroe Islands, Lebanon, Overseas Countries and Territories (OTCs), the Palestinian Authority, San Marino, and Syria. The EEA was signed between the European Community and the EFTA countries, except Switzerland. Some EFTA countries later joined the European Community (now Union). The remaining EFTA countries that belong to the EEA are Iceland, Lichtenstein, and Norway. Switzerland has signed separate bilateral agreements with the European Community that also cover both trade in goods and in services. When we refer to the EEA, we will use the term loosely to cover all agreements that have been concluded between EFTA countries, including Switzerland, and the EC.
Source: World Trade Organization (WTO), European Commission (DG External Relations), and Office of the U.S. Trade Representative.

To shed light on our central issue – whether the EC and U.S. agreements provide for "more of the same" relative to the WTO agreements, or impose obligations in areas other than those already covered in the WTO agreements – we classify the fifty-two policy areas into two broad groups: WTO-plus (WTO+) and WTO-extra (WTO-X). The former is meant to include obligations relating to policy areas that are already subject to some form of commitment in the WTO agreements. The PTA can here either reconfirm existing commitments or provide for further obligations. The archetypal obligation here would be the formation of a FTA, because this would be a reduction in tariffs going beyond what is already committed to in the WTO context. Examples of other areas we have classified as WTO+ include obligations concerning SPS (sanitary and phytosanitary) measures, TBT (technical barriers to trade) measures, antidumping, state aid, and obligations covered by the GATS. We have also included those intellectual property rights provisions that address issues falling under the Trade-Related Aspects of Intellectual Property Rights (TRIPs) agreement. Finally, we have also included export taxes, although the WTO contains no precise commitment in this area. Nonetheless, WTO members could negotiate commitments on export taxes under GATT Article II, so it can be argued that a WTO instrument already exists in this area.

A WTO-X designation is, on the other hand, meant to capture an obligation in an area that is qualitatively new, relating to a policy instrument that has not previously been regulated by the WTO. For instance, there are no undertakings with regard to environmental protection in the WTO. We thus classify an environmental obligation as WTO-X. Other such clear examples are obligations concerning labor laws or movement of capital.

2.4. The Legal Enforceability of Identified Areas

To determine the impact of the EC and U.S. preferential trade agreements, it is important not only to identify the areas in which the agreements contain provisions, but also to determine the extent to which these provisions are legally enforceable. Unclearly specified undertakings, and undertakings that parties are only weakly committed to undertake, and that can be seemingly fulfilled with some token measure, are not likely to be successfully invoked by a complainant in a dispute settlement proceeding, and would presumably therefore also have little impact. To shed light on the extent to which this is an issue in practice, we have evaluated each provision in each agreement for the extent to which it specifies at least some obligation that is clearly defined, and that is likely effectively to bind the parties.

With a view to maintaining some degree of objectivity, we have classified certain terms as either implying enforceable or nonenforceable obligations. The following are some examples of terms that we interpret as creating legally enforceable obligations:

- "The parties shall allow the free movement of capital"
- "Neither party may expropriate or nationalize a covered investment"
- "If a party does not accept the technical regulation that is equivalent of its own it shall, at the request of the other party, explain the reasons"
- "By the end of (exact date) a party shall accede to the following international conventions:"
- "Neither party may impose performance requirements or enforce any commitment or undertaking, in connection with the establishment, acquisition, expansion, management, conduct, operation, or sale"
- "Each party shall not fail effectively to enforce labor (environmental) laws"

As can be seen, the word "shall" appears in many of these examples.

The following examples illustrate formulations that we define to be in the opposite category, not meeting the test of effectively binding the parties:

- "The parties shall cooperate" –It is likely to be very difficult to prove that a party has not "cooperated."

- "Dialogue shall be established" – It would require almost complete silence from the respondent for the complainant successfully to argue that no dialogue has been established.
- "Special attention shall be paid to" – How could it be verified that special attention has not been devoted to an issue?
- "Measures necessary for development and promotion of" – It is likely to be very hard for a complainant in a dispute to prove either that a measure is necessary or that it is not necessary for development.
- "Parties may conclude" – This phrase does not impose any restriction on the parties.
- "Parties shall strive (aim) to" – It would be difficult to prove absence of best endeavors.

Distinguishing the degree of legal enforceability in this way cannot be defended only from the point of view of practical experience, but also from the point of view of the principles of international law. One of the requirements in Article 2 of the Vienna Convention on the Law of Treaties for an agreement to be a treaty is that it is "governed by international law." This is normally interpreted to require the parties to intend that the agreement has legal effect under international law. The terminology of an agreement may indicate the extent to which such intent exists.

3. WTO+ Areas

This section discusses the extent to which the various WTO+ areas we have identified are covered in the twenty-eight EC and U.S. agreements, whether existing obligations are legally binding, and the extent to which they entail substantive undertakings.[6]

3.1. Coverage of WTO+ Areas

The coverage of WTO+ areas in the EC and U.S. agreements is displayed under the heading "AC" (for area covered) in, respectively, Tables 5.2 and 5.3, where a dark box indicates that a particular agreement contains an obligation in a particular area.

As can be seen, there is generally speaking a very high degree of coverage in both EC and U.S. agreements. There are three areas for which all EC and all U.S. agreements contain obligations: Industrial Products, Agricultural Products, and TRIPs. All the EC agreements also include obligations concerning Customs Administration, TBT, Antidumping, and Countervailing Measures. Most (but not all) of the U.S. agreements also cover these areas. All the U.S. agreements include obligations concerning Public Procurement and Export Taxes, and so do all but

---

[6] Section 4 will undertake a parallel analysis of WTO-X areas. Although we will discuss some findings in the respective sections, we will save the broader discussion for Section 5.

Table 5.2. *Classification of WTO+ areas in EC agreements*

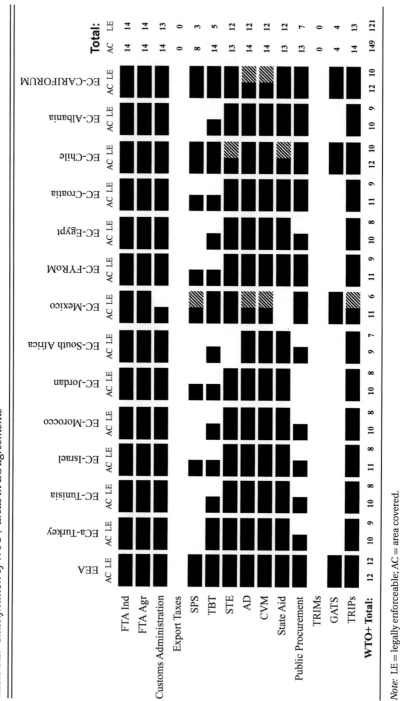

	EEA		ECa-Turkey		EC-Tunisia		EC-Israel		EC-Morocco		EC-Jordan		EC-South Africa		EC-Mexico		EC-FYRoM		EC-Egypt		EC-Croatia		EC-Chile		EC-Albania		EC-CARIFORUM		Total:	
	AC	LE	AC	LE	AC	LE	AC	LE	AC	LE	AC	LE	AC	LE	AC	LE	AC	LE	AC	LE	AC	LE	AC	LE	AC	LE	AC	LE	AC	LE
FTA Ind																													14	14
FTA Agr																													14	14
Customs Administration																													14	13
Export Taxes																													0	0
SPS																													8	3
TBT																													14	5
STE																													13	12
AD																													14	12
CVM																													14	12
State Aid																													13	12
Public Procurement																													13	7
TRIMs																													0	0
GATS																													4	4
TRIPs																													14	13
WTO+ Total:	12	12	10	9	10	8	11	8	10	8	10	8	9	7	11	6	11	9	10	8	11	9	12	10	10	9	12	10	149	121

Note: LE = legally enforceable; AC = area covered.

158

Table 5.3. *Classification of WTO+ areas in U.S. agreements*

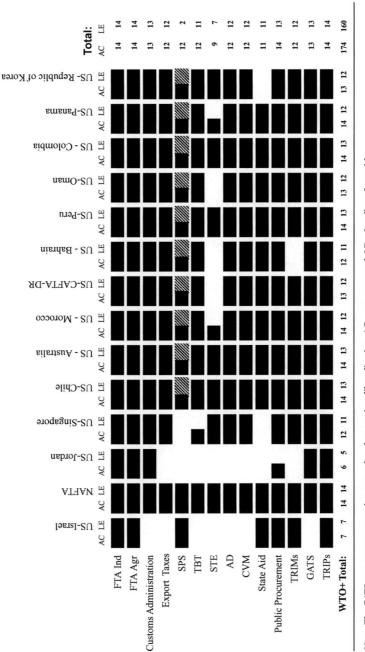

Note: The GATS area covers commitments related to services liberalization. AC = area covered; LE = legally enforceable.

159

one or two of the EC agreements. Also, most EC and U.S. agreements include provisions concerning State Trading Enterprises and State Aid. There is thus a fairly high degree of similarity between the two sets of agreements when it comes to the coverage of WTO+ areas. Both contain obligations in more or less the same areas.

There are, however, a few important differences between the two sets of agreements in terms of coverage. First, GATS obligations are included in all U.S. agreements, but only in four EC ones. Second, most U.S. agreements include Trade Related Investment Measures (TRIMs) obligations, whereas none of the EC ones has anything explicit on this.[7]

3.2. The Enforceability of WTO+ Obligations

So far we have discussed the areas that appear in the two sets of agreements. We next seek to identify those obligations that are legally enforceable. The "LE" in Tables 5.2 and 5.3 shows the areas where undertakings are legally enforceable.

A dark box indicates that the language is sufficiently precise or committing to provide a legally enforceable obligation. A cross-hatched box indicates that the language is sufficiently precise or committing but that it is nonenforceable because of an explicit statement that dispute settlement is not available.

Let us start by pointing to the areas that are exempt from dispute settlement. As can be seen, the EC agreement with Mexico has four such exemptions, for SPS, Antidumping, Countervailing Measures, and TRIPs; the EC agreement with CARIFORUM has exemptions for the latter two areas, and the EC–Chile agreement has exemptions for State Trading Enterprises and State Aid. The U.S. agreements contain exemptions from dispute settlement only in the context of SPS, but they do so for ten agreements, allowing dispute settlement regarding SPS measures only in the agreement with Israel and in NAFTA.

In areas that are nonenforceable as a result of imprecise language, we note that, with respect to the EC agreements, in seven of the fourteen agreements Public Procurement undertakings are not enforceable; in nine out of the fourteen agreements TBT undertakings are not enforceable; and in ten out of twelve agreements SPS undertakings are not enforceable. The U.S. agreements, on the other hand, contain relatively speaking substantially fewer areas where legally nonenforceable language has been included, both in absolute numbers and relative to the number of covered areas.

Turning to the areas with enforceable obligations, we observe that both sets of agreements include such obligations for all their agreements with regard to tariff liberalization (FTAs) for both industrial and agricultural products, and with

---

[7] Note, however, that by reaffirming the Article III and XI GATT rights and obligations in its PTAs, the EC effectively introduces obligations with respect to the two forms of TRIMs currently sanctioned by the multilateral system, that is, export performance and local content types of investment measures.

respect to twelve out of the fourteen agreements in the areas of Customs Administration, Export Taxes, Antidumping, Countervailing Measures, State Aid, and TRIPs.

3.3. Main Observations Concerning WTO+ Undertakings

Our initial conclusions concerning the WTO+ parts of the agreements are the following:

1. Both the EC and U.S. sets of agreements have a large number of legally enforceable obligations with significant undertakings in areas covered by the current WTO mandate, such as tariff cuts in goods, Customs Administration, Export Taxes, Antidumping, Countervailing Measures, Agriculture, and TRIPs.
2. Commitments in the "new WTO areas" (GATS, TRIPs) figure prominently in both sets of agreements, although more so in U.S. PTAs as far as services are concerned.
3. The extent of the overlap between the two sets of agreements notwithstanding, we still observe some notable differences: the U.S. agreements have substantial, legally enforceable obligations concerning TRIMS, TBT, and GATS, whereas the EC agreements contain significantly more obligations of this kind concerning State Trading Enterprises.
4. Both sets of agreements opt for staged tariff liberalization with respect to both industrial and farm goods. Still, it is very difficult to pronounce on their consistency with the WTO rules in light of the confusion surrounding the meaning of the terms appearing in GATT Article XXIV, and the lack of practice regarding the interpretation of GATS Article V.[8]

4. WTO-X Areas

We now turn our attention to the WTO-X areas, which refer to provisions regarding commitments in policy areas not covered by the current mandate of the WTO.

4.1. The Coverage of WTO-X Areas

Tables 5.4 and 5.5 provide information about the coverage of the two sets of agreements for WTO-X areas.

We will start by describing the overlap between the two sets of agreements and then revert to the differences among them. We should note at the outset, however, that the two sets of agreements differ significantly in their WTO-X subject matter. Four areas – Environment, Intellectual Property, Investment,

---

[8] See Mavroidis (2007).

Table 5.4. *WTO-X areas covered in EC Agreements*

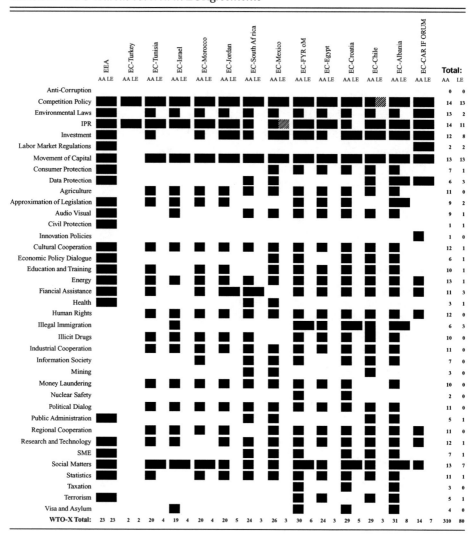

Area	Total AA	Total LE
Anti-Corruption	0	0
Competition Policy	14	13
Environmental Laws	13	2
IPR	14	11
Investment	12	8
Labor Market Regulations	2	2
Movement of Capital	13	13
Consumer Protection	7	1
Data Protection	6	3
Agriculture	11	0
Approximation of Legislation	9	2
Audio Visual	9	1
Civil Protection	1	1
Innovation Policies	1	0
Cultural Cooperation	12	1
Economic Policy Dialogue	6	1
Education and Training	10	1
Energy	13	1
Fiancial Assistance	11	3
Health	3	1
Human Rights	12	0
Illegal Immigration	6	3
Illicit Drugs	10	0
Industrial Cooperation	11	0
Information Society	7	0
Mining	3	0
Money Laundering	10	0
Nuclear Safety	2	0
Political Dialog	11	0
Public Administration	5	1
Regional Cooperation	11	0
Research and Technology	12	1
SME	7	1
Social Matters	13	7
Statistics	11	1
Taxation	3	0
Terrorism	5	1
Visa and Asylum	4	0
WTO-X Total:	**310**	**80**

WTO-X Total by agreement: EEA 23 23; EC-Turkey 2 2; EC-Tunisia 20 4; EC-Israel 19 4; EC-Morocco 20 4; EC-Jordan 20 5; EC-South Africa 24 3; EC-Mexico 26 3; EC-FYR oM 30 6; EC-Egypt 24 3; EC-Croatia 29 5; EC-Chile 29 3; EC-Albania 31 8; EC-CARIFORUM 14 7.

Note: LE = legally enforceable.

and Movement of Capital – appear in both sets of agreements; twelve of the fourteen EC agreements include commitments in these areas, and so do eleven of the fourteen U.S. agreements. There is also some overlap with regard to Competition: all EC agreements include such a commitment, whereas seven of the U.S. agreements also do.

U.S. agreements typically also include commitments in two additional areas: Labor Market Regulation, an item that has been included in thirteen U.S. agreements, and Anti-Corruption, where the corresponding number is ten.

Table 5.5. *WTO-X areas covered in U.S. Agreements*

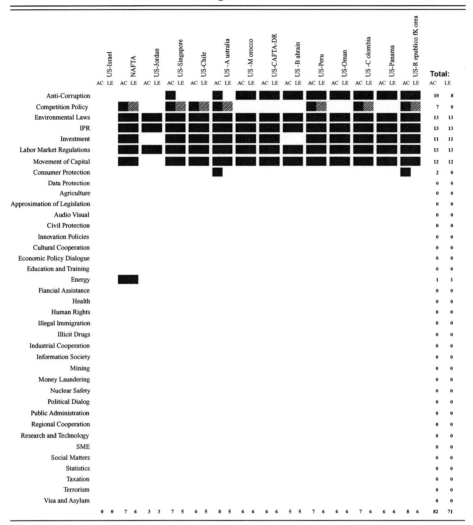

Note: AC = area covered; LE = legally enforceable.

Besides these areas, U.S. agreements contain commitments in two additional WTO-X areas – Data Protection, which has been included in two agreements, and Energy, which has been included in one.

All of the thirty-eight WTO-X areas – except Anti-Corruption – are covered in at least one of the fourteen EC agreements. Of the fourteen agreements, ten include provisions concerning Agriculture,[9] Cultural Cooperation, Education and Training, Energy, Financial Assistance, Human Rights, Illicit Drugs, Industrial Cooperation, Money Laundering, Political Dialogue, Regional Cooperation,

[9] We refer to commitments that lie outside the current WTO mandate.

Research and Technology, Social Matters, and Statistics. The only agreement that stands out in terms of coverage is the one with Turkey, which contains commitments in only two areas: Competition and Intellectual Property Rights.

4.2. The Enforceability of WTO-X Obligations

Although the EC agreements contain a larger number of WTO-X areas, it is the U.S. agreements that contain the (proportionately speaking) higher number of legally enforceable obligations in these areas.

The U.S. agreements contain few areas with nonenforceable provisions:

1. The main source of nonenforceability is the exemption of Competition-related disciplines from dispute settlement (illustrated by a cross-hatched box under the heading "LE" in Table 5.2); all seven agreements that include a Competition provision explicitly exclude the commitments from dispute settlement.
2. There are four further instances of nonenforceability: two regarding Anti-Corruption and two concerning Consumer Protection. In total, only 13 percent (eleven out of eighty-two) of the covered provisions are deemed to be nonenforceable.

By contrast, nearly 75 percent (230 out of 310) of the provisions included in the EC agreements are nonenforceable. The EC agreements contain enforceable obligations in only five WTO-X areas in a significant number of agreements:

1. Competition (in thirteen out of the fourteen agreements that contain commitments in this area);
2. Intellectual Property Right (IPR; eleven out of fourteen);
3. Movement of Capital (thirteen out of thirteen);
4. Investment (eight out of twelve); and
5. Social Matters (seven out of thirteen).

For each of the remaining thirty-three areas, there are no legally enforceable obligations in more than three agreements signed by the EC. Most obligations are not enforceable at all. One agreement represents an outlier, the European Economic Area (EEA), an agreement that involves the EC and some of its Western European trading partners with whom there is a long tradition of multilevel cooperation.

4.3. Main Observations Concerning WTO-X Undertakings

Our initial conclusions concerning the WTO-X parts of the agreements are as follows:

1. Whereas the U.S. agreements typically contain few areas where enforceable obligations have been agreed, the EC agreements contain a smaller (proportional to the overall) number of areas with enforceable obligations, and a

much larger number of areas where exhortatory language has been agreed. It thus seems that, whereas the United States has adopted a rather "functionalist" approach (ensuring legal enforceability of the selected areas), the EC has opted for "legal inflation," whereby a large number of areas are included in the agreement, but very few of them are coupled with legally enforceable obligations.

2. Altogether, only eight of the thirty-eight WTO-X areas involve legally enforceable obligations in a significant number of agreements.
3. Three of these eight areas concern both EC and U.S. agreements: Intellectual Property Rights, Investment, and Movement of Capital.
4. Three areas concern mostly or solely U.S. agreements: Anti-Corruption, Environment, and Labor.
5. Two areas involve EC agreements only: Competition and Social Matters.
6. Finally, provisions concerning Terrorism, Illegal Immigration, Visa and Migration, and Illicit Drugs appear in some of the EC agreements (in five, six, three, and ten agreements, respectively), but typically the obligations are not enforceable. Contrary to what may have been expected, these national security-related areas are not present in U.S. agreements.

5. PTAs and the WTO – More of the Same or Ventures into New Areas?

A central issue in the policy debate concerning PTAs has been whether they support or hinder multilateral trade liberalization. This issue has received a new twist during the past decade, because of the common claim that these agreements are no longer about deeper integration in areas where the multilateral system already provides a degree of integration but are instead mainly to be seen as ventures into new policy areas. Having so far analyzed the WTO+ and the WTO-X areas separately, in this section we will discuss the balance in the EC and U.S. PTAs between the WTO+ and the WTO-X areas. Our purpose is to distill an overall picture of where the *center of gravity* of these agreements lies. Are they essentially about further integration along the same lines as in the GATT/WTO, or are they mainly about providing integration in new policy areas? As before, we will put particular emphasis on the extent to which identified obligations are likely to be legally enforceable, and we will seek to characterize the areas where legal inflation is most pervasive, and also whether it is likely to be an intentional feature of certain areas.

5.1. Differences in Coverage of EC and U.S. PTAs

To detect the center of gravity of the EC and U.S. agreements in terms of coverage, Figure 5.1 plots the number of covered WTO+ areas (measured on the vertical axis) against the number of covered WTO-X areas (measured on the

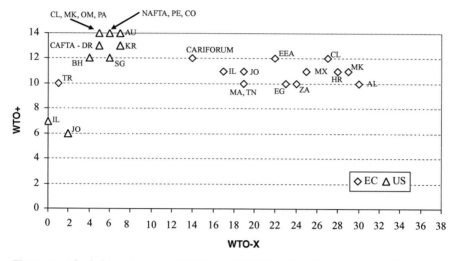

Figure 5.1. The balance between WTO+ and WTO-X undertakings in terms of coverage. *Source:* Author's calculations based on Table 3.1, Table 3.2, Table 4.1, and Table 4.2.

horizontal axis) for each of the twenty-eight agreements. As can be seen, a very pronounced pattern emerges: all the EC agreements (with one exception) are positioned to the southeast of the U.S. agreements. That is, *in terms of coverage, the EC agreements have more WTO-X and fewer WTO+ areas than the U.S. agreements.* Hence, while both the EC and the U.S. agreements cover a large proportion of WTO+ areas (between ten and twelve for the EC and between twelve and fourteen for the United States, out of a maximum of fourteen), the EC PTAs cover a much greater proportion of WTO-X areas (reaching around thirty in recent agreements, out of a maximum of thirty-eight) than U.S. agreements (with fewer than ten areas covered, even in the most recent agreements).

5.2. Center of Gravity of EC and U.S. PTAs Adjusted for Legal Enforceability

Discarding nonenforceable obligations, the picture that emerged earlier changes dramatically. As shown in Figure 5.2, although the number of WTO+ areas remains slightly larger for U.S. agreements (ranging between eleven and thirteen) compared to EC agreements (ranging between eight and ten), the number of WTO-X areas with legally enforceable provisions is now slightly higher for U.S. (ranging between five and six) than for EC (ranging mostly between three and five) agreements.[10] The EC agreements thus evidence a very considerable degree of "legal inflation" in WTO-X areas, a phenomenon that is much less

[10] One agreement stands out in each set: the EEA agreement on the EC side, with twenty-three legally binding provisions, and the U.S.–Israel agreement, with zero.

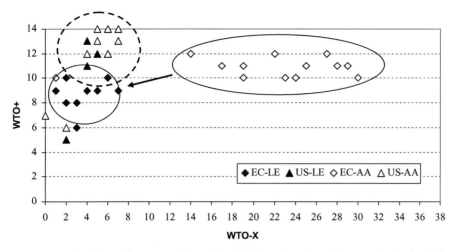

Figure 5.2. The balance between WTO+ and WTO-X undertakings, discounting for the lack of legal enforceability. *Source:* Author's calculations based on Table 2.1, Table 3.1, Table 3.2, Table 4.1, and Table 4.2. *Note:* LE=legally enforceable; AC=areas covered.

prevalent in the EC agreements for WTO+ areas or in the WTO+ and WTO-X areas of the U.S. PTAs.

It should be noted that the two latest EC agreements, with Albania and the CARIFORUM, contain slightly more legally enforceable WTO-X provisions than do the U.S. agreements. In this respect, the EC–CARIFORUM agreement resembles more the U.S. PTAs than any other EC PTA: it covers relatively few WTO-X areas, of which many contain legally enforceable provisions.[11] Still, only half of the fourteen WTO-X areas that are covered contain enforceable obligations. And the EC–Albania agreement, while having eight areas with enforceable obligations, features the same degree of legal inflation – twenty-three out of the thirty-one areas in the EC–Albania agreement are classified as nonenforceable – as the other EC agreements.

5.3. In Which Areas Is Legal Inflation Most Pervasive?

Table 5.6 somewhat reorganizes the data on coverage and legally enforce-ability in order to highlight the type of areas where legal inflation is most per-vasive. The table divides all areas (i.e., both WTO+ and WTO-X areas) into five broad groups, along different lines than the WTO+/WTO-X distinction, which was designed to capture the nature of each area relative to the WTO agree-ments. In Table 5.6 the intention is instead to capture the content of each area

---

[11] The EC–Albania PTA is a more traditional EC agreement in this respect: it covers thirty-one WTO-X areas, of which only eight contain legally binding provisions.

Table 5.6. *Legal inflation by groups of areas*

	EU PTAs			U.S. PTAs		
	AC	LE	Legal Inflation	AC	LE	Legal Inflation
1. Trade- and Investment-related Obligations	107	98	8%	113	113	0%
2. GATS/TRIPs/IPR	32	28	13%	40	40	0%
3. Migration-related Regulations	23	10	57%	–	–	–
4. Domestic Trade-related Regulations	104	60	42%	103	78	24%
Total Trade and Regulations:	**266**	**196**	**26%**	**256**	**231**	**10%**
5. Other	206	17	92%	1	1	0%
Total all areas:	**472**	**213**	**55%**	**257**	**232**	**10%**

Note: AC = area covered; LE = legally enforceable.

in terms of policy objectives or instruments. Group 1, trade- and investment-related obligations, is meant to capture obligations that address policy instruments affecting goods trade and investment, and that are applied at the border. Group 2, GATS/TRIPs/IPR, and Group 3, migration-related regulations, are self-explanatory. Group 4, domestic trade-related regulations, is intended to include obligations concerning domestic (behind-the-border) regulations. Finally, Group 5, labeled "Other," includes all remaining areas and mainly contains development-related provisions from EC agreements. Although this grouping of areas is heuristic, we believe that it is informative in that it reflects sharp differences in legal inflation across groups as the discussion next indicates.

Table 5.6 gives, group by group, the number of times each legal inflation within the group occurs in EU or U.S. agreements; it then gives, group by group, the number of instances each area within that group occurs with enforceable obligations. In addition, it calculates an index of legal inflation, which is defined as the number of instances of legally nonenforceable obligations in a group of areas relative to the total number of times that group of areas occurs.

There are two main findings that emerge from the table. First, and once again, there is a striking difference between the EC and the U.S. agreements. Taking all areas together, the inflation rate is 55 percent for the EC PTAs compared to only 10 percent for the U.S. agreements. Second, there are significant differences across areas. Distinguishing between the Trade and Regulations areas (i.e., Groups 1–4) on the one hand and "Other" areas on the other hand, one observes a second striking difference. For the EC the inflation rate is only 26 percent in the former grouping as opposed to 92 percent in the latter. Moreover, the difference in inflation rates between the EC and the United States is much less for Trade and Regulations (26 percent versus 10 percent) than it is for the total of all areas.

We now detail these differences across the five groups. As can be seen from the table, there are clearly systematic differences in the extent of legal inflation in the different groups. At one end we have the trade and investment group, which displays literally zero legal inflation for the U.S. agreements, and only

9 percent for the EC agreements, with most of the latter explained by obligations in the WTO-X investment area. Furthermore, not only is there little or no inflation, these areas are also covered in almost all agreements of both the EC and the United States (with the exception of Export Taxes, and TRIMs in EC agreements), and they very often involve substantial undertakings. The GATS/TRIPs/IPR group displays a very similar pattern.

At the other end of the spectrum in terms of legal inflation is the "Other" group, which largely consists of development-related undertakings appearing in the cooperation parts of the EC agreements. The U.S. agreements effectively have no instances of this group of areas, and are therefore irrelevant here. For this group, which contains a large number of areas that are covered in a large number of EC agreements, the legal inflation rate is 92 percent! This average is higher than the inflation rate for any of the other groups, and is even higher than each individual area in all other groups, with the exception of two areas: the Visa, Border Control, and Asylum area, and the Human Rights area. Based on this observation, we would argue that, to the extent that these agreements promote development, it is not because of the enforceability of their legal commitments.

Provisions related to domestic regulations, in the broad sense of the term, can be found in both WTO+ and WTO-X areas. In the group domestic trade-related regulations we have tried to distinguish regulations that have more obvious potential to be used as legal arguments in a trade dispute from those that do not seem to have such potential. It is for this reason that, for instance, Labor and Environment areas are grouped together with the SPS and TBT areas, while areas such as Nuclear Safety and Money Laundering – which can also be said to address domestic regulation – are kept under the "Other" label. It is also for this reason that the Environment and Labor areas are classified as potentially affecting trade.

Turning to the numbers, we see that this group reveals a more complicated pattern than the other groups. However, there is a significant difference in legal inflation in the group for the EC and the U.S. agreements, with 42 percent of the areas covered in EC agreements being nonenforceable, compared to only 24 percent for the United States.

An issue of particular interest with regard to EC and U.S. PTAs is the extent to which they can be seen as a means of transferring the regulatory regimes of the EC and the United States to other countries. The scattered pattern that emerges for this group makes it difficult to draw unambiguous conclusions in this regard, and may also indicate that the groups need to be redefined to answer this question properly. However, it is noteworthy that in almost all the areas in this group, the PTAs extend either international or EU/U.S. domestic regulatory standards to partner countries. Because the EU and the United States already broadly meet the international or domestic regulatory standards contained in the PTAs, these agreements could indeed potentially be vehicles for transferring regulatory rules of the EC and the United States to their PTA partners. One might imagine various ways in which such a transfer occurs. For instance, the formation of the PTAs may affect domestic policy discussions concerning the choice of regulatory regime. However, for these agreements to affect such a transfer by legally binding the partner countries to a hub's regulatory regime, they must contain enforceable provisions. As we have seen, the picture seems to be mixed in this regard.

5.4. Closing Remarks

The general picture that emerges from comparing the undertakings in the WTO+ and WTO-X areas for the two sets of PTAs is the following:

1. The EC agreements go much further than the U.S. agreements in covering areas outside the scope of the WTO agreements. There has also been an increasing tendency to this effect.
2. When adjusting for nonenforceable language, one observes significant "legal inflation" in non-WTO parts of the EC agreements. In fact, the EC agreements are similar to the U.S. agreements in that much of the emphasis of enforceable language is on existing WTO areas.
3. Both EC and U.S. PTAs contain non-WTO areas with substantial undertakings. An important aspect of both sets of agreements is thus that they combine substantial undertakings in WTO areas and in non-WTO areas.
4. A significant proportion of the substantial, legally enforceable obligations are in areas where domestic or international regulations are important, but the specific regulatory areas differ for the two hubs.

6. Conclusion

There is growing concern about preferential trading agreements and the role they should play in the multilateral trading system. Not only are they becoming increasingly prevalent, there is also a perception that many recent PTAs, especially those centered on the EC and the United States, go far beyond the scope of the current WTO agreements.

With a view to shedding light on whether the previous perception corresponds to reality, this study has assessed in some detail all the PTAs signed by the EC or the United States and other WTO members by dividing all the areas they include into two categories: WTO+ obligations, which are areas already covered by the present WTO agreements, and WTO-X obligations, which are areas currently falling outside these agreements.

Our examination of the two sets of PTAs yields two main findings.

First, both EC and U.S. agreements contain a significant number of WTO+ and WTO-X obligations. However, EC agreements go much further in terms of WTO-X coverage than U.S. agreements. When discounting for "legal inflation" the picture remains largely the same for U.S. agreements, but it changes dramatically for EC agreements. Adjusting for "legal inflation," U.S. agreements actually contain more legally binding provisions, both in WTO+ and WTO-X areas, than EC agreements.

It is thus clear that the EU and the United States have chosen markedly different strategies for including provisions in their PTAs that go beyond the WTO agreements. In particular, EC agreements display a fair deal of "legal inflation," a phenomenon almost totally absent in U.S. agreements. The study does not permit us to draw precise conclusions about this asymmetry of behavior between the EU and the United States, but the fact that much of the "legal inflation" occurs in development-related provisions, which are unique to the EC agreements, suggests that the EU has a greater need than the United States to portray its PTAs as not driven solely by commercial interests. Our feeling is that this may reflect a lack of consensus on the part of EU member-states about the ultimate purpose of these PTAs, the wide variety of provisions of weak legal value representing a compromise between various interests among EU members.

Second, although EC and U.S. preferential trade agreements do go significantly beyond the WTO agreements, the number of legally enforceable WTO-X provisions contained in EC and U.S. PTAs is still in fact quite small. Provisions that can be regarded as really breaking new ground compared to existing WTO agreements are few and far between: environment and labor standards for U.S. agreements, and competition policy for EC agreements. These provisions clearly all deal with regulatory issues. The other enforceable WTO-X provisions found in EC and U.S. PTAs concern domains that more or less relate to existing WTO agreements, such as investment, capital movement, and intellectual property, which also concern regulatory matters.

The fact that the new, legally enforceable WTO-X provisions all deal with regulatory issues suggests that EC and U.S. agreements effectively serve as a means for the two hubs to export their own regulatory approaches to their PTA partners. The study does not permit us to draw conclusions about the respective costs and benefits of this situation for the hubs and the spokes, but our feeling is that it serves primarily the interests of the two "regulators of the world." This feeling is based on the fact that the legally enforceable WTO-X provisions included in EC and U.S. agreements have all been the subject of earlier, but failed, attempts by the EU and/or the United States to incorporate them in WTO rules, against the wishes of developing countries. To the extent that our conclusion is correct, it supports the view expressed inter alia by WTO Director-General Pascal Lamy that PTAs might be breeding concern about unfairness in trade relations.

What the implications of our findings are for the "regionalism versus multilateralism" issue is beyond the scope of this chapter. However, what is clear is that a serious discussion of this matter needs to start from a detailed assessment of the nature of EC and U.S. PTAs, including the findings reported in this study.

REFERENCES

Baldwin, R. E., 2006. Multilateralising Regionalism, Spaghetti Bowls as Building Blocks on the Path to Global Free Trade, *World Economy*, 29: 1451–518.

Bartels L., 2008. *Social Issues: Labor, Environment and Human Rights, in Bilateral and Regional Trade Agreements: Commentary, Analysis and Case Studies*, ed. by Simon Lester and Bryan Mercurio, Cambridge: Cambridge University Press.

Bhagwati, 2008. *Terminates in the Trade System: How Preferential Agreements Undermine Free Trade*, Oxford: Oxford University Press.

Bourgeois, J., K. Dawar and S. J. Evenett, 2007. *A Comparative Analysis of Selected Provisions in Free Trade Agreements, Study commissioned by DG Trade*, Brussels: European Commission, mimeo.

Cordonier Segger J. M., 2007. *Sustainable Development in RTAs, in Regional Trade Agreements and the WTO Legal System*, ed. by Bartels L. and Ortino H., Oxford: Oxford University Press.

Dawar K., 2008. Assessing Labour and Environmental Regimes in Regional Trading Arrangements, Society of International Economic Law (SIEL), Inaugural Conference, Working Paper No. 55/08.

Desta M. and N. Barnes, 2007. Competition Law in Regional Trade Agreements: An Overview, in *Regional Trade Agreements and the WTO Legal System*, ed. by Bartels L. and Ortino H., Oxford: Oxford University Press.

Elliott, K. A., 2006. Labor Standards, in Trade Relations Between Colombia And the United States, ed. by J.J. Schott, *Policy Analysis in International Economics*, no. 79/2006, Washington, DC: Peterson Institute for International Economics.

Krajewski, M., 2007. Services liberalization in RTAs: Lessons for GATS unfinished business, in *Regional Trade Agreements and the WTO Legal System*, ed. by Bartels L. and Ortino H., Oxford: Oxford University Press.

Lesser, C., 2007. Do Bilateral and Regional Approaches for Reducing Technical Barriers to Trade Converge Towards the Multilateral Trading System?, OECD Trade Policy Working Papers, No. 58.

Mavroidis, P. C., 2007. *Trade in Goods*, Oxford: Oxford University Press.

McCaffery, S., 2006. *Understanding International Law*, Newark: LexisNexis.

Mercurio, B., 2007. TRIPS-Plus provisions in FTAs: Recent Trends, in *Regional Trade Agreements and the WTO Legal System*, ed. by Bartels L. and Ortino H., Oxford: Oxford University Press.

Ortino, F., 2008. RTAs and Trade in Services, in Lester S. and Mercurio B. eds., *Bilateral and Regional Trade Agreements: Commentary, Analysis and Case Studies*, Cambridge: Cambridge University Press.

Pugatch, M.P., 2007. A Transatlantic Divide? The EU and U.S. approach to the international regulation of Intellectual Property Trade-Related Agreements, ECIPE Working Paper 02/2007.

Reuter P., 1989. *Introduction to the Law of Treaties*, London: Pinter Publishers.

Roy M., J. Marchetti, and H. Lim, 2006. Services liberalization in the New Generation of PTAs: How much further than GATS?, WTO Staff Working Paper ERSD-2006–07.

Sapir A., 2007. *Europe and the Global Economy, in Fragmented Power: Europe and the Global Economy*, ed. by Sapir A., Brussels: Bruegel.

GARY N. HORLICK

Straightening the Spaghetti Bowl

There are numerous reasons of economics, trade policy, and international relations why global/multilateral trade rules may be preferable to bilateral or plurilateral trade rules. As Jagdish Bhagwati points out, the proliferation of free trade agreements (FTAs), regional trade agreements (RTAs), and preferential trade agreements (which encompasses all of them) has created a "spaghetti bowl." In part, this is because none of those agreements (even "template" agreements signed by a large economy with numerous small economies) line up perfectly with each other. These dissimilarities seem inevitable, as each agreement represents a different set of negotiating priorities, at a different point in time, by different negotiators (it is human nature to be unable to resist tinkering with a previous negotiator's text!). As a result, these agreements create different tariff levels among different countries with different rules of origin, different phase-in periods, different marking rules, and so on. Not to mention different systems of investment protection, intellectual property protection, labor and human rights and environment provisions, and so on. Each of these differences may all have understandable bases, and even laudable ones, but the result is a system of such complexity that perhaps as much as 50 percent of all trade supposedly "freed" by these agreements ignores the benefits in favor of the certainty of MFN – usually WTO – tariffs.

This is not a theoretical problem, but rather a distinctly real-world one. Let us imagine that a client calls me to ask me what the rule of origin is for a laptop computer under the U.S.–Morocco FTA. I will further assume that I know the rules of origin under NAFTA very well, and I know that the U.S.–Morocco FTA follows the NAFTA rules of origin very closely. If I know that the U.S.–Morocco FTA rules of origin are identical to the NAFTA rules of origin, I could answer the client's question immediately, and would not bother charging her for that

The views expressed herein are the sole responsibility of the author. He gratefully acknowledges assistance from two anonymous reviewers.

service. However, I know that three or four changes were made to the NAFTA rules of origin in each of the succeeding FTAs negotiated by the United States. That means I cannot answer the client's question immediately, but must tell her that I have to research it to make sure that I am giving her the right answer. At that point, I have to charge her for my services. This creates inefficiency and dead-weight loss, not to mention a sense of irritation in large companies about government's inability to do things right. There are undoubtedly good lobbyist reasons why a rule of origin was changed in a new FTA, but no one counts the cost of doing so. Worse, there is to date no simplified computerized search mechanism that lets me easily compare the rules of origin in all U.S. FTAs, much less all preferential agreements around the world, so the research is not always easy. And the cost is multiplied when comparing different services commitments, investment regimes, and so on among the world's preferential agreements.

Thus, here are three obvious suggestions to start straightening out the spaghetti bowl (assuming that in the short term it will be impossible to restrain politicians' lust to negotiate these deals):

1. We should standardize rules of origin for goods (which would be aided immensely by a WTO agreement, now long overdue).
2. We should create a common computerized format for tariff schedules, rules of origin, and services schedules.
3. More adventurously, we should create or attempt to re-create standardized investment agreements (with standardized options), as well as other provisions for FTAs.
4. I realize I only said "three suggestions," but a lot of this could be solved by multilateral agreements.

5.1 Comments on "Beyond the WTO? Coverage and Legal Inflation in EU and U.S. Preferential Trade Agreements"

According to the WTO, in July 2007 there were about 205 preferential trade agreements (PTAs) in force and by 2010 no fewer than 400 PTAs are expected to be implemented. This wave of PTAs, which started in the 1990s, is unprecedented both in terms of the number of countries and the breadth of issues they cover. Therefore it is imperative to get the basic facts about these agreements straight before we draw normative conclusions and make any detailed policy prescriptions. The paper by Horn, Mavroidis, and Sapir provides an excellent first step in this direction. The authors provide a careful and systematic classification of the policy areas covered by the reciprocal PTAs of the United States and European Union (EU) as well as the extent of their legal enforceability.

The areas are usefully divided into ones that are covered in some way in the WTO (WTO+) and those that are currently excluded from it (WTO-X). The main findings are the following. First, the obligations in WTO+ areas contained in these PTAs are often similar to the obligations in the WTO itself. Second, there are thirty-eight distinct WTO-X areas but only about eight appear to be legally enforceable. These are typically related to Intellectual Property, Investment, and Movement of Capital (both in U.S. and EU PTAs); Competition and Social Matters (EU); and Anti-Corruption, Environment, and Labor (U.S.). Third, EU agreements include more WTO-X areas than the United States but the authors argue that most of these are not legally enforceable (the authors name this phenomenon "legal inflation").

The paper provides an exhaustive classification of important features of PTAs that have taken years for large research institutions to compile, with some of them still in the middle of such a process, so this paper will prove to be a useful resource. Moreover, the voluminous information from the agreements is presented in an intelligible and intelligent way. I learned a number of interesting facts and also gained insight on how to classify the legal enforceability of an issue. Given how unexplored this topic still is, there are many directions for further research and that will be the main focus of my comments.

This area of research has the potential to uncover the areas where PTAs can have truly large welfare effects. Traditional trade gains for PTA members are difficult to quantify because it is well known that PTAs may have negative effects, for example, trade diversion toward costlier exports of a PTA partner just because it faces no tariff. Moreover, it is often difficult to generate large benefits from trade creation (at least in static models) and yet we see a huge proliferation of these agreements. Partly this could be accounted for by political economy reasons; a PTA allows an exporter to receive protection in the partner's market. However, it may also be due to benefits arising from all the nontrade areas that recent PTAs cover. It would therefore be useful to point out explicitly that an important motivation for studying such PTAs is that they can (i) improve cooperation on nontrade issues with cross-border spillovers (immigration, environment, terrorism, etc.), which may be difficult to enforce in a separate agreement (Limão, 2007) and/or (ii) provide a commitment mechanism for small countries seeking reform (on labor, competition, etc.).

In terms of the scope of the agreements covered in the paper, I found it a good idea to start with the United States and EU given their size in world trade, the fact that they are the hubs of many PTAs and also the source of much market regulation and of templates for agreements. In the future it would be interesting to analyze other countries, but prior to that I would suggest extending the scope to additional types of preferences provided by these two countries.

The authors focus on *reciprocal* PTAs under Article XXIV by the United States and EU, but these countries participate in other preferential agreements. For example, why not also analyze (i) EU accessions; (ii) EU preferences to former colonies (the African, Caribbean and Pacific Group of States [ACP] agreements previously granted under an MFN waiver); (iii) U.S. preferences to Andean, African, and Caribbean countries (under a MFN waiver); and (iv) the U.S. and EU Generalized System of Preferences (GSP), which that applies to many developing countries (under the Enabling Clause)?

Broadening the scope as suggested earlier is important for this line of research for two reasons. First, because the authors use a count to measure the importance of different types of areas, we must know what the number of relevant agreements is. Second, the omitted set of agreements is more likely to contain WTO-X areas and thus omitting those biases the results against these areas. For example, the title of the act containing the U.S. preferences to Colombia, Peru, Bolivia, and Ecuador is the "Andean Trade Promotion *and Drug Eradication Act.*" This and other WTO-X motives are also central in the U.S. preferences to Caribbean countries. More broadly, Jackson (1997) states that developed countries "often use...the [GSP] preference systems as part of "bargaining chips" of diplomacy" (p. 160).

There is another important motive to include unilateral preferences in the analysis, which is that they may provide additional evidence of whether WTO-X and WTO+ areas are actually important and enforced. The GSP preferences have a long history from which we learn that some countries have lost eligibility for its preferences "because of worker rights or intellectual property concerns" as described in the U.S. GSP Handbook. A more recent example occurred in 2005 when the United States revoked Cote d'Ivoire's eligibility for preferences under the African Growth and Opportunity Act (AGOA) because of its failure to comply with the United Nations' cease-fire resolution.

One difficulty that the authors faced was how to determine what areas are actually covered by an agreement. This is currently based on the headings of articles and chapters contained in the agreements, which seems sensible given it is objective and somewhat comparable across agreements. However, this approach may miss important motives for agreements. Several WTO-X areas are contained in letters, annexes, and side agreements (e.g., NAFTA's Labor and Environmental side agreements). The preamble of agreements and their pre- or postnegotiation documents are also likely to be an important omitted source. To see how such omissions could affect the results, note for example that, according to the authors, no U.S. agreement mentions terrorism but, according to the U.S. Trade Representative, the recent wave of U.S. "free trade agreements in the Middle East carry out the recommendation in the 9/11 Commission Report" that "a comprehensive U.S. strategy to counter terrorism should include economic policies that encourage development, more open societies, and opportunities for people to improve the(ir) lives" (USTR press release on the agreement with Oman).

The potential omission bias due to the sources of classification of the areas covered has two dimensions that are relevant for the key findings of this paper. First, the omission biases us against finding that WTO-X areas are important, because these are often more sensitive and difficult to put on paper. Second, this bias is stronger for the United States because its negotiators are probably more likely not to include chapters/headings that cannot be explicitly enforced than the EU. (I have no hard evidence for the last point but suspect it could be justified by the legal background of U.S. negotiators and the emphasis the EU places on soft power.)

Collecting and classifying these data is important in and of itself. However, to really learn from it we must aggregate it. Currently this is done via simple counts and, although this is a useful first step, I would suggest considering additional measures that weight observations by their importance. For example, in addition to distinguishing between old and new agreements – as the authors already do – one could also place more weight on the new agreements that are thought to be templates and thus likely to be replicated, for example, U.S.–Chile. A more mechanical suggestion would be to consider using weighted frequencies, for example, by partner country population (?) to provide some idea of how many people are potentially affected by changes in WTO-X and WTO+ areas.

A significant way in which the authors do provide information about the relative importance of different areas in agreements is by asking if they are legally enforceable. This is a difficult question, particularly because we want to maintain comparability within and across PTAs. Nonetheless, the authors provide a reasonable approach. I question only one of the criteria used. They define articles with statements such as "The parties shall cooperate" as not being legally enforceable, but if there is a clause requiring that a party present valid reasons why "a party does not accept the technical regulation" then the area is legally enforceable. Yet proving that a party has not cooperated seems no more difficult than proving the reasons it does not accept a regulation are invalid. I am unsure if both or neither should be included as criteria for enforceability but it was not obvious to me why they should be in opposite categories.

I would have liked to see more discussion on why we should focus only on legal enforceability. This focus is sensible from the perspective of international law and is probably the one that is easiest to quantify. However, given the absence of formal dispute settlement in some PTAs, is a "legally enforceable" clause (as defined in the paper) any more relevant than any other that is enforced by an implicit threat? This is a difficult issue but a key one for the paper, and thus it warrants at least some discussion.

One of the central motives for the interest in PTAs is that they can affect not only its members but also its nonmembers. This can happen in a variety of ways, for example, by changing the incentive of the United States and the EU to negotiate multilateral tariff negotiations. This fear that PTAs can be a stumbling block to multilateral liberalization extends back to the early 1990s. The authors' motivation is related to this fear because they aim to determine the relative importance of WTO-X versus WTO+ areas and argue this can inform us about whether the PTAs are more likely to slow multilateral liberalization. The introduction suggests that PTAs with WTO-X areas are less likely to be a stumbling block, but I do not understand why that should be so. In fact, previous theoretical work shows that X-PTAs are likely to be an important stumbling block (Limão, 2007). This occurs because even countries that are small from a trade perspective can generate a gain in nontrade issues that are important for large partners such as the United States and EU, so the latter choose to keep higher MFN tariffs to provide a preference. There is now detailed evidence for this effect for the United States (Limão, 2006) and the EU (Karacaovali and Limão, 2008).

Turning to future work, we see there are two main outstanding questions. First, the authors clearly state that their aim in this paper is not to explain why the EU and the United States include WTO-X obligations in their PTAs. However, answering this question is important if we want to evaluate the impacts of PTA on members and nonmembers. Two plausible motives why these issues have been pursued in PTAs and not the WTO are as follows.

1. The WTO-X issues generate "regional" or partner-specific spillovers. Thus, to get cooperation in them, countries want to target trade concessions, which they cannot do in the WTO because of the MFN clause.

2. The United States and EU have higher bargaining power when negotiating bilaterally than in the WTO.

However, these motives do not necessarily imply that in the future some of these issues will not be included in the WTO. This may occur because MFN tariffs in the United States and EU are very low, which drives down the preference margins they can offer.

The second outstanding question is which PTAs are indeed driven by interest in cooperation in WTO-X areas and whether the obligations in those PTAs are actually implemented. The authors' contribution is a crucial initial step in addressing this question: providing basic facts about what areas are included in PTAs and whether they are legally enforceable. Future work should expand the scope of agreements in terms of countries and areas covered as well as codify and test which provisions translate into policy adoption and changes in outcomes. Only then will we be able to provide informed prescriptions relevant for the current wave of PTAs.

REFERENCES

Jackson, John, 1997. *The World Trading System: Law and Policy of International Economic Relations*, 2nd ed. Cambridge, MA: MIT Press; xi, 441.
Karacaovali, Baybars, and Nuno Limão, 2008. "The Clash of Liberalizations: Preferential vs. Multilateral Trade Liberalization in the European Union," *Journal of International Economics*, 74(2): 299–327.
Limão, Nuno, 2007. "Are Preferential Trade Agreements with Nontrade Objectives a Stumbling Block for Multilateral Liberalization?," *Review of Economic Studies*, 74(3): 821–55.
————, 2006. "Preferential Trade Agreements as Stumbling Blocks for Multilateral Trade Liberalization: Evidence for the U.S.," *American Economic Review*, 96(3): 896–914.

6 Labor Clauses in EU Preferential Trade Agreements – An Analysis of the Cotonou Partnership Agreement

1. Introduction

Over the past fifteen years, the promotion of labor rights has moved from the periphery to the center of the European Union's (EU's) international relations agenda.[1] From relatively cautious beginnings under the European Economic Community (EEC) Treaty, a linkage has progressively evolved between, on the one hand, the EU's interconnected trade, development, and foreign policies and, on the other hand, the obligations it expects from partner countries regarding respect for human rights and observance of international labor standards. As the enlarged EU has sought to exert its growing influence as a "global actor," so this linkage has become inextricable and a feature of what the EU wishes to present as a coherent strategy designed to tilt the axis of globalization toward its "social dimension."[2]

Section 2 of this chapter outlines the main reasons for the EEC's initial caution in international relations and proceeds to identify several factors that have contributed to the emergence of a strict requirement of human rights conditionality as an "essential element" of preferential trade agreements (PTAs) and provided a basis for separate clauses reaffirming the parties' commitment to specified international labor standards. To explore the practical application of this strategy, Section 3 analyzes the most prominent example of a transformed PTA, the Cotonou Partnership Agreement (CPA), signed jointly in 2000 by the EU

The EU's Treaty of Lisbon entered into force on December 1, 2009, after submission of this chapter for publication. The most relevant treaty changes are referred to on pages 190–92.

[1] On the status of the external dimension of social policy in the early 1990s, see C. Barnard, "The External Dimension of Community Social Policy: The Ugly Duckling of External Relations," in N. Emiliou and D. O'Keeffe (eds.), *The European Union and World Trade Law* (Chichester: Wiley, 1993), 149–64.

[2] See the European Commission's Communication, *The Social Dimension of Globalization – The EU's Policy Contribution on Extending the Benefits to All*, COM (2004, 383. The Communication was published as a response to the report of the ILO's *World Commission on the Social Dimension of Globalization*, February 24, 2004: www.ilo.org/public/english/wcsdg/.

and its member-states and seventy-eight members of the African, Caribbean, and Pacific Group of States (ACP).[3] The purpose of this case study is to evaluate the substantive role of the labor clause in the CPA in the context of the integrated trade, development, human rights, and foreign policy objectives of this hugely ambitious model agreement that seeks to replace trade preferences with reciprocal regional partnerships and be fully World Trade Organization (WTO) compliant over time. Section 4 offers some concluding remarks on the effectiveness of measures such as the CPA and the potential of the next generation of regional partnership agreements as evolutionary mechanisms for integrating the economic and social dimensions of trade and development.

2. The Changing Shape of EU International Relations

The EEC was born as a "child of the [General Agreement on Tariffs and Trade] GATT"[4] with a mission to construct a regional common market based on principles of nondiscrimination and market liberalization. The rapid attainment of the European common market was a quid pro quo for exceptional arrangements that, although not intended to raise barriers to nonmembers of the EEC, permitted measures, including PTAs, that were designed to achieve "closer integration"[5] but would otherwise be irreconcilable with the Most Favored Nation (MFN) treatment obligation under the GATT.[6] Labor clauses were not a feature of this initial equation for two principal reasons. First, although the EEC was committed to the achievement of "improvements in living and working conditions"[7] through a process of harmonization of social policies in its member-states, such a development was considered to be axiomatic in the dynamic process of market construction. Hence, in the formative period of the Community, the need to maintain or extend labor standards to avoid social dumping was regarded as an internal matter to be addressed at the national level.[8] As the Community

---

[3] Decision 1/2000 of the ACP–EU Council of Ministers of July 27, 2000, OJ 2000 L195/46, effective from April 1, 2003. For the text see OJ 2000 L317/3 as rectified at OJ 2004 L385/88. The agreement was revised on June 25, 2005, in Luxembourg and rendered legally effective from July 1, 2008, Decision 2008/373/EC, OJ 2008 L129 and L132. For the revised text see ec.europa.eu/development/geographical/cotonouintro_en.cfm.

[4] See M. Cremona, "Neutrality or Discrimination? The WTO, the EU, and External Trade," in G. de Búrca and J. Scott (eds.), *The EU and the WTO: Legal and Constitutional Issues* (Oxford: Hart, 2001), 151–84 at 151.

[5] GATT Art. XXIV.   [6] Art. I GATT.

[7] EEC Art. 117 (now Art. 136 of the European Community [EC] Treaty).

[8] EEC Art. 119 (now EC Art. 141) on equal pay between men and women was an exception to this approach reflecting concern about the economic risks of divergence between national regimes. As the European Court of Justice reasoned in Case 43/75 *Defrenne v Sabena II* [1976] ECR 455, at para. 9, the primary purpose of EEC Art. 119 was "to avoid a situation in which undertakings established in States which have actually implemented the principle of equal pay suffer a competitive disadvantage in intra-Community competition as compared with undertakings established in States which have not yet eliminated discrimination against women workers as regards pay."

closely adhered to its remit under the GATT, and was mindful of the EEC Treaty's exceptional and somewhat exposed position as a permitted regional trade agreement, labor standards were not recognized as a trade issue to avoid the taint of protectionism. Neither the Yaoundé Conventions, as early PTAs with French-speaking African countries from 1964, nor the successor Lomé Conventions, with the broader ACP group of countries from 1975, contained specific labor clauses although they did have a political dimension and were designed to promote "economic, social, and cultural development."[9]

One explanation for the Community's circumspect approach lies with its limited competence under a system of strictly conferred Treaty powers. In the exercise of its legal personality,[10] the Community has always had the capacity to conclude agreements with one or more states or international organizations in areas where the Treaty so provides.[11] In the external trade sphere, the Common Commercial Policy (CCP) contains express competences for the Community to act exclusively both in the exercise of autonomous powers, such as its General System of Trade Preferences (GSP) targeted at developing countries, and when negotiating and concluding bilateral or multilateral trade agreements that fall within its ambit.[12] Exclusivity has the effect of preempting unilateral action by the member-states who are constrained by a duty of close cooperation.[13] The CCP places emphasis on uniform principles and trade liberalization aiming to contribute to "the harmonious development of world trade, the progressive abolition of restrictions on international trade, and the lowering of customs barriers."[14] It was not until the late 1970s that the European Court of Justice (ECJ) ruled that the reach of the CCP extended to aspects of development and economic policy insofar as such content in PTAs is necessary, for reasons of uniformity and effectiveness, to keep pace with shifts in global trade policy.[15] Nevertheless, the CCP is not an open-ended or general external relations policy of the Community.[16] In itself, it does not provide a firm foundation for attaching human rights or labor clauses to "pure" trade agreements.[17] The conferred

---

[9] For an overview, see L. Bartels, "The Trade and Development Policy of the European Union," in M. Cremona (ed.), *Developments in EU External Relations Law* (Oxford: OUP, 2008), 128–71.

[10] EC Art. 281.   [11] EC Art. 300(1).

[12] See, especially, EC Arts. 131 and 133. The Community has legal personality in external relations under EC Art. 281 and has powers to enter into international agreements under EC Art. 300.

[13] EC Art. 10. For analysis, see M. Cremona, "Defending the Community Interest: The Duties of Cooperation and Compliance," in M. Cremona and B. de Witte (eds.), *EU Foreign Relations Law: Constitutional Fundamentals* (Oxford: Hart, 2008), 125–69.

[14] EC Art. 131.

[15] *Opinion 1/78* (re: International Agreement on Natural Rubber) [1979] ECR 2871, paras. 44–45.

[16] See, especially, *Opinion 1/94* (re: WTO Agreement) [1996] ECR I-5267.

[17] See A. C. L. Davies, "Should the EU Have the Power to Set Minimum Standards for Collective Labour Rights in the Member-States?," in Alston P. (ed.), *Labour Rights as Human Rights* (Oxford: OUP, 2005), 177–213 at 185.

powers principle has ensured that any social dimension in an exclusive PTA between the Community and third countries negotiated as part of the CCP, or in GSP measures, must be an ancillary or secondary impulse to the primary market liberalization objective of these Treaty provisions.

Although it was, and remains, possible for the Community to enter into international agreements in areas such as social policy where it does not have express external powers, it must normally have hitherto exercised complementary internal harmonization in that field.[18] Hence, the exercise of implied external powers must be necessary for the attainment of a parallel European Community (EC; ex-EEC) Treaty objective. Social policy is, however, an area of shared competence in which the role of the EU is to support and complement the activities of the member-states in specified fields of labor law.[19] From 1987 onward, the Community has been granted extended powers to adopt binding directives laying down "minimum requirements" in these fields,[20] but this does not prevent the member-states from maintaining or introducing "more stringent protective measures" so long as they are compatible with the Treaty.[21] To meet these complementary requirements, when International Labor Organization (ILO) Convention No. 170 on the safety of chemicals at work was under discussion in 1991, falling within the specified Community field of protecting workers' health and safety,[22] the ECJ rejected arguments brought by the European Commission for an exclusive role for the Community in concluding the Convention at the ILO and instead ruled that it was necessary for there to be concurrent action by the Community and the member-states concerning both the negotiation and implementation stages.[23] Parallel action was necessary to present a common front at the international institutional level but only for avoiding contradictions in the external activities of the Community or negative coherence.[24]

An additional limiting factor has been that, by contrast with the Community's full membership status under the GATT and now the WTO, membership of the ILO has remained an exclusive preserve of the individual EU member-states. The European Commission only has observer status at the ILO.[25] Although the EU has developed its own system of social dialogue between management and labor, operating as an adjunct to its standard legislative process, its formal decision-making structures do not fit with the fully fledged tripartite system of

---

[18] See Case 22/70 *Commission* v *Council* (re: ERTA) [1971] ECR 263.

[19] EC Art. 137(1).   [20] EC Art. 137(2) (ex Art. 118a EEC).

[21] EC Art. 137(4).   [22] EC Art. 137(1)(a).

[23] *Opinion 2/91* (re: ILO) [1993] ECR I-1061.

[24] For discussion of coherence as a function of EU legal principles, see C. Hillion, "*Tours pour un, un pour tous!* Coherence in the External Relations of the European Union," in Cremona, note 9 above, 10–36.

[25] *Opinion 2/94* (re: ECHR) [1996] ECR I-1759, indicates that, as with the ECHR, the EU, as the Community, does not have competence to accede to the ILO. For discussion, see T. Novitz, "'A Human Face' for the Union or More Cosmetic Surgery? EU Competence in Global Social Governance and Promotion of Core Labor Standards," 9 *Maastricht Journal of European and Comparative Law* 231 (2001).

the ILO. Moreover, the EU's internal legislative competence over core areas of labor law is strictly limited. Areas such as wage setting and the right to take collective action are regarded as intrinsic features of the labor law frameworks and bargaining systems of each member-state and have been ring-fenced as national competences under the EC Treaty.[26] Prior to 2001, when an exchange of letters between the European Commission and the ILO heralded a change of direction toward more systematic international policy coordination and constructive dialogue,[27] the relationship was one of cordial but often platitudinous diplomatic cooperation. Such exchanges are indicative of a convergence of interest between the EU and ILO but have not yet led to the establishment of a formal interinstitutional deliberative process to enforce international labor standards.[28]

From the early 1990s, there has been a gradual but distinct shift in the orientation of the EU's international relations policy. As the Community took on the mantle of the European Union in 1993,[29] and sought to "assert its identity on the international scene,"[30] there was concern that the incipient Union's leading role in the emergent WTO, when compared with its lack of direct participation in ILO structures, was symptomatic of an asymmetry between economic and social objectives in both regional and global governance. In responding to this challenge, the EU began to develop a rationale that would enable it to take proactive measures including new-style PTAs, within the scope of its conferred Treaty powers, to promote international labor standards as part of a somewhat inchoate international relations policy encompassing trade, development, human rights, and foreign policy objectives. Such measures would have to be delicately calibrated not only to find a balance between economic and social policy objectives while being WTO compliant, but also to be regarded as not jeopardizing what is often suggested as the "comparative advantage" of developing countries in world trade associated with maintaining lower labor costs,[31] especially wages

---

[26] EC Art. 137(5). See further, B. Ryan, "Pay, Trade Union Rights, and European Community Law," 13 *International Journal of Comparative Labor Law and Industrial Relations* 305 (1997).

[27] OJ 2001 C165/23.

[28] For critical analysis, see T. Novitz, "The European Union and International Labour Standards: The Dynamics of Dialogue between the EU and the ILO," in Alston, note 17 above, 214–41.

[29] Following the entry into legal effect of the Treaty on European Union (TEU).

[30] TEU Art. 2.

[31] In essence, the "comparative advantage" theory can be rationalized by reference to the lower labor standards that prevailed during the period of development of what are now "developed" countries. On this basis, it is suggested that to impose today's European labor standards on developing countries would be to put the latter at a competitive disadvantage and slow down the process of development. The comparative advantage theory is not, however, intended to extend to situations where countries actually lower labor costs in response to increasing competition, leading to a "race to the bottom." See further, C. McCrudden and A. Davies, "A Perspective on Trade and Labor Rights," *Journal of International Economic Law* 43 at 49 (2000).

that, it is argued, can only improve with the economic growth that market access brings.[32]

Several factors combined to bring about this change of outlook. First, the completion of the Internal Market in 1993 was accompanied by a program of harmonization of labor standards in the EU intended to create a European "social space" to reduce, if not wholly prevent, the risk of social dumping between member-states as companies took advantage of market liberalization to relocate within the EU. However, it was apparent that, as unemployment increased in the EU in the early 1990s, jobs were increasingly being exported, along with production, outside of the EU to economies with lower labor costs, mainly in the Far East. The demands of globalization negated the effects of a purely internal response to social dumping, for, as the European Commission noted in its 1994 White Paper on Social Policy,[33]

> The Union recognizes that other regions may need to compete on the basis of lower labor costs, based on lower wages, longer hours, and more difficult conditions, but it is not in the interests of international cooperation that the exploitation of workers should become an instrument of international competition.

Reading between the lines, such statements might be interpreted as signifying a new wave of protectionism. It was swiftly realized that it would be necessary for the EU to weave together a narrative that would justify utilizing its expanding external powers in trade and development to seek to improve global labor conditions, in alignment with ILO standards, and in a manner consistent with transformational approaches to human rights and international development at global level, and yet also in concordance with its WTO obligations.[34] To demonstrate its own credibility and international leadership on this issue, the EU has evolved the concept of the European social model (ESM) as a core of distinctive values based on high labor standards, equality of opportunity, and social solidarity.[35] The spillover of the ESM into the external dimension now appeared to offer a tantalizing opportunity for a kind of Europeanization beyond Europe by positing an alternative social model to the dominant neoliberal agenda.

---

[32] See the Communication from the Commission to the Council, COM(1996) 402, on the link between the trading system and internationally recognized labor standards, and point 5 of the *ILO Declaration on Fundamental Principles and Rights at Work*, adopted by the International Labor Conference at its 86th session, June 16, 1998 (Geneva: ILO, 1998): www.ilo .org.

[33] COM(94) 333.

[34] For the clearest signal of the shift toward an external dimension of EU social policy, see the preamble of the European Council Resolution of December 6, 1994, *On Certain Aspects of European Social Policy: A Contribution to Economic and Social Convergence in the Union*, OJ 1994 C386/6.

[35] See J. Kenner, *EU Employment Law* (Oxford: Hart, 2003), 303–4.

Second, irrespective of market factors, from the early 1990s the EU has sought recognition as a leading protagonist on the international political stage. The Treaty on European Union (TEU) had, as its centerpiece, the establishment of a Common Foreign and Security Policy (CFSP) as an overarching feature of EU international relations. Although the CFSP is governed by a distinct regime or "Treaty pillar" of intergovernmental cooperation that restrains but does not displace national sovereignty,[36] setting it apart from the established Community principle of conferred powers, it now provides the motor for the EU's international relations policy.[37] The priorities of the CFSP, inter alia, the promotion of human rights and democratization, conflict resolution in the European "neighborhood," security, and combating terrorism after 9/11, drive the EU's choices not only when it seeks partners for trading relations and development assistance, but also when it decides to impose sanctions. As the activities of the CFSP broaden and relate more directly to individual rights, there is increasing concern that such policy choices are unduly influenced by security and counterterrorism concerns and are deficient in both democratic and judicial accountability.[38]

Third, and of equal importance, there has been an alignment between the EU's trade, development, and human rights policies following the introduction of Title XX of the EC Treaty on Development Cooperation as part of the TEU amendments. The Development Title provides a legal basis for external action, including the negotiation and conclusion of international agreements,[39] to advance broad objectives in which observance of internationally recognized labor standards is an integral part of the policy mix. The ECJ is prepared to uphold the legality of such agreements so long as they have development cooperation, as defined in Title XX, as their essential objective even if ancillary provisions cover other matters.[40] Such agreements, even if they are negotiated and concluded exclusively under Community powers, always operate as complementary "mixed agreements" in the sense that the EU member-states, whether or not they are signatory parties, retain sovereignty to negotiate and conclude concurrent

---

[36] See C. Hillion & R. Wessel, "Restraining External Competences of EU Member-States under CFSP," in Cremona and de Witte, note 13 above, 79–121, who argue that in practice the relationship between the CFSP and the Community "pillar" is interconnected and operates to restrain the external competences of member-states.

[37] The most powerful CFSP instrument directed at specific situations is the Joint Action, which is designed to "commit the member-states in the positions they adopt and in the conduct of their activity" (TEU Art. 14). Joint Actions are not subject to the jurisdiction of the ECJ and, although the TEU is not explicit on this point, do not give rise to directly effective rights for individuals in national courts. See further, A. Dashwood, "The Law and Practice of CFSP Joint Actions," in Cremona and de Witte, note 13 above, 53–77.

[38] For a critique, see E. Spaventa, "Fundamental What? The Difficult Relationship between Foreign Policy and Fundamental Rights," in Cremona and de Witte, note 13 above, 233–55.

[39] EC Art. 181.

[40] See Case C-268/94 *Portugal v Council* [1996] ECR I-6177. This case concerned the Cooperation Agreement with India on Partnership and Development, OJ 1994 L223/23. Clauses in the agreement concerned tourism, energy, culture, and the prevention of drug abuse.

development cooperation agreements as long as they act in close cooperation with the EU and conform to Treaty objectives.

Combating poverty and fostering "sustainable economic and social development" of developing countries, by giving support to the most disadvantaged among them,[41] now forms part of an interinstitutional European Consensus on Development (ECD) that presents a postcolonial "vision" based on the principle of ownership of development strategies by partner countries.[42] The EU has often been accused of using its dominance in trade and development assistance to impose its own values on other countries,[43] but its approach chimes with a fast-moving global agenda. Policies designed to encourage adherence to international labor standards can be presented as an important contribution to "sustainable development"[44] and eradicating poverty as set out the UN's Millennium Development Goals (MDGs) and reiterated in the ECD. Under the ECD, the EU is committed to a set of common principles based on the ILO's "Core Labor Standards" (CLS),[45] and its parallel campaign for "decent work,"[46] into national and

---

[41] EC Art. 177.   [42] OJ 2006 C46/1.

[43] For example, see P. Leino, "The Journey Toward All that is Good and Beautiful: Human Rights and 'Common Values' as Guiding Principles of EU Foreign Relations Law," in Cremona and de Witte, note 13 above, 259–89.

[44] The Implementation Plan following the UN World Summit on Sustainable Development, held in Johannesburg, September 2–4, 1992, contains several references to the priority of promoting labor standards such as increasing "income-generating employment opportunities," para. 10(b), and "elimination of the worst forms of child labor," para. 12. The Plan calls for support for the ILO and encouragement of "its ongoing work on the social dimension of globalization," para. 47(c): See www.un.org/esa/sustdev/documents/WSSD_POI_PD/English/POIToc.htm. The European Commission has added its own gloss in its Communication entitled *Toward a Global Partnership for Sustainable Development,* COM (2002) 82, leading directly to changes in the GSP and a review of PTAs "to help developing countries benefit from the global trading system."

[45] See the *ILO Declaration on Fundamental Principles and Rights at Work,* note 32 above, and the European Commission's follow-up Communication: *Promoting Core Labor Standards and Improving Social Governance in the Context of Globalization,* COM(2001) 416. The CLS comprise four fundamental principles and rights at work to be observed by all ILO member countries regardless of whether or not those countries have ratified the relevant ILO Conventions, namely (1) freedom of association and the effective recognition of the right to collective bargaining; (2) the elimination of all forms of forced or compulsory labor; (3) the effective abolition of child labor; and (4) the elimination of discrimination in respect of employment. For critical analysis and debate on the CLS method, see P. Alston, "'Core Labor Standards' and the Transformation of the International Labor Rights Regime," 15 *European Journal of International Law* 457 (2004), and B. A. Langille, "Core Labor Rights – The True Story," 16 *European Journal of International Law* 409 (2005), discussed in Section 3 of this chapter.

[46] See *Decent Work,* Report of the Director General to the 87th session of the International Labor Conference (Geneva: ILO, 1999): www.ilo.org. The aim of the decent work agenda is to encourage all forms of productive work "in conditions of freedom, equity, security, and human dignity" and thus contribute to the eradication of poverty. See also the Ministerial Declaration by the UN Economic and Social Council on *Full Employment and Decent Work,* 2006, UN Doc. GA, 61st Session, Supp. No. 3 (A/61/3/Rev. 1), chap. III, para. 50, and UN ECOSOC Resolution 2008/18, July 24, 2008. See further, B. Hepple, *Labor Laws and Global*

regional strategies to promote sustainable development and eradicate poverty. Moreover, the broad scope of the ECD provides a basis for a wide reading of the Development Cooperation provisions of the EC Treaty by the ECJ even where there is an overlap, in funding and technical assistance, between development cooperation and CFSP objectives.[47]

Fourth, human rights and fundamental freedoms are now established among the foundational principles of the Union and core elements of the CFSP.[48] Human rights objectives are thus mainstreamed across the fields of EU external relations even though there is no clear Treaty basis to pursue them independently of trade, development, or foreign policy.[49] Specifically, in the development context, Article 177(2) of the EC requires that development cooperation policy must contribute to respect for human rights. The EU's own reference point, in seeking human rights' conditionality in the broader international relations dimension, is its self-declared Charter of Fundamental Rights (CFR)[50] adopted in 2000 and adapted in 2007.[51] The CFR provides an institutional imperative for the EU and its member-states to uphold a set of universal and indivisible human rights as drawn from the international obligations of the member-states.[52] Although not legally binding per se, the CFR represents a negotiated consensus between the EU institutions and the member-states reached at the highest level[53] and, as such, has become the ultimate point of reference for evaluating the substance of human rights both internally and externally, including by the ECJ. Most significantly, it places "fundamental social rights" sourced explicitly from the European Social Charter of the Council of Europe[54] and the Community Charter of the Fundamental Social Rights of Workers[55] at the center of its human rights agenda[56]

Trade (Oxford: Hart Publishing, 2005), 63–6. For the EU's response, see the Commission Communication: *Promoting Decent Work for All: The EU's Contribution to the Implementation of the Decent Work Agenda in the World,* COM(2006) 249, and the Council Conclusions on *Decent Work for All,* December 1, 2006: www.consilium.europa.eu.

[47] See Case C-91/05 *Commission* v *Council (ECOWAS),* Judgment of the ECJ of May 20, 2008, OJ 2008 C171/2. Discussed by C. Hillion and R. Wessel, "Competence Distribution in EU External Relations after Ecowas: Clarification or Continued Fuzziness?," 46 *Common Market Law Review* 551 (2009).

[48] EU Arts. 6 and 11.   [49] See Davies, note 17 above, at 184–90.

[50] OJ 2000 C364/1.   [51] OJ 2007 C303/1.

[52] See J. Kenner, "Economic and Social Rights in the EU Legal Order: The Mirage of Indivisibility," in Hervey T. K. & Kenner J. (eds.), *Economic and Social Rights under the EU Charter of Fundamental Rights* (Oxford: Hart, 2003), 1–25.

[53] The CFR was drawn up by a broadly representative "European Convention" and adopted as an Inter-Institutional Declaration of the EU. See G. de Búrca, "The Drafting of the European Union Charter of Fundamental Rights," 26 *European Law Review* 126 (2001).

[54] 1961, 529 UNTS 89.

[55] COM(89) 248, reproduced in *Social Europe* 1/90.

[56] For specified sources of the CFR, see the separately published "explanations," OJ 2007 C303/17. Under the Treaty of Lisbon amending the TEU and the EC Treaty, December 17, 2007, OJ 2007 C306 (as yet unratified), the status of the CFR would be further enhanced to have the "same legal value" as the EU Treaties, although this would not necessarily lead to the creation of justiciable rights for individuals. See Art. 6(1) of the consolidated text of the TEU, OJ 2008 C115.

and subject to the oversight of its specially established Agency for Fundamental Rights (FRA).[57]

Specified labor rights in the "Solidarity" Title of the CFR include, inter alia, the right to collective bargaining and action and the right to protection in the event of unjustified dismissal,[58] both of which, however, are subject to "national laws and practices." Moreover, in the cases of *Viking Line* and *Laval*,[59] the ECJ, while drawing on the CFR to recognize the right of workers to take collective action as a fundamental right that is integral to EU law, has interpreted the scope of that right narrowly in the context of the foundational EC Treaty provisions on free movement in the internal market.[60] The ECJ ruled in *Viking Line* that where the right to take collective action, including strike action, is likely to restrict free movement in the internal market, it can only be exercised for the purpose of the protection of workers if, firstly, it can be shown before a national court that jobs are jeopardized or under serious threat and, secondly, that collective action is suitable for ensuring the achievement of the objective pursued and does not go beyond what is necessary to attain that objective, to satisfy the requirement of proportionality.[61] This is an extremely strict test to satisfy and is a clear indication that the duty of the courts to uphold the economic freedoms in the EC Treaty trumps the fundamental social right to take collective action guaranteed in the CFR.

Nevertheless, in the external relations context, it is no longer institutionally possible, or indeed credible, for the EU to pursue its trade and development policy objectives without addressing human rights' considerations including labor rights.[62] The EU has an imperative to promote observance of universal labor standards in its external relations as part of its *acquis communautaire*,[63] notwithstanding that the role of labor rights is highly contested in the context of globalization and often marginalized at the international level.[64] To put these policies into effect, human rights clauses have been elaborated as an "essential

---

[57] The FRA was established on March 1, 2007, under Council Regulation 168/2007/EC, OJ 2007 L53/1. Note, however, that the FRA was instituted under EC Treaty powers and has no oversight of the CFSP regime.

[58] CFR Arts. 28 and 30.

[59] Case C-438/05 *International Transport Workers' Federation and Finnish Seamen's Union v Viking Line ABP and OÜ Viking Line Eesti* [2007] ECR I-10779 and Case C-341/05 *Laval un Partneri Ltd* v *Svenska Byggnadsarbetareförbundet and others* [2007] ECR I-11767.

[60] Specifically, EC Art. 43 on the right of establishment in *Viking Line* and EC Art. 49 on free movement of services in *Laval*.

[61] *Viking Line*, paras. 83–4.

[62] For the apotheosis of this approach, see the Commission's Communication, COM (2001) 252, on the EU's role in promoting human rights and democratization in third countries.

[63] See E. Riedel & M. Will, "Human Rights Clauses in External Agreements of the EC," in Alston P. (ed.), *The EU and Human Rights* (Oxford: OUP, 1999), 723–4 at 732.

[64] See P. Alston, "Labor Rights as Human Rights: The Not So Happy State of the Art," in Alston (ed.), note 17 above, 1–24. As an example of the marginalization of labor rights on the international stage, Alston, at p. 7, refers to the UN Conference on Trade and Development (UNCTAD) held in Sao Paolo in June 2004 where the negotiated consensus "made not a single reference to labor standards, labor rights, workers' rights, or core standards."

element" of PTAs and other trade and/or development measures.[65] The parties commit themselves to respecting fundamental human rights by reference to observance of shared international obligations. In some cases, specific reference is made to "fundamental social rights" within the conception of respect for human rights and it is now commonplace to find a separate labor clause referring to the ILO's CLS although, as in the CPA, discussed next, the latter do not necessarily form part of the "essential elements" of the agreement. Separate provisions allow for a procedure to be established for "appropriate measures" to be taken in the event of violation of an "essential element" allowing for suspension of the PTA in whole or in part for a "material breach" within the meaning of Article 60 of the Vienna Convention on the Law of the Treaties.[66] For reasons of coherence, this process was formalized by two Council Regulations designed to standardize and synchronize the requirements for implementing EU operations in development cooperation and other areas in accordance with the emerging policy consensus.[67] To reinforce these measures, on their expiration at the end of 2006, a replacement Regulation (the European Instrument for Democracy and Human Rights) was introduced to provide resources, within the framework of EU development cooperation policy, for the "promotion of human rights and democracy worldwide" for the period 2007–2013.[68] Significantly, among the array of fields identified for assistance and monitoring under this Instrument, there is a specific reference to "the promotion of core labor standards and corporate social responsibility"[69] within the framework of the central objective of contributing to "respect for all human rights and fundamental freedoms."[70]

The EU presents its human rights policy as "positive conditionality" and rejects accusations of imposing Western values or a sanctions-based approach to human rights and labor standards. Most importantly, in the present analysis, it seeks to align its approach with the emergent human rights dimension of global trade and the linkage between trade and sustainable development in the WTO's Doha Development Agenda.[71] In a marked departure from the narrow emphasis

---

[65] See, for example, Art. 5(1) of the Lomé IV ACP–EC Convention, as revised in 1995, OJ 1998 L156/3, discussed in Section 3 of this chapter.

[66] See E. Fierro, "Legal Basis and Scope of the Human Rights Clauses in EC Bilateral Agreements: Any Room for Positive Interpretation?," 7 *European Law Journal* 41 (2001).

[67] Council Regulation 975/1999/EC concerning development cooperation operations, OJ 1999 L120/1, and Council Regulation 976/1999/EC concerning Community operations other than development cooperation, OJ 1999 L120/8. These measures were subsequently amended by, respectively, European Parliament and Council Regulation 2240/2004/EC, OJ 2004 L390/3, and Council Regulation 2242/2004/EC, OJ 2004 L390/21. See further, A. Gatto, "The Integration of Social Rights Concerns in the External Relations of the European Union," in G. de Búrca and B. de Witte (eds.), *Social Rights in Europe* (Oxford: OUP, 2005), 339–65.

[68] Regulation 1889/2006/EC, OJ 2006 L386/1, and OJ 2007 L200/549. The financial envelope for the implementation of this Regulation, under Art. 19, is €1,104,000,000.

[69] Art. 2(1)(a)(viii).   [70] Art. 1.

[71] See the November 2001 Declaration of the Fourth WTO Ministerial Conference in Doha, Qatar: www.wto.org/english/tratop_e/dda_e/dda_e.htm.

of the CCP on trade liberalization, the Treaty of Lisbon, 2007, would, if ratified, commit the EU to pursuing both "free and fair trade" in its relations with the wider world[72] and would reinforce the linkage between trade and other policies by bringing all of the Union's external relations activities within a single legal framework.[73]

Each of these factors is indicative of a greater awareness within the EU, following the fall of the Berlin Wall and eastward enlargement, of its unique role as the "world's biggest trader," accounting for 20 percent of global imports and exports,[74] and the "foremost donor of development aid," accounting for 55 percent of the total, including national contributions of member-states.[75] The EU's status is not just about the quantum of trade and development it oversees but also its capacity, as a regional polity with genuine supranational powers, to act externally in these areas. The EU's awareness of its global actorliness was revealed in the Laeken Declaration of 2001, where the European Council proclaimed that[76]

> Europe needs to shoulder its responsibilities in the governance of globalization. The role it has to play is that of a power … seeking to set globalization within a moral framework, in other words to anchor it in solidarity and sustainable development.

The European Council's rhetoric is laden with assumptions.[77] First, it is assumed that the pace and shape of globalization can be directed proactively by the EU as a power player within an international rule-based legal order.[78] Second, it is assumed that the EU has an institutional vocation to help reduce an imbalance between the economic and social dimensions of global governance. Third, it is implicit that the EU has both the international credibility and the legal and political capacity to perform the role of a global actor in the arena of social policy. Fourth, and most controversially, it is assumed that the EU's "moral framework," later described more subtly as "common values" in the Treaty of Lisbon,[79] offers a superior model to be followed by other countries.

---

[72] TEU Art. 3(5) in the consolidated Lisbon text, note 56 above. See also the earlier Communication of the European Commission on *fair trade*, COM (1999) 619.

[73] The Title on External Action is contained in Part V of the Treaty on the Functioning of the European Union, Arts. 205–222 of the consolidated Lisbon text, note 56 above.

[74] See the European Commission, *European Union in the World*, March 18, 2007: ec.europa .eu/world/what/trade_policy/index_en.htm.

[75] See further, the European Commission, *More and Better Aid*: ec.europa.eu/development/ how/more-and-better-aid_en.cfm.

[76] Annex I of the Presidency Conclusions, Laeken European Council, December 2001, p. 19.

[77] These arguments are developed further in J. Kenner, *The EU and Global Labour Law* (Oxford: Hart, 2012, forthcoming).

[78] See especially, F. Snyder, "Governing Economic Globalization: Global Legal Pluralism and European Law," 5 *European Law Journal* 334 (1999).

[79] TEU Art. 2 in the consolidated text, note 56 above.

The general provisions on the Union's external action in the Treaty of Lisbon[80] would, if ratified, specifically require the EU to advance "the principles which have inspired its own creation" on the international scene, including, inter alia, the "universality and indivisibility of human rights, respect for human dignity, the principles of equality and solidarity, and respect for the principles of the United Nations Charter and international law." Most pointedly, the Union would seek to develop relations and build partnerships only with countries and international, regional, or global organizations that "share [the EU's] principles." Thus, the Union does not seek explicitly to export its principles but it does regard adherence to them as a condition of trading relations and development assistance with organizations such as the ACP and its member countries.

Under this model, the EU, acting as a superpower, at least in the fields of trade and development assistance, has a "global vocation"[81] to exercise its influence and deploy its resources in such a way as to require observance of international labor rights by reference to the CLS and ratified ILO conventions and, more broadly, to support policies attuned to the ILO's Decent Work Agenda and the principles in its Declaration on Social Justice and Fair Globalization,[82] which requires regional organizations such as the EU to have a key role in implementation. It follows that the EU's own rhetorical commitments and the thrust of the international agenda requires its institutions and member-states to act to "*reinforce* global social governance."[83] The EU's exchange of letters with the ILO in 2001,[84] and its subsequent actions in forming a strategic partnership with the ILO in the field of development,[85] reveal a desire to instill in global labor law a higher normative authority than has hitherto been possible,[86] and, in so doing, respond to the ILO's request to help end the neglect of the social dimension of globalization.[87] Nevertheless, when requiring labor clauses in PTAs, the EU's scope for maneuver is limited, not least because it must ensure that it complies with WTO rules and recognize the comparative advantages of developing countries arising from lower labor standards that are not regarded by the ILO as incompatible with the CLS.[88] The EU can exert influence over global social policy by punching above its weight, but it cannot govern globalization.

---

[80] See especially TEU Art. 21 in the consolidated text, note 56 above.
[81] See M. Cremona, "Rhetoric or Reticence: EU External Commercial Policy in a Multilateral Context," 38 *Common Market Law Review* (2001), 359–96 at 359.
[82] Adopted by the 97th International Labor Conference, Geneva, June 10, 2008.
[83] See especially, Novitz, note 25 above.   [84] OJ 2001 C165/23.
[85] Signed on July 15, 2004: ec.europa.eu/development/icenter/repository/memorandum-of-understanding-EC-ILO-signed percent20–15-07–2004_en.pdf.
[86] See N. Walker, "The EU and the WTO: Constitutionalism in a New Key," in De Búrca and Scott, note 4 above, 31–57 at 37.
[87] See the letter from the Director General of the ILO to the European Commission, May 14, 2001, note 27 above.
[88] Point 5 of the *ILO Declaration*, note 32 above.

3.   The ACP–EU Cotonou Partnership Agreement

Formed in 1975, the ACP represents a diverse grouping of states from Sub-Saharan Africa, the Caribbean, and the Pacific.[89] For more than twenty-five years, from the first Lomé Agreement in 1975 until the signing of the CPA in Benin, the Community targeted nonreciprocal trade preferences and development aid at partners in the ACP group, many of whom had gained independence from the member-states of the emergent EEC during the period of decolonization in the 1950s and 1960s.[90] The relationship was often described as one of donor and recipient rather than a true partnership,[91] but it represented the most advanced model of North–South development cooperation yet devised.[92] By 2000, more than 90 percent of ACP exports were entering the EU duty and quota free and upwards of €30 billion of economic assistance had been channeled through the European Development Fund (EDF), and yet thirty-nine out of the sixty-three UN designated Least Developed Countries (LDCs) at that time were ACP states and 95 percent of the ACP population, concentrated in Sub-Saharan Africa, had experienced successive falls in income from the 1980s, resulting in 292 million people living on less than $1 a day.[93] ACP countries' share of the Community market declined from 6 percent in 1976 to 3 percent in 1998.[94] Many factors, largely outside the control of the Community, contributed to these problems, ranging from, inter alia, wars, political instability, food insecurity, environmental degradation, health crises and HIV/AIDS, endemic corruption, and inefficiency in some ACP states, and competition from more efficient, fast-growing non-ACP states in neighboring regions. The Lomé I–IV agreements were regarded as, at best, only a partial success for the best placed ACP countries, and a fundamental rethink of the evolving ACP–EU relationship was overdue long before the CPA was negotiated.[95]

---

[89] The Georgetown Agreement, June 6, 1975, 1247 UNTS 148. The ACP comprises forty-eight countries from Sub-Saharan Africa, sixteen from the Caribbean, and fifteen from the Pacific. For further details see the ACP Web site: www.acpsec.org/en/about_us.htm.

[90] The legal relationship of the EC with many of the now-ACP countries is defined by Part IV of the EC Treaty concerning the association of overseas countries and territories, EC Arts. 182–88 and Annex II.

[91] See J. A. McMahon, "Negotiating in a Time of Turbulent Transition: The Future of Lomé," 36 *Common Market Law Review* (1999), 599 at 622.

[92] See N. J. Udombana, "Back to Basics: The ACP-EU Cotonou Trade Agreement and Challenges for the African Union," 40 *Texas International Law Journal* (2004–2005), 59 at 65. Lomé's emphasis on an equitable approach to international trade and economic relations was heavily influenced by the UN Declaration of 1974 on a *New International Economic Order*, G. A. Res. 3201 (S-VI), UN Doc. A/9559.

[93] See O. Babarinde and G. Faber, "From Lomé to Cotonou: Business as Usual?," 9 *European Foreign Affairs Review* (2004), 27 at 34–5.

[94] See the European Commission overview at ec.europa.eu/development/geographical/cotonouintro_en.cfm.

[95] See COM(96) 570, "Green Paper" on EU–ACP relations.

As the EU's preeminent trade and development agreement, the CPA is of particular significance for our analysis because its scope extends to all areas of EU external relations policy – trade, development, environment, foreign policy, and security – and has both human rights and labor standards clauses. It would be tempting to discuss the labor clause immediately but it is important to appreciate its context in this multistranded and now revised text.[96]

Although concluded as an international agreement under EC Treaty powers,[97] the CPA is not an exclusive trade agreement of the kind falling within the CCP, but rather, its development policy orientation required a mixed agreement signed by the Community and all EU member-states as contracting parties with seventy-eight ACP member-states.[98] The CPA offers a long-term framework, based on reciprocal rights and obligations, lasting until 2020, subject to adaptation and a new financial protocol every five years.[99] Resources under the EDF have increased by 65 percent from €13.8 billion in 2000–2007 to €22.7 billion between 2008 and 2013.[100]

To achieve WTO compliance, new trade arrangements had to be concluded by the end of 2007.[101] Under the CPA there is a gradual shift toward trade liberalization on a region-by-region basis replacing old-style uniform trade preferences that, although subject to a temporary WTO waiver,[102] have to be phased out except for the LDCs in the ACP group. The LDCs are entitled to choose to maintain preferential nonreciprocal arrangements, which should include "essentially all products,"[103] under the "Everything But Arms" (EBA) Regulation.[104] Subject

---

[96] For references, see note 3 above.　　　　　　[97] EC Arts. 300(2) and 310.

[98] In accordance with Art. 181 EC. Among the ACP countries, only Cuba is not a signatory. Certain of the provisions do not apply to South Africa as set out in Protocol 3 of the CPA.

[99] CPA Art. 95. Further revision is anticipated in 2010.

[100] See the Internal Agreement between representatives of the governments of the member-states, meeting within the Council, of July 17, 2006, OJ 2006 L247/30, as modified by a Council Decision of July 16, 2007, OJ 2007 L202/45.

[101] Two GATT panel reports in the 1990s had found that the nonreciprocal trade preferences under Lomé were no long justified under GATT Art. XXIV: *EEC-Bananas I*, DS32/R, 1993 and *EEC-Bananas II*, DS38/R, 1994. For discussion, see Bartels, note 9 above, 147–51.

[102] GATT Doc L/7604, December 19, 1994. Extended to 2007 by WTO Decision of November 14, 2001: WT/MIN(01)/15, with separate arrangements for continuation of banana quotas until December 31, 2005: WT/MIN(01)/16. To allow more time for negotiations and ensure WTO compliance, duty-free and quota-free access was offered to all countries negotiating EPAs, subject to permitted exceptions: European Commission, "EC Market Access Offer in EPAs," April 4, 2007. For analysis of EPAs, see Bartels, note 9 above, pp. 166–69.

[103] CPA Art. 37(9).

[104] EBA allows for duty-free access on imports of all products from LDCs for "essentially all products" except arms without any quantitative restrictions with the exception of fresh bananas, rice, and sugar, all of which must be liberalized by September 2009; see Council Regulation 416/2001/EC, OJ 2001 L60/43. Forty-one of the fifty countries covered by the EBA initiative are members of the ACP. The EBA is intended to comply with the WTO's Doha Ministerial Declaration adopted on November 14, 2001, WT/MIN(01)/DEC/1. Para. 42 declares that "We commit ourselves to the objective of duty-free, quota-free market access for products originating from LDCs."

to this exception, the provisions of the CPA require differentiated regional integration agreements in the form of bilateral and reciprocal Economic Partnership Agreements (EPAs), which are free trade agreements in all but name.[105] An example is the CARIFORUM–EU EPA established with fifteen Caribbean ACP members in 2008 to open up "substantially all trade" between the partners subject to permitted WTO exceptions for certain goods and, ultimately, leading to full integration of those countries into the world economy.[106] These agreements, in turn, form part of the evolutionary development of the CPA, including elaboration of its labor rights' clause. The labor provisions of the CARIFORUM–EU EPA are discussed in Section 4.

Those ACP members who are neither LDCs nor signatories of an EPA are effectively designated as the weaker partners. Members of this group are entitled only to a narrower range of trade preferences and subject to stricter rules of origin under the EU's unilateral GSP.[107] Differentiation and regionalization are defined among the "fundamental principles" of the CPA precisely to address the variable levels of development needs of ACP states and permit special treatment of LDCs.[108] Thus, with the exception of LDCs, who have the option of leaving an EPA, there is an incentive for ACP country groups to move toward regional integration. Differentiation is intended to augur political stability within each region, better targeting of EDF resources, and a sharper focus on the CPA's development priorities and monitoring of human rights obligations and other "essential" and "fundamental" elements of the agreement.[109] The main concern is that the withdrawal of trade preferences through the EPA method may tend to marginalize the weaker ACP states and the poorest members of their societies, contrary to the CPA's core development objectives.[110]

Economic integration of the ACP countries into the world economy through regional agreements is one strand of the CPA, but equally important is political integration and advancing the EU's development and foreign-policy priorities to the extent that these are shared with the ACP group. Thus, the first stated

[105] CPA Art. 37(1). EPAs are based on three principles: reciprocity; regionalism; and special treatment for the poorest. LDCs are entitled to have equally favorable market access even if they are not able to be part of an EPA under Art. 37(6). See further, S. R. Hurt, "Cooperation and Coercion? The Cotonou Agreement between the European Union and ACP States and the End of the Lomé Convention," 24 *Third World Quarterly* (2003), 161 at 168; and Udombana, note 92 above, at 81–84.

[106] For the text of the agreement signed on October 15, 2008, see OJ 2008 L289/3. An interim EPA has also been signed with the Ivory Coast, COM(2008) 438 and 439, and further proposals concern the Central African states of Cameroon and Ghana, the South African Development Community group of states (SADC), the East African Community (EAC), the Pacific countries and East and Southern Africa (ESA). See the General Report on the Activities of the European Union 2008: europa.eu/generalreport/en/rg2008en.pdf, p. 192.

[107] See Babarinde and Faber, note 93 above, at 39–42.   [108] CPA Art. 2.

[109] As Bartels observes, note 9 above at 169, how much "asymmetry" is permitted under GATT Art. XXIV is uncertain.

[110] Hurt, note 105 above, at 169.

objective of the partnership is to "promote and expedite the economic, cultural, and social development" of ACP states "with a view to contributing to peace and security and to promoting a stable and democratic political environment."[111] Significantly, the revised CPA text of 2005, reflecting the international environment after 9/11, reinforces the CFSP dimension with detailed additional provisions on the "fight against terrorism" and "cooperation in countering the proliferation of weapons of mass destruction."[112] Although these provisions are not drafted in the form of strict conditionality and form part of an "integrated approach," there is an inevitable linkage, if only in perception, between progress in these areas and the relative prioritization of the trade, development, and other political dimensions of the CPA, including the human rights and labor standards provisions.

The post-TEU priorities of the EC Development Title are reflected in the CPA's central goal "of reducing and eventually eradicating poverty consistent with the objectives of sustainable development."[113] This is reinforced in the revised CPA that, incorporating the ECD agenda, identifies goal and targets from the MDGs and measures progress using a range of indicators. Although there are references to increasing the share of women in waged employment in the non-agricultural sector and cutting the unemployment rate of young people,[114] these indicators do not expressly refer to labor conditions.

Equally important, among the "fundamental principles" in Article 2 is "equality of the partners and ownership of development strategies." The onus for implementation is to be determined by the ACP states "with due regard" to the essential elements including respect for human rights. Although the central government of each ACP country is the main partner, participation in the partnership is "open to different kinds of other actors" to encourage the integration of all sections of society. Such participation is regarded as a "fundamental principle" but is no more than aspirational in practice, albeit that it is intended to extend to the private sector and civil society, including, implicitly, trade unions and employers' organizations. This, in turn, raises concerns about the representativeness of such actors in a partnership based on democratic principles.[115] Ownership of development strategies and participation in the partnership is to be delivered by "dialogue" and the fulfillment of mutual obligations.[116] The CPA contains a solidarity clause, modeled on Article 10 of the EC Treaty, designed to guarantee the fulfillment of the obligations that the parties have contracted to attain.[117]

The "pivotal role" to be played by dialogue is reinforced in Title II on the "political dimension," including the provisions concerning the three "essential elements" of respect for human rights, democratic principles, and the rule of

---

[111] CPA Art. 1.   [112] Arts. 11(a) and 11(b) of the revised CPA.
[113] CPA Art. 1.
[114] Indicators 11 and 45 annexed to the revised CPA.
[115] See Davies and McCrudden, note 31 above, at 61.
[116] CPA Art. 2.   [117] CPA Art. 3.

law and the separate, somewhat weaker "fundamental element" regarding "good governance," the latter being a euphemism for combatting corruption.[118] In connecting political dialogue, including wider participation in the partnership and capacity building within civil society,[119] with respect for human rights, the CPA marks a significant advance on previous efforts to introduce a human rights dimension into ACP–EU relations.[120] Lomé IV, as revised in 1995, had declared that respect for human rights is recognized as "a basic factor for real development" and constitutes, along with "democratic principles and the rule of law," "an essential element" of that Convention,[121] consistent with the emerging requirements of conditionality being applied by the EU.[122] Under the revised Lomé IV, however, there was, save in cases of special urgency, only a power to hold consultations in the event of an alleged failure to fulfill an obligation in respect of one of the essential elements. Ultimately, in the event of urgency or refusal of consultations, the party that invoked the failure was entitled to "take appropriate steps" to partially or fully suspend the application of the Convention to the party concerned but only as a measure of last resort.[123] During the 1990s, development assistance to Haiti, the Sudan, and Togo was suspended because of persistent violations of the essential elements provisions.[124]

The CPA is stronger than the revised Lomé IV both in the human rights language it expresses and, to a lesser extent, its enforcement mechanisms. Turning first to Article 9 as an expression of the parties' formal commitment to human rights, we see the CPA has a number of novel and interesting features.

First, the concept of "sustainable development," as the core objective of the CPA as a whole, is to be "centered on the human person" as the main protagonist and beneficiary of development and, hence, "this entails respect for and promotion of all human rights."[125] Respect for human rights, along with the

---

[118]CPA Art. 9. The EU failed in its attempts to include "good governance" as an "essential element" as part of the negotiations. The significance of the distinction between an "essential element" and a "fundamental element" of the agreement lies with the fact that a breach of the good governance provisions concerning the latter cannot lead to suspension procedures. See further, M. Holland, "20/20 Vision? The EU's Cotonou Partnership Agreement," *The Brown Journal of World Affairs* (Winter/Spring 2003), Vol. 9/2, 161 at 165–7.

[119]See CPA Arts. 4–7.

[120]The first such attempt can be traced back to the "Uganda Guidelines" of 1977, Bull EC 6–1977. See further, Bartels, note 9 above, p. 152.

[121]Art. 5(1) states, "Respect for human rights, democratic principles, and the rule of law, which underpins relations between the ACP States and the Community and all provisions of the Convention, and governs the domestic and international policies of the Contracting Parties, shall constitute an essential element of this Convention." For the revised text, see OJ 1998 L156/3.

[122]See Commission Communication: *The Inclusion of Respect for Democratic Principles and Human Rights in Agreements between the Community and Third Countries*, COM (95) 216.

[123]Art. 366a of Lomé IV as revised.

[124]See the country profiles for details: ec.europa.eu/development/geographical/regions countries_en.cfm.

[125]CPA Art. 9(1).

other essential elements, is thus regarded as an "integral part of sustainable development."[126] The greater significance of this terminology arises not so much from the linkage between development objectives and human rights but rather the positive conditionality with which it is imbued.

Second, the definition of human rights and fundamental freedoms, as essential elements of the CPA, includes, for the first time in EU–ACP relations, respect specifically for "fundamental social rights."[127] Article 9 does not define this term but the preamble stresses that the parties are "anxious to respect basic labor rights taking account of the principles laid down in the relevant conventions of the [ILO]" and refers to a wider list of UN texts from which labor rights can be drawn, including the International Covenant on Economic, Social, and Cultural Rights.[128] Moreover, in Article 9(2), the parties refer to their "international obligations and commitments concerning respect for human rights," which are deemed "universal, indivisible, and interrelated" and, moreover, "undertake to promote and protect all fundamental freedoms and human rights, be they civil and political, or economic, social, and cultural" and, in this context, they "reaffirm the equality of men and women." The parties conclude that respect for human rights, thus defined, along with democratic principles and the rule of law, together "underpin the ACP–EU Partnership" and constitute the "essential elements" of the CPA.[129] This language is strikingly similar to the content of the EU's own CFR and references in the EC Treaty to sources of "fundamental social rights," indicating that the EU is seeking to reinforce or even export social values that it regards as forming part of the ESM.

Third, the existing procedures for political dialogue and, ultimately, suspension under the essential elements provisions are refined, if not necessarily strengthened, in the CPA and the 2005 revisions.[130] The purpose of political dialogue is to assess progress regularly in all areas of cooperation, including the essential elements, and to resolve disputes. Political dialogue is intended to be "flexible" but becomes more "systematic and formalized"[131] to prevent situations in which one party might "deem it necessary" to have recourse to the formal consultation procedures in the event of alleged failure of another party to fulfill one of the essential elements.[132] Under the revised CPA, except in cases of "special urgency," "all possible options for dialogue" must be exhausted prior to the initiation of formal "consultation procedures" under Article 96 relating to the essential elements.[133] The term "special urgency" refers to exceptional cases of "particularly serious and flagrant violation" of one of the essential elements

---

[126] Ibid.   [127] Ibid.
[128] 993 UNTS 3 (1966). For a further reference to "basic social rights" see CPA Art. 25(g) in the section on "Social and Human Development."
[129] CPA Art. 9(2).
[130] CPA Arts. 8, 9, and 96 as revised, and the new Annex VII.
[131] Art. 8(6a) as revised. See Annex VII for the detailed modalities.
[132] CPA Art. 8(2) as revised.   [133] CPA Art. 96(1a) as revised.

that require an "immediate" reaction.[134] Such action would be appropriate in the event of a coup d'état, but in other cases the form and level of consultation is left to the parties, with disputes normally resolved by the governing body, the joint ACP–EU Council of Ministers.[135] The time period for consultation varies according to the nature and gravity of the violation.[136] Ultimately, if consultations do not lead to a solution acceptable to the parties, "appropriate measures" may be taken.[137] Article 96 defines "appropriate measures" as measures taken "in accordance with international law, and proportional to the violation." In accordance with the principle of proportionality, priority must be given to those measures that least disrupt the application of the CPA, and it is understood that suspension would be a measure of "last resort."[138]

The process leading to suspension under the CPA is highly convoluted, except in a "special urgency" situation, as in the case of Liberia,[139] but it has been invoked, following dialogue and consultations, against Fiji,[140] Guinea-Bissau,[141] Ivory Coast,[142] and, repeatedly, against Zimbabwe.[143] The EU has applied a range of measures including withdrawal of EDF resources and, against Zimbabwe, restrictions on capital payments and freezing of funds of government members.[144] The violations cited in the letters sent to governments of these states typically refer to a failure to respect human rights in general or to hold democratic elections, but in none of these cases has there been a direct reference to violations of fundamental social rights or specified breaches of ILO conventions. This is despite the fact that, for example, in Zimbabwe, there have been a number of substantiated incidents of systematic denial of labor rights and brutal treatment of trade unionists.[145]

---

[134] CPA Art. 96(2)(b). If measures are taken by one of the parties in a case of special urgency that party must, under Art. 96(2)(c), notify the other party and the joint ACP–EU Council of Ministers and this may, in turn, lead to further consultations and ultimately be resolved through the dispute settlement procedure in Art. 98.

[135] For analysis of the institutional structures, see Udombana, note 92 above, 86–8.

[136] CPA Art. 96(2)(a) as revised. Consultations shall begin no later than 30 days after the procedure is initiated and must not last longer than 120 days.

[137] Ibid. Note also that these measures "shall be revoked" as soon as the reasons for taking them no longer prevail.

[138] CPA Art. 96(2)(c). Under Art. 98 these procedures are subject to a binding dispute settlement process involving international arbitrators.

[139] Council Decision 2003/63/EC, OJ 2003 L220/3. The suspension has now been lifted by Council Decision 2006/450/EC, OJ 2006 L179/51.

[140] Council Decision 2007/641/EC, OJ 2007 L260/15.

[141] Council Decision 2004/680/EC, OJ 2004 L311/27.

[142] Council Decision 2001/510/EC, OJ 2001 L183/38.

[143] Council Decision 2002/148/EC, OJ 2002 L50/64.

[144] See Bartels, note 9 above, 152–3. Suspension of aid to Zimbabwe has been renewed and extended annually since 2002. See Council Decision 2009/148/EC, OJ 2009 L49/15 for the most recent extension.

[145] For a recent example, see reports of the arrest of more than sixty-nine trade unionists, assaults against members of the Zimbabwe Congress of Trade Unions, and the arrest of its

In addition to the essential elements provisions, and for the first time in ACP–EU relations, the CPA includes a specific labor clause, Article 50 on "trade and labor standards." See paragraph 1:

> The parties reaffirm their commitment to internationally recognized core labor standards, as defined by the relevant [ILO] Conventions, and in particular the freedom of association and the right to collective bargaining, the abolition of forced labor, the elimination of the worst forms of child labor and nondiscrimination in respect of employment.

In order to fulfill this commitment, the parties agree to "enhance cooperation in this area" in particular fields, including educational awareness, exchange of information on legislation, "the formulation of national labor legislation and strengthening of existing legislation," and "enforcement of adherence to national legislation and work regulation."[146] Finally, in a statement that reiterates point 5 of the ILO Declaration containing the CLS, the parties agree that "labor standards should not be used for protectionist trade purposes."[147]

When we unpack the contents of Article 50, a number of questions arise. First, what is the purpose and effect of the inclusion of a specific labor clause in the CPA? It might be suggested that by simply restating a commitment to the CLS this provision is merely declaratory and serves to do no more than reaffirm "standards" that, critics have forcefully argued, do not, in themselves, create hard obligations and are, at best, promotional in nature, and may even undermine the ILO's supervisory system.[148] Such a response would be persuasive if Article 50 were to be viewed in isolation, but in the context of the CPA as a whole, the effect of this clause is to crystallize within a sophisticated trade and development regime the essentially soft legal commitments that the parties have signed up to internationally in the ILO Declaration and convert them into a binding bilateral obligation to adhere to the "relevant [ILO] conventions." On this interpretation, the parties have bound themselves to, where necessary, introduce laws and regulations and, in all cases, ensure their effective application in respect of, at least, the eight core conventions referred to in the ILO Declaration.[149] Although the agreement of the parties to enhance cooperation in these fields might appear

---

Secretary General in December 2008, as strongly condemned by the International Trade Union Confederation: www.ituc-csi.org/spip.php?article2605.

[146] CPA Art. 50(2).   [147] CPA Art. 50(3).

[148] For example, see Alston, note 45 above, who refers, at 511, to the Annex to the Declaration, which proclaims that the follow-up to the CLS is of a "strictly promotional nature" although such action can be presented as complementary to ILO supervision.

[149] ILO Declaration, point 2, note 32 above. The "relevant conventions" are freedom of association and collective bargaining (87 and 98); forced labor (29 and 105); nondiscrimination (100 and 111); minimum age in employment (138); and elimination of the worst forms of child labor (182). Alston, note 45 above at 490, contends that, although the CLS are sourced from the specified conventions, the precise relationship between the CLS and the detailed text of the conventions is expressed in an "opaque formula."

somewhat vacuous, the CPA framework provides a basis not merely for a tick-box approach to ratification of ILO conventions that the parties have already signed up to, but rather for monitoring compliance in practice by improving the quality of labor legislation and enforcement of labor standards on the ground. As Hepple has explained, the "unique legal character" of the Declaration is that "obligations are placed on all [ILO] member-states not by reason of ratification of the named conventions, but from the very fact of membership."[150] The ILO has set a target of 2015 for universal ratification of these conventions and significant progress has been made in this direction, including in Africa.[151]

Article 50 has the effect of mainstreaming the CLS, as recommended by the World Commission on the Social Dimension of Globalization,[152] on the basis that the ILO is unable to realize its objectives acting alone but is more likely to pursue them effectively with the assistance of powerful actors such as the EU and ACP.[153] This approach is also reinforced by the inclusion of the CLS within the UN Global Compact.[154] The "constitutional obligation"[155] that flows from the Declaration is thus rendered more effective through its transposition directly into the CPA and is therefore subject to the collective oversight of the parties and, more broadly, coordinated action under the strategic partnership between the European Commission and the ILO.[156]

Article 50 is therefore best understood as more than a mere declaration, but this leads us to a second question. The trade and labor clause is located within the chapter on "trade-related areas" in the Title on Economic and Trade Cooperation in Part 3 of the CPA setting out Cooperation Strategies. What therefore is the relationship between the somewhat remotely situated Article 50 and the core "essential elements" provisions in the "Political Dimension" in Part 1? More specifically, does Article 50 add weight to or detract from the parties' agreement to uphold "fundamental social rights" in line with their international obligations and to act on alleged violations under the procedure in Article 96? If the CLS equate to "fundamental social rights" within the meaning of Article 9, it follows that Article 50 may serve as a conduit for the EU to take such action in the event of reported violations, especially in cases where such reports emanate from the ILO.

In seeking answers to this question, it is necessary, at least tentatively, to enter into the polarized debate between those, such as Langille, who regard the CLS as core labor rights that positively reinforce the noncore conventions in the international labor code as part of a coherent "constitutional" framework[157] and those, notably Alston, who are concerned about an excessive reliance on

---

[150] Hepple, note 46 above, p. 59.
[151] Hepple, ibid. p. 60.
[152] See note 2 above.
[153] See Alston, note 64 above, p. 8.
[154] Launched in 2000 and signed up to by business leaders: www.unglobalcompact.org.
[155] See Hepple, note 46 above, p. 59.
[156] See note 87 above.
[157] Langille, note 45 above, at 409.

"principles" that are "delinked from corresponding standards and thus effectively undefined."[158] According to Alston, the concentration on the CLS produces major flaws, including "an ethos of voluntarism in relation to implementation and enforcement, an unstructured and unacceptable decentralization of responsibility, and a willingness to accept soft 'promotionalism' as the bottom line."[159] In response to this debate, it is important to note that although the 1998 Declaration is, of itself, inherently soft in international law terms, in the sense that it promotes rather than sets standards, somewhat contrary to the ILO tradition, its aim is the bigger prize of triggering adherence to and enforcement of the specified conventions. The CLS are presented as a set of human rights' norms to be applied under international law irrespective of either the traditional ILO method of ratification or a country's level of development.[160]

As a mainstreaming clause, Article 50, when read in conjunction with the essential elements provision, is best understood as aiding this theoretical leap toward the actual attainment of the CLS. On this reading, such an alignment arises in part through a straightforward reinforcement of the parties' obligations to adhere to the "relevant" ILO conventions, providing ballast to the Declaration's reference to the CLS as "fundamental rights."[161] Moreover, when account is taken of the essential elements provisions (which cannot be ignored under the scheme of the CPA), the promotion of these rights must be understood as additional to the binding requirement on the parties, under their international law obligations, to observe all ILO conventions they have ratified including those not listed among the core. Inevitably, the selection of the core creates a presumption of a hierarchy of labor standards that may detract states from formally ratifying "noncore" conventions arguably leading to an irrational prioritization, albeit one based on international consensus. The ILO's more recent "Decent Work Agenda," which focuses on many of the standards left out of the core, may rigidify this distinction by promoting soft programmatic solutions in areas such as employment and income.[162]

The essential elements and labor clauses in the CPA, however, interpreted positively, are capable of transcending this distinction and, to a certain extent, the academic debate, on the basis that the CLS can be understood as fully subsumed within the "fundamental social rights" in the CPA and cannot be distinguished from, or raised above, the "hard law" status of ratified ILO conventions.

[158] Alston, note 45 above, at 457. In Alston's assessment, at 483, "principles" are placed ahead of "rights" and the former are employed in general international law to "denote either a norm of lesser status than a right or a broad general principle very different in nature" from the principles proclaimed in the Declaration.
[159] Alston, note 45 above, at 457.
[160] See R. Blackwell, *Business and Human Rights* (Harvard Law School, Human Rights Program, 1999). Discussed by McCrudden and Davies, note 31 above, at 50.
[161] Para. 2 of the Declaration, note 32 above.
[162] See note 46 above and the critique of Alston, note 45 above, at 488.

Thus, even though the follow-up system under the CLS is a reporting mechanism and not sanctions, and is not subject to the normal ILO supervisory system,[163] the process is designed to increase the number of ratifications of, at least, the core conventions in combination with action arising through mainstreaming instruments and international agreements such as the CPA. On this basis it follows that, within the revised ACP–EU *acquis*, both "core" and "noncore" conventions falling within these categories are "relevant" and subject to political dialogue and, ultimately, the consultation procedure in Article 96.

Discussion of the issues surrounding this question lead us a third related question. If it is accepted, even by CLS sceptics, that violations of fundamental social rights, at least in the form of ratified ILO conventions among the core, can be pursued under the CPA, why has the EU been so cautious? The answer, in part, is that the EU's silence on labor rights issues in its actions under the consultation procedure does not necessarily negate the argument presented earlier regarding the potential of pursuing violations. Rather, it may indicate a degree of caution on the part of the EU when deciding whether or not to emphasize violations of labor rights in cases involving multiple breaches of the essential elements. Such caution may simply reflect the fact that, consistent with the requirement of proportionality,[164] the first and easiest step is to pursue other grounds, such as alleged breaches of democratic principles on the basis that once these issues are resolved by, for example, simply holding an election, any human rights violations can be addressed later.[165] The EU has to be satisfied that the violation is sufficiently serious to justify restrictions on market access that may run counter to its economic interests and, more importantly, the immediate needs of the population of the country in question. It also reflects the reality that the ground for any conflict over violations of labor rights has to be carefully chosen and the proposed measures have to be proportionate to ward off any charges of protectionism. This also ties in with a more general problem in international labor law that states facing such allegations may be able to point to formal ratification of the relevant conventions and have sufficient support among other states in their region to resist pressure from the ILO.[166] Regionalization and differentiation in the CPA may inadvertently serve to reinforce such resistance. If the EU's caution persists in cases where there is strong evidence of violations of ratified ILO conventions, or of the CLS specifically, it would be unfortunate because such reticence tends

---

[163] See further, Hepple note 46 above, pp. 60–2.   [164] CPA Art. 96(2)(c).

[165] See Davies, note 17 above at 186, who contends that full suspension of the CPA is only likely to be invoked in cases of grave violations such as the collapse of democracy, and, even if freedom of association is violated, it would be unlikely, alone, to constitute grounds for suspension.

[166] Zimbabwe, for example, has ratified the conventions on freedom of association and the right to organize.

to reinforce the widely held perception that "social rights are like paper tigers, fierce in appearance, but missing in tooth and claw."[167]

Concerns about the balance to be struck between trade liberalization and labor rights lead us to a fourth and final question concerning the purpose of Article 50, specifically the final paragraph declaring that "labor standards should not be used for protectionist purposes." Following the inclusion of a similar caveat in point 5 of the ILO Declaration, its reiteration here is hardly surprising, but what is its effect on the CPA as a whole? In addressing this question, it is important to note at the outset that the "comparative advantage" theory has received strong support from many ACP countries represented among the group of 113 that pressed for the inclusion of the corresponding paragraph in the Declaration.[168] There is little doubt that the ACP delegation at Cotonou would not have been prepared to accept an explicit trade-labor clause without the refinement of labor rights in the CLS and the caveat against protectionism. The decision of such a large number of developing nations to accept the CLS as an integral part of a PTA does, however, mark an important development that is indicative of an implicit acceptance that increased trade between the EU and ACP countries goes hand in hand with the safeguarding of labor rights.[169] Such claims are not yet proven but the driving force of globalization is such that the pressure to fall back on a minimum set of "core" labor rights as a means of preserving a social dimension has become irresistible. In turn, this helps to explain the compromises involved in the choice of core conventions that form the CLS. The selected conventions are designed to balance "social progress and economic growth."[170] Conventions concerning working hours, night work, and unemployment are not included because they might be regarded, if raised to the level of obligatory human rights norms, as a threat to economic competitiveness.[171] The CLS are also significantly narrower in scope than the labor rights enumerated in the EU's own CFR.[172] Moreover, as McCrudden and Davies note, none of the conventions directly concern the level of wages as part of a "clear attempt to lessen the accusation of protectionism and the erosion of comparative advantage."[173] What remains is a selection of conventions that, from the classical perspective of labor law, is incomplete and incoherent, but there is an underlying logic to choosing those labor rights that command the widest consensus, reflect freedom of contract, and avoid conflict with the prevailing drive for trade liberalization.[174]

---

[167] See B. Hepple, "Enforcement: the Law and Politics of Cooperation and Compliance," in B. Hepple (ed.), *Social and Labour Rights in a Global Context* (Cambridge: CUP, 2002), 238–57 at 238.
[168] Hepple, note 46 above, p. 61.   [169] Ibid., p. 51.
[170] See the preamble of the ILO Declaration, note 32 above.
[171] Hepple, note 46 above, p. 59.   [172] Alston, note 45 above, at 487.
[173] McCrudden and Davies, note 31 above, at 51–2.
[174] Ibid.

The inclusion of both the CLS and the caveat against protectionism in the CPA was an inevitable outcome of the EU's own approach to the social dimension and the international posture of many ACP countries, but nevertheless it has the distinct advantage of enabling the EU to act, within the constraints discussed previously, to enforce the essential elements, including labor rights recognized as human rights norms – the CLS and ratified ILO conventions – without breaching WTO rules. In this context, it can be argued that consultations under Article 96 flowing from alleged violations of ILO conventions must be regarded as wholly separate from trade issues on the basis that the ILO has functional autonomy over labor standards. The EU is able to justify its actions as objective and proportionate with trade liberalization objectives. From this standpoint, trade preferences can be suspended without violating the WTO's MFN clause. Indeed, the requirement for such a defense mechanism has only increased following India's successful challenge to the EU's GSP in 2002, which, although it applies only to special rules concerning GSPs and did not directly address labor conditionality, has highlighted the importance placed by the WTO on the need for the EU to have objective processes for determining the rules for granting trade preferences to developing countries and differentiating between them.[175]

Positive conditionality under the CPA, tying in with the need to promote social rights to meet the global challenge of sustainable development, can thus be presented as nonprotectionist and wholly consistent with WTO law. The EU acknowledges the difficulty of advancing labor rights in this context but, by accepting caveats concerning protectionism, it is able to extoll but not necessarily export its social model and, also, is choosing to work within the boundaries of the international legal order when pursuing its "moral" obligation as a global actor.

4.   Concluding Remarks and Ways Forward

The EU's approach to international relations has been transformed in recent years in both philosophy and practice. Labor rights are merely a singular thread among a complex web of issues that underlie the dynamic of trade, development cooperation, environment, human rights, and foreign policy. In its external posture, the EU upholds the virtues of market liberalism and accepts its hegemonic dominance in the global order.[176] From this starting position the EU believes,

---

[175] WTO Appellate Body Report, WT/DS246/AB/R, April 7, 2004. Discussed by G. M. Grossman and A. O. Sykes, "A Preference for Development: The Law and Economics of GSP," in G. A. Bermann & P. C. Mavroidis (eds.), *WTO Law and Developing Countries* (New York: CUP, 2007), 255–82 and, in the same volume, J. Kenner, "The Remodeled European Community GSP+: A Positive Response to the WTO Ruling?," 292–305.

[176] See, for example, the Commission's Communication: *The Social Dimension of Globalization*, note 2 above, Executive Summary, para. 1, in which it proposes a policy approach that "contributes to maximizing the *benefits of globalization* for all social groups in all its partner

somewhat bombastically, that it has the capacity to extend the reach of its policies beyond its formal powers by "shaping globalization" based on *our* common values and principles."[177] Statements of this kind, frequently reiterated, are in many ways unhelpful because they tend to reinforce the view that, even when echoing consensus-based international legal obligations such as the CLS, the EU is spouting universal language as a guise for promoting its own objectives.[178] In turn, this leads to suspicion that terms such as partnership in the context of a "*European* Consensus on Development" are mere figments deployed by the EU to avoid charges of neocolonialism.[179] Such fears will only be exacerbated if foreign policy considerations appear to be influencing choices concerning trade preferences, levels of development assistance, and the selection of states who should or should not face "appropriate measures" for alleged human rights' violations. Moreover, there is a real danger that the assertion of human rights as a precondition to the right to development, if applied negatively or disproportionately, will engender a relationship not of cooperation but coercion.[180] The EU, as the stronger party in the relationship, has to remind itself that, notwithstanding the language of "dialogue" and "consultations," in practice, conditionality only works one way[181] and, as cases such as *Laval* and *Viking Line* vividly demonstrate,[182] it too has to balance economic and social considerations when applying fundamental social rights in its internal market and should not impose double standards on its weaker partners.[183] When it comes to the assertion of labor rights, in particular, there is the additional problem of convincing trading partners, and indeed the WTO, that the EU's external actions are not motivated by a desire to protect the interests of European workers, not least in a period of global recession and rising unemployment.

What this analysis of the CPA has served to demonstrate is that, for the first time in ACP–EU relations, core labor rights are included within a shared conception of "fundamental social rights" but, as an integral part of a finely balanced package, they cannot be detached from trade issues and are inextricably tied to progress toward sustainable development, especially in the poorest regions and countries. The case for and against the CLS as a selection of labor rights is finely

---

countries and regions" (emphasis added). For an incisive critique of the EU's strategy based on a neo-Gramscian analysis, see Hurt, note 105 above.

[177] *EU Declaration on Globalization*, Annex of the Council of the EU Presidency Conclusions, December 14, 2007, p. 25. Emphasis added.

[178] Leino, note 43 above, p. 264.   [179] Ibid., p. 273.

[180] See especially the critique of Hurt, note 105 above.

[181] K. Arts, *Integrating Human Rights into Development Cooperation: The Case of the Lomé Convention* (The Hague: Kluwer Law International, 2000), p. 193.

[182] See note 59 above.

[183] On this point, see the analysis of Novitz, note 28 above, who cites several examples of failures by EU member-states to uphold their obligations under ratified ILO conventions. Also, Leino, note 43 above at p. 269, observes that more powerful non-ACP partners, such as China, are able to insist on a dialogue-only approach to human rights with no realistic prospect of sanctions.

balanced but labor lawyers should not lose sight of the bigger picture. What the CLS undoubtedly provide is a basis for mainstreaming norms that are regarded as compatible with international trade without detracting from the obligations of the parties in international law. The effectiveness of the CPA in this respect should not be assessed crudely by reference to the volume of political dialogue or the frequency with which procedures are launched under Article 96. Instead, progress is dependent on positive advances that, over time, make the comparative advantage theory less salient. Above all, such changes require a deepening of the partnership "based on a balance of interests and mutual respect"[184] through the evolving EPA process. Such a development must take account of the reality of survival in a world where 1.5 billion people, one-third of the working-age population, are either unemployed or unable to earn enough to lift themselves or their families out of poverty.[185] In this context, it is essential to take account of the level of social and technological development in each country and the impact on their economy of decisions of powerful private actors, both multinational corporations and financiers, when making investment choices.

As an indicator of the potential of the CPA, and the broader strategy of regionalization and differentiation going forward, the substance of the CARIFORUM–EU EPA suggests a more sophisticated approach extending significantly beyond the terms of the CPA.[186] First, by contrast with the CPA, there is a specific reference in the preamble of the EPA to the need to respect "basic labor rights" in line with the commitments the parties have undertaken within the ILO directly linked to the need for "economic and social progress for their people in a manner consistent with sustainable development." This statement indicates significant progress, and a degree of comfort on the part of both sets of parties, in linking labor rights with development policy, referring to labor rights rather than standards or principles, and referencing ILO commitments that must be taken to extend beyond the CLS and include, at least, all ratified conventions. Second, contained among the cooperation priorities is a commitment to enhancing the technological and research capabilities of the CARIFORUM states so as to "facilitate development of, and compliance with … internationally recognized labor and environmental standards."[187] In this way, the fulfillment of international labor standards is being mainstreamed into core development objectives. Third, in perhaps the most innovative feature of the agreement, the "behavior of investors" is directly addressed. Investors are required to "act in accordance with core labor standards" as required by the ILO.[188] More powerfully, under Article 73 on "maintenance of standards," the parties "shall ensure" that "foreign

---

[184] See the "Algiers Declaration" of the Organization of African Unity, OAU Assembly, 35th Ord. Session p. 8, OAU Doc. AHG/Decl. 1 (XXXV), July 1999.

[185] UN statistics from 2006. See the preamble of the UN ECOSOC Resolution 2008/18, note 46 above.

[186] See note 106 above.   [187] CARIFORUM–EU EPA Art. 8(v).

[188] CARIFORUM–EU EPA Art. 72.

direct investment is not encouraged by lowering domestic environmental, labor, or occupational health and safety legislation and standards" or "by relaxing core labor standards." Although the actual enforcement of this policy is left to each country, the message it sends to potential investors is clear. Moreover, this provision represents a clear rejection of social dumping and incorporates the established EU principle that states are expected to maintain a floor of basic labor standards.[189]

Finally, the CARIFORUM–EU EPA has a separate chapter on "social aspects" of trade, Articles 191–196. This chapter reiterates the provisions of CPA Article 50 regarding the CLS, including the caveat on protectionism. However, it also seeks to encourage "high levels" of social and labor standards "consistent with internationally recognized rights," subject to the social development priorities of each state.[190] In addition, it contains a provision on "upholding levels of protection"[191] that broadens and reinforces the parties' commitment to maintain and improve standards by agreeing "not to encourage trade or foreign direct investment or maintain a competitive advantage" by "(a) lowering the level of protection provided by domestic social and labor legislation" or "(b) derogating from, or failing to apply, such legislation or standards."[192] This is backed up by a detailed procedure for consultation and monitoring, including a facility to appoint a Committee of Experts and seek advice from the ILO.[193]

In addressing the relationship between trade and labor issues, the CARIFORUM–EU EPA shifts the emphasis in a positive direction. In a remarkable statement it expresses unconditional support for linking trade, labor standards, and "decent work."[194] In Article 191(3), it makes this declaration:

> The Parties recognize the beneficial role that core labor standards and decent work can have on economic efficiency, innovation, and productivity, and they highlight the value of greater policy coherence between trade policies, on the one hand, and social policies on the other.

This paragraph is nuanced and open to a variety of interpretations but it represents, at least, a shared appreciation of what McCrudden and Davies describe as the "positive synergies between trade liberalization and labor rights."[195] This first EPA would have been easier to negotiate with the smaller CARIFORUM group and, without doubt, the EPAs to be finalized for Africa present a greater challenge, but it may yet serve as a model for subsequent regional partnerships. The EU now recognizes that its economic and social model "cannot simply be transposed to other parts of the world"[196] but can be adapted, subject to democratic

[189] EC Art. 137(4).
[190] CARIFORUM–EU EPA Art. 192.
[191] CARIFORUM–EU EPA Art. 193.
[192] Ibid.
[193] CARIFORUM–EU EPA Art. 195.
[194] CARIFORUM–EU EPA Art. 191(2).
[195] McCrudden and Davies, note 31 above, at 48.
[196] See the European Commission's Communication: *The Social Dimension of Globalization*, note 2 above, Executive Summary, para. 1.

support, where conditions suit, in conjunction with strategies to ensure that obligations to uphold international labor standards are met. Suspension of trade preferences and development assistance remains an option, as a last resort, but the case for linkage between trade and labor standards is not about sanctions.[197] As the world enters a period of deep recession both the positive benefits and negative side effects of globalization are widely understood. In this difficult climate, there is now the potential for agreement on a positive, more confident, and, above all, equitable approach to trade, development, and labor issues upon which genuine regional partnerships can be based.

[197] See C. Barry and S. J. Reddy, *International Trade & Labor Standards* (New York: Columbia University Press, 2008), p. 5.

JUAN A. MARCHETTI

7 Do PTAs Actually Increase Parties' Services Trade?

World Trade Organization

Preferential liberalization of trade in services is not a new phenomenon, but it has become a more common and prominent feature of the latest generation of bilateral preferential trade agreements (PTAs) negotiated in this decade.[1] As of September 15, 2008, fifty-six such accords have been notified to the World Trade Organization (WTO) under Article V of the General Agreement on Trade in Service (GATS; see Table 7.1). Most of those notifications arrived after 2001 – fifty compared to six before the year 2000. In addition, many more agreements are currently being negotiated.

One might expect that countries entering these PTAs do so with the objective of eliminating barriers to trade in services, but more importantly, in the hope that the agreements will actually increase bilateral services trade between the parties. Lack of reliable data on trade in services (especially of bilateral flows) has made it almost impossible to carry out empirical studies of the determinants of bilateral services trade flows and – in particular – of the effects of PTAs on trade flows in services. However, the availability of statistics on trade in services has improved over the past year, particularly among Organization for Economic Cooperation and Development (OECD) countries. Taking those developments in the statistical field into account, the main purpose of this chapter is to provide an initial quantitative estimate of the effect of PTAs on bilateral trade in services, using the standard gravity model.

The author would like to thank Gene Grossman, Petros C. Mavroidis, and Roberta Piermartini for helpful comments, discussions, and suggestions on an earlier version of this chapter. All remaining errors are my own. The views expressed are personal and do not necessarily represent those of the WTO Members or the WTO Secretariat.

[1] Even prior to the advent of the WTO General Agreement on Trade in Services (GATS), preferential liberalization of services trade had already been included in the EC Treaty (and moreover when the internal market initiative was introduced), and in NAFTA. Moreover, even before the end of the twentieth century, services liberalization had already been envisaged in such agreements as Mercosur, ASEAN, and the Andean Community.

Table 7.1. *PTA agreements on services trade notified to the WTO (as of September 2008)*

Agreement	Date of entry into force	Date notified by Parties
T1Brunei Darussalam–Japan	31-Jul-08	31-Jul-08
Iceland–Faroe Islands	1-Nov-06	10-Jul-08
ASEAN–China	1-Jul-07	26-Jun-08
Japan–Indonesia	1-Jul-08	27-Jun-08
Chile–Panama	7-Mar-08	17-Apr-08
Pakistan–Malaysia	1-Jan-08	19-Feb-08
Japan–Thailand	1-Nov-07	25-Oct-07
Chile–Japan	3-Sep-07	24-Aug-07
EC 27	1-Jan-07	26-Jun-07
Trans–Pacific SEP	28-May-06	18-May-07
India–Singapore	1-Aug-05	3-May-07
Panama–Singapore	24-Jul-06	4-Apr-07
MERCOSUR	7-Dec-05	5-Dec-06
U.S.–Bahrain	1-Aug-06	8-Sep-06
Costa Rica–Mexico	1-Jan-95	17-Jul-06
EFTA–Korea	1-Sep-06	23-Aug-06
Japan–Malaysia	13-Jul-06	12-Jul-06
Jordan–Singapore	22-Aug-05	7-Jul-06
Guatemala–Mexico	15-Mar-01	3-Jul-06
Honduras–Mexico	1-Jun-01	20-Jun-06
El Salvador–Mexico	15-Mar-01	23-May-06
U.S.–CAFTA–DR	01-Mar-06	17-Mar-06
Korea–Singapore	2-Mar-06	21-Feb-06
U.S.–Morocco	1-Jan-06	30-Dec-05
Thailand–New Zealand	1-Jul-05	1-Dec-05
Mexico–Nicaragua	1-Jul-98	26-Oct-05
EC–Chile	1-Mar-05	28-Oct-05
Japan–Mexico	1-Apr-05	31-Mar-05
Panama–El Salvador	11-Apr-03	24-Feb-05
Thailand–Australia	1-Jan-05	27-Dec-04
U.S.–Australia	1-Jan-05	22-Dec-04
EFTA–Chile	1-Dec-04	3-Dec-04
EC 25	1-May-04	26-Apr-04
Korea–Chile	1-Apr-04	8-Apr-04
Chile–El Salvador	1-Jun-02	5-Feb-04
China–Macao, China	1-Jan-04	27-Dec-03
China–Hong Kong, China	1-Jan-04	27-Dec-03
U.S.–Singapore	1-Jan-04	17-Dec-03
U.S.–Chile	1-Jan-04	16-Dec-03
Singapore–Australia	28-Jul-03	25-Sep-03
CARICOM	1-Jul-97	17-Jan-03
EFTA–Singapore	1-Jan-03	14-Jan-03
EFTA	1-Jun-02	3-Dec-02
Japan–Singapore	30-Nov-02	8-Nov-02
United States–Jordan	17-Dec-01	15-Jan-02
EC–Mexico	1-Oct-00	21-Jun-02
Chile–Costa Rica	15-Feb-02	16-Apr-02

(*cont.*)

Table 7.1 *(continued)*

Agreement	Date of entry into force	Date notified by Parties
New Zealand–Singapore	1-Jan-01	4-Sep-01
EFTA–Mexico	1-Jul-00	25-Jul-01
Chile–Mexico	1-Aug-99	27-Feb-01
Canada–Chile	5-Jul-97	30-Jul-97
EEA	1-Jan-94	13-Sep-96
CER	1-Jan-89	22-Nov-95*
EC (Treaty of Rome)	1-Jan-58	10-Nov-95*
NAFTA	1-Jan-94	1-Mar-95*
EC accession of Austria, Finland, and Sweden	1-Jan-95	20-Jan-95*

Source: WTO.

Another very important question, particularly when analyzing PTAs from a "law and economics" perspective, is whether different PTAs have a different impact on trade in services – in other words, whether some of them are more effective than others in promoting trade in services. This question will also be addressed in the chapter by, first, describing the different modalities adopted by PTAs and, second, by factoring those differences into the gravity equation.

The chapter is organized as follows. Section 1 gives a brief overview of the basic economics of trade in services. Section 2 looks into the law of PTAs. In doing so, the chapter takes a broad view of preferential integration in services to cater for not only negative integration agreements, basically the new-generation PTAs, but also positive integration agreements, such as the European Communities. Section 3 provides a selective survey of the gravity equation in international trade. Section 4 reviews previous literature on the application of the gravity equation to trade in services. Section 5 presents the empirical specification and the data used in this chapter. Section 6 presents the estimation results. The final section concludes.

1. The Basic Economics of Trade in Services

Simply put, *services* are a diverse group of economic activities distinct from manufacturing, mining, and agriculture. From the point of view of consumption, a distinction can be made between producer and consumer services. The former are input into the production of goods and other services, while the latter are destined to final consumption. Producer services include communication, transport and storage, retail and wholesale distribution, banking, insurance, finance, advertising, marketing, computer-related services, and professional services. Consumer services include both personal services, consumed by individuals and households as part of private consumption (e.g., tourism, cultural and entertainment activities, domestic services), and collective services, consumed by groups of persons as part of public consumption (e.g., public services, health and social services, education, water supply, sanitation and sewerage services, waste collection and disposal). It is clear that many of these services, such as telecommunications, have a dual role, being at the same time inputs into the production process and services for final consumption.

Economists have long debated the differences between goods and services. Services are usually characterized as intangible, nonstorable, and requiring simultaneous production and consumption; goods, in contrast, are tangible and storable, and hence do not typically require simultaneity of supply and use. Intangibility is a common feature of services. One can physically touch a manufactured product, but services are intangible. One cannot touch a piece of legal advice or a journey, although one can often see the results.

Arguably the most important difference between the goods and services is that the latter must be consumed as they are produced, and hence do require simultaneous interaction between the producer and the consumer. For many services, whose number is growing because of technological advances, this key feature is of course not necessary. Think of a variety of financial, entertainment, information, professional, education, and communication services that can be produced in one country and delivered to consumers in another country, either through electronic means or stored in some medium (e.g., paper, CD-ROM). However, a good number of services do require proximity between the consumer and the producer to make trade possible, and therefore call for the movement of one or the other. Examples of such services are construction, tourism, haircuts, or most medical services, among many others. Even for the services that can actually be supplied at a distance, the personal contact between suppliers and consumers is often seen as necessary to complete the transactions, build trust, and compensate for information asymmetries between suppliers and clients.

The interaction between producers and consumers implies that a definition of trade in services must go beyond our traditional understanding of trade to encompass provider and consumer mobility across national borders. We will see in the next section that agreements dealing with services trade (both at the bilateral and multilateral levels) have taken account of this specific feature.

The specific features of services have critical implications for what we understand as trade policy in services. Border measures, particularly tariffs, are almost impossible to apply to trade in services for the simple reason that customs agents will not be able to see the service cross the border. What customs agents, as well as most of us, will observe are service suppliers (either firms or persons) or consumers crossing the frontier. Price-based measures, such as taxes, may be applied to services (including foreign services) but will not be levied on the border but rather within a country's borders. Additionally, if services trade requires the movement of suppliers and/or consumers, then the ability of governments to impede international transactions on services will depend on regulations affecting the entry, establishment, and operations of service suppliers (be they firms or persons) or the movement of consumers.

However, as explained elsewhere (Marchetti and Mavroidis, 2004) regulations are very heterogeneous, and although some may have been designed as protectionist devices others may be necessary to achieve legitimate economic or social objectives. The GATS, and all the bilateral PTAs dealing with services, solve the question by distinguishing between trade restrictions and "domestic regulations." The disciplines on market access and national treatment are meant to capture the most outrageous or explicit forms of protection of national service industries, that is, discriminatory measures or specifically identified limitations on market access, whereas the disciplines on "domestic regulation" deal with more implicit forms of barriers to trade in services stemming from licensing and qualification requirements, procedures, and technical standards.

2. The Different Liberalization Approaches – From Simple PTAs to Deeper Integration

For the sake of this chapter, I take a rather broad view of PTAs, going from those providing for deeper integration (positive integration type of agreements seeking harmonization of regulations) to those envisaging the liberalization of specific restrictions to trade in services without aiming at regulatory harmonization (negative integration type of agreements). The European Union (EU) and the European Economic Area (EEA) belong to the first category; all the other PTAs negotiated in the past decade belong to the second one. This second category can be further divided into those agreements providing for a GATS-type gradual approach to opening services markets, those adopting an immediate North American Free Trade Agreement (NAFTA)-type liberalization approach, and those adopting a hybrid approach (mixture of the previous two).[2] A full analysis of the plethora of agreements covering trade in services would certainly be beyond the scope of this chapter.[3] Instead, I will focus on the liberalization modalities and principles adopted by the different groups of agreements now in place.

2.1. GATS-Type Agreements

GATS-type agreements contain one chapter dealing with (almost) all aspects of services trade.[4] These agreements apply to "measures affecting trade in

---

[2] GATS stands for General Agreement on Trade in Services.
[3] For an analysis of liberalization commitments in several PTAs negotiated in this decade, see Roy, Marchetti, and Lim (2006, 2007, and 2008).
[4] See, for example, the following PTAs: EFTA (European free Trade Association)–Korea, EFTA–Chile, EFTA–Mexico, EC–Chile, EC–Mexico, Association of Southest Asian Nations (ASEAN), and Mercosur's protocol on services.

services," with trade being defined by reference to four modes of supply that, as explained in the previous section, take account of the different modalities through which services can be supplied. The four modes are the following:

- Cross-border trade or mode 1, that is, the supplier and the consumer interact over distance, and it is the "service" that actually "crosses" the border;
- Consumption abroad or mode 2, that is, the consumer "moves" (most probably physically but possibly also "virtually" through the Internet) to the supplier's jurisdiction and "consumes" the service there;
- Commercial presence or foreign suppliers or mode 3, that is, the producer sells services directly to consumers in the latter's jurisdiction, through commercial establishments such as subsidiaries or branches; and
- Temporary presence of foreign natural persons supplying services or mode 4, that is, the supplier (in this case a natural person, either employed or self-employed) supplies services directly to the consumers in the latter jurisdiction, through his or her temporary presence in the consumer's territory.

Save for a few exceptions (e.g., sectoral exclusions in the PTA between Australia and Thailand, or the exclusion of financial services from the PTA between [European Free Trade Association] EFTA countries and Chile), the sectoral coverage of these agreements is the widest possible – all services are covered, except for the bulk of air transport services and "services supplied in the exercise of governmental authority," which are those supplied neither in competition nor on a commercial basis.[5]

Market access and national treatment are central obligations in PTAs. Market access provisions are aimed at prohibiting a specific set of governmental measures restricting the supply of services. In GATS-type agreements, six types of market access limitations are contemplated: (a) limitations on the total number of suppliers; (b) limitations on the total number of transactions or assets; (c) limitations on the total value of operations or output; (d) limitations on the total number of employees; (e) restrictions on the type of legal entity required to supply services; and (f) restrictions on foreign equity participation. These correspond to the measures listed in Article XVI:2(a)–(f) of the GATS. The national treatment obligation is usually defined in GATS-type agreements as in Article XVII:1 of the GATS, as the obligation to "accord to services and service suppliers of [the other party], in respect of all measures affecting the supply of services, treatment no less favorable than that it accords to its own like services and service suppliers." Unlike the market access obligation, the national treatment obligation does not identify specific limitations, and hence any measure applied to the detriment of like foreign service and service suppliers, either de jure or de facto, would qualify as a departure from national treatment.

---

[5] For a discussion on "services supplied in the exercise of governmental authority," see Marchetti and Mavroidis (2004).

Market access and national treatment are not general and unconditional obligations in GATS-type agreements. In other words, these agreements do not contain any obligation to grant access to, or avoid discrimination of, foreign services and services suppliers. Rather, under these agreements the freedom to access the market through any of those modes of supply, as well as the extent of national treatment, are subject to negotiations, and the resulting commitments are entered into national schedules. Because of this approach, unless the agreement provides for periodic rounds of negotiations, such as Mercosur and ASEAN, liberalization of services trade (understood as the granting of access and national treatment to foreign services and services suppliers) may be quite incomplete or, rather, cover a limited number of sectors.

A critical element of any trade agreement covering services is its negotiating modality, which determines the sectoral coverage of those liberalization commitments (i.e., the sectors that will be subject to market access and national treatment obligations, and the extent to which these obligations will apply). GATS-type agreements adopt a so-called positive-list or bottom-up modality whereby the liberalization obligations (market access and national treatment) only apply to the sectors listed and are subject to any limitations or conditions inscribed in the schedule of commitments. Limitations may be inscribed with respect to any of the six market access measures described earlier, and with respect to any discriminatory measure.[6] Under a positive-list approach, limitations may be introduced for existing nonconforming measures or for future measures. Moreover, because only "measures" are bound, no indication is given of the relevant laws/regulations on which these are based, which accentuates the lack of transparency of this scheduling mechanism.

Agreements generally adopting a GATS-type approach include Mercosur, ASEAN, Thailand–Australia, Singapore–Australia, Singapore–Japan, New Zealand–Singapore, the PTAs signed by the EC, and the PTAs subscribed by EFTA countries.

2.2. NAFTA-Type Agreements

These agreements have both a services chapter ("cross-border trade in services") and an investment chapter. The services chapter applies then to measures affecting cross-border trade in services, which is defined as including the

[6] Actually, three levels of commitments are possible in GATS-type schedules: (1) Full commitments, whereby a country commits itself not to apply any of the six market access limitations and not to discriminate foreign services and service suppliers. This is indicated by inscribing the word "none" in the sector and model of supply concerned; (2) partial commitments, whereby the country indicates which market access limitations may apply, and any applicable limitation on national treatment; and (3) no commitment at all, whereby the country reserves the right to impose any of the six market access limitations or to discriminate like foreign services and service suppliers. This is indicated by inscribing the word "unbound" in the sector and mode of supply concerned.

equivalent to GATS modes 1, 2, and 4, but does not cover the supply of a service through foreign direct investment (FDI), which is instead covered by a specific chapter on investment.[7] Further provisions on the temporary movement of some categories of natural persons are also typically found in an additional chapter.

With regard to sectoral coverage, NAFTA-type agreements also differ from the GATS type in that they list the categories of services that parties to the agreement will not be prevented to supply, such as law enforcement, correctional services, income security or insurance, social security or insurance, social welfare, public education, public training, health, and childcare. Some of the new agreements signed by the United States do contain "public services" carve-outs (i.e., exceptions) similar to the ones contained in the GATS.

Older PTAs, such as NAFTA and Canada–Chile, do not have a specific provision on "market access" but contain a somewhat similar discipline addressing "quantitative restrictions," which are defined as nondiscriminatory measures that impose quota-type limitations on (a) the number of service providers or (b) the operations of any service provider.[8] Depending on the interpretation of the "limitations on the operations of any service supplier," this apparently more limited list of restrictions (compared to the six included in GATS Article XVI) may have a similar or broader coverage compared to the GATS list of market access limitations.

The new generation of NAFTA-type agreements, including those signed by the United States, do contain a market access provision modeled on GATS Article XVI, but excluding foreign equity restrictions from the list of market access limitations. This omission, however, does not seem to modify the liberalization content of the cross-border services chapter in these agreements because foreign equity limitations may be captured by the national treatment principle.

NAFTA-type agreements also have a national treatment obligation, defined differently than in the GATS, as treatment no less favorable than the one accorded "in like circumstances" to one's own service providers. The comparator then is different: "like" services and service suppliers in the GATS, and "like circumstances" in the NAFTA-type agreements. This difference may have relevant implications in the protection afforded by the national treatment principle in the different agreements.

As in the GATS, market access (or quantitative restrictions) and national treatment are not immediate and unconditional obligations, but negotiable

---

[7] Article 1201 of NAFTA provides that Chapter 12 on "Cross-Border Trade in Services" applies to measures relating to cross-border trade in services where "cross-border trade in services" is defined as the "provision of a service (a) from the territory of a Party into the territory of another Party, (b) in the territory of a Party by a person of that Party to a person of another Party, or (c) by a national of a Party in the territory of another Party, but does not include the provision of a service in the territory of a Party by an investment, as defined in Article 1139 (Investment – Definitions), in that territory."

[8] See NAFTA Article 1213 and Canada–Chile Article H-12.

obligations. In other words, parties to these agreements can impose limitations on market access and/or national treatment when making a liberalization commitment. In addition, limitations (or reservations, as they are called in this type of agreement) can be entered with regard to the most-favored-nation principle and the obligation to refrain from imposing a "local presence" requirement as a precondition for the cross-border supply of a service.

In terms of their liberalization modality, NAFTA-type agreements are based on a "top-down" or "negative-list" approach, whereby all sectors are supposed to be subject to the obligations on market access, national treatment, MFN, and local presence, unless otherwise specified in lists of reservations. Reservations are typically for existing nonconforming measures (Annex 1) and for future measures (Annex 2). Contrary to PTAs following the GATS approach, NAFTA-type agreements provide a high degree of transparency because, save for the normally limited number of Annex 2 reservations, the actual level of openness is spelled out, along with an indication of the piece of legislation (e.g., law, regulation) giving ground to the measure.

2.3. "Deeper Integration" Agreements

This category includes the European internal market. The central principles governing the internal market for services are set out in the EC Treaty. This guarantees the freedom to EC services suppliers to establish themselves in other member-states, and the freedom to provide services on the territory of another EC member-state other than the one in which they are established. The free movement of services (complemented by the freedom of establishment) is one of the four fundamental freedoms on which the EC internal market is founded.[9]

Any discrimination concerning the provision of services based on nationality is prohibited directly by the EC Treaty, without the need of specific Community legislation. Services covered under this "freedom" include all the activities of an industrial or commercial character or of craftsmen and the activities of the professions. Services do not include transport, banking, and insurance, which have their own liberalization frameworks.[10]

The EC Treaty provisions have direct effect. This means, in practice, that member-states must modify those national laws that restrict freedom of establishment, or the freedom to provide services, that are incompatible with these principles. Member-states may only maintain restrictions if they are justified by reasons of general interest (e.g., on grounds of public policy, public security, or public health), and provided they are proportionate.

---

[9] The other freedoms include the free movement of goods, the free movement of persons, and the free movement of capital.

[10] The free movement of services rules can also be extended to nationals of a non-EU country who provide services and are established within the EU.

Although the Treaty refers to the freedom to provide services, the European Court of Justice (ECJ) has held that the freedom established by the Treaty includes the freedom, for the recipient of services (such as tourists, persons seeking medical treatment, people traveling for business or study purposes) to go to another member-state to receive the service there. Therefore, this freedom is not just the freedom to provide (akin to mode 1 of the GATS) but also the freedom to consume services anywhere across the EU (akin to mode 2 of the GATS).

The principles of freedom of establishment and free movement of services have been clarified and developed over the years through the case law of the ECJ. In addition, important developments and progress in the field of services have been brought about through specific legislation in fields such as financial services, telecommunications, broadcasting, and the recognition of professional qualifications.

Home-country regulation and mutual recognition are essential to this approach. In other words, if a service is lawfully authorized in one EC member-state, it must be open to users in the other member-states without having to comply with every detail of the legislation of the host country, except those concerning consumer protection. Over the years, however, numerous national barriers were found to prevent the full development of the internal market and made it necessary to take specific actions to remove barriers affecting both the freedom of establishment for providers in member-states and the free movement of services between member-states. This is the aim of the Services Directive adopted in 2006 that establishes a general legal framework facilitating the exercise of the freedom of establishment for service providers and the free movement of services.[11] That framework is "based on a dynamic and selective approach consisting in the removal, as a matter of priority, of barriers which may be dismantled quickly and, for the others, the launching of a process of evaluation, consultation, and complementary harmonization of specific issues, with a view to achieving a genuine internal market for services by 2010."

In the case of the freedom of establishment, the Directive provides for a new framework for authorization schemes including conditions for the granting of authorization, duration, procedures, and so on. Member-states will be able to establish or maintain authorization schemes only if certain conditions are met and these schemes will have to be nondiscriminatory, necessary, and proportionate. The Directive also provides for the creation of single points of contact in each EC (in fact, EEA) member-state through which providers can complete all procedures and formalities.

In the case of freedom to provide services, member-states shall no longer be able to prevent a foreign service provider from offering his or her services on their territory. Member-states may still stipulate their own national requirements, but only for reasons of public policy, public security, public health, or protection

[11] Directive 2006/123.

of the environment. Such national requirements must also respect common internal market principles of nondiscrimination, proportionality, and necessity. To make it easier to monitor such requirements, and to give service providers better and easier access to information on national requirements, all member-states are obliged to report and justify their national requirements to the Commission.

Services covered by the Directive are all business-related services, such as management consultancy services; testing and certification services; advertising and marketing services; distribution services; recruitment services; legal and fiscal advisory services; estate agency services; installation and maintenance services; building and construction services; car rental and travel agency services; and tourism, sport, and entertainment services. Public services (water, electricity, and gas) and waste management services are covered by the provisions related to the freedom of establishment, but not by the provisions relating to cross-border trade in services. Additionally, the Directive does not deal with services of noneconomic general interest (education and health), social services provided for by the state, audiovisual services, including cinematographic services, gambling, activities connected with the exercise of official authority, private security services, and services provided by notaries. Finally, the Directive does not apply to services that are already covered by Community legislation, such as financial services, telecommunication services, and transport services.

The Agreement on the EEA, which entered into force on January 1, 1994, brought together the EC member-states (now twenty-seven) and three EFTA countries (Iceland, Liechtenstein, and Norway) in a single market for services.[12]

3. An Introduction to the Gravity Equation in International Trade

Tinbergen (1962) pioneered the use of the gravity equation in international trade. Since then, the gravity equation has been a popular instrument in empirical foreign trade analysis, and it has been successfully applied to flows of varying types such as workers' remittances, foreign direct investment, cross-border lending, and of course, international trade flows. According to this equation, which

---

[12] Switzerland is not part of the EEA Agreement but has a series of bilateral agreements with the EU, including an insurance agreement signed in 1989. The Vaduz Convention between the four EFTA countries, which entered into force in June 2002, introduced provisions on investments and trade in services (defined as covering the equivalent to modes 1, 2, and 4 of the GATS) into the EFTA framework. Under the Convention, trade and investment in services between EFTA states is liberalized, subject to reservations lodged by each EFTA state at the conclusion of the negotiations. Liberalization was thus subject to a negative-list approach. These reservations are to be reviewed with a view to their removal. It is worth noting that Iceland, Liechtenstein, and Norway as member-states of the EEA had already lifted most of these limitations to investment and trade in services among themselves and vis-à-vis the other EC member-states, although this is not the case in respect of Switzerland. Most of the reservations maintained by the EFTA states under the revised Convention reflect their current commitments under the GATS.

draws from Newton's law of gravity, exports from country i to country j (Xij) are explained by the economic sizes of the two countries, typically measured by gross domestic product (GDP) (Yi and Yj), and the geographic distance between them, Dij (usually measured center to center).

$$Xij = G\frac{YiYj}{Dij}$$

In log linear form, the equation is usually expressed in the following manner:

$$\ln(X_{ij}) = \beta_0 + \beta_1 \ln(Y_i) + \beta_2 \ln(Y_j) + \beta_3 \ln(\text{Distance}_{ij}) + \varepsilon_{ij} \qquad (1)$$

The gravity equation can be thought of as a representation of supply and demand forces. If country i is the origin, then Yi represents the total amount it is willing to supply to all customers, while Yj represents the total amount destination j demands. Distance may be interpreted as a sort of tax "wedge" that imposes trade costs and results in lower equilibrium trade flows. The expected signs are therefore positive for β_1 and β_2, and negative for β_3.

Over time, the original equation was "augmented" to include other explanatory variables of foreign trade, such as income per capita, geographical adjacency, common language, colonial links, institutions, and infrastructure. The equation has also been used to estimate the effects of various economic integration frameworks, such as the WTO, regional trade agreements, and currency unions.

In spite of its empirical success, the equation remained a purely empirical proposition to explain bilateral trade flows for a long time, with little or no theoretical underpinnings. However, since the end of the 1970s, the gravity equation has been "legitimized" by a series of theoretical articles by prominent economists that demonstrated that the basic equation was indeed consistent with various models of trade. Anderson (1979) made the first formal attempt to derive the gravity equation from a model that assumed product differentiation. Bergstrand (1985, 1989) also explored the theoretical determination of bilateral trade in a series of papers in which gravity equations were associated with simple monopolistic competition models. Helpman and Krugman (1985) used a differentiated product framework with increasing returns to scale to justify the gravity model. More recently, Deardorff (1995) has proven that the gravity equation characterizes many models and can be justified from standard trade theories. Finally, Anderson and Wincoop (2001) derived an operational gravity model that helps solve the so-called border puzzle (more on this later).

Additionally, several authors have discussed the econometric specification of the gravity equation, contributing to the improvement of its performance (e.g., Cheng and Wall, 2005); Egger, 2000; Feenstra, 2004; Baldwin and Taglioni, 2006).

4. The Gravity Equation and Trade in Services

Only a few studies using the gravity equation have been devoted to services, mainly because of the lack of reliable and consistent data on bilateral trade. Grunfeld and Moxnes (2003) apply a gravity equation to bilateral export of services and FDI flows for 1999. Data for services trade come from the OECD, and cover twenty-two OECD members and their trading partners, including non-OECD countries. Their regressors (or explanatory variables) include the level of GDP and GDP per capita in the importing and exporting countries, the distance between them, a dummy variable if they are both members of a free trade area (FTA), a measure of corruption in the importing country, and a trade restrictiveness index (TRI) to measure the barriers to services trade in the importing country. The TRI is the augmented frequency index based on research by the Australian Productivity Commission. Its results suggest that the standard gravity model effects found in studies on trade in goods apply to services too. Trade between two countries is positively related to their size and negatively related to the distance between them and barriers to services in place in the importing country (measured by the TRI). They find that the presence of a FTA is not significant in the case of services. This result might be expected, as many of the FTAs covered at the time did not cover trade in services.

Kimura and Lee (2006, but the original working paper had been circulated in 2004) apply the standard gravity framework to services trade with the aim of comparing the results to the estimates for trade in goods. They also use OECD statistics on trade in services, but for the years 1999 and 2000. They use the standard explanatory variables (GDP, distance), plus adjacency, common language, and the existence of a regional trade agreement (RTA) between the countries concerned. They innovate by including as regressors a measure of remoteness (a trade-weighted measure of the distance between the two countries), and a measure of trade restrictiveness (the Economic Freedom of the World Index developed by the Fraser Institute). Kimura and Lee estimate their gravity equation using a mixture of ordinary least-squares (OLS) and time-fixed effects. The major difference they report is that distance between countries is more important in services trade than in goods trade. They suggest this implies there are higher transport costs for services but fail to provide any reason why this may be the case. Common language between the importer and the exporter is not found to be significant, whereas RTAs are found to correlate positively with trade in services, which contradicts the finding by Grünfeld and Moxnes. Kimura and Lee argue that while many FTAs do not explicitly cover trade in services, their presence may indirectly facilitate the process.

Walsh (2006) also estimates a gravity equation of services trade, using import data for twenty-seven OECD countries and up to fifty trading partners over a three-year period (1999–2001). The gravity model is estimated with total services, government services, transport services, travel, and other commercial services as dependent variables. He includes a dummy variable to cater for membership in the European Union. The standard gravity framework explains the determinants of services well. The GDP per capita of the importing and exporting countries and a common language are found to be the most important determinants of trade between two countries. However, adjacency and membership of the European Union are not found to increase services trade. Walsh's results also show that distance is not a significant determinant of services trade flows.

In another paper, Ceglowski (2006) estimated a gravity equation for services trade in a sample of twenty-eight OECD countries, for the period 1999–2000. Apart from standard gravity variables, the study includes a dummy variable to cater for membership in various preferential trading arrangements, namely closer economic relations (CER; here those between Australia and New Zealand), the EFTA, the EU, NAFTA, and the EEA. She finds that geographical and linguistic proximity are key determinants of services trade. Additionally, common membership in a PTA has a significant, positive effect on bilateral services trade. According to the author, much of this effect of PTAs appears to reflect the impact of bilateral trade in goods on services trade.

5. Methodology and Data

In its most basic form, the gravity model estimates the trade between two countries as a positive function of their economic sizes and a negative function of the distance between them. As explained before, I will use an "augmented" gravity equation to cater for other determinants of bilateral trade in services, including preferential trade agreements. In log linear form, the equation to be used will take the following form:

$$\ln(X_{ijt}) = \beta_0 + \beta_1 \ln D_{ij} + \beta_2 \ln(Y_{it}) + \beta_3 \ln(Y_{jt}) + \beta_4 \text{Comlang}_{ij}$$
$$+ \beta_5 \text{Cont}_{ij} + \beta_6 \text{EI} A_{ijt} + e_{ijt} \qquad (2)$$

where i and j denote trading partners (exporter and importer, respectively); t denotes time; and the variables are defined as follow:

X_{ijt} denotes services exports from i to j at time t,
Y_{it} is the exporter's current GDP in dollars,
Y_{jt} is the importer's current GDP in dollars,
D_{ij} is the distance between the exporter and the importer, measured as the distance between the most populated cities in each country,
Cont_{ij} is a binary "dummy" variable that is unity if the exporter and the importer share a land border,
Comlang_{ij} is a binary dummy variable that is unity if the exporter and the importer share the same language,

EIA_{ijt} is a binary dummy variable that is unity if both countries are parties to any type of economic integration agreement (i.e., free trade area or a common market) covering services trade in year t, and

e_{ijt} represents the omitted other influences on bilateral trade.

We should expect positive signs for all the coefficients of the explanatory variables, except for the one on distance, which should be negative. In the case of GDP, a higher income level in the exporting country should be positively related to the country's ability to produce more services for export, while a higher level of income in the importing country should indicate a higher level of demand for services (produced domestically or imported).

One should also expect the distance variable to yield a negative coefficient. Physical distance may be considered a proxy of various transaction costs affecting trade in services, such as travel costs, costs associated with cultural unfamiliarity with the foreign market, costs associated with communications, costs of market research, and costs of establishing trust and reputation (which are essential in services that in many cases are affected by asymmetric information). Therefore, the larger the distance between the seller and the buyer, the more difficult for the former to actually sell (export) his or her services. By the same token, common language and contiguity may be considered as "positive" forces that would help diminish the adverse effects of transaction costs; thus their expected positive signs.

The signs of more interest to me in this exercise are of course β_6, which measure the effect on bilateral trade if both countries belong to a common market or free trade area covering services trade. This EIA dummy is an all-encompassing variable, capturing every type of agreement on trade in services. The agreements included in this dummy, based on the availability of data on bilateral trade in services, are the following: Australia–New Zealand, Australia–Singapore, Australia–Thailand, Australia–United States, Canada–Chile, Hong Kong–China, EC25, EC–Chile, EC–Mexico, EEA, EFTA, Japan–Mexico, Japan–Singapore, NAFTA, United States–Chile, and United States–Singapore. See Table 7.2 for the agreements included in this variable, and the direction of trade flows.

However, as has been explained earlier in Section 2, FTAs (or PTAs *stricto sensu*) and common market initiatives involve different degrees of liberalization and economic integration. Therefore, to isolate the impact of each type of agreement, I also estimate an extension of equation (2), where the EIA variable is actually decomposed according to the different types of economic integration agreement. Accordingly, I will also estimate the following equation:

$$\ln(X_{ijt}) = \beta_0 + \beta_1 \ln D_{ij} + \beta_2 \ln(Y_{it}) + \beta_3 \ln(Y_{jt})$$
$$+ \beta_4 \text{Comlang}_{ij} + \beta_5 \text{Cont}_{ij} + \beta_6 \text{PTA}_{ijt} + \beta_7 \text{EC}_{ijt} + e_{ijt} \qquad (3)$$

where PTA_{ijt} is a binary dummy variable that is unity if both countries are parties to a PTA (typically known as free trade areas) covering services trade; and where

Table 7.2. *Economic integration agreements covered by the study (and direction of trade flow)*

Agreement	Date of entry into force
Australia–New Zealand	1-Jan-89
Australia–Singapore	28-Jul-03
Australia–Thailand	1-Jan-05
Australia–U.S.	
U.S.–Australia	1-Jan-05
Canada–Chile	5-Jul-97
China–Hong Kong, China	1-Jan-04
EC 15 (intra-EC15 trade)	1-Jan-95
EC 25 (intra-EC25 trade)	1-May-04
EC–Chile (exports from individual EC member-states to Chile)	1-Mar-05
EC–Mexico (exports from individual EC member-states to Mexico)	1-Oct-00
EEA (exports from EC countries to Iceland, Liechtenstein, and Norway)	1-Jan-94
EFTA (exports from Iceland, Liechtenstein, and Norway to Switzerland)	1-Jun-02
Japan–Mexico	1-Apr-05
Japan–Singapore	30-Nov-02
NAFTA	
Canada–Mexico	
Canada–U.S.	1-Jan-94
U.S.–Mexico	
U.S.–Canada	
U.S.–Chile	1-Jan-04
U.S.–Singapore	1-Jan-04

EC_{ijt} is a binary dummy variable that takes the value 1 if the exporter and the importer are both EC member-states. The EC variable includes the ten countries that joined the EC in 2004. In the case of the EC member-states, then, the internal market will be basically covered by this variable, while the PTAs between the EC and Chile, and between the EC and Mexico, will be covered by the PTA variable.

Further detail on the construction of these dummies is warranted. First, the bilateral PTA dummy includes all the bilateral agreements entered into force between 1999 and 2006, or already in force throughout that period, between the pairs of countries for which there are data on bilateral services trade. Agreements such as ASEAN and Mercosur, whose members do not report figures of services exports or imports broken down by partner, have been therefore omitted. Other more "ancient" agreements, such as the Australia–New Zealand Closer Economic Realtions Trade Agreement (ANZCERTA) and NAFTA, have been included in the sample. See Table 7.2 for a list of the agreements covered.

Second, to assign the date of entry into force to the different agreements, I used the following rule: the agreement that entered into force before the end of June of a given year will carry as a date of entry into force that same year, while the agreement that entered into force as of July 1 of a given year will carry as the date of entry into force the following year. For example, if the agreement entered into force on February 1, 2003, the date of entry into force will be 2003; and if the agreement entered into force on December 1, 2003, the date of entry into force will be 2004. The date of entry into force is the one that prompts the value "1" for the dummy variable.

Third, in the case of European countries, I have used data on individual countries' services exports, which allows capturing the effect of both intra-EC trade and extra-EC trade. Intra-European trade among the twenty-five European member-states will be captured by the EC dummy, which will, for example, take the value 1 for the period 1999–2006 for France's exports to Germany, and the value 1 as of 2004 for France's exports to the Czech Republic. Extra–EC trade (e.g., France or Czech Republic's exports to Chile) will be captured by the PTA dummy.

Some clarifications with regard to the estimation are also in order. First, to be closely aligned with theories surrounding the gravity equation, I focus on uni-directional trade in services, and not on total trade. In particular, I focus on services from country i to country j as the dependent variable. The reason for this is that, as explained by Baldwin and Taglioni (2006) and Subramanian and Wei (2007), the basic theory tells us that the gravity equation is a modified expenditure function; it explains the value of spending by one nation on the goods produced by another nation. In other words, the gravity equation explains unidirectional bilateral trade. In this case, the choice of exports of services, instead of imports, has been on purpose. Indeed, contrary to trade in goods, where import figures are generally more reliable than export figures, in the case of services, the contrary is true – export figures are more reliable than import figures, because surveys of domestic exporters in specific sectors are generally more reliable than surveys of importing entities throughout the whole economy.[13]

Second, I use country (importer and exporter) fixed effects, to cater for the so-called multilateral resistance term. As explained by Anderson and van Wincoop (2003), many omitted factors can influence trade between pairs of countries. The most important of these omitted factors is the so-called multilateral resistance term. Trade between any two countries depends negatively on the trade barriers of each country relative to the average barrier of the two countries with all trade partners. In other words, when multilateral trading costs (the barriers vis-à-vis the "rest of the world") rise relative to bilateral costs (the barriers vis-à-vis the bilateral trading partners), trade flows rise between the country pair i and j; and vice versa. Anderson and van Wincoop argue that multilateral

---

[13] I thank Andreas Maurer and Joscelyn Magdeleine, from the WTO, for pointing this out to me.

resistance cannot be measured by using remoteness variables based on measures of distance, as these do not capture border effects; rather the gravity equation must be solved by taking into account the impact of barriers on prices. Anderson and van Wincoop show that the estimation of the gravity equation can be greatly improved by incorporating what they refer to as multilateral resistance measures. The importance of Anderson's and van Wincoop's (2003) contribution is acknowledged in the literature. However, as Feenstra (2004) and others has noted, it has not been widely adopted in empirical research given the difficulties in its implementation (a customized program is needed as the endogenous nature of the price terms requires a nonlinear solution). Feenstra (2004) shows that the inclusion of country-specific fixed effects generates the same results as Anderson and van Wincoop (2003) with little loss of efficiency. Because trade between any two countries depends on the multilateral resistance of both importers and exporters, I will use time-varying fixed effects for both importers and exporters to account for factors specific to each country, such as the level of barriers (see Subramanian and Wei, 2007, for a similar approach).

Third, following Baldwin's and Taglioni's (2006) recommendation, I use (undeflated) nominal trade and GDP data combined with time (year) dummies. As explained by these authors, the usual procedure of deflating trade and GDP figures back to a common year by using, for example, the U.S. price index can introduce important biases. They therefore recommend the use of time-fixed effects (or time dummies) to cater for variations in inflation. These time-fixed effects would also cater for other changing factors, such as the value of the dollar, the global business cycle, and so forth.

Although data on total services trade, as well as trade in selected Balance-of-Payments (BoP) categories such as transport, travel, and other commercial services, have been generally available for a long time, only a few countries had offered a breakdown of these data (at least for total services) by trading partner. This explains the fact that previous gravity studies on services trade had to focus on very short periods of time – one, two, or three years at the utmost. However, data availability has improved markedly over the past few years, prompted by initiatives at the international level to improve services data collection with a view to inter alia match the GATS definitions of trade and the sectoral classification used in negotiations.[14] There are currently three main sources of BoP services trade data at the international level: Eurostat, OECD, and the UN. The country and time coverage offered by these sources are not identical, however.

In a nutshell, the Eurostat Cronos database offers the longest time series but focuses only on European countries and their partners (seventy in total, including partner regions). The UN Services Trade Database covers around eighty

---

[14] See the *Manual of Statistics of International Trade in Services*, issued in 2002 by Eurostat, the IMF, OECD, the UN, the World Bank, and the WTO, and which was recently reviewed. The new version was completed in 2009 and published in 2010.

reporters, with data broken down by partner (although not in all cases). Data are available since 2000. This data set covers many reporters not included in the OECD database. Finally, the OECD Statistics on International Trade in Services includes data since 1999, for twenty-seven OECD countries, plus Hong Kong and the Russian Federation.[15] It contains data broken down by partner, covering fifty-five partner countries and partner regions. This is the database used in this study. I used data on total services exports for the period available as of the date of writing (1999–2006).

It is worth noting that bilateral BoP figures correspond *grosso modo* to modes 1, mode 2 (through the category Travel), and partially mode 4. See Maurer et al. (2008) for further details.

Data on GDP were taken from the World Bank World Development Indicators. Data on distance, contiguity, and common language were taken from the geographical database compiled by CEPII (Centre d'Etudes Prospectives et d'Informations Internationales). The distance variable used in this study is the distance between the most populated cities in the two countries concerned.

As said, the regressand is the natural log of services exports. I first estimated the gravity equation by using only as regressors the "traditional" gravity variables: GDP, distance, contiguity, and common language. I applied successively OLS with year-fixed effects; and then OLS with year, importer, and exporter fixed effects. I then repeated the same procedures but adding the dummies capturing the different PTA arrangements. In all cases, I computed robust standard errors.

6. Estimation Results

As can be seen from the results in Table 7.3, the model works well for trade in services, with R-squares between 71 percent and 84 percent, with 90 percent, 95 percent, and 99 percent confidence intervals.

The signs of the traditional gravity variables are as expected: negative for the distance variable, and positive for GDP, contiguity, and common language. The results improve significantly – in terms of their goodness of fit – with the simultaneous introduction of year, importer, and exporter fixed effects. The distance coefficient is significant (around 1), when year, importer, and exporter fixed effects are introduced. In all cases, contiguity and common language appear as important determinants of services trade, and in all cases more significant than the dummies catering for economic integration agreements, PTAs, and the EC.

---

[15] The thirty member countries of OECD are Australia, Austria, Belgium, Canada, Czech Republic, Denmark, Finland, France, Germany, Greece, Hungary, Iceland, Ireland, Italy, Japan, Korea, Luxembourg, Mexico, the Netherlands, New Zealand, Norway, Poland, Portugal, Slovak Republic, Spain, Sweden, Switzerland, Turkey, United Kingdom, and United States. However, Korea, Mexico, and Switzerland do not publish data broken down by partner country.

Table 7.3. *Estimation results*

	(1)	(2)	(3)	(4)	(5)	(6)
Log exporter's	0.82***	0.94***	0.82***	1.02***	0.82***	1.02***
GDP	(0.01)	(0.08)	(0.01)	(0.08)	(0.01)	(0.08)
Log importer's	0.78***	0.61***	0.77***	0.65***	0.78***	0.64***
GDP	(0.01)	(0.07)	(0.01)	(0.07)	(0.01)	(0.07)
Log distance	−0.63***	−0.94***	−0.60***	−0.93***	−0.60***	−0.93***
	(0.01)	(0.02)	(0.01)	(0.02)	(0.01)	(0.02)
Contiguity	0.57***	0.61***	0.60***	0.62***	0.59***	0.62***
	(0.07)	(0.07)	(0.07)	(0.07)	(0.07)	(0.07)
Common	1.39***	0.80***	1.39***	0.80***	1.39***	0.80***
language	(0.04)	(0.04)	(0.04)	(0.04)	(0.04)	(0.04)
EIA			0.27***	0.11***		
			(0.03)	(0.03)		
PTA					0.39***	0.12***
					(0.05)	(0.04)
EC25					0.30***	0.14***
					(0.03)	(0.03)
Observations	9,942	9,942	9,942	9,942	9,942	9,942
R^2	0.71	0.84	0.71	0.84	0.71	0.84

Notes: Regressand: log of services exports. Ordinary least-squares (OLS) estimates of a log-linear gravity model are given. Robust standard errors are in parentheses. Equations (1), (3), and (5) have been estimated with OLS and year-fixed effects. Equations (2), (4), and (6) have been estimated with OLS, and year, importer, and exporter fixed effects.
* Significant at 10%; ** significant at 5%; *** significant at 1%.

The estimated coefficients for GDP variables are all significant. When the year, importer, and exporter fixed effects are introduced, the exporter's GDP coefficient becomes much larger than the importer's GDP coefficient. This could be interpreted as evidence of a "home market effect" in services trade, as derived by Krugman (1980). The home market effect is the tendency for large countries to be net exporters of products (in this case, services) with high transport costs and strong scale economies. In the presence of fixed costs, and thus scale economies, firms prefer to concentrate global production of a product or service in a single location; in the presence of transport costs, it makes sense for this location to be a market with high product demand. The home market effect implies a link between market size and exports that does not exist in models in which trade is based solely on comparative advantage. In terms of the gravity equation, this effect should translate into a significantly higher coefficient for the exporter's GDP variable than for the importer's GDP (see also Feenstra et al., 1998).

The effect of membership in an economic integration agreement, whether a free trade area or a common market, is positive and significant. In column 3, the coefficient of EIA implies that services trade between EIA signatories is 31 percent higher than for other country pairs, after controlling for economic size, distance, adjacency, and linguistic ties.[16] Controlling for country-specific (importer and exporter) fixed effects in column 4 reveals a smaller effect of membership in an EIA, suggesting intra-bloc services trade is just 12 percent higher.

The effect of membership in an economic integration agreement covering services trade may depend on the type of agreement. For the sake of this empirical estimation, I have distinguished between typical free trade areas, like the NAFTA, or the agreement between Australia and the United States, and deeper integration agreements, primarily exemplified by the European internal market. A relevant question in that regard is this: Is there any difference in the effect of these different types of agreements on services trade? The answer may be no. In column 5, computing only year-fixed effects, both types of agreements appear to have very significant effects on bilateral services trade – 35 percent for the EC and 47 percent for bilateral PTAs. However, controlling for importer and exporter fixed effects in column 6 reveals again a smaller effect (between 13 percent and 15 percent), with a slight advantage to deeper integration agreements.

7. Concluding Remarks

The main motivation for this chapter was to discuss the law and economics of preferential liberalization of trade in services. The chapter took a deliberate empirical approach on both accounts.

From a legal perspective, the chapter showed that PTAs covering trade in services can take different forms, from so-called deeper integration agreements to more straightforward free trade arrangements. There was no theoretical discussion of the pros and cons of each type of agreement – simply a review of their main features, as shown by practice.

Tackling the issue from an economic perspective, the chapter looked into the determinants of bilateral services trade, paying particular attention to the effects of PTAs. Although preliminary, and most probably incomplete, the empirical exercise has led to some interesting findings that would certainly deserve further research. First, my findings show that distance (which here probably represents transaction costs in general rather than the costs of physical distance between markets) is relevant for trade in services. In fact, it turns out to be very significant once time- and country-fixed effects are taken into account. Second, there seems to be evidence of a home market effect in services, which would deserve further attention with a view to achieving a better understanding of trade in services.

Third, and most importantly for the sake of this chapter and this volume, PTAs appear to have positive effects on bilateral services trade, of the order of 12 to 15 percent. It has not been possible to find, however, a significant difference – in terms of their effect on services trade – between free trade areas and a deep

[16] The formula to compute these effects is $(e^{\beta i} - 1) \times 100$, where βi is the estimated coefficient.

integration initiative like the European internal market. This may be due also to the inherent limitations of the methodology followed in this chapter – the gravity equation – that can only give a partial indication of the effect of agreements on bilateral services trade.

Further research is certainly needed. Apart from methodological issues that need to be further explored (such as the existence of zero flows, or the endogenous nature of PTAs), it would be interesting to consider the effect of PTAs on trade in different services (not just on total trade), and particularly taking into account that service sectors differ in their tradability. Additionally, a more complete assessment of the effects of PTAs on trade in services would call for an analysis of the effects on trade through commercial presence (mode 3 in GATS parlance), which is arguably the most relevant mode of supplying services. The key issue here is data availability – no doubt about it. However, data permitting, these avenues are worth exploring to get a better understanding not only of services trade but also of economic integration in general.

REFERENCES

Anderson, James E., 1979. "A Theoretical Foundation for the Gravity Equation," *American Economic Review*, 69, 106–16.

Anderson, James E., and Eric van Wincoop, 2003. "Gravity with Gravitas: A Solution to the Border Puzzle," *American Economic Review*, 93 (March: 170–92).

Baldwin, Richard, and Dara Taglioni, 2006. "Gravity for Dummies and Dummies for Gravity Equations," NBER Working Paper 12516 (September).

Baier, S., and J. Bergstrand, 2005. "Do Free Trade Agreements Actually Increase Members' International Trade?," Federal Reserve Bank of Atlanta Working Paper No. 2005–3.

Bergstrand, Jeffrey H., 1985. "The Gravity Equation in International Trade: Some Microeconomic Foundations and Empirical Evidence," *The Review of Economics and Statistics*, 67(3):474–81.

Bergstrand, Jeffrey H., 1989. "The Generalized Gravity Equation, Monopolistic Competition, and the Factor-Proportions Theory in International Trade," *The Review of Economics and Statistics*, 71(1):143–53.

Ceglowski, Janet, 2006. "Does Gravity Matter in a Service Economy?," *Review of World Economics*, 142(2).

Cheng, I-Hui, and Howard J. Wall, 2005. "Controlling for Heterogeneity in Gravity Models of Trade and Integration," *Federal Reserve Bank of St. Louis Review*, January/February, 87(1):49–63.

Deardorff, Alan V., 1998. "Determinants of Bilateral Trade: Does Gravity Work in a Neoclassical World?," In Jeffrey A. Frankel (ed.), *The Regionalization of the World Economy*. Chicago: University of Chicago Press (for NBER).

Deardorff, Alan V., 1995. "Determinants of Bilateral Trade: Does Gravity Work in a Neo-Classical World?," National Bureau of Economic Research Working Paper Series No. 5377.

Deardorff, Alan, and R. Stern, 1997. "Measurement of Non-Tariff Barriers," Organisation for Economic Cooperation and Development Economics Department Working Paper No. 179.

Egger, Peter, 2000. "A Note on the Proper Econometric Specification of the Gravity Equation," *Economic Letters* 66(25):31.

Evenett, Simon J., and Wolfgang Keller, 2002. "On Theories Explaining the Success of the Gravity Equation," *The Journal of Political Economy* 110(2): 281–316.

Feenstra, Robert C., 2004. *Advanced International Trade Theory and Evidence*. Princeton, NJ: Princeton University Press.

Feenstra, Robert C., James R. Markusen, and Andrew K. Rose, 2001. "Using the Gravity Equation to Differentiate among Alternative Theories of Trade," *The Canadian Journal of Economics*, 34(2): 430–47.

Feenstra, Robert C., James R. Markusen, and Andrew Rose, 1998. "Understanding the Home Market Effect and the Gravity Equation: The Role of Differentiating Goods," NBER Working Paper No. 6804.

Grunfeld, L., and A., Moxnes, 2003. "The Intangible Globalisation: Explaining Patterns of International Trade in Services," Norwegian Institute of International Affairs Paper No. 657.

Helpman, Elhanan, and Paul Krugman, 1985. *Market Structure and Foreign Trade*. Cambridge, MA: MIT Press.

Kimura, F., and H.-H., Lee, 2004/2006. "The Gravity Equation in International Trade in Services," *Review of World Economics*, 142(1).

Krugman, Paul, 1980. "Scale Economies, Product Differentiation, and the Pattern of Trade," *American Economic Review*, 70: 950–9.

Marchetti, Juan, and Martin Roy, 2009. "Services Liberalization in the WTO and in Preferential Trade Agreements," in Marchetti and Roy (eds.), *Opening Markets for Trade in Services* New York: Cambridge University Press.

Marchetti, Juan, and Petros Mavriodis, 2004. "What Are the Main Challenges for the GATTs Framework? Don't Talk about the Revolution," *European Business Organization Law Review*, 5:11–62.

Maurer, Andreas, Y. Markus, J. Mageleine, and B. D'Andrea, 2008. "Measuring Trade in Services," In Mattoo, Stern, and Zannini (eds.), *Handbook on International Trade in Services*. New York: Oxford University Press.

Rose, Andrew K., 2000. "One Money, One Market: The Effects of Common Currency on Trade," *Economic Policy* 30, (April) 9–45.

Roy, M., J. Marchetti, and H. Lim, 2006. "Services Liberalization in the New Generation of Preferential Trade Agreements: How Much Further than the GATS?," WTO Staff Working Paper ERSD-2006-7.

Roy, M., J. Marchetti, and H. Lim, 2007. "Services Liberalization in the New Generation of Preferential Trade Agreements: How Much Further than the GATS?," *World Trade Review*, 6(2): 155–92.

Roy, M., J. Marchetti, and H. Lim, 2008. "The Race Towards Preferential Trade Agreements in Services: How Much Is Really Achieved?," in Panizzon, Pohl, and Sauvé, (eds.), *The GATS and the International Regulation of Trade in Services*. New York: Cambridge University Press.

Subramanian, Arvind and Shang-Jin Wei, 2007. "The WTO Promotes Trade, Strongly but Unevenly," *Journal of International Economics*, 72(1): 151–75.

Tinbergen, J., 1962. *Shaping the World Economy: Suggestions for an International Economic Policy*. New York: Twentieth Century Fund.

Walsh, Keith, 2006. "Trade in Services: Does Gravity Hold? A Gravity Model Approach to Estimating Barriers to Services Trade," IIIS Discussion Paper No. 183.

WILLIAM J. DAVEY

8 A Model Article XXIV: Are There Realistic Possibilities to Improve It?

The creation of the World Trade Organization (WTO) in the Uruguay Round of multilateral trade negotiations was a spectacular success. Within nine months of signing the Uruguay Round results, all of the major trading nations that took part in the General Agreement on Tariffs and Trade (GATT) had ratified those results and brought the WTO into existence as of January 1, 1995. This grand success appeared to usher into existence a new era of comprehensive multilateralism in world trade. Now, viewed a decade and a half later, the creation of the WTO seems to represent the high point of multilateralism. While the WTO's dispute settlement system has continued to function reasonably well, its other chief role – to serve as a forum for further negotiations on market liberalization – has not. For those interested in trade negotiations, the plodding, on-again, off-again WTO negotiations do not compare well in terms of effectiveness with the negotiating processes that have lead to a rapid expansion in the number of preferential trade agreements (PTAs) in recent years.[1]

This phenomenal growth in the number of PTAs[2] has raised concerns about their relationship with and effect on the multilateral trading system embodied

---

[1] In this chapter, the term "preferential trade agreements" or "PTAs" is generally used as opposed to the WTO jargon "regional trade agreements" or the GATT Article XXIV categories of "free trade agreements" and "customs unions." The use of "PTA" reflects current practice among economists and the fact that many PTAs are not regional in any sense. Although the range of preferential agreements is quite extensive, the term "PTA" as used herein does not include any arrangements that are not claimed to fall within the ambit of GATT Article XXIV (or its analogs in GATS [Article V] and the Enabling Clause). Many PTAs, as the term is used herein, now include provisions on non-WTO subjects (e.g., on labor and environmental issues) or what are sometimes called WTO-plus provisions (e.g., on intellectual property rights). In theory, the inclusion of some such provisions might affect their compliance with WTO requirements for PTAs, but those additional provisions – whatever their intrinsic merit – generally are not relevant to the question of whether a PTA is WTO compliant.

[2] As of January 1, 1995, when the WTO came into existence, there were fewer than 100 PTAs in force. See WTO Secretariat, Regionalism and the World Trading System, Appendix Table 1 (1995). As of November 1, 2008, there were 227 PTAs in force. Report (2008) of the Committee on Regional Trade Agreements to the General Council, WT/REG/19, para. 4 (November

233

in the WTO.[3] In principle, the interrelationship of PTAs and the multilateral trading system is governed by GATT Article XXIV.[4] However, there is more or less universal agreement that Article XXIV has not functioned well. Although PTAs are usually notified as required, and many have been discussed in great detail, almost no decisions on their conformity with GATT rules have been taken because of a lack of consensus over the meaning of various terms in Article XXIV and over how Article XXIV's rules should be applied to specific PTAs.

Not surprisingly, there has long been interest in revising Article XXIV, or, at a minimum, clarifying the meaning of its provisions. However, given the experience to date, it seems that implementing significant changes may well be impossible. On the one hand, almost all WTO members participate in PTAs and any proposed changes will likely be automatically opposed by those who think their own PTAs might be called into question by such changes. It is difficult to imagine much in the way of substantive change to Article XXIV or even clarification of the contested terms that would not call into question some PTAs and therefore generate opposition. Moreover, developing countries benefit from an even less stringent regime for PTAs among themselves, and they seem loathe surrendering any special and differential treatment that they now enjoy. On the other hand, even among those who might be willing to support some change or clarification, it is not clear what the goal of changing or clarifying Article XXIV really is. Is it to improve PTAs by making them less trade distortive? Or is it to discourage their use because of their various undesirable effects on the multilateral trading system? This split in goals may further complicate the process of achieving consensus on specific changes or clarifications.

This chapter explores the extent to which the growth and coverage of PTAs threaten the WTO and the multilateral trading system in general. It then considers what responses the WTO might take through amending Article XXIV to control the spread of PTAs, or, at a minimum, to reduce their deleterious effects on the multilateral system. The chapter commences with a brief overview of the existing position of PTAs under WTO/GATT rules.

28, 2008). There may be some double counting that exaggerates these statistics, but it is not disputed by anyone that recent years have seen a rapid growth in the number of PTAs.

[3] There have been a number of major official studies of this issue. WTO Secretariat, World Trade Report 2003 ("Secretariat Report"); the so-called Sutherland Report (Peter Sutherland et al., *The Future of the WTO*, 2004; Warwick Commission, *The Multilateral Trade Regime: Which Way Forward*, 2007). See also Jagdish Bhagwati, *Termites in the Trading System* (Oxford, 2008) and Ross Buckley, Vai Io Lo, and Laurence Boulle, *Challenges to Multilateral Trade: The Impact of Bilateral, Preferential, and Regional Agreements* (Wolters Kluwer, 2008).

[4] There is an analogous provision in GATS – Article V – that will not be discussed here. Although there are some salient differences, the basic issues are similar, although to date there has been much less experience with its application. PTAs may also be entered into between developing countries pursuant to the Enabling Clause.

1. Preferential Trade Agreements in the WTO/GATT System[5]

1.1. The Evolution of PTAs in the WTO/GATT System

The most-favored-nation (MFN) principle, which requires that tariff and other trading advantages given to one country must be given unconditionally to all WTO/GATT members, is one of the basic obligations in the WTO/GATT system.[6] The MFN rule would have precluded PTAs, a few of which did exist at the time GATT was negotiated. Probably to reflect that fact, the original U.S. proposal for an international trade organization, which ultimately led to GATT, included an exception for customs unions.[7] During the course of the negotiations, the exception for customs unions was broadened to also include free trade areas.[8] The basic difference between a customs union and a free trade area is that while both eliminate duties and other barriers to trade among members, a customs union also imposes a common commercial policy toward nonmembers. The North American Free Trade Agreement – NAFTA – is an example of a free trade agreement, whereas the European Community (EC) is an example of a customs union.

The expansion of the Article XXIV exception to include free trade areas meant that it would potentially be used more frequently, as it is much easier to negotiate a free trade area than a customs union because free trade areas are not

---

[5] This section and much of the next are based on "Regional Trade Agreements and the WTO: General Observations and NAFTA Lessons for Asia," a 2003 paper presented at a conference of the Japan Association of International Economic Law and reprinted in William J. Davey, *Enforcing World Trade Rules* 159–83 (Cameron, May 2006).

[6] GATT Article I. For historical and other materials on the MFN Clause, see John H. Jackson, William J. Davey, and Alan O. Sykes, *Legal Problems of International Economic Relations*, ch. 10 (5th ed., 2008).

[7] A customs union is defined in GATT Article XXIV:8(a) as the substitution of a single customs territory for two or more customs territories, so that duties and other restrictive regulations of commerce are eliminated on substantially all trade between the constituent members of the union and substantially the same duties and other regulations of commerce are applied by members of the union to nonmembers.

[8] A free trade area is defined in GATT Article XXIV:8(b) as a group of two or more customs territories where duties and other restrictive regulations of commerce are eliminated on substantially all trade between the constituent members of the free trade area. The rationale for the addition of free trade areas to Article XXIV is not clear. The addition was proposed by Syria and Lebanon and supported by other developing countries and France. According to the WTO Secretariat, it was apparently accepted as a way of blunting developing-country demands for legitimizing preferences more generally. WTO Secretariat, *supra* note 2, at 8. It has been suggested that it was added to accommodate a possible U.S.–Canada FTA. Although secret negotiations were held on that subject in 1948, no agreement was forthcoming. Peter Morici, "The Environment for Free Trade," in Peter Morici (ed.), *Making Free Trade Work: The Canada–United States Agreement* 1, 24 n. 13 (Council on Foreign Relations, 1990). Wilcox notes that Article XXIV was drafted in light of plans for increasing economic unification of Western Europe, but does not mention North American integration. Clair Wilcox, *A Charter for World Trade* 71 (1949).

required to have a common commercial policy.[9] However, at the time that the Article XXIV exception was negotiated, it was not clear that it was in fact likely to be used extensively. Indeed, only a few PTAs were notified to GATT in the 1940s and 1950s.[10] Basically, customs unions and free trade areas were not particularly controversial at the time because there were only a few in existence.[11] It was easy to view them as a major step in trade liberalization in a world of 40 percent tariffs. Moreover, the theoretical concerns of trade-diverting versus trade-creating effects of such agreements were not explored by Viner until some years after Article XXIV was negotiated.[12]

In contrast to the initial years of GATT, the WTO has experienced a mushrooming of PTAs.[13] According to recent reports, more than 100 have come into force since the start of the Doha Round.[14] Of particular significance is that much of the PTA activity has involved countries that traditionally eschewed PTAs in favor of the multilateral system – the United States (until the 1980s), Japan, and Korea (until this decade). Almost all WTO members now seem to embrace PTAs heartily.

What explains this increasing popularity of PTAs? In a 2003 report, the WTO Secretariat mentions two reasons why standard economic analysis would justify a country's decision to pursue preferential trade agreements – first, in a world of second best, a case may be made for an individual country to reduce trade barriers on a selective basis; second, some countries may be able, through trade diversion, to secure gains that they could not otherwise achieve.[15] Nevertheless, standard economic analysis also suggests that it is difficult to predict accurately when such gains would be available and very difficult to achieve them in a world where trading partners may be tempted to take similar actions or counteractions to promote or protect their own trading interests.

Perhaps more importantly, governments may prefer a multilateral approach but conclude that a regional or preferential approach is more viable. This may arise, for example, because further integration under the multilateral approach

---

[9] The United States apparently believed that technical difficulties in forming free trade areas (origin issues?) would push their members toward establishing full customs unions. WTO Secretariat, *supra* note 2, at 8, n. 5, citing W. Brown, *The United States and the Restoration of World Trade* 156 (Brookings, 1950).

[10] The GATT Analytical Index lists only five agreements that came into force prior to 1960 and that were notified under Article XXIV; see GATT Analytical Index 858 (6th rev. ed., 2005). The Benelux customs union predated GATT.

[11] There were, of course, major concerns at this time about trade preferences not in the form of customs unions or free trade areas. For an explanation of the differences between preferences and customs unions, see Wilcox, *supra* note 8, at 69–71, quoted in WTO Secretariat, *supra* note 2, at 8 n.4. Indeed, a major U.S. goal in the GATT/ITO negotiations was to restrict the British system of imperial preferences.

[12] Joseph Viner, *The Customs Union Issue* (1950).

[13] See *supra* note 2.

[14] "Afta Doha," *The Economist*, September 6, 2008, at 85.

[15] Secretariat Report, *supra* note 3, at 49.

is stymied by the opposition of some countries, thus making it very time consuming.[16] A regional or preferential approach may also be followed because of a desire to protect market access,[17] to signal a commitment to market liberalization generally, and/or to attract foreign direct investment.[18] The Secretariat Report also cites various political reasons for pursuing PTAs.[19] Increasingly, it seems that countries feel pressured to join PTAs to maintain existing preferences and to avoid being left out of regional integration plans.

In any event, given this growth in the significance of PTAs, how does the WTO system deal with them?

1.2. The Control of PTAs in the WTO/GATT System

1.2.1. The Basic Rules of Article XXIV

GATT Article XXIV specifies conditions that must be met for a PTA to qualify as an exception to the overriding MFN principle that is normally applicable.[20] In particular, GATT Article XXIV:4 provides as follows:

> [WTO] Members recognize the desirability of increasing freedom of trade by the development, through voluntary agreements, of closer integration between the economies of the countries parties to such agreements. They also recognize that the purpose of a customs union or of a free trade area should be to facilitate trade between the constituent territories and not to raise barriers to the trade of other [WTO] Members with such territories.

Although Article XXIV:4 sets outs GATT's basic philosophy with respect to PTAs, it is unclear whether it imposes any obligation. The following paragraph, paragraph 5 of Article XXIV, commences with the word "Accordingly," suggesting that paragraph 4 sets out a general principle that is put into practice by paragraph 5. Paragraph 4 is important, however, because its states the general principles, one of which is that PTAs should not raise trade barriers vis-à-vis nonmembers.

[16] Id.

[17] The Canada–U.S. Free Trade Agreement is an example of this motivation (on the part of Canada).

[18] Secretariat Report, *supra* note 3, at 50.   [19] Id.

[20] GATS Article V provides a similar exception and is treated in the WTO in the same fashion as GATT Article XXIV, although there is obviously less experience with it, given its recent vintage and the fact that not all PTAs cover services. In addition, for developing countries, the so-called Enabling Clause allows the formation of regional or global arrangements among developing WTO members. See the decision of November 28, 1979, 26th Supp. BISD 203. Unlike GATT Article XXIV, which contains requirements that PTAs must meet, inter alia, in respect of product coverage, the Enabling Clause decision imposes no conditions on PTAs and applies to the mutual reduction, as well as the elimination of tariffs. It allows for mutual reduction or elimination of nontariff barriers in accordance with criteria or conditions that may be prescribed by WTO members. Such criteria or conditions have not been prescribed to date.

Paragraph 5 is essentially concerned with the level of restrictions applied to nonmembers before and after the PTA is brought into effect. For customs unions, paragraph 5(a) specifies that

> the duties and other regulations of commerce imposed at the institution of any such [customs] union ... in respect of trade with [WTO] Members not parties to such union ... shall not on the whole be higher or more restrictive than the general incidence of the duties and regulations of commerce applicable in the constituent territories prior to the formation of the union.

A similar result is required of free trade areas, where the duties and other regulations of commerce of each of the constituent members of the area are not to be higher or more restrictive than the corresponding duties and regulations existing in the member prior to formation of the area.

Paragraph 5(c) specifies that if the customs union or free trade area is implemented over time, which is the usual case, then the ultimate formation of the union or area should occur within a reasonable period of time. The 1994 Uruguay Round Understanding on Article XXIV specifies that the reasonable period of time should exceed ten years only in exceptional cases.[21] Historically, some PTAs have had very long transition periods.[22]

Paragraph 8 of Article XXIV also provides substantive control of the formation of PTAs, through its definition of what qualifies as a customs union or free trade area.[23] Paragraph 8 defines a customs union as follows:

> A customs union shall be understood to mean the substitution of a single customs territory for two or more customs territories, so that
>
> (i) duties and other restrictive regulations of commerce (except where necessary those permitted under Articles XI, XII, XIII, XIV, XV, and XX) are eliminated with respect to substantially all the trade between the constituent territories of the union or at least with respect to substantially all the trade in products originating in such territories, and,
>
> (ii) ... substantially the same duties and other regulations of commerce are applied by each of the members of the union to the trade of territories not included in the union.

The definition of a free trade area is essentially that contained in paragraph (i).

Over the years, the WTO/GATT system has had considerable difficulty in interpreting these terms. Foremost among the problems have been defining the

---

[21] Understanding on the Interpretation of Article XXIV of GATT 1994, para. 3.

[22] GATT Analytical Index, *supra* note 10, at 808–10.

[23] Although phrased as general definitions, it is understood that paragraph 8 contains obligations that must be complied with. See Understanding on the Interpretation of Article XXIV of GATT 1994, para. 1: "[PTAs] to be consistent with Article XXIV, must satisfy, *inter alia*, the provisions of paragraphs 5, 6, 7, and 8 of that Article."

terms "other regulations of commerce," "other restrictive regulations of commerce," and "substantially all the trade." For example, are there limits on how restrictive a PTA's rules of origin may be? Are antidumping rules permitted to exist in free trade areas? Is it possible to exclude to a substantial degree a significant sector, such as agriculture, from the coverage of a free trade agreement? Does it matter that there has traditionally been little trade in that sector? The inability to reach consensus on the meaning of these and other terms has made it difficult for the WTO/GATT system to review and oversee the operation of PTAs. After considering the current mechanisms for review of PTAs – the WTO Committee on Regional Trade Agreements and dispute settlement – we will consider the status of the Doha negotiations on PTAs, which are one of the subjects of the so-called rules negotiations.

1.2.2. Review and Oversight of PTAs by WTO Members

Paragraph 7 of Article XXIV requires that parties deciding to enter a PTA must "promptly notify" the WTO of that agreement and make such information available as will enable the WTO to make such reports or recommendations in respect of the PTA as may be appropriate.[24] In addition, periodic reporting on the operation of PTAs is also required.[25] Traditionally, PTAs notified under GATT were examined by an ad hoc working party established for that purpose. Early on, the WTO changed that procedure through the creation of a Committee on Regional Trade Agreements (CRTA), whose charge was to examine all PTAs, other than those notified under the Enabling Clause, which are reviewed by the Committee on Trade and Development. Unfortunately, because of the consensus requirements for decisions in WTO/GATT and the above-noted imprecision in the definition of several key terms for applying the requirements of Article XXIV, the GATT working parties and the CRTA have been incapable of reaching any conclusions on the WTO consistency of PTAs that have been reviewed by them.[26] Although hope springs eternal, it is not clear that the situation will soon change,

---

[24] The notification requirements are elaborated upon in the Understanding on the Interpretation of Article XXIV of GATT 1994, paras. 7–11.

[25] Understanding on the Interpretation of Article XXIV of GATT 1994, para. 11.

[26] A 1995 Secretariat Report noted that conformity with Article XXIV had been found explicitly in only six cases. See WTO Secretariat, *supra* note 2, at 16–17. See also GATT Analytical Index, *supra* note 10, at 817. Since then, there have been no other decisions taken on notified PTAs. As to the six approvals, the one clear approval involved the Czech–Slovak agreement that was entered into when Czechoslovakia split. In looking at the other five agreements, there are issues as to how to count or evaluate the "approvals": The South Africa–Rhodesia approval was subject to further reports and completion of the customs union, which never occurred (see L/381, July 27, 1955). The two Nicaragua FTAs were with non-GATT parties and provided for further review. Reports were regularly filed by Nicaragua but there does not seem to have been further review, although there was consideration of an expansion of the second agreement to Costa Rica and Panama, where it appears that it was concluded by the Council that the terms of Article XXIV had not been met (see L/1770, May 17, 1962). It is this latter unapproved agreement – establishing the Central

which has raised the question of whether it would be possible to control use of PTAs through dispute settlement.[27]

1.2.3. Review of PTAs in Dispute Settlement

Paragraph 12 of the 1994 Uruguay Round Understanding on Article XXIV specifies the following:

> The provisions of Article XXII and XXIII of GATT 1994 as elaborated and applied by the Dispute Settlement Understanding may be invoked with respect to any matters arising from the application of those provisions of Article XXIV relating to customs unions, free trade areas, or interim agreements leading to the formation of a customs union or free trade area.

Although there were some questions raised in the WTO as to whether this language was sufficient to give the dispute settlement system general jurisdiction over claims arising under PTAs, two Appellate Body decisions made clear that this was the way that the previous text should be interpreted.

The principal case, which was directly on point, was the *Turkey–Textiles* case, in which India challenged certain quotas that Turkey had imposed on textile imports from India.[28] Turkey's defense was that it was required to impose such quotas because of its entry into a customs union with the EC. The key issue

American Common Market – that is currently in force. The two Caribbean agreements concerning CARICOM were approved without conditions, although the conclusions of the two reports, which were identical because the agreements were closely related, mentioned concerns about the agricultural sector. At present, of the approved agreements, only CARICOM is in force and the services aspects of CARICOM have not yet been approved by the CRTA.

[27] In fact, the new transparency procedures put in place provisionally in 2006, which should improve significantly the quality of information supplied to the Committee on Regional Trade Agreements, seem to foresee better-informed discussions and consideration of PTAs in lieu of any decisions on WTO compatibility. See Section 4 *infra*. As in the case of the Trade Policy Review Mechanism, the Secretariat reports under the new transparency procedures are not to be used as a basis for dispute settlement. See WTO Agreement, Annex II: Trade Policy Review Mechanism, para. A(i); General Council Decision of December 14, 2006, Transparency Mechanism for Regional Trade Agreements, WT/L/671 (December 18, 2006), para. 10.

[28] Turkey – Restrictions on Imports of Textiles and Clothing Products, WT/DS34, Panel and Appellate Body reports adopted on November 19, 1999. The second case involved an attempt by India to invoke the GATT Article XVIII balance-of-payments exception to defend its comprehensive system of import quotas and controls. The 1994 understanding on balance-of-payments exceptions contained language related to dispute settlement similar to that contained in the 1994 understanding on Article XXIV. Indeed, while the language related to the jurisdiction of dispute settlement in balance-of-payments cases was arguably less clear than that applicable to Article XXIV, the panel and Appellate Body both found that the dispute settlement system could assess the legitimacy of the justification for invocation of the balance-of-payments exception. See India – Quantitative Restrictions on Imports of Agricultural, Textile, and Industrial Products, WT/DS90, Panel and Appellate Body reports adopted on September 22, 1999.

in the case was whether the Turkish measures could be justified under Article XXIV. The panel found that they could not be so justified.[29] This was confirmed on appeal. As explained by the Appellate Body, Article XXIV does not permit the adoption of GATT-inconsistent measures on formation of a customs union unless the absence of those measures would prevent the formation of a customs union. In connection with that, it noted that the definition of a customs union in Article XXIV:8(a) allows a degree of flexibility in the extent to which constituent members must adopt the same regulations of commerce vis-à-vis nonmembers of the union. Accordingly, Turkey could have entered into the customs union without imposing the quotas at issue. Indeed, it noted that the problem could have been handled through application of rules of origin.[30]

Turkey–Textiles is significant for two other reasons as well. First, in its discussion of Article XXIV, the Appellate Body noted that it provided a defense to a charge of a GATT violation. As such, in the first instance, a member invoking Article XXIV has the burden of proving that the free trade area or customs union at issue complies with the definitional requirements for such entities, as they are specified in Article XXIV.[31] In that regard, the Appellate Body criticized the panel for avoiding that issue by assuming for purposes of its analysis that the EC–Turkey customs union met the terms of Article XXIV. The Appellate Body also indicated indirectly its view that panels have jurisdiction to review whether a free trade area or customs union meets the requirements of Article XXIV, a question that the panel had left open.[32]

At this juncture, it remains to be seen whether the dispute settlement system will become the principal mechanism by which the conformity of PTAs is checked. Given the complex economic issues that would be involved, it would not be an easy task for it to perform, particularly in close cases. However, because the results of dispute settlement are adopted quasi-automatically, it could perform such a role. Because, as noted in the next section, the Committee on Regional Trade Agreements will apparently not attempt to decide on conformity in the future, dispute settlement may be by default the only route for review of PTAs.

1.2.4. The Doha Negotiations on PTAs

As noted earlier, there has been considerable controversy over the years as to the requirements imposed by GATT Article XXIV, as well as the other WTO provisions on PTAs. As will be discussed in Part III, many of these issues have received some attention in the Doha negotiations, but at this juncture it may well be that the only outcome of the Doha negotiations on PTAs will be the General Council

---

[29] Panel Report, *Turkey–Textiles*.

[30] Appellate Body Report, *Turkey–Textiles*, paras. 42–63.

[31] Id. at para. 58.

[32] Id., para. 60. On the latter point, the Appellate Body simply referred to its decision in *India–QR*; see note 28 *supra*.

decision already taken on enhanced transparency.[33] This decision will be useful in helping to provide more timely and specific information on PTAs for their consideration by the CRTA, but it seems to foresee that there will only be discussions of PTAs in the CRTA, and that the CRTA will not attempt to decide on PTA conformity with WTO rules in the future. It is worth noting again here that negotiations on PTAs are complicated by the fact that virtually all WTO members are parties to some PTAs. Thus, the limited results are not surprising. Nonetheless, there is evidence that the new system is more functional – along with improved notification procedures, a standard Secretariat analysis of a notified PTA is prepared, and the PTA is discussed at a CRTA meeting within a given timeframe. It may well be that these changes will result in closer scrutiny of PTAs than at present and consequently even improve their overall WTO compatibility in the future.[34]

1.2.5. Summary

The WTO rules actually seem reasonably drafted so as to minimize any adverse effects of PTAs on the multilateral trading system. The requirement that tariffs and other commercial regulations affecting non-PTA members should not become more restrictive as a result of the PTA helps to reduce the possibility of harmful trade diversion. The requirements that substantially all trade be covered and that tariffs and other restrictive commercial regulations be eliminated between PTA members helps to ensure that only bona fide PTAs are entered into – which helps ensure that PTAs are not used to eliminate MFN rules in only certain sectors. Unfortunately, agreement on the precise meaning of these rules has never been achieved and the review mechanisms designed to ensure compliance with them have never functioned at all. Although the dispute settlement system seems to be available to help ensure compliance with the rules, it has yet to have been used for that purpose in a general challenge to a PTA and, as a consequence, it is not clear that it could successfully resolve a broad-based challenge to a PTA. How serious are these deficiencies? Ultimately, whether they pose a real threat to the WTO and the multilateral trading system depends on whether the effects of PTAs on that system are really all that bad. The next section explores that question.

---

[33] General Council Decision of December 14, 2006, Transparency Mechanism for Regional Trade Agreements, WT/L/671 (December 18, 2006).
[34] The new Transparency Mechanism will not result in improved periodic reviews of PTAs. The new provisions on subsequent notifications are in id., paras. 14–17. Although WTO members are required to notify the CRTA of changes in PTAs and provide information on their operation, as well as to provide a report at the end of a PTA's implementation period, the WTO Secretariat will not prepare an analysis similar to what it prepares in connection with the initial notification of a PTA. Such an analysis done on a periodic basis, with discussion in the CRTA, would in my view be a valuable addition to the indirect reviews of PTAs done in the trade policy reviews of individual WTO members who are parties to PTAs. It would be a valuable source of information on what actually occurs in PTAs.

2. The Effects of Preferential Trade Agreements on the Multilateral Trading System

There is considerable controversy over whether PTAs are desirable in general economic terms for the world at large or compatible with the multilateral trading system. As noted earlier, there have been three major WTO-related studies in the past five years that have given considerable attention to the perceived problems of PTAs. In 2003, the WTO's *World Trade Report* analyzed PTAs in some depth and was generally quite critical of the growth of PTAs and their effect on the multilateral trading system. In 2004, the so-called Sutherland Report, authored by an eminent persons group appointed by the WTO's Director-General to advise him on *The Future of the WTO*, was also quite critical of the growth of PTAs. Indeed, Jagdish Bhagwati, a member of the group, published in 2008 a biting critique of PTAs – *Termites in the Trading System* – that expands on the concerns raised in the Sutherland Report. Finally, in 2007, the Warwick Commission report on *The Multilateral Trading Regime: Which Way Forward?* also raised concerns about the impact of PTAs on the WTO and its rules-based multilateral trading system. Interestingly, a 1995 WTO Secretariat Report – *Regionalism and the World Trading System* – was much more sanguine about the WTO–PTA relationship and viewed regional efforts as more complementary to the WTO than in competition with it.[35] The difference in tone in the more recent studies cited in this paragraph probably reflects the recent surge in the numbers of PTAs, the expansion of the topics they cover,[36] and their growing use by major trading countries.

Despite the many critiques of PTAs, it is not always easy to draw clear conclusions on their effects – economic or otherwise. In this section, I first consider several overall attempts to analyze the economic effects of PTAs, based on surveys of the economic literature. From this evaluation, I conclude that the actual economic impact of PTAs is probably somewhat negative but may not be all that great. Second, I consider the other effects of PTAs on the multilateral system. In this regard, I find a number of negative impacts of PTAs on that system. Third, I contrast the relatively desirability of multilateral and preferential approaches, which highlights why it is necessary to take seriously the PTA threat to the multilateral trading system.

2.1. The Economic Effects of PTAs

There is much controversy over the economic effects of PTAs on the multilateral trading system. The basic question that has been asked since Viner's classic work on the economics of PTAs is whether such arrangements are trade creating

---

[35] WTO Secretariat, *supra* note 2, at 62.

[36] The 1995 report noted that the WTO was often more comprehensive than PTAs. Ibid. That is less true today as many recent PTAs cover WTO-plus issues (e.g., intellectual property) and non-WTO issues (e.g., labor and environment).

or trade diverting – a consideration that in any event is only suggestive but not determinative of whether they are welfare enhancing or not. This is obviously an economic (not a legal) question, and economists have quite differing views on the issue. This diversity of viewpoints arises because of the difficulty of measuring the economic effects of PTAs. Although this might seem to be a straightforward empirical issue, it is more complicated than that. Whether one attempts to measure the effects of a PTA after the fact or predict them in advance, one is always forced to speculate on what would have happened without the PTA in question, and that can never be known with any certainty. For example, how would markets have evolved in absence of the PTA and would other trade liberalization have occurred? This section of the chapter will only summarize briefly some recent general surveys of economic studies that touch on the basic questions surrounding the economic impact of PTAs.

In a 2001 OECD review, the authors reviewed the economics literature on the effects of PTAs on trade and investment flows.[37] In examining recent *ex post* studies, the review concludes that results are "mixed." Some studies showed significant increases in intra-bloc trade, but others did not. As to trade diversion, there was no indication found that it is a major problem, although some evidence indicated that it may exist to a limited degree. The review reports that *ex post* studies on the economic growth effects of PTAs suggest that they "have had little impact on economic growth."[38] The *ex ante* studies reviewed showed "weak evidence of trade diversion, but that the recent wave of regionalism has been trade creating on a net basis and welfare improving for member countries and trading blocs as a whole."[39]

The *World Trade Report 2003*, a WTO publication, concluded that for the most part there is not strong evidence of trade creation in most PTAs. Positive evidence is found in respect of some PTAs, but not in others.[40] In respect of the more general issue of trade creation versus trade diversion, it notes a divergence of opinion among economists and studies of specific PTAs.[41] The WTO report also notes that not all trade in PTAs is preferential – often because of the cost of complying with rules of origin and other administrative requirements – and that certain sectors often remain protected under PTAs. Both of these factors would help explain findings that the economic effect of PTAs on trade creation may not be as great as might otherwise be expected.[42] It is also worth noting that as MFN tariffs continue to fall, the preferences provided by PTAs shrink. Likewise, as networks of PTAs proliferate, the amount of preference provided by any one PTA also shrinks.

---

[37] Regional Integration: Observed Trade and Other Economic Effects, OCED Doc. TD/TC/ WP(2001)19/FINAL (October 19, 2001).

[38] Id., para. 2.

[39] Id., para. 3. The review notes that the results vary widely, depending on the precise model used. Models based on imperfect competition showed greater positive results.

[40] Secretariat Report, *supra* note 3, at 55–7.   [41] Id., at 58–9.   [42] Id., at 59–62.

Works that are more recent also note that many studies have found ambiguous results. For example, a recent paper commences by stating that "[m]any recent papers have pointed to ambiguous trade effects of developing [country] regional trade agreements, calling for a reassessment of their economic merits."[43] The paper's own evaluation found that there had been a positive impact on trade between members, although only seven agreements were studied. Even then, there was a negative impact in one case, and in another the positive impact had dissipated over time.[44]

The conclusion to be drawn by a noneconomist would seem to be straightforward. The negative economic impact of PTAs may not be all that great. Does this mean that the creation of PTAs may not be a major problem for the multilateral trading system? This does not necessarily follow because PTAs produce more than economic effects on the multilateral trading system, and the next section considers those.

2.2. Other Effects of PTAs

The WTO report lists four reasons why PTAs may be inimical to the multilateral trading system.[45] First, it notes the claim that some trade diversion will occur because of the complexity of typical PTA rules of origin. From the noneconomic perspective, the complexity of these rules raises compliance costs in the multilateral system. This argument seems irrefutable. It has often been noted that the complexity of administrative rules in PTAs often leads traders to forego benefits under a PTA, such that a significant amount of trade under preferential arrangements does not benefit from available preferences.[46] Indeed, it may also explain why the economic impact of PTAs is less than might otherwise be expected (i.e., rules of origin are drafted to limit such impact). This argument, however, mainly suggests that entry into PTAs, particularly complex networks of PTAs with varying rules of origin, may not make good policy sense. It does not necessarily follow that this complexity will hinder development of the multilateral system. Indeed, the simplicity of the multilateral system is highlighted in comparison.

The second problem raised by the WTO report concerns transparency. For the most part, this is because of the administrative complexities discussed in the

---

[43] Souleymane Coulibaly, "Evaluating the Trade Effect of Developing Regional Trade Agreements: A Semi-parametric Approach," World Bank Policy Research Working Paper 4220, May 2007, at 1.

[44] Ibid.

[45] Secretariat Report, *supra* note 3, at 65. For a somewhat similar list, see Bhagwati, *supra* note 3.

[46] Id., at 59. *The Economist* reports that many imports are made without benefitting from preferences because the documentary requirements to justify them are viewed as too complex by the businesses that would have to comply with them. For example, only 5 percent of ASEAN trade takes advantage of the available preferences. "Afta Doha," *The Economist*, September 6, 2008, at 85.

preceding paragraph. However, it is broader than that. To the extent that different PTAs take different approaches to resolving trade issues (rules on standards, services regulation, etc.), they may significantly increase the transaction costs to businesses of engaging in international trade.[47] Divergent rules may not only undermine multilateral rules, they may make multilateral rules more difficult to negotiate in the long run, as it may be more difficult to reconcile differences in a few competing rules championed by different PTA networks than many different rules each supported by only individual states.[48]

The third problem seen in the WTO report is that PTAs may slow down multilateral liberalization because groups in a country desiring liberalization may be largely satisfied with that achieved in PTAs, whereas those in sectors wanting protection may be able to gain exclusion from the PTA. Thus, pressures for multilateral liberalization will be undermined, and opposition will remain as strong. In addition, it is feared that the creation of preferences will inevitably create lobbies for their retention – a problem that has arisen in the Doha negotiations. A related problem arises in countries where PTAs are controversial. The political capital spent to obtain legislative approval of minor PTAs may sour the atmosphere for future consideration of all trade agreements, including multilateral agreements that might not otherwise be particularly controversial.[49]

The fourth concern is a related one – that the negotiation of PTAs will detract from the multilateral negotiations simply because of the limited resources available to many countries. Although PTAs often follow basic patterns, they all have to be "customized" to the concerns of the pair of countries involved. The resources needed to do that inevitably will reduce those available for multilateral negotiations. Whereas proponents of trade liberalization will presumably remain in favor of multilateral liberalization, their attention and resources will also be diverted. Thus, it would seem that a policy of pursuing multiple PTAs is inevitably going to undermine the multilateral system.[50]

---

[47] OECD, Regional Trade Agreements and the Multilateral Trading System: Consolidated Report, TD/TC(2002)8/FINAL, at 19 (November 20, 2002).

[48] Id. Of course, in some instances PTA rules may end up serving as models for the multilateral system. Id., at 20. Thus, it is argued that PTAs may be "building blocks" rather than "stumbling blocks" to freer trade on a multilateral basis. See generally Robert Z. Lawrence, "Emerging Regional Arrangements: Building Blocks or Stumbling Blocks," in Richard O'Brien (ed.), *Finance and the International Economy* (1991). As long as divergent rules exist, however, they clearly increase the cost of trade.

[49] Bhagwati, *supra* note 3, at 87. In the United States, PTAs may be more controversial because it is perceived that the United States has a much increased negotiating leverage in most PTA negotiations compared to its position in multilateral negotiations. As a result, there is an expectation that the PTA should be a better deal for the United States and provide rules, for example, on TRIPS plus, labor, and the environment that would obviously not be attainable in multilateral negotiations.

[50] Of course, during PTA negotiations, trade negotiators may obtain a deeper understanding of domestic trade policy concerns in their own country that will be useful for them in multilateral negotiations as well.

All of these issues seem significant, but, of course, there is cause for concern only if it is clear that the multilateral trading system is in fact superior to expanding networks of PTAs and if such expansion precludes progress at the multilateral level. These two questions are taken up in the following subsection.

2.3. The Desirability of PTAs and the Multilateral Trading System Compared

In comparing the effectiveness of PTAs and the multilateral trading system, it is quite noteworthy that the economic benefits of PTAs do not seem to be so clear. Although there would seem to be an overall gain, it does not seem to be that significant and may lead to undesirable trade diversion. Thus, the multilateral system, which over decades has clearly produced significant economic benefits, seems clearly superior.[51]

If one thinks systemically, the multilateral system's superiority turns on a number of factors in addition to broader economic benefits – (i) *the nondiscrimination principle*, which in the long run is in the interest of all nations (and especially the smaller and weaker); (ii) *comprehensiveness* – the ability to deal with all issues, including those such as subsidies and general rules that PTAs typically do not address (and often simply cannot because of their global dimensions); (iii) *trade facilitation* – the ability to simplify trade, as compared to the complexities that PTAs add through rules of origin and nonstandardized rules; (iv) *predictability*, in that a world of proliferating PTAs results in trade instability as each new PTA changes the relative advantages theretofore enjoyed by all other traders as opposed to the stability of the multilateral system; (v) *fairness*, in that smaller countries have a more effective voice in negotiations, whereas PTAs, at least between a powerful and a weaker state, seem to be one sided and offered on a take-it-or-leave-it basis; and (vi) *more effective dispute settlement*, and in particular, fairer dispute settlement that is less power based than in PTAs.

Given the clear superiority of the multilateral trading system, the question becomes to what extent the continuing expansion of PTAs undermines (i) the multilateral trading system as it exists today and (ii) multilateral negotiations, such as the Doha Round, designed to expand and improve the multilateral system. I doubt that continued expansion of PTAs threatens the WTO as it currently stands. Indeed, so much was achieved in the Uruguay Round that much of the WTO membership is still engaged in the implementation process. Thus, the WTO and the multilateral trading system are not about to become irrelevant, particularly in light of its vast current coverage and the advantages listed earlier. Nevertheless, over time, I have become increasingly worried about the

---

[51] Bhagwati notes that economists using the Michigan CGE model of world production and trade "have calculated that the gains under multilateral trade liberalization dominate significantly those from a policy of PTAs." Bhagwati, *supra* note 3, at 56, n. 7.

effect of the growing numbers of PTAs on the future evolution of the multilateral system. Fifteen years ago, PTAs seemed complementary to the multilateral
trading system, as found by the 1995 Secretariat report. Indeed, the work done
in the European Union (EU) and in NAFTA on services, trade-related aspects
of intellectual property rights (TRIPS), and other issues arguably facilitated the
Uruguay Round negotiations on these topics. More recently, however, the expansion in the numbers and topics covered by PTAs causes me to fear that they are
now impeding liberalization at the multilateral level. Although the clear inherent superiority of the multilateral system should ensure its long-run success, in
my view PTAs are presenting an increasing challenge to the WTO. Indeed, given
the ambiguous economic results of PTAs, it seems clear that political reasons are
a major factor in propelling countries to enter PTAs. Thus, there is no reason to
think that the explosive recent growth in PTAs will not continue. The problems in
concluding the Doha Round underline this. The Doha difficulties call into question advantages (ii) and (iii) previously cited and give credence to the argument
that the only practical way forward toward trade liberalization is through PTAs.
The resulting increase (discussed earlier) in divergent standards and effect on
domestic political support for multilateral liberalization will clearly complicate
conclusion of the Doha Round and future multilateral initiatives.

Although I do not want to overstate the problem (as noted earlier, the WTO
is not about to become irrelevant), it seems to me that the WTO cannot just take
the position that nations will eventually see its inherent superiority or that falling
MFN tariff rates will eventually marginalize PTAs. It must take some action to
solidify its superiority over PTAs and to blunt their deleterious effects (such as
complexity) on the multilateral trading system. What actions might be taken? A
number of proposals have been made in recent years that are evaluated in the
following section.

3.   Proposals for Enhancing WTO Control of PTAs

If it is accepted that the recent and explosive growth in the number of PTAs
poses some degree of threat to the multilateral trading system, what can be done?
In this section, I look at suggestions made by the three groups that recently have
made proposals on how the WTO might control PTAs – the WTO Secretariat
Report, the Sutherland Report, and the Warwick Commission Report. Second, I
consider some proposals made in the Doha negotiations for improving the substance of Article XXIV through clarifications and modifications of existing text.
Finally, I look at some other limited actions that might be more politically plausible than the changes considered in the second part. In particular, I examine
whether giving WTO members the right to participate in the activities of PTAs to
which they are not parties – a sort of transparency plus requirement for PTAs –
might reduce the negative effects of PTAs on the multilateral trading system.

3.1. The WTO Report, Sutherland Report, and Warwick Commission

Each of the three WTO-related studies cited earlier – the 2003 WTO Secretariat Report, the Sutherland Report, and the Warwick Commission – contained suggestions on how to minimize the harmful impacts of PTAs on the WTO. This section looks at each of those recommendations.

The WTO Secretariat report suggested one major mechanism to blunt the adverse effects of PTAs. It proposed that WTO rules should be modified to require that nations entering into a PTA undertake to multilateralize the PTA's trade liberalization over time, and it proposed a monitoring system to ensure that would happen.[52] Effectively, this would mean that over time parties to a PTA would have to lower their MFN tariffs to zero. The time period over which that would have to occur was not specified.[53] Although this would indeed "solve" the problems of PTAs vis-à-vis the WTO, it is frankly hard to believe that the WTO membership would agree to such a change given the widespread use of PTAs and the membership's long-term failure to regulate them seriously.[54]

The Sutherland Report suggested three approaches to combatting PTAs. The simplest and what would be the most effective was the suggestion that all developed-country tariffs should be bound at zero in WTO schedules at some future agreed-upon point.[55] This is also seen by Bhagwati as the most effective approach in his recent book.[56] Although the effectiveness of the approach cannot be questioned, at least if major developing countries are included, its practicality seems rather limited given the great difficulty in trying to get agreement on lowered tariffs in the Doha Round.[57] It would seem from that experience that developed countries are not prepared to reduce tariffs unilaterally, but rather

---

[52] Secretariat Report, *supra* note 3, at 66.

[53] Professor Srinivasan supports this approach and says that it would require implementation within five years. He would also require that any PTA provisions on intellectual property, labor, and the environment that go beyond the applicable WTO provisions be brought into conformity with the WTO provisions within five years as well. Such requirements would certainly make PTAs less attractive, but it is not clear to me why parties cannot supplement the WTO in the three areas mentioned. Such supplemental agreements must not violate the applicable WTO rules, but because the WTO does not purport to cover all issues, it seems inappropriate for it to prevent countries from negotiating and agreeing on non-WTO issues in non-WTO fora.

[54] Bhagwati finds it unlikely that PTA members would agree to phase out their preferences unilaterally. Bhagwati, *supra* note 3, at 91. This idea bears some resemblance to the principles of "open regionalism," as espoused by C. Fred Bergsten in "Open Regionalism," 20 *The World Economy* 545 (1997). To date, it does not appear that open regionalism has "caught on."

[55] Sutherland Report, *supra* note 3, Recommendation 3, at 79.

[56] Bhagwati, *supra* note 3, at 97.

[57] It is worth noting that the previously described Secretariat approach would be less comprehensive and therefore perhaps a bit more practical because it would require zero tariffs only where they had been agreed in a PTA context.

expect serious reductions in tariffs by major developing countries. Because such reductions would probably be beneficial for all, it is hard to defend a position that would exempt the major developing countries. In any event, as noted, agreement on zero tariffs seems unlikely in the near term.

Second, the Sutherland Report suggested that the WTO adopt more effective disciplines for and better reviews of PTAs,[58] but it did not propose any specifics beyond increased transparency and discussion,[59] which arguably have been occurring gradually over time in any event. Finally, the Sutherland Report called for restraint in the use of PTAs and called for WTO members to ensure that their PTAs did not adversely affect third parties.[60]

Not surprisingly, the Sutherland Report recommendations were not well received. For example, Hufbauer calls all three simply "implausible."[61] Cottier notes that the report "refrains from making suggestions for reform that would be in a position to address these concerns more effectively. There is an obvious and disturbing discrepancy in the report."[62]

The recommendations of the Warwick Commission report are similar to those made by the Sutherland Report. The Commission calls for restraint in the conclusion of PTAs, and in particular suggests that the major developed and major developing nations should not enter into PTAs among themselves.[63] Despite this suggestion, the difficulties in concluding the Doha Round would seem to make such a development more likely.[64] It also noted support for a move to zero tariffs.[65] The Warwick Commission also called for the clarification of WTO disciplines for PTAs and improvements in review procedures.[66] Finally, it called for the strengthening of transparency and for the establishment of a code of best practices.[67] Although the Commission's report did not go into much detail on the specific improvements it had in mind, it did cite the example of origin rules, which it thought could be standardized and provide for broader cumulation possibilities.[68] The skepticism that greeted the Sutherland Report's recommendations on PTAs would seem to be equally applicable to those of the

---

[58] Sutherland Report, *supra* note 3, Recommendation 4, at 79.
[59] These were suggested in the body of the report. Id., at para. 105, p. 26.
[60] Sutherland Report, *supra* note 3, Recommendation 2, at 79.
[61] Gary Clyde Hufbauer, "Inconsistency Between Diagnosis and Treatment," 8 *JIEL* 291, 293 (2005). Hufbauer is particularly critical of the discrimination inherent in the suggestion that only developed countries undertake to lower their tariffs to zero.
[62] Thomas Cottier, "The Erosion of Non-Discrimination: Stern Warning Without True Remedies," 8 *JIEL* 595, 596–7 (2005).
[63] Warwick Commission, *supra* note 3, Recommendation 2, at 53.
[64] A blue-ribbon panel of former high-ranking U.S. government officials noted in December 2008 that "there is considerable interest in potential FTAs with the [EU] and/or Japan." See "High-Powered Panel Urges Obama to Avoid Supporting New Round of WTO Trade Talks," *BNA International Trade Daily*, December 16, 2008.
[65] Warwick Commission, *supra* note 3, Recommendation 2, at 51.
[66] Id., Recommendation 1, at 53.   [67] Id., Recommendation 3, at 53.
[68] Id. at 52.

Warwick Commission. However, what about the one specific proposal in the Warwick Commission report not found in the Sutherland Report, that is, the idea of harmonizing or standardizing PTA provisions? Although there would be definite advantages in doing so, critics have argued that the task would be extremely complex and would ultimately not do enough to counter the PTA problem.[69]

Despite the eminence of those who produced these reports, it seems that they have not produced particularly useful suggestions – the ideas that would clearly work (phase out of preferences or multilateral zero tariffs) seem impracticable; the other ideas are rather imprecise. So, what else might be done that would be plausible?

3.2. Clarifications and Modifications to the Text of Article XXIV

As noted earlier, there have been a number of interpretative difficulties in respect of Article XXIV. In particular, there have been disagreements over

(i) how to measure whether a PTA liberalizes substantially all trade between the parties, as required by Article XXIV:8;
(ii) how to assess whether the level of duties and other regulations of commerce prevailing after formation of the PTA exceed those in force prior thereto, as required by Article XXIV:5, including how to define "other regulations of commerce" (e.g., does that phrase include rules of origin and/or technical or SPS standards?);
(iii) how to define "other restrictive regulations of commerce" in Article XXIV:8, which has an impact on whether PTAs can retain the possibility for their members to apply safeguards and antidumping duties against each other;
(iv) how to interpret the "exceptional circumstance" exception to the general rule that PTAs should be implemented within ten years; and
(v) the extent to which there should be special and differential treatment of developing country PTAs, beyond the already loose standards of the Enabling Clause.

The possibility of amending Article XXIV to deal with these and other issues has been a topic of discussion in the "rules" negotiations in the Doha Round.[70]

---

[69] Bhagwati, *supra* note 3, at 92–7. The difficulty of harmonizing origin rules is highlighted by the never-ending negotiations in the WTO on nonpreferential rules of origin. Those negotiations were supposed to be completed by 1997, but are still progressing at a snail's pace. In this regard, it is noteworthy that APEC's attempt to make PTAs more WTO friendly by development of PTA best practices or model clauses has not achieved much. Hufbauer and Schott concluded, "To date, the guidelines have not had a perceptible impact on trade negotiations," although they note that the process has had an educational benefit. Gary Clyde Hufbauer and Jeffrey J. Schott, "Fitting Asia-Pacific Agreements into the WTO System," at 34 (paper presented at WTO Conference on Multilateralizing Regionalism, *infra* note 98).

[70] In connection with the Doha negotiations, the WTO Secretariat has prepared a number of very useful background documents. See Compendium of Issues Related to Regional

So far, there has been agreement on improving transparency and the procedures used to review PTAs in the CRTA, and those improvements have been put in place in 2006 on a provisional basis.[71] Since the beginning of 2006, there does not appear to have been much consideration of these issues. The chair of the rules negotiating group did not include any Article XXIV-related proposals in his chair drafts of 2007 and 2008,[72] although he did refer to the Article XXIV negotiations in his July 2008 report to the Trade Negotiations Committee.[73]

3.2.1. Defining "substantially all the trade"

To qualify as a WTO-consistent PTA, Article XXIV:8 specifies that

> "duties and other restrictive regulations of commerce...are eliminated on substantially all the trade [SAT] between the constituent territories."

It has long been disputed whether this should be interpreted by applying a quantitative test or a qualitative test or both.[74] In the case of a quantitative test, the EC once proposed 80 percent of trade volume.[75] Others have argued that the

Trade Agreements, TN/RL/W/8/Rev. 1 (August 1, 2002); Coverage, Liberalization Process, and Transitional Provisions in Regional Trade Agreements, WT/REG/W/46 (April 5, 2002); Rules of Origin Regimes in Regional Trade Agreements, WT/REG/W/45 (April 5, 2002); Basic Information on Regional Trade Agreements: Agreements Notified to the GATT/WTO and in force as of January 31, 2002, WT/REG/W/44 (February 7, 2002); Mapping of Regional Trade Agreements, WT/REG/W/41 (October 11, 2000); Synopsis of "Systemic" Issues Related to Regional Trade Agreements, WT/REG/W/37 (March 2, 2000); Inventory of Non-Tariff Provisions in Regional Trade Agreements, WT/REG/W/26 (May 5, 1998); Systemic Issues Related to "Other Regulations of Commerce," WT/REG/W/17/Rev. 1 (February 5, 1998); Systemic Issues Related to "Substantially all the Trade," WT/REG/W/21/Rev. 1 (February 5, 1998); Systemic Implications of Regional Trade Agreements and Regional Initiatives for the Multilateral Trading System, WT/REG/W/8 (August 28, 1996). In addition, papers on procedures for review were prepared and served as background for the negotiations that led to the transparency mechanism decision.

[71] Transparency Mechanism for Regional Trade Agreements, General Council Decision of December 14, 2006, WT/L/671 (December 18, 2006). See text accompanying notes 33–4 *supra*.

[72] See the WTO Web site at http://www.wto.org/english/tratop_e/rulesneg_e/rulesneg_e.htm# work (last visited November 8, 2008). Nor were such proposals contained in his December 2008 text. TN/RL/W/236 (December 19, 2008).

[73] Negotiating Group on Rules, Report by the Chairman to the Trade Negotiations Committee, TN/RL/22, para, 8, July 17, 2008. According to the chairperson, "I will continue to consult Members [on the systemic issues relating to PTAs]. My impression is that no one is disputing the fundamental importance of the issues and to continuing discussions on systemic issues. Nevertheless, as I have argued before, the Group cannot advance and conclude its work in this area without text-based proposals by Members. . . . I hope we will see text-based proposals from Members . . . in time for the next meeting of the Group in October and to bring these negotiations to a successful conclusion."

[74] For a bit of history, see GATT Analytical Index, *supra* note 10, at 824–6. In the *Turkey–Textiles* case, the Appellate Body indicated that there are both quantitative and qualitative aspects to this issue. *Turkey–Textiles*, Appellate Body Report, para. 49.

[75] GATT Analytical Index, *supra* note 10, at 824.

threshold should be higher and that a qualitative test is needed because existing trade volumes may reflect existing barriers to trade that reduce trade far below what it would otherwise be. Among the ideas to address this issue would be to require that no sectors be excluded from liberalization.

In the current negotiations, the most detailed proposal that I am aware of has been made by Australia.[76] It proposed that to meet the SAT requirement, a PTA must liberalize initially 70 percent of harmonized system (HS) six-digit tariff lines, rising to 95 percent within a ten-year transition period. In order to prevent the 5 percent exclusion from being used to shield significant sectors from liberalization, Australia also proposed that by year 10, all highly traded products would have to be liberalized, with highly traded products defined as, for example, the fifty most imported products by one PTA member from another.

Other WTO members seemed to prefer the quantitative method. Turkey noted that it was "not ... in conformity with economic realities" to require that no major sectors be excluded from a PTA.[77] The EU noted that a quantitative test based on trade flows had been "traditionally favored" and that although it would consider a tariff-line test as a supplement, it was necessary to balance the need to clarify the term with past interpretations by WTO members in entering into PTAs.[78]

In short, it appears that some useful work has been done on this issue, but there does not appear to be any consensus in the offing. It is noteworthy, as has been noted earlier, that one problem in clarifying the meaning of Article XXIV is that those members who have entered into PTAs in the past hesitate to agree to a clarification that would suggest that their past PTAs did not (and often still do not) comply with Article XXIV.[79]

3.2.2. Banning Trade Remedies after Transition Periods

Most, but not all, PTAs permit the use of safeguard, countervail, and antidumping[80] measures on intra-PTA trade. It has been questioned whether this is consistent with the Article XXIV:8 requirement that liberalization apply to "duties and other restrictive regulations of commerce (except, where necessary, those permitted under Articles XI, XII, XIII, XIV, XV, and XX)." On the one hand, it is hard to argue that the parenthetical list should be exclusive because it includes Article XI (quotas), but not Article XXI (national security), which would seem

---

[76] See TN/RL/W/173/Rev.1 (March 3, 2005); TN/RL/W/180 (May 13, 2005).

[77] TN/RL/W/32, at 3 (September 25, 2005).   [78] TN/RL/W/179 (May 12, 2005).

[79] It is worth noting that tightening the trade-coverage standards for PTAs would likely increase the potential for PTAs to have negative (trade-diverting) effects, although such effects could be offset to the extent that the tighter standards resulted in fewer PTAs.

[80] The lack of an economic rationale for having antidumping rules has often been pointed out. See William J. Davey, "Antidumping Laws: A Time for Restriction," in William J. Davey (ed.), *Enforcing World Trade Rules: Essays on WTO Dispute Settlement and GATT Obligations*, ch. 8 (Cameron, May 2006). They are nonetheless a permanent feature of the world trading system.

odd. It is also questioned whether safeguard, countervail, and antidumping measures are restrictive regulations of commerce because they are time limited and
address specific problems on a nondiscriminatory basis.[81] On the other hand,
one can argue that after an appropriate transition period, such measures should
not be needed. Even if safeguard, countervail, and antidumping measures are
permitted by Article XXIV:8, there is also the question of whether such measures
may be applied in a more favorable manner to PTA members, a preference often
found in PTAs.[82]

Given that most PTAs allow application of safeguard, countervail, and
antidumping measures to intra-PTA trade, it seems unlikely that there could be
an agreement banning that practice. Similarly, an attempt to ban more favorable
treatment of PTA members seems unlikely as well, although there is a bit of support for that.[83]

3.2.3. Establishing Tests for Assessing Whether a PTA Raises Barriers to the Trade of Third Parties
Article XXIV:5 specifies that

> [T]he duties and other regulations of commerce maintained in each of the
> constituent territories and applicable at the formation of such free-trade
> area...to the trade of [WTO] Members not included in such [free trade]
> area...shall not be higher or more restrictive than the corresponding duties
> and other regulations of commerce existing in the same constituent territo-
> ries prior to the formation of the free-trade area.

The idea is easy to grasp. It is essentially an attempt to operationalize the statement in Article XXIV:4 that "the purpose of a...free-trade area should be to facilitate trade between the constituent territories and not to raise barriers to the trade
of the other Members with such territories." There have been some difficulties in
interpreting the phrase "other regulations of commerce" (called ORC for short)
and measuring whether the formation of a PTA has made them more restrictive.

The discussions in the Doha negotiations have focused on such issues as
whether rules of origin and technical or sanitary and phytosanitary (SPS) measures are ORCs. The diversity of viewpoints is seen in arguments presented by
India, which has argued that rules of origin are ORCs, but that technical barriers
to trade (TBT) and SPS measures are not.[84] The consequence, according to India,

---

[81] Although individual safeguard, countervail, and antidumping measures may effectively target specific countries, the rules under which they are applied do not discriminate.

[82] It has been pointed out to me that there is some tension regarding the goals to be achieved
by possible reforms in this area. Requiring members to eliminate trade remedies in intra-
PTA trade involves requiring greater discrimination against non-PTA partners; presumably
it is desirable only to the extent it raises the bar and makes PTAs less likely to start with.
The "no more favorable treatment" idea goes in exactly the opposite direction, proposing
to limit discrimination in respect of trade remedies.

[83] See, e.g., WT/REG/W/29 (July 29, 1998), Japan; TN/RL/W/114 (June 6, 2003), India.

[84] TN/RL/W/114, at 3–5 (June 6, 2003).

is that rules of origin cannot be more stringent and that TBT and SPS rules cannot discriminate against third parties (because they are not necessary for the formation of a PTA, Article XXIV does not protect discriminatory TBT and SPS rules). Korea has argued that all nontariff trade measures are ORCs.[85] The EU has argued that different approaches may be needed to determine if different ORCs are neutral, and that if an ORC is consistent with applicable WTO agreements, it should be permissible.[86] In short, the diversity of viewpoints on this issue seems rather broad.

3.2.4. Reasonable Period of Time and Exceptional Circumstances

The 1994 Understanding on Article XXIV essentially suggests that, except in exceptional circumstances, PTAs should be phased in over a time period not to exceed ten years. It appears that many recent (post-2000) PTAs have longer phase-in periods.[87] As a result, there have been discussions as to how to define exceptional. This issue is, of course, one that would lend itself to claims for special and differential treatment for developing countries. The chair of the negotiating group has indicated considerable divergence in views on this issue.[88]

3.2.5. Development-Related Issues

The sort of development-related issues that have arisen are suggested by a paper submitted by the ACP countries, which argued inter alia that developing-country PTAs should benefit from longer transition periods (e.g., at least eighteen years), that it is necessary to protect CRTA decisions from dispute settlement, and that developing-country PTAs should be subject to less onerous notification/transparency requirements.[89] Others questioned the need for this.[90] More generally, developing countries have argued that special and differential treatment should be applied to any improvements in Article XXIV. Given the relatively higher tariffs in developing countries and consequent increased possibility of trade diversion, weakening current or new rules would not seem to be desirable, especially given the expansive definition of "developing country" in the WTO and the greatly increased importance of many advanced developing countries in international trade in recent years.

3.2.6. Desirability and Plausibility of Reform Proposals

It would obviously be desirable to clarify the meaning of Article XXIV's key provisions. In that regard, I would strongly support a clarification of SAT along

[85] TN/RL/W/116, at 2–3 (June 11, 2003).   [86] TN/RL/W/179, at 4 (May 12, 2005).
[87] Id. at 3 (EU).
[88] Report by the Chairman to the Trade Negotiations Committee, TN/RL/15 (September 30, 2005).
[89] TN/RL/W/155 (April 28, 2004).
[90] See, e.g., TN/RL/W/165 (October 8, 2004), Japan.

the lines proposed by Australia. In addition, it seems to me that any measure that affects trade should be considered an ORC, subject to consideration in the analysis of whether the trade of third parties has been subjected to higher duties or more restrictive ORC than the corresponding duties and ORC existing prior to the formation of the PTA. I would also support a definition of exception circumstances that would tighten the requirement that a PTA normally be implemented within ten years. In the absence of rules on competition in a PTA, I find it difficult to support a complete ban on safeguards and other trade remedies. The problem with these proposals is that even if they are presented as a way to ensure compliance with Article XXIV so as to make PTAs more economically compatible with the multilateral system and the original intent of GATT's framers (i.e., by helping to minimize trade diversion), they will be viewed as making PTAs much more difficult to negotiate and as such are likely to be unpopular with many WTO members.

In any event, as noted in the foregoing discussion, these proposals do not seem to have much of a chance of achieving consensus. The proposals to clarify the meanings of ORC and "other restrictive regulations of commerce" (ORRC) have not received much serious attention. So far, the main focus of the negotiations on systemic issues has been on three topics: defining SAT, defining the exception to the ten-year phase-in rule, and development-related issues (special and differential treatment and the relationship of the Enabling Clause PTA provisions to Article XXIV). However, as explained earlier, it does not seem likely that agreement on these three issues is likely in the near future.

3.3. Transparency Plus: WTO Control of PTA Dispute Settlement and Expanded Third-Party Participation

Given the implausibility of the proposals discussed so far, are there any remaining alternatives to consider? It would seem to me that two additional approaches might be considered. The first – expanded use of dispute settlement – has always existed, but might prove more useful in the future. The second – expanded transparency and third-party participation requirements – might be achievable and help reduce the potentially undesirable impacts of PTAs and ease their ultimate incorporation into the multilateral system.

3.3.1. WTO Dispute Settlement[91]

In the first instance, it is worth recalling that the conditions that PTAs are required to meet are, in principle, enforceable through dispute settlement. As

---

[91] In recent years, a new WTO/PTA issue has arisen in respect of dispute settlement. How should WTO panels treat PTA cases and dispute settlement provisions (such as those purporting to give exclusive jurisdiction over certain disputes to PTA dispute settlement)? Although this issue is beyond the scope of this paper, I would note my views that (i) PTA parties cannot divest WTO dispute settlement panels of jurisdiction unless the WTO

previously noted, the WTO Appellate Body made it clear that is the case in
Turkey–Textiles.[92] The dispute settlement process could precisely define the SAT,
ORC, and ORRC concepts, as well as specify what sort of exceptional circumstances would justify exceeding the normal ten-year phase-in period. It would
not be difficult for the dispute settlement system to perform this task; defining terms found in the WTO agreements is what the system does all the time.
Of course, it would be much harder to determine if the restrictive effect of
ORCs had increased. Indeed, it is commonly acknowledged that the economic
and legal analysis required to make such an evaluation would be extremely
complex, but it could be done.[93] After all, the dispute settlement system has
been charged with evaluating rather complex economic issues in connection
with aircraft, cotton, and tax subsidies. Because the dispute settlement process – although lengthy – cannot be blocked by parties, a decision on the WTO
consistency of a PTA can be expected, in contrast to the CRTA process, where
such decisions are never produced. There would remain the problem of enforcing the decision, but WTO members tend to comply with dispute settlement
decisions.[94]

Accordingly, over time, one could expect that the WTO's rules on PTAs would
become much clearer and that new PTAs would be more WTO consistent from
the outset. The process would probably take many, many years, however, as the
nature of dispute settlement systems – the WTO's included – is to avoid difficult issues as long as possible.[95] The process would also engender considerable
bitterness and controversy – bitterness on the part of those whose PTAs are first
to be challenged and controversy as the rules become defined in ways opposed

membership has waived DSU Article 23 in respect of the PTA provision and (ii) WTO panels
are not generally bound by prior rulings of PTA dispute settlement, although such rulings
may be taken into consideration in WTO dispute settlement proceedings. William J. Davey
and André Sapir, "The *Soft Drinks* Case: The WTO and Regional Agreements," 8 *World Trade
Review* (2009).

[92] In *Brazil–Tyres*, the Appellate Body reiterated that panels should consider Article XXIV
issues where necessary to decide a case. *Brazil–Tyres*, WT/DS332, Appellate Body Report,
paras. 253–7.

[93] Folsom has proposed that the WTO should give up on trying to review PTAs in the CRTA
and simply require transparency and leave it to the dispute settlement system to ensure
compliance with the rules. Ralph H. Folsom, "Bilateral Free Trade Agreements: A Critical
Assessment and WTO Regulatory Reform Proposal," University of San Diego School of Law,
Legal Studies Research Paper No. 08–070, September 2008 (available at http://ssrn.com/
abstract=1262872). For another, rather ambitious, and probably impractical approach, see
Colin B. Picker, "Regional Trade Agreements v. The WTO: A Proposal for Reform of Article
XXIV to Counter this Institutional Threat," 26 *University of Pennsylvania Journal of Interna-
tional Economic Law* 267 (2005).

[94] William J. Davey, "The WTO Dispute Settlement System: The First Decade," 8 *JIEL* 17–50
(2005).

[95] It is worth recalling that in *Turkey–Textiles*, the panel assumed that the customs union at
issue was WTO compliant and only considered the validity of the specific quotas challenged as WTO illegal. Although the Appellate Body indicated that as a first step a panel
should consider the WTO consistency of the PTA at issue, it would not be surprising to

by some (or many) members. Nonetheless, to the extent that the first decisions were narrowly based, one can easily imagine that over time the bitterness and controversy would subside as a body of clearer rules developed and the GATT compatibility of PTAs improved. There is no doubt, however, that this approach would be very controversial, which probably explains why there have been no broad-based challenges to PTAs in the decade since *Turkey–Textiles* was decided, even though there are certainly PTAs that would be hard to defend.[96] Thus, given the lengthy time and great controversy that reliance on dispute settlement would involve, what else might be considered?

3.3.2. Transparency and Participation[97]

One theme that emerges in the various studies of the PTA problem is that it would be desirable to increase transparency about PTAs and to encourage their integration into the multilateral system.[98] This would be particularly useful to ensure that PTAs in fact do not raise barriers to trade vis-à-vis nonparties. Although transparency is often thought of in terms of having the parties to a PTA supply information to the WTO, transparency in WTO terms also involves making sure that trade-related information is available to those who may be affected by it. Indeed, the accession negotiations with China focused particular attention on this issue. Along these lines, it would be useful to require increased transparency in the operation of PTAs. To be precise, I would propose that WTO members who are not parties to a PTA should have the right to participate in

---

me if panels continue to try to avoid that issue as long as possible given its complexity. For an argument as to why they should do so, see Youri Devuyst and Asja Serdarevic, "The World Trade Organization and Regional Trade Agreements: Bridging the Constitutional Credibility Gap," 18 *Duke Journal of Comparative and International Law* 55–72 (2007). However, it seems inevitable that in some cases, the overall issue of WTO consistency will not be avoidable without inappropriately deserved relief to wrong parties. See also note 96 *infra*.

[96] Professor Srinivasan takes a dim view of using dispute settlement to resolve these issues. I agree that it may be more desirable for PTAs to be vetted by the WTO membership than by a dispute settlement panel. However, in the absence of a workable vetting system, I see no alternative to dispute settlement. Otherwise, those adversely affected by noncompliant PTAs will have no recourse at all. The WTO membership should not be heard to complain about this result because they have failed to improve the operation of the CRTA in this regard. William J. Davey, "A Comment on Are the Judicial Organs of the World Trade Organization Overburdened?," in R. Porter, P. Sauvé, A. Subramanian, and A. Beviglia Zampetti (eds.), *Efficiency, Equity and Legitimacy: The Multilateral Trading System at the Millennium* 329–33 (Brookings, 2001).

[97] On instituting periodic reviews of existing PTAs in a TPRM-like process, see note 34 *supra*.

[98] On this subject generally, see papers presented at the Conference on "Multilateralizing Regionalism," held September 10–12, 2007, in Geneva. The papers presented are available on the WTO Web site: www.wto.org/english/tratop_e/conference_sept07_e.htm (last visited December 19, 2008).

or observe certain PTA functions. In particular, I would require PTAs to allow such WTO members to participate in PTA dispute settlement processes as third parties and to attend various PTA committee and working group meetings as observers.

Third-Party Rights in PTA Dispute Settlement: It seems clear that nonparties to PTAs are often affected by dispute settlement decisions in PTAs.[99] Indeed, in the many cases where there are overlapping obligations, parties to a PTA have a choice of bringing an action in the WTO or under the PTA's dispute settlement provisions. When brought in the WTO, the rest of the WTO membership has a right to observe and participate in the dispute as a third party, yet it has no rights at all if the dispute is brought under the PTA dispute settlement provisions. André Sapir and I have recently proposed that the WTO impose the requirement that all PTA dispute settlement systems contain provisions giving nonparty WTO members third-party rights in PTA disputes.[100] This would ensure greater transparency of PTA dispute settlement and enable third parties to defend their rights if necessary through subsequent action in the WTO. Such a change would seem to be plausible as the WTO membership generally seems to support expanding third-party rights in dispute settlement panel proceedings.[101] In addition, it might help make PTA dispute settlement systems more balanced, at least where there is considerable disparity in the economic power of the parties, as is often the case.[102]

Third-Party Participation in PTA Administration: PTAs typically have many working groups involved in the functioning and governance of the PTA. Such groups typically deal with technical issues regarding specific aspects of the PTA's operation. For example, there may be a group that focuses on customs issues, such as the operation of rules or origin and customs clearance procedures. The work that these groups do is often similar to that undertaken by the various committees in the WTO, such as those on licensing, rules of origin, valuation, technical standards, and SPS measures. Opening such group meetings would enable nonmembers of a PTA to monitor what the PTA was doing in areas that are more generally dealt with in the WTO. Although I agree with Bhagwati that trying to

---

[99] Davey and Sapir, *supra* note 91.   [100] Ibid.

[101] This general support is not inconsistent with the fact that some members attempt to block third-party rights in specific cases where they arguably have a right to do so.

[102] It has also been proposed to require PTA dispute settlement to occur under WTO auspices and rules. Professor Srinivasan advocates this as well. See Picker, *supra* note 93; Lim Chin Leng and Henry Gao, "Saving the WTO from the Risk of Irrelevance: The WTO Dispute Settlement Mechanism as a 'Common Good' for RTA Disputes," 11 *JIEL* 899 (2008). I feel that this would be an advantage for PTAs and that the WTO should not provide such advantages because PTAs may ultimately undermine it. Our proposal to give WTO members third-party rights in PTA dispute settlement is enough to ensure that WTO member interests are protected.

standardize PTA practices in these various areas would be impossible to negotiate in the WTO,[103] increasing PTA transparency and opportunities for WTO
member participation in PTA activities of this sort would probably lead to more
harmonization over time, even if complete standardization were never achieved.
At a minimum, it would provide a sort of early warning system, so that the rest of
the WTO membership could react to PTA activities that raise WTO issues or otherwise threaten to affect adversely the multilateral trading system. This proposal
would perhaps be more difficult to implement than the third-party proposal outlined earlier because it might be viewed as potentially giving rise to unwelcome
meddling, but because the nonparties would be observers only, it seems to me
that it could be accepted, especially because outside input might often be quite
useful on technical issues.

Summary: It has to be admitted that these two proposals would have only
a limited impact, but that in itself may make them achievable. Besides, as noted
earlier, the PTA threat to the WTO is not a matter of life or death for the WTO.
Thus, modest proposals are not out of place. In any event, the impact would not
be inconsequential. PTA disputes will often have ramifications for other WTO
members, particularly where such disputes are settled. Giving nonparty WTO
members third-party rights in such disputes would increase their awareness of
such ramifications. Increasing their involvement in the administration of PTAs
would help promote the multilateralization of the outcomes, thereby making
PTAs more building blocks than stumbling blocks – particularly in respect of
technical trade issues. Indeed, it could be expected to make eventual harmonization in respect of such issues more likely to occur sooner.[104]

4. Conclusion

PTAs pose a problem for the WTO. Although their economic impacts may
not be that great, they undermine the multilateral trading system in various
ways. Because of the inherent superiority of the multilateral system, it is essential to blunt their deleterious effects and to try, at a minimum, to ensure that
PTAs comply with existing WTO rules. Recent attempts to recommend ways to
deal with this problem by the WTO Secretariat, Sutherland Report, and the Warwick Commission have not produced ideas of much practical, near-term use.

---

[103] See note 69 *supra*. As indicated there, such efforts may have a useful educational aspect.

[104] Both of these changes would require an amendment to GATT Article XXIV to be legally binding, and it is very difficult to amend WTO rules. Thus, consideration would have to be given
to putting such "requirements" in a General Council decision (such as was done in respect
of the new transparency procedures), with the understanding that the decision would not
be enforceable in dispute settlement. It is likely that most members would comply with the
requirements of such a decision, however, because they would have participated in its consensus adoption.

Although it would, of course, be preferable to strengthen and clarify the existing WTO rules, that does not seem achievable in the near-to-medium term. Thus, this chapter makes some more modest proposals that are more likely to be acceptable and yet still have some desirable benefits for the multilateral system in its struggle with the proliferation of PTAs.

T. N. SRINIVASAN

8.1 *Comments on "A Model Article XXIV:*
Are There Realistic Possibilities to Improve It?"

Professor Davey has written a very interesting chapter on preferential trade agreements (PTAs). Such trade preferences are, by definition, restricted to members of the PTA, but not extended to other members. As such, prima facie, they violate the cardinal principle of nondiscrimination among members of GATT/WTO as enshrined in the Most Favored Nation (MFN) clause of Article I.1 of the GATT agreement of 1947 (hereafter GATT, 1947). This agreement was incorporated (with subsequent amendments) as GATT (1994) as part of the multilateral agreements signed in 1994 that concluded the Uruguay Round of Multilateral Negotiations, among which the agreement to found the WTO with effect from January 1, 1995, with the then set of contracting parties (CPs) of GATT as founder members, was one. However, the original CPs of GATT had explicitly exempted from the MFN clause, albeit under certain conditions specified in Article XXIV, namely customs unions (CUs) and free trade areas (FTAs). They also grandfathered and capped the then existing trade preferences (such as those of the UK, France, the United States, and a few other CPs) through Articles I.2–I.4.[105] While recognizing "the desirability of increasing freedom of trade by the development, through voluntary agreements, of closer integration between the economies of the parties to such agreements," they also recognized that "the purpose of customs union or a free trade area should be to facilitate trade between the constituent territories and not to raise barriers to the trade of other members with such territories" (Article XXIV:4). In pursuance of this purpose, Part 5 of the article laid down certain conditions by elaborating the content of the phrase "not to raise barriers to the trade of other members with such territories" in Article XXIV:4. Part 8 added others by defining CUs and FTAs. There can be no doubt that the CPs considered only such CUs and FTAs that fulfilled the definitions and conditions of Article XXIV that would be deemed consistent with the objectives of the CPs laid out in the preamble to GATT. These were "raising standards

[105] GATT (1947) included many more exceptions to MFN and a procedure to obtain a waiver from MFN.

of living, ensuring full employment and a large and steadily growing volume of real income and effective demand, developing the full use of the resources of the world and expanding the production and exchange of goods." These were to be achieved by "entering into reciprocal and mutually advantageous arrangements directed to the substantial reduction of tariffs and other barriers to trade and to the elimination of discriminatory treatment in international commerce" (WTO, 1994, p. 486).

GATT (1947) also required parties intending to enter into a CU or FTA to notify the GATT promptly of their intention. It also set up an ad hoc mechanism consisting of a working party of CPs to examine the consistency of any notified CU or PTA with GATT principles and report to the entire group of CPs.

The CPs of GATT (1947) did not view PTAs that are agreements for *preferential* and *not* free trade among its members as desirable from the perspective of the purpose laid out in Article XXIV:4. This is clear from the fact that CPs explicitly grandfathered and capped the then existing trade preferences. This being the case, I am not convinced that the framework laid out in Article XXIV for CUs and FTAs is appropriate, let alone adequate, for analyzing the consistency of the contemporary PTAs with a liberal nondiscriminatory multilateral global trading system and the threat posed by their proliferation. For this reason, while I share Professor Davey's conclusion that the proliferation of PTAs is a grave threat to the multilateral system, I do not share his faith that, by merely amending Article XXIV along the lines he suggests in the chapter, the grave threat posed by PTAs could be mitigated. Although I have yet to read Jagdish Bhagwati's latest potential bestseller on PTAs as termites in the global trading system, I agree with his description of them as termites. I do not see any meaningful approach to the infestation of termites other than their extermination. Controlling their ravenous appetite or their "fertility" in proliferation could help contain their threat for a while, but sooner or later they have to be eliminated.

To understand why the CPs of the GATT did not consider PTAs other than CUs and FTAs as desirable, one has to go back to the origins of GATT (see Srinivasan, 1988, chapter 2 for details). Briefly, the GATT was an agreement signed in October 1947 among twenty-three distinct customs of jurisdictions (not necessarily sovereign nations, though most of them were). It resulted from negotiations that originated from the U.S. government's *Proposals for the Expansion of World Trade and Employment*, published in December 6, 1945, and forwarded to all countries of the world. At the same time, the United States invited fifteen countries (including the Soviet Union) to negotiate reciprocal reductions in tariffs and other trade barriers. GATT was intended to be subsumed in the commercial policy chapter of the chapter for an International Trade Organization (ITO), which was itself to be the outcome of the United Nations Conference on Trade and Employment that opened in Havana on November 21, 1947. The conference was the result of the resolution proposed by the United States and approved by the United Nations Economic and Social Council (ECOSOC) in 1946. There was a large overlap between the group that was negotiation reduction of trade barriers and the preparatory committee for the conference. Moreover, the discussion in the committee was based on the suggested charter for an ITO submitted by the United States. The committee placed this draft with some relatively minor changes before the Havana Conference. The conference approved the charter in March 1948 after extensive debate. It was signed by fifty-three of the fifty-six participants at the conference (including the United States). However, the ITO never came into being, primarily because the United States did not ratify the charter, with President Truman having withdrawn it from further consideration by the U.S. Senate at the end of 1950. The dominant role of the United States in the GATT has a lot to do with many of its articles, including Article XXIV.

Fearing that reciprocal tariff reductions incorporated in the GATT signed in October 1947 might unravel before GATT was formally subsumed in the ITO, the contracting parties decided to bring Parts I and II of GATT into force in early 1948 through a provisional protocol of application. Technically, GATT was an executive agreement that did not require approval by the U.S. Senate and not a treaty that established an ITO that would have required such approval. All subsequent attempts to establish an organization failed: to quote John Jackson (1989, p. 89), "The GATT has limped along for nearly forty years with almost no 'basic constitution' designed to regulate its organizational activities and procedures."

The negotiators of the Uruguay Round of Multilateral Trade Negotiations (1986–92) who agreed to establish the WTO could have reconsidered articles of GATT (1947) as amended until then before bodily incorporating them as GATT (1994) in their agreement concluding the Round. However, they did not, except for agreeing on understandings relating to some of the articles. In particular, they chose not to review considerations that led the original CPs to confine Article XXIV to CUs and FTAs. Although the United States as a CP of GATT was opposed to the preferential trade between the UK and France with their colonies and believed that CUs are better vehicles for liberalizing trade than preferential trade, nonetheless it agreed to a compromise by accommodating and grandfathering the trade preferences granted by the UK and France but capping them in GATT. In his classic work on the Havana Conference and the charter for the ITO, Wilcox (1949, p. 70) noted the logical inconsistency in being against a PTA in which discrimination against trade among nonmembers applies only for part of trade and being in favor of a CU in which such discrimination applies for substantially all trade. Nevertheless, he explained the then dominant view in favor of a CU as follows:

> A customs union creates a wider trading area, removes obstacles to competition, makes possible a more economic allocation of resources and this operates to increase production and raise planes of living. A preferential

system, on the other hand, retains internal barriers, obstructs economy in production, and restrains the growth of income and demand. It is set up for the purpose of conferring a privilege on producers within the system and imposing a handicap on external competitors. A customs union is conducive to the expansion of trade on a basis of multilateralism and nondiscrimination; a preferential system is not.

This is not the occasion to review the extensive literature on a comparison between partial and complete discrimination, except to note that the conditions laid down in Article XXIV that abolition of trade barriers should cover substantially all trade and that the process toward such abolition should be completed within a relatively short time made sense in light of the then belief in the superiority of CU.

Let me now turn to Professor Davey's chapter in some detail. He says that the exemption from MFN in Article XXIV first covered CUs and then extended to FTAs. In fact, the exemption for both was in the original GATT agreement. He is also not quite right that, at the time of GATT negotiations, PTAs were not particularly controversial. Certainly CUs and FTAs were not, but PTAs were, as is evident from Wilcox (1949, p. 70).

I am afraid throughout the chapter Professor Davey uses the acronym "FTAs" to cover agreements that are not FTAs strictly speaking as defined in Article XXIV:8. Most of the PTAs in force are not only not FTAs, but some also go beyond matters relating to trade in goods and services and into investment, competition policy, labor and environmental standards, and intellectual property that may or may not be trade related. Merely improving Article XXIV, which at best covers CUS and FTAs limited to trade, is not enough.

The working party mechanism of GATT for examining the consistency with GATT of CUs and FTAs notified to GATT pronounced only six of the ninety-eight such agreements during the life of GATT (1948–94), and the six notably did not include the CU of the European Economic Community (EEC) and the European Free Trade Area (EFTA). The working party that examined the compatibility of the Treaty of Rome that established EEC concluded "no agreement was reached on the compatibility of the Treaty of Rome with Article XXIV, and the contracting parties agreed that because 'there were a number of important matters on which there was not at this time sufficient information ... to complete the examination of the Rome Treaty' ... this examination and the discussion of the legal questions involved in it could not be usefully pursued at the present time." The examination of EEC was never taken up again in GATT. The Committee on Regional Trade Agreements (CRTA) in the WTO that replaced the GATT mechanism has not done much better either.

Professor Davey gives the impression that this abject failure is largely because of the difficulty in defining and interpreting the terms "other regulations of commerce," "other restrictive regulations of commerce," and "substantially all trade." It is true that there was disagreement on the meaning of these terms, and given the convention that decisions of GATT/WTO have to be based on consensus, any forward movement based on the views of a majority was precluded. Still, the reason for the failures of the GATT/WTO mechanisms for examining PTAs goes deeper as the annual reports of the WTO and the thorough analysis in WTO (1995) have repeatedly emphasized. The annual report of 2007 (WTO 2007) explains the reasons well:

> Despite improvements in transparency and procedural issues achieved with the new Transparency Mechanism, there has been no further progress on its mandate of consistency assessment of RTAs, due to long-standing institutional, political, and legal difficulties. Since the establishment of the WTO, Members have been unable to reach consensus on neither the format nor the substance, of the reports on any of the examinations entrusted to the CRAT.

I am not convinced that clarifying the terms used and making other technical improvements in Article XXIV will obviate all the "long-standing, institutional, political, and legal" difficulties. Although I had no expectation that the Rules negotiations in the Doha Round would have effectively addressed them, as Professor Davey points out, the latest negotiation draft of the chair of the Rules negotiation group does not say anything on Article XXIV. In any case, the Doha Round is in a coma if not already dead.

Professor Davey discusses the empirical studies on economic effects of PTAs and emphasizes their divergent conclusions. One reason for such divergence is that most of the empirical analysis depends on regression analysis based on some variant of cross-country gravity models of bilateral trade flows. Their conclusions naturally depend on the variant used, time periods of analysis, and the countries as well as PTAs included. I am one of those who believe that because of their methodological infirmities there is very little of policy relevance that one can learn from such cross-country regressions. Only a few of the studies include the nontrade components of PTAs and their interaction with trade components. Two such recent studies – Adams et al. (2003) and De Rosa (2007) – come to diametrically opposite conclusions on trade diversion effects of recent PTAs! Incidentally, it is well known in theory that trade diversion need not necessarily imply welfare loss, and the fact that most such regressions focus on trade creation and diversion and not on welfare has to be kept in mind. Let me say that I agree with much of what Professor Davey says on the noneconomic effects of PTAs and his argument on superiority of multilateral trading systems relative to PTAs.

Professor Davey approves of the Australian proposal for clarifying the term "substantially all trade" by requiring that a PTA must liberalize initially 70 percent of six-digit tariff lines, within ten years raise it to 95 percent, and include highly traded products (defined as the fifty most imported products by one PTA member from another). In his view, it is unlikely that PTAs banning measures such as antidumping and safeguard measures would be acceptable. He does not therefore support their ban in the absence of competition rules in a PTA. Incidentally, he wrongly includes antidumping among nondiscriminatory measures. They do discriminate not only among a country's trading partners who export to it but also among exporting firms from its exporting partner. Only safeguard measures that have to be imposed on a MFN basis by definition are not discriminatory. He does not recognize that there is virtually no economic rationale for antidumping measures anyway. With safeguards already available in the WTO, the pernicious antidumping should be eliminated altogether. He rightly argues for including any measure besides tariffs that affects trade in other regulations of commerce mentioned in Article XXIV. Professor Davey is not in favor of proposing any modifications of Article XXIV that make PTAs more difficult to negotiate because they will make them unpopular with WTO members. I would view anything that makes PTAs more difficult to negotiate as desirable! If the members of WTO prefer to practice discrimination, they should be open about it and abandon MFN altogether. I am convinced that leaving the task of definition of the terms used in Article XXIV and evaluating the complex analysis of the economic and legal effects of restrictive measures to the Dispute Settlement System of the WTO, as Professor Davey suggests, would be extremely undesirable. To do so would be an abrogation of "legislative" rights of WTO members to the judiciary. It is an invitation for judicial outreach, as is already happening.

I do not have much to add to his discussion of the report of the WTO Secretariat in 2003 as well as those of the Sutherland and Warwick Commissions. The report of WTO (1995) that he does not mention is also relevant. In fact, in my paper (Srinivasan, 1998) I had proposed that, instead of modifying WTO rules to require that PTAs be required to multilateralize their preferences over time as the WTO Secretariat Report 2003 proposes, we should repeal Article XXIV altogether and replace it by two simple requirements of notification of proposed PTAs and of commitment to extend their preferences to all members of the WTO on a MFN basis within five years. I would add now a third requirement that any provisions in PTAs on investment, competition policy, intellectual property, labor and environmental standards, and so on that go beyond what has been agreed in the WTO should be brought into conformity with WTO provisions within five years. I have been told several times that my proposal is unrealistic and would not be accepted by WTO members because it would effectively kill PTAs. Perhaps so, but it treats termites as they should be treated.

Finally, instead of requiring that all PTA dispute settlement systems give members of the WTO who are not members of the PTAs third-party rights in PTA disputes, I would prefer that all PTAs are required to transfer to the WTO dispute settlement system for resolution any disputes among its members that could affect the rights of WTO members who are not members of the PTAs.

REFERENCES

Adams, Richard, Phillipa Dee, Jyothi Goli, and Greg McGuire, 2003. "The Trade and Investment Effects of Preferential Trading Arrangement – Old and New Evidence," Staff Working Paper. Canberra: Australia Productivity Commission.

Davey, William, 2008. *A Model Article XXIV: Are There Realistic Possibilities to Improve It?* University of Illinois College of Law.

De Rosa, Dean A., 2007. "The Trade Effects of Preferential Arrangements: New Evidence from the Australia Productivity Commission," Working Paper Series No. WP 07–1. Washington: Peterson Institute for International Economics.

Jackson, John, 1989. *Restructuring the GATT System.* London: Pinter.

Srinivasan, T. N., 1998. "Regionalism and the WTO: Is Non-Discrimination Passé?," in Anne Krueger (ed.), 1998, *The WTO as an International Organization*, (chapter 12). Chicago: University of Chicago Press, 329–52.

Srinivasan, T. N., 1988. *Developing Countries and the Multilateral Trading System: From the GATT to the Uruguay Round and the Future* Boulder, CO: Westview Press.

Wilcox, Clair, 1949. *A Charter for World Trade.* New York: Macmillan.

WTO, 2007. *Annual Report.* Geneva: World Trade Organization. Accessed at http://www.wto.org/english/res_e/booksp_e/anrep_e/anrep07_e.pdf. Pg. 52.

WTO, 1994. *The Results of the Uruguay Round of Multilateral Trade Negotiations: The Legal Texts.* Geneva: World Trade Organization.

WTO, 1995. *Regionalism in the World Trading System.* Geneva: World Trade Organization.

Index